Computational Propaganda

Oxford Studies in Digital Politics

Series Editor: Andrew Chadwick, Professor of Political Communication in the Centre for Research in Communication and Culture and the Department of Social Sciences, Loughborough University

Using Technology, Building Democracy: Digital Campaigning and the Construction of Citizenship
Jessica Baldwin-Philippi

Expect Us: Online Communities and Political Mobilization
Jessica L. Beyer

If... Then: Algorithmic Power and Politics
Taina Bucher

The Hybrid Media System: Politics and Power
Andrew Chadwick

The Only Constant Is Change: Technology, Political Communication, and Innovation Over Time
Ben Epstein

Tweeting to Power: The Social Media Revolution in American Politics
Jason Gainous and Kevin M. Wagner

Risk and Hyperconnectivity: Media and Memories of Neoliberalism
Andrew Hoskins and John Tulloch

Democracy's Fourth Wave?: Digital Media and the Arab Spring
Philip N. Howard and Muzammil M. Hussain

The Digital Origins of Dictatorship and Democracy: Information Technology and Political Islam
Philip N. Howard

Analytic Activism: Digital Listening and the New Political Strategy
David Karpf

The MoveOn Effect: The Unexpected Transformation of American Political Advocacy
David Karpf

Prototype Politics: Technology-Intensive Campaigning and the Data of Democracy
Daniel Kreiss

Taking Our Country Back: The Crafting of Networked Politics from Howard Dean to Barack Obama
Daniel Kreiss

Media and Protest Logics in the Digital Era: The Umbrella Movement in Hong Kong
Francis L.F. Lee and Joseph M. Chan

Bits and Atoms: Information and Communication Technology in Areas of Limited Statehood
Steven Livingston and Gregor Walter-Drop

Digital Cities: The Internet and the Geography of Opportunity
Karen Mossberger, Caroline J. Tolbert, and William W. Franko

Revolution Stalled: The Political Limits of the Internet in the Post-Soviet Sphere
Sarah Oates

Disruptive Power: The Crisis of the State in the Digital Age
Taylor Owen

Affective Publics: Sentiment, Technology, and Politics
Zizi Papacharissi

The Citizen Marketer: Promoting Political Opinion in the Social Media Age
Joel Penney

China's Digital Nationalism
Florian Schneider

Presidential Campaigning in the Internet Age
Jennifer Stromer-Galley

News on the Internet: Information and Citizenship in the 21st Century
David Tewksbury and Jason Rittenberg

The Civic Organization and the Digital Citizen: Communicating Engagement in a Networked Age
Chris Wells

Networked Publics and Digital Contention: The Politics of Everyday Life in Tunisia
Mohamed Zayani

Computational Propaganda

POLITICAL PARTIES, POLITICIANS, AND POLITICAL MANIPULATION ON SOCIAL MEDIA

EDITED BY SAMUEL C. WOOLLEY AND PHILIP N. HOWARD

OXFORD
UNIVERSITY PRESS

Oxford University Press is a department of the University of Oxford. It furthers
the University's objective of excellence in research, scholarship, and education
by publishing worldwide. Oxford is a registered trade mark of Oxford University
Press in the UK and certain other countries.

Published in the United States of America by Oxford University Press
198 Madison Avenue, New York, NY 10016, United States of America.

CIP data is on file at the Library of Congress
ISBN 978–0–19–093141–4 (pbk.)
ISBN 978–0–19–093140–7 (hbk.)

9 8 7 6 5 4 3 2 1

Paperback printed by Sheridan Books, Inc., United States of America
Hardback printed by Bridgeport National Bindery, Inc., United States of America

Contents

Part I   THEORETICAL INTRODUCTION AND
ANALYTICAL FRAME

Introduction: Computational Propaganda Worldwide   3
   SAMUEL C. WOOLLEY AND PHILIP N. HOWARD

Part II   COUNTRY-SPECIFIC CASE STUDIES

1. Russia: The Origins of Digital Misinformation   21
   SERGEY SANOVICH

2. Ukraine: External Threats and Internal Challenges   41
   MARIIA ZHDANOVA AND DARIYA ORLOVA

3. Canada: Building Bot Typologies   64
   ELIZABETH DUBOIS AND FENWICK MCKELVEY

4. Poland: Unpacking the Ecosystem of Social Media Manipulation   86
   ROBERT GORWA

5. Taiwan: Digital Democracy Meets Automated Autocracy   104
   NICHOLAS J. MONACO

6. Brazil: Political Bot Intervention During Pivotal Events   128
   DAN ARNAUDO

7. Germany: A Cautionary Tale   153
     LISA-MARIA N. NEUDERT

8. United States: Manufacturing Consensus Online   185
     SAMUEL C. WOOLLEY AND DOUGLAS GUILBEAULT

9. China: An Alternative Model of a Widespread Practice   212
     GILLIAN BOLSOVER

Part III   CONCLUSIONS

Conclusion: Political Parties, Politicians, and Computational
     Propaganda   241
     SAMUEL C. WOOLLEY AND PHILIP N. HOWARD

Author Bios   249
Index   253

Computational Propaganda

Part I

THEORETICAL INTRODUCTION AND ANALYTICAL FRAME

Introduction

Computational Propaganda Worldwide

SAMUEL C. WOOLLEY AND PHILIP N. HOWARD

What Is Computational Propaganda?

Digital technologies hold great promise for democracy. Social media tools and the wider resources of the Internet offer tremendous access to data, knowledge, social networks, and collective engagement opportunities, and can help us to build better democracies (Howard, 2015; Margetts et al., 2015). Unwelcome obstacles are, however, disrupting the creative democratic applications of information technologies (Woolley, 2016; Gallacher et al., 2017; Vosoughi, Roy, & Aral, 2018). Massive social platforms like Facebook and Twitter are struggling to come to grips with the ways their creations can be used for political control. Social media algorithms may be creating echo chambers in which public conversations get polluted and polarized. Surveillance capabilities are outstripping civil protections. Political "bots" (software agents used to generate simple messages and "conversations" on social media) are masquerading as genuine grassroots movements to manipulate public opinion. Online hate speech is gaining currency. Malicious actors and digital marketers run junk news factories that disseminate misinformation to harm opponents or earn click-through advertising revenue.

It is no exaggeration to say that coordinated efforts are even now working to seed chaos in many political systems worldwide. Some militaries and intelligence agencies are making use of social media as conduits to undermine democratic processes and bring down democratic institutions altogether (Bradshaw & Howard, 2017). Most democratic governments are preparing their legal and regulatory responses. But unintended consequences from over-regulation, or

regulation uninformed by systematic research, may be as damaging to democratic systems as the threats themselves.

We live in a time of extraordinary political upheaval and change, with
political movements and parties rising and declining rapidly (Kreiss, 2016;
Anstead, 2017). In this fluctuating political environment, digital technologies
provide the platform for a great deal of contemporary civic engagement
and political action (Vaccari, 2017). Indeed, a large amount of research has
shown that social media play an important role in the circulation of ideas and
conversation about politics and public policy. Increasingly, however, social
media platforms are also vehicles for manipulative disinformation campaigns.
Political campaigns, governments, and regular citizens around the world
are employing combinations of people and bots—automated software built
to mimic real users—in an attempt to artificially shape public life (Woolley,
2016; Gallacher et al., 2017). But there are still open, and difficult to answer,
questions about the specific mechanisms of influence for particular voters,
and how governments, news organizations, and civil society groups should
respond. How do new forms of civic engagement affect political outcomes?
To what extent do online echo chambers and selective exposure to information promote political extremism? How can civil activists respond effectively
to "trolling" by hostile political agents?

Computational propaganda is a term that neatly encapsulates this recent
phenomenon—and emerging field of study—of digital misinformation and
manipulation. As a communicative practice, computational propaganda
describes the use of algorithms, automation, and human curation to purposefully manage and distribute misleading information over social media networks
(Woolley & Howard, 2016a). As part of the process, coders and their automated software products (including bots) will learn from and imitate legitimate social media users in order to manipulate public opinion across a diverse
range of platforms and device networks. These bots are built to behave like real
people (for example, automatically generating and responding to conversations
online) and then let loose over social media sites in order to amplify or suppress
particular political messages. These "automated social actors" can be used to
bolster particular politicians and policy positions—supporting them actively
and enthusiastically, while simultaneously drowning out any dissenting voices
(Abokhodair, Yoo, & McDonald, 2015). They can be managed in conjunction
with human troll armies to "manufacture consensus" or to otherwise give the
illusion of general support for a (perhaps controversial) political idea or policy,
with the goal of creating a bandwagon effect (Woolley & Guilbeault, 2017).
Computational propaganda therefore forms part of a suite of dubious political
practices that includes digital astroturfing, state-sponsored trolling, and new
forms of online warfare known as PsyOps or InfoOps wherein the end goal is

to manipulate information online in order to change people's opinions and, ultimately, behavior.

However, trying to understand computational propaganda only from a technical perspective—as a set of variables, models, codes, and algorithms—plays into the hands of those who create it, the platforms that serve it, and the firms that profit from it (Bolsover & Howard, 2017). The very act of describing something as purely "technical" or in very mechanistic terms may make it seem unbiased and inevitable. This is clearly a dangerous position to take, and we must look to the emerging discipline of "social data science" to help us understand the complex socio-technical issues at play, and the influence of technology (including computational propaganda) on politics. As part of this process, social data science researchers must maintain a critical stance toward the data they use and analyze, so as to ensure that they are critiquing as they go about describing, predicting, or recommending changes in the way technology interacts with our political systems. If academic research on computational propaganda does not engage fully with the systems of power and knowledge that produce it (that is, the human actors and motivations behind it), then the very possibility of improving the role of social media platforms in public life evaporates (Bolsover & Howard, 2017). We can only hope to understand and respond appropriately to a problem like computational propaganda's impact on our political systems by undertaking computational research alongside qualitative investigation—by addressing the computational as well as the political.

Computational propaganda, with this in mind, can therefore be understood to incorporate two important components: the technical and the social. As a technical phenomenon, we can define computational propaganda as the assemblage of social media platforms, autonomous agents, algorithms, and big data tasked with the manipulation of public opinion (Woolley & Howard, 2016b). "Computational" propaganda is of course a recent form of the propaganda that has existed in our political systems for millennia—communications that deliberately subvert symbols, appealing to our baser emotions and prejudices and bypassing rational thought, to achieve the specific goals of its promoters—with computational propaganda understood as propaganda created or disseminated by computational means. Automation, scalability, and anonymity are hallmarks of computational propaganda. The pernicious advantage of computational propaganda is in enabling the rapid distribution of large amounts of content, sometimes personalized in order to fool users into thinking that messages originate in their extended network of family and friends. In this way, computational propaganda typically involves one or more of the following ingredients: bots that automate content delivery; fake social media accounts that require some (limited) human curation; and junk news—that is, misinformation about politics and public life.

The political bots we have already mentioned as being integral to the spread of computational propaganda are software programs or agents that are created to perform simple, repetitive, typically text-based tasks. Generally speaking, bots are used to computationally enhance the ability of humans to get work done online, both in terms of volume and speed. This work can be benign and extremely useful: most of the internal links that allow us to navigate Wikipedia are created and maintained by bots. When bots are programmed with human attributes or abilities—in order to pass as genuine social media users, for instance—they are referred to as *social bots* or *chat bots*. They can be used to perform mundane tasks like gathering information, but they can also interact with people and systems. This could involve simple tasks like delivering news and information—automated updates about the weather, sports news, and share values, for example. They can also be used to support more malicious activities, such as spamming and harassment. But regardless of whether they are put to a benign or malicious task, they are able to rapidly deploy messages, interact with other users' content, and even affect or manipulate trending algorithms—all while passing as human users. Political bots—that is, social bots used for political manipulation—thus represent an effective tool for driving online propaganda and hate campaigns. One person, or a small group of people, can fairly easily create and coordinate an army of political bots on Twitter, YouTube, or Instagram to give the illusion of a large-scale consensus or interest in a particular issue.

Governments and political actors around the world have used political bots—programmed to appear and behave like genuine citizens—to drown out and harass the opposition and to push their own messages. Political campaigns (and their civilian supporters) have deployed political bots and computational propaganda during recent elections in order to swing the vote, or to defame and intimidate the opposition. Anonymous political actors have spread false news reports, and coordinated disinformation campaigns and troll mobs to attack human rights defenders, civil society groups, and journalists. Computational propaganda is an extremely powerful new communication tool—and it is being used against democratic actors and institutions worldwide.

Automation and Algorithms as Tools for Political Communication

The term *computational propaganda* can be used to describe the recent series of digital attacks on civic society. The "computational" part of the equation is an important one. Data-driven techniques and tools like automation (bots) and algorithms (decision-making code) allow small groups of actors to megaphone highly specific, and sometime abusive and false, information into mainstream online environments. Rapid cycles of sharing, repurposing, and further dissemination often ensue.

During the 2016 US presidential election, for instance, far-right users on the 8chan imageboard spread a meme featuring Hillary Clinton, the Star of David, and a background of money. This image was then disseminated on sites like Facebook and subsequently shared and re-shared by mainstream conservatives. Presidential candidate Donald Trump then re-tweeted the image. The media picked up on the massive uptick in online chatter and began writing stories on the subject. The tactic—using hate and the viral spread of disinformation to undermine opposition—is not necessarily an new one. Russian propagandists and others have made healthy use of it in recent years (Castle, 2015). However, the rate at which this information is now routinely seeded—and the degree of confusion created by its rapid growth and spread online—is new.

The history of computational propaganda is of course brief, relative to the much longer history of traditional forms of political propaganda. But over the last six years state and nonstate political actors—from candidates for office to hacking collectives—have successfully swayed opinion and behavior during critical elections, security crises, and other important political events (Woolley, 2016). Powerful (and often anonymous) political actors have used computational propaganda techniques to perpetrate political attacks, to spread disinformation, censor and attack journalists, and create fake trends. In the last five years clear-cut cases of this have been observed in Argentina (Rueda, 2012), Australia (Peel, 2013), Azerbaijan (Pearce, 2013), Bahrain (Owen Jones, 2017), Brazil (Cordova, Doneda, & Almeida, 2016), China (King et al., 2013), Iran (Wendling, 2016), Italy (Cresci et al., 2015), Mexico (Savage et al., 2015), Russia (Tucker, 2017), South Korea (Sang-hun, 2013), Saudi Arabia (Freedom House, n.d.), Turkey (Saka, 2014), the United Kingdom (Howard & Kollanyi, 2016), the United States (Kollanyi, Howard, & Woolley, 2016), and Venezuela (Forelle et al., 2015).

Automation and anonymity lie at the heart of computational propaganda, and underpin what is both interesting and important about it as a new field of academic enquiry. "Computational" doesn't just mean that these acts of persuasion happen on a computer or online. Rather, it underscores the fact that these political strategies rely on *computational enhancement*. Automation allows propaganda attacks to be scaled. Anonymity allows perpetrators to remain unknown. In 2015, the security firm Incapsula published a study finding that bots generate almost half of all Web traffic—an extraordinary proportion (Zeifman, 2015). Within the social media sphere, estimates suggest that over a third of Twitter's users are in fact bots—automated software-driven accounts built to pass as real people. Estimates claim that within two years bots will generate around

10 percent of all activity on popular social media sites. These broad estimates of bot activity might sound rather horrifying (if we value social media as a space of genuine, unmediated connection with other people), but the details are even more so—many bots now maintain a parallel presence on several social media sites concurrently, to lend themselves an aura of human credibility. They also mimic human lifestyles—adhering to a believable sleep-wake cycle, making them harder to identify based on usage patterns alone.

Social bots on dating apps like Tinder are programmed to not respond immediately to human advances, but to delay their response as a human might (Melendez, 2015). Indeed, as has been pointed out by Chu et al. (2010), on Twitter a bot can do nearly everything a human can do through the Twitter API, and they note the ever-increasing difficulty of distinguishing between scripts generated by humans, bots or cyborgs (that is, a bot-aided human, or a human-aided bot).

Many bots are launched via a social media platform's application programming interface (API). Some sites, like Twitter, have more open APIs and less strict policies around bot use. On Twitter, bots can be directly plugged into one of many APIs. They can process information and activity on Twitter in real time, and respond to any comments and users that are relevant to their script (for example, that are identifiable as promoting or following a particular user or view). Facebook has more stringent policies about the use of automation, and maintains a "real name" policy that requires every user to verify their (unique, human) identity, but it still has problems with manipulative or otherwise problematic automation. In fact, in 2012 Facebook publicly announced that it intended to combat the fake accounts present on the social network, which amounted to 8.7 percent of all accounts (Wasserman, 2012). This percentage might seem small at first glance, but it represented 83 million accounts; equivalent to the entire population of Germany. Facebook was explicit in stating that these fake accounts and their "fraudulent likes" were antithetical to its purpose:

> Real identity, for both users and brands . . . is important to not only Facebook's mission of helping the world share, but also the need for people and customers to authentically connect to the Pages they care about . . . Facebook was built on the principle of real identity and we want this same authenticity to extend to Pages. We undoubtedly expect that this will be a positive change for anyone using Facebook. ("Improvements To Our Site Integrity Systems," 2012)

However, Facebook—in common with all the world's most popular social media platforms—continues to struggle with the bot problem.

In 2014 a bot named "Eugene Goostman" passed the Turing Test for the first time; meaning that it fooled a third of the judges into believing mistakenly that it was human, following a five-minute conversation between bot and judge (Aamoth, 2014). Bots are becoming increasingly humanlike in their speech and behavior, and thus more difficult to detect. They can be bought cheaply, with armies of bots built to like particular content or send message "bombs" costing less than 100 US dollars.

The Social Data Science of Political Communication

Algorithms and other computational tools now play an important political role in areas like news consumption, issue awareness, and cultural understanding (Gillespie, 2012; Sandvig et al., 2016)—leading to concern within the social sciences, especially within media studies and science and technology studies, about their impact on social life. The various problems thrown up by this intersection are also explored in the information and computer sciences literature. Working in conversation with research from the computer sciences (Mitter, Wagner, & Strohmaier, 2014; Ferrara et al., 2016), communication and media oriented work has shown that political actors around the globe are using social media bots in efforts to both facilitate and control communication (Woolley & Howard, 2016a, 2016b; Woolley, 2016). Bots have been used by political campaigns and candidates in order to manipulate public opinion by disrupting activist attempts to organize, and also to create the illusion of popularity and consensus. This work highlights the increasing sophistication of modern social bots, and also their potential to threaten civic life both online and offline.

One particularly damaging form of computational propaganda is false news reports, widely distributed by bots over social media platforms like Twitter, Facebook, Reddit, and beyond. These social media platforms have served significant volumes of fake, sensational, and other forms of "junk news" during sensitive political moments over the last several years. However, most platforms reveal little about how much of this content there is, or what its impact on users may be. But in a marker of how important this problem might actually be, the World Economic Forum recently identified the rapid spread of misinformation online as among the top 10 perils to society (World Economic Forum, 2014). Previous research has found that social media favors sensationalist content, regardless of whether the content has been fact-checked or is from a reliable source (Vicario et al., 2016). When distribution of this junk news is backed by automation, either via political bots or through the platform operator's own dissemination

algorithms, political actors have a powerful set of tools for computational propaganda. Both state and nonstate political actors can deliberately manipulate and
amplify nonfactual information online, to their own ends.

Building and using bots has also been discussed as a kind of "agnostic com-
mercialism." Bot builders act as hired guns, selling bots on freelancing platforms
like Fiverr, with little concern for how they will be used or by whom. Using
bots to spread advertisements or to attack opponents online has a long history, existing in email and other chat mediums before spreading to social media
platforms like Twitter and Facebook. These newer forms can gather information
on users in order to push a particular argument or agenda, often via hashtags
(Hwang, Pearce, & Nanis, 2012). Experiments on the efficacy of such bots have
shown that they can infiltrate social networks on sites like Facebook with a high
degree of success, and that they can bypass the security systems intended to protect users from just such attacks (Boshmaf et al., 2013). In our own interviews
with programmers who build and deploy such bots, many have told us that their
work is purely mercenary—that they are apolitical in their views, and driven
solely by a desire to make money online.

Of course, voter manipulation existed long before bots became mainstream
on social media. Over a decade ago, Howard (2005) established the study of
political "astroturf" movements, defining astroturfing as the process of seeking
electoral victory or legislative relief for grievances by helping political actors find
and mobilize a sympathetic public using the Internet. This campaign strategy can
be used to create the image of public consensus where there is none, or to give a
false impression of the popularity of a candidate or public policy idea. Almost as
soon as social media took off as arguably the most important means of receiving
news and communicating with our peers, network automation was used to support political communication in similar ways. Ratkiewicz et al. (2011) examined
the ways in which Twitter bots were deployed before and during the 2010 US
midterm congressional campaigns. They explored social bot-driven attacks
upon candidates for the House and Senate, and suggested that these technological actors formed part of larger "astroturf" political efforts. Social bots, or "sock
puppets," were harnessed in this context for their anonymity and ubiquity.

While there is a great deal of academic work exploring the tremendous democratic potential of the Internet, recent research has also shown how the liberating
uses of the Internet can be compromised when governing elites use them as tools
for social control. Within- and between-country digital divides may also have an
impact on how social media are used in public life—analysis by Schradie (2011)
suggests that there is a class-based gap between producers of online content, and
consumers. Still others argue that the now widespread political normalization
of social media systems has allowed the politically powerful to leverage these
tools for coercion and control (Karpf, 2012). Indeed, states that have exercised

firm control over their own Internet development from the beginning—such as China, Singapore, and Iran—have proven success in online control (Kalathil & Boas, 2010).

A Mixed-Method Approach for Understanding Computational Propaganda

Media scholars have been concerned with the study of propaganda, and its effect upon public opinion, at least since the seminal work of Lazarsfeld (1941) and Lasswell (1948). Our own multi-year study of computational propaganda worldwide, which we present in this edited volume, picks up this line of research in order to understand the ways in which algorithms, automation, and social media are being used to promote the messages of political actors in many different kinds of democratic and authoritarian regimes around the world. The case studies we present all begin with a basic set of research questions crafted for comparability. Does computational propaganda occur as part of a country's current political landscape? What are its forms, types, or styles? What is its impact on public life? Each case study also considers the impact of the observed phenomena on the country's political institutions. How might political bot activity run afoul of its election law? Which computational propaganda campaigns had a significant impact, and how might they be prevented in the future?

In keeping with our previous point about the importance of tackling this area from both the technical and social side, the findings we present are the result of knowledge generated via multiple social and data science methods. Our research team made use of both qualitative and quantitative methods of analysis. This mixed-method approach enables the case studies to speak to concerns at the intersection of several disciplines, especially those focused on social science, law, and computer science. We have conducted qualitative and quantitative content analysis of news coverage about computational algorithms. We have performed big data analysis of large networks of Facebook, Twitter, and Weibo users. Researchers have used a variety of methods in cataloguing their country-specific case studies including, but not limited to interviews with the victims of attacks, interviews with those who have worked to produce political bots and social media-based propaganda, process tracing, participant observation, and social network analysis. Each case required different approaches and tools.

The research team involved 12 researchers across nine countries who, altogether, interviewed 65 experts, analyzed tens of millions of posts on seven different social media platforms during scores of elections, political crises, and national security incidents. The researchers were chosen for their knowledge of particular political cultures, their ability to conduct in-country interviews in the relevant languages, and their skills at analyzing large datasets of social media content. This edited collection therefore features some of the best work that can come from collaboration across the social, policy, and computer sciences. Five different families of research methods were used by the team, depending on the context of each case. These included the following.

Computational Social Science. The research team applied a suite of machine learning techniques, including regression analysis, k-core analysis, and topic discovery methods in order to analyze public data collected from social networking sites, from surveys, and interviews. The goal of these methods is usually to map social influence, identify region-specific hot button issues that polarize social groups—like race, religion, immigration, and gender—and to track the use of online misinformation campaigns to influence voters.

Qualitative Ethnography, Participant Observation, and Fieldwork. Spending time with the designers of social media platforms or political communication experts yielded significant insights into how the affordances of these technical systems can limit citizens' choices for self-expression. Systematic interviews with political consultants, data mining firms, and civil society victims of attacks, reveal much about the economic incentives and market structure of political manipulation techniques. Increasingly, state of the art social science involves methodological collaboration—computational analysis of data can reveal underlying patterns of information and behavior, but only in combination with ethnography can we undertake a theoretically meaningful interpretation of them. By combining both methods, this book considers both the broad patterns of computational propaganda in our online information environment and the deep-seated political, economic, and sociocultural forces that operate to encourage, promote, and leverage it.

Social Network Analysis. The research team applied social network analysis techniques to integrate large datasets from social networking platforms with existing survey and polling data, in order to understand how the structure of social networks bounds our opportunities for political learning, engaging with political leaders, and empathizing with social problems. Mapping advert networks on social media can reveal how far a misinformation campaign has traveled and what made it go viral, while mapping social networks can reveal how users may self-select into "echo chambers."

Surveys and Public Opinion Polling. Several of the chapters in this volume take advantage of existing survey instruments to trace the impact of algorithmic manipulation on public opinion. Surveys can be useful in generalizing user opinion on the political use of social media. Open-ended questionnaires allow users to elaborate on elements of digital political manipulation and harassment that researchers might not otherwise have encountered or considered. Scaled questions allow researchers to ascertain whether or not, and to what extent, users believe computational propaganda to be a problem they have experienced.

Comparative Policy Analysis. The legal research methodologies used in this edited collection examine how governments, and other jurisdictions where relevant, have implemented the key privacy and data protection principles and safeguards of leading privacy and data protection instruments. In most cases, national governments do not have electoral laws that help political actors make good decisions about the complex range of political communication technologies currently on offer. Wherever possible, chapter authors have discussed the rules that should apply in election campaigning—or that perhaps should have been applied.

Computational Propaganda: Addressing a Global Problem

We have already mentioned that the World Economic Forum has identified the rapid spread of misinformation online as one of the top 10 perils to society. In this book we present new, original evidence about how this manipulation and amplification of disinformation is produced, managed, and circulated by political operatives and governments. We measure how Russian Twitter conversation is constrained by highly automated accounts. We demonstrate how highly automated accounts in the United States have moved from peripheral social networks to engage with core groups of humans. We also trace the source of some forms of junk news and automated accounts to programmers and businesses in Germany, Poland, and the United States.

Our interviews with political party operatives, freelance campaigners, and elections officials in seven countries provide further evidence that social media bots—and computational propaganda more broadly—have been used to manipulate discussion online. This manipulation is underscored, and indeed facilitated, by the fact that some social media platforms, in particular political contexts, are either fully controlled by or dominated by governments and organized disinformation campaigns. Almost half of the Twitter activity in Russia is managed by highly automated accounts. Significant portions of political tweeting in Poland are produced by just a handful of alt-right accounts.

Computational propaganda also plays a role in particular events, especially during elections and security crises. It played a significant role during three recent political events in Brazil: the 2014 presidential elections, the impeachment of former president Dilma Rousseff, and the 2016 municipal elections in Rio de Janeiro. Analysis of how the Ukrainian conflict has played out on social media provides perhaps the most detailed case of computational propaganda's role during a global security crisis, and Russia's ongoing involvement in information wars. Numerous online disinformation campaigns have been waged against Ukrainian citizens on VKontakte, Facebook, and Twitter. The industry that drives these efforts at manipulation has been active in Ukraine since the early 2000s.

Computational propaganda also flourished during the 2016 US presidential election (Howard, Kollanyi, & Woolley, 2016), with numerous examples of misinformation distributed online with the intention of misleading voters or simply earning a profit. Multiple media reports have investigated how "fake news" may have propelled Donald J. Trump to victory (Dewey, 2016; Parkinson, 2016; Read, 2016). In Michigan, one of the key battleground states, junk news was shared just as widely as professional news in the days leading up to the election (Howard et al., 2017). Surveys have suggested that many people who saw fake news during the election believed those headlines (Silverman & Singer-Vine, 2016), though we have yet to see firm long-term interference with political learning.

There is a difference in how computational propaganda is used by authoritarian and democratic governments. Increasingly, however, this gap is closing. Our case studies show that authoritarian governments direct computational propaganda at both their own populations and at populations in other countries. Campaigns directed by China have targeted political actors in Taiwan, and Russian-directed campaigns have targeted political actors in Poland and Ukraine. But in democracies as well, individual users design and operate fake and highly automated social media accounts. Political candidates, campaigners, and lobbyists rent larger networks of social media accounts for purpose-built campaigns, while governments have assigned public resources to the creation, experimentation, and use of such accounts. And this doesn't just rely on automation and AI technology; when it comes to effective use of computational propaganda, the most powerful forms will involve both algorithmic distribution and human curation—software bots and human trolls working together. Our Taiwanese study reveals that Chinese mainland propaganda over social media is not fully automated but is in fact heavily coordinated by humans.

It's not all bad news. There are important examples of positive contributions made by algorithms and automation over social media. In Canada, civic actors are using complex algorithms to do constructive public service—albeit, with an as-yet uncertain overall impact. Bot builders in the United States have constructed small groupings of social bots with mandates for making information about political processes more public and easier to understand, for creating art aimed at critiquing particular policies or social issues, and for connecting social or political groups with similar interest groups.

Our motive in undertaking this multi-case analysis of computational propaganda is to better understand the global reach of political bots, digital disinformation, junk news, and other similar problems. In presenting the first systematic exposé and analysis of computational propaganda for a number of country-specific case studies, we have paid particular attention to the themes inherent in propaganda generally, but also try to illuminate crucial details surrounding particular attacks and events. Ultimately, we hope to understand who is behind misinformation campaigns while also explaining who the victim groups are, what they experience, and what they—and others fighting this global problem—can do about it.

Bibliography

Aamoth, D. (2014, June 9). Interview with Eugene Goostman, the Fake Kid Who Passed the Turing Test. *Time*. Retrieved from http://time.com/2847900/eugene-goostman-turing-test/.

Abokhodair, N., Yoo, D., & McDonald, D. W. (2015). Dissecting a Social Botnet: Growth, Content and Influence in Twitter. In *Proceedings of the 18th ACM Conference on Computer Supported Cooperative Work & Social Computing* (pp. 839–851). New York, NY: ACM. Retrieved from https://doi.org/10.1145/2675133.2675208.

Anstead, N. (2017). Data-Driven Campaigning in the 2015 United Kingdom General Election. *The International Journal of Press/Politics*, 22(3), 294–313. Retrieved from https://doi.org/10.1177/1940161217706163.

Bolsover, G., & Howard, P. (2017). Computational Propaganda and Political Big Data: Moving Toward a More Critical Research Agenda. *Big Data*, 5(4), 273–276. Retrieved from https://doi.org/10.1089/big.2017.29024.cpr.

Boshmaf, Y., Muslukhov, I., Beznosov, K., & Ripeanu, M. (2013). Design and Analysis of a Social Botnet. *Computer Networks: The International Journal of Computing and Telecommunications Networking*, 57(2), 556–578. Retrieved from https://www.sciencedirect.com/science/article/pii/S1389128612002150?via%3Dihub

Bradshaw, S., & Howard, P. N. (2017). *Troops, Trolls and Troublemakers: A Global Inventory of Organized Social Media Manipulation* (Working Paper No. 2017.12) (p. 37). Oxford, England: Project on Computational Propaganda. Retrieved from http://comprop.oii.ox.ac.uk/2017/07/17/troops-trolls-and-trouble-makers-a-global-inventory-of-organized-social-media-manipulation/.

Castle, S. (2015, February 13). A Russian TV Insider Describes a Modern Propaganda Machine. *The New York Times*. Retrieved from https://www.nytimes.com/2015/02/14/world/europe/russian-tv-insider-says-putin-is-running-the-show-in-ukraine.html.

Chu, Z., Gianvecchio, S., Wang, H., & Jajodia, S. (2010). Who Is Tweeting on Twitter: Human, Bot, or Cyborg? In *Proceedings of the 26th Annual Computer Security Applications Conference* (pp. 21–30). Austin, TX: ACM. Retrieved from http://dl.acm.org/citation.cfm?id=1920265.

Cordova, Y., Doneda, D., & Almeida, V. (2016, June). Tropical Bot Wars Timeline. Retrieved February 24, 2017, from http://www.tropicalbots.live.

Cresci, S., Di Pietro, R., Petrocchi, M., Spognardi, A., & Tesconi, M. (2015). Fame for Sale: Efficient Detection of Fake Twitter Followers. *Decision Support Systems*, 80, 56–71. Retrieved from https://doi.org/10.1016/j.dss.2015.09.003.

Dewey, C. (2016, November 17). Facebook Fake-News Writer: "I Think Donald Trump Is in the White House Because of Me." *The Washington Post*. Retrieved from https://www.

washingtonpost.com/news/the-intersect/wp/2016/11/17/facebook-fake-news-writer-i-think-donald-trump-is-in-the-white-house-because-of-me/?utm_term=.30dba5468d15.

Ferrara, E., Varol, O., Davis, C., Mencaer, F., & Flammini, A. (2016). The Rise of Socialbots. *Communications of the ACM*. Retrieved from https://cacm.acm.org/magazines/2016/7/204021-the-rise-of-social-bots/fulltext

Forelle, M., Howard, P., Monroy-Hernández, A., & Savage, S. (2015). Political Bots and the Manipulation of Public Opinion in Venezuela. *arXiv:1507.07109 [physics]*. Retrieved from http://arxiv.org/abs/1507.07109.

Freedom House. (n.d.). Freedom on the Net 2013: Saudi Arabia. New York, NY: Freedom House.

Gallacher, J., Kaminska, M., Kollanyi, B., Yasseri, T., & Howard, P. N. (2017). Social Media and News Sources during the 2017 UK General Election. Retrieved from comprop.oii.ox.ac.uk.

Gillespie, T. (2012). The Relevance of Algorithms. In *Media Technologies: Essays on Communication, Materiality and Society*. Cambridge: MIT Press. Retrieved from http://citeseerx.ist.psu.edu/viewdoc/download?doi=10.1.1.692.3942&rep=rep1&type=pdf.

Howard, P. N. (2005). *New Media Campaigns and the Managed Citizen*. New York, NY: Cambridge University Press.

Howard, P. N. (2011). *Castells and the Media*. New York, NY: Polity Press.

Howard, P. N. (2015). *Pax Technica: How the Internet of Things May Set Us Free*. New Haven, CT: Yale University Press.

Howard, P. N., Bolsover, G., Kollanyi, B., Bradshaw, S., & Neudert, L.-M. (2017). Junk News and Bots during the U.S. Election: What Were Michigan Voters Sharing Over Twitter? Data Memo 2017.1. Oxford, UK: Project on Computational Propaganda. Retrieved from http://comprop.oii.ox.ac.uk/2017/03/26/junk-news-and-bots-during-the-u-s-election-what-were-michigan-voters-sharing-over-twitter/.

Howard, P. N., & Kollanyi, B. (2016). *Bots, #Strongerin, and #Brexit: Computational Propaganda during the UK–EU Referendum* (Working Paper No. 2016.1) (p. 6). Oxford, UK: Project on Computational Propaganda. Retrieved from http://dx.doi.org/10.2139/ssrn.2798311.

Howard, P. N., Kollanyi, B., & Woolley, S. C. (2016). Bots and Automation Over Twitter during the US Election. *Computational Propaganda Project: Working Paper Series*.

Howard, P. N., & Parks, M. R. (2012). Social Media and Political Change: Capacity, Constraint, and Consequence. *Journal of Communication*, 62(2), 359–362. Retrieved from https://doi.org/10.1111/j.1460-2466.2012.01626.x.

Hwang, T., Pearce, I., & Nanis, M. (2012). Socialbots: Voices from the Fronts. *Interactions*, 19(2), 38–45. Retrieved from https://www.researchgate.net/publication/254004076_Socialbots_Voices_from_the_fronts

Improvements To Our Site Integrity Systems. (2012, August 31). Retrieved June 23, 2016, from https://www.facebook.com/notes/facebook-security/improvements-to-our-site-integrity-systems/10151005934870766/.

Kalathil, S., & Boas, T. C. (2010). *Open Networks, Closed Regimes: The Impact of the Internet on Authoritarian Rule*. Washington, DC: Carnegie Endowment.

Karpf, D. (2012). *The MoveOn Effect: The Unexpected Transformation of American Political Advocacy*. Oxford, UK: Oxford University Press.

King, G., Pan, J., & Roberts, M. E. (2013). How Censorship in China Allows Government Criticism but Silences Collective Expression. *American Political Science Review*, 107(02), 326–343. Retrieved from https://doi.org/10.1017/S0003055413000014.

Kollanyi, B., Howard, P. N., & Woolley, S. C. (2016). *Bots and Automation over Twitter during the U.S. Election* (Data Memo No. 2016.4) (p. 5). Oxford, UK: Project on Computational Propaganda. Retrieved from http://www.politicalbots.org.

Kreiss, D. (2016). *Prototype Politics: Technology-Intensive Campaigning and the Data of Democracy* (First Edition). New York, NY: Oxford University Press.

Lasswell, H. D. (1948). *The Structure and Function of Communication in Society*. New York, NY: Institute for Religious and Social Studies.

Lazarsfeld, P. (1941). Remarks on Critical and Administrative Communications Research. In *Studies in Philosophy and Social Science* (Vol. 9, pp. 1–17). Frankfurt: Institute of Social Research.

Margetts, H., John, P., Hale, S., & Yasseri, T. (2015). *Political Turbulence: How Social Media Shape Collective Action*. NJ: Princeton University Press.

Melendez, S. (2015, February 10). Tinder Bots Have Evolved to Mimic the Girl Next Door. Retrieved June 23, 2016, from http://motherboard.vice.com/read/tinder-bots-next-door.

Mitter, S., Wagner, C., & Strohmaier, M. (2014). Understanding the Impact of Socialbot Attacks in Online Social Networks. *arXiv*. Retrieved July 5, 2018, from https://arxiv.org/abs/1402.6289

Owen Jones, M. (2017, February). Irreverence and Analysis on Bahrain, Bots, and the History of the Persian Gulf. Retrieved February 24, 2017, from https://marcowenjones.wordpress.com/.

Parkinson, H. J. (2016, November 14). Click and elect: how fake news helped Donald Trump win a real election. *The Guardian*. Retrieved from https://www.theguardian.com/commentisfree/2016/nov/14/fake-news-donald-trump-election-alt-right-social-media-tech-companies.

Pearce, K. (2013, March 10). Cyberfuckery in Azerbaijan | Katy Pearce. Retrieved May 14, 2014, from http://www.katypearce.net/cyberfuckery-in-azerbaijan/

Peel, T. (2013, August 26). The Coalition's Twitter Fraud and Deception. Retrieved May 14, 2014, from http://www.independentaustralia.net/politics/politics-display/the-coalitions-twitter-fraud-and-deception,5660.

Ratkiewicz, J., Conover, M., Meiss, M., Gonçalves, B., Flammini, A. and Menczer, F. Detecting and tracking political abuse in social media. In *Proceedings of the 5th International AAAI Conference on Weblogs and Social Media* (2011). 297–304.

Read, M. (2016, November). Donald Trump Won Because of Facebook. *New York Magazine*. Retrieved from http://nymag.com/selectall/2016/11/donald-trump-won-because-of-facebook.html.

Rueda, M. (2012, December 27). 2012's Biggest Social Media Blunders in LatAm Politics. Retrieved February 24, 2017, from http://abcnews.go.com/ABC_Univision/ABC_Univision/2012s-biggest-social-media-blunders-latin-american-politics/story?id=18063022.

Saka, E. (2014). The AK Party's Social Media Strategy: Controlling the Uncontrollable. *Turkish Review*, 4(4), 418–423. Retrieved from https://doi.org/N/A.

Sandvig, C., Hamilton, K., Karahalios, K., & Langbort, C. (2016). When the Algorithm Itself is a Racist: Diagnosing Ethical Harm in the Basic Components of Software. *International Journal of Communication*, 10, 20.

Sang-hun, C. (2013, November 21). Prosecutors Detail Attempt to Sway South Korean Election. *The New York Times*. Retrieved from http://www.nytimes.com/2013/11/22/world/asia/prosecutors-detail-bid-to-sway-south-korean-election.html.

Savage, S., Monroy-Hernández, A., & Hollerer, T. (2015). Botivist: Calling Volunteers to Action Using Online Bots. *arXiv Preprint arXiv:1509.06026*. Retrieved from https://doi.org/10.1145/2818048.2819985.

Schradie, J. (2011). The digital production gap: The digital divide and Web 2.0 collide. *Poetics*, 39(2), 145–168. Retrieved from https://doi.org/10.1016/j.poetic.2011.02.003.

Silverman, C., & Singer-Vine, J. (2016, December 7). Most Americans Who See Fake News Believe It, New Survey Says. Retrieved March 3, 2017, from https://www.buzzfeed.com/craigsilverman/fake-news-survey.

Tucker, J. (2017, February 24). Turning the Virtual Tables: Social Media, Opposition, and Government Responses in Russia and Venezuela. Retrieved February 24, 2017, from http://data.washington.edu/seminar/2016/tucker/.

Vaccari, C. (2017). Online Mobilization in Comparative Perspective: Digital Appeals and Political Engagement in Germany, Italy, and the United Kingdom. *Political Communication*, 34(1), 69–88. Retrieved from https://doi.org/10.1080/10584609.2016.1201558.

Vicario, M. D., Bessi, A., Zollo, F., Petroni, F., Scala, A., Caldarelli, G., . . . Quattrociocchi, W. (2016). The Spreading of Misinformation Online. *Proceedings of the National Academy of Sciences, 113*(3), 554–559. Retrieved from https://doi.org/10.1073/pnas.1517441113.

Vosoughi, S., Roy, D., & Aral, S. (2018). The spread of true and false news online. *Science, 359*(6380), 1146–1151. Retrieved from https://doi.org/10.1126/science.aap9559.

Wasserman, T. (2012, August 2). 83 Million Facebook Accounts Are Fake. Retrieved June 23, 2016, from http://mashable.com/2012/08/02/fake-facebook-accounts/#_daGF3AAxqqg.

Wendling, M. (2016, March 16). Who's at the Controls of Iran's Bot Army? *BBC News.* Retrieved from http://www.bbc.co.uk/news/blogs-trending-35778645.

Woolley, S. C. (2016). Automating Power: Social Bot Interference in Global Politics. *First Monday, 21*(4). Retrieved from http://firstmonday.org/ojs/index.php/fm/article/view/6161.

Woolley, S. C., & Guilbeault, D. (2017). *Computational Propaganda in the United States of America: Manufacturing Consensus Online* (Computational Propaganda Working Paper Series No. 2017.5) (p. 37). Oxford, United Kingdom: Oxford Internet Institute, University of Oxford.

Woolley, S. C., & Howard, P. N. (2016a). Automation, Algorithms, and Politics| Political Communication, Computational Propaganda, and Autonomous Agents—Introduction. *International Journal of Communication, 10*(0), 9.

Woolley, S. C., & Howard, P. N. (2016b). Social Media, Revolution, and the Rise of the Political Bot. In P. Robinson, P. Seib, & R. Frohlich (Eds.), *Routledge Handbook of Media, Conflict, and Security.* New York, NY: Routledge.

World Economic Forum. (2014). 10. The Rapid Spread of Misinformation Online. Retrieved March 8, 2017, from http://wef.ch/GJAfq6.

Zeifman, I. (2015, December 9). 2015 Bot Traffic Report: Humans Take Back the Web, Bad Bots Not Giving Any Ground. Retrieved June 23, 2016, from https://www.incapsula.com/blog/bot-traffic-report-2015.html.

Part II

COUNTRY-SPECIFIC CASE STUDIES

1

Russia

The Origins of Digital Misinformation

SERGEY SANOVICH

Introduction

The goals and precise impact of the alleged Russian activities around US elections and several other important recent political contests in the West are still subject to a vigorous debate (Kofman, 2017; Bialik & Arthur, 2016; Hopkins, 2016; Enten, 2016; Applebaum, 2016a, 2016b; Applebaum & Lucas, 2016). However, if Russia simply wanted to convince other world powers of its ability to stage a prolonged, multifaceted and global campaign of influence, it has won an unquestionable and impressive victory (Marusic, 2016; Musgrave, 2016). In this campaign, no tool employed by the Russian government attracted more attention than cyber operations of various kinds. Of course, chief among them was the alleged hacking of the email accounts of the Democratic National Committee and Hillary Clinton's campaign chairman. However, all inquiries into the matter emphasize that getting the hacked information across and framing its meaning to the general public was as important as acquiring it in the first place. The United States intelligence community report on Russian activities specifically mentions that "Russia's state-run propaganda machine—comprised of its domestic media apparatus, outlets targeting global audiences such as RT[1] and Sputnik,[2] and a network of quasi-government trolls—contributed to the influence campaign by serving as a platform for Kremlin messaging to Russian and international audiences" (National Intelligence Council, 2017, p. 3). Similarly, a European Parliament resolution issued in November 2016 states that "the Russian Government is employing a wide range of tools and instruments, such as think tanks and special foundations (e.g., Russkiy Mir), special authorities (Rossotrudnichestvo), multilingual TV stations (such as RT), pseudo news agencies and multimedia services (e.g., Sputnik), cross-border social and religious groups (...) social media and internet trolls to challenge democratic values, divide Europe, gather domestic support and create the perception of failed states in the EU's eastern neighbourhood" (European Parliament 2016, Section 8).[3]

The intentions and capability demonstrated by Russia in the domain of cyber propaganda took many Western observers by surprise. Indeed, as opposed to the widely discussed issue of the builders of the Great Firewall of China (MacKinnon, 2011; King, Pan, & Roberts, 2013), the Russian government prior to 2014 was considered neither particularly artful nor even interested in intervening in the online flows of information (Groves, 2007; see also Kovalev, 2010). In search of an explanation, US defense analysts turned to a 2013 article they discovered in an obscure Russian military–industrial magazine. The article, written by the Chief of the Russian General Staff and General of the Army, Valery Gerasimov, discussed at length different elements of "ambiguous warfare," including the information war. Army and navy analysts concluded that online media tools deployed by the Kremlin to brainwash the Ukrainian population and whitewash Russian actions in the West were part of an elaborate strategy clandestinely developed by Russian military planners (Connell & Evans, 2015; Dickey et al., 2015; cf. McDermott, 2016; Bartles, 2016).

The concern over the alleged "digital propaganda gap"—the New Cold War reincarnation of the original "missile gap"—prompted an intense debate about the impact of and potential responses to Russian foreign propaganda activities. The European Parliament, the British Legatum Institute and the US Center for Strategic and International Studies, among others, published reports on the issue (Conley, Stefanov, Vladimirov, & Mina, 2016; European Union Institute for Security Studies, 2016; Pomerantsev & Lucas, 2016; Russell, 2016). The United States (Timberg, 2016), France (Gramer, 2017), and Germany (Reuters, 2017) have recently appropriated additional funding for various counter-propaganda and cyber defense measures. Worried about the influence of bots in particular,[4] the US Defense Advanced Research Projects Agency (DARPA) launched a bot detection program and ran a competition among scientists to build the best detecting algorithm (Subrahmanian et al., 2016).

It is worth noting that in its broad campaign of so-called active measures in Eastern Europe and beyond, Russia is leveraging its traditional advantages: a well-trained intelligence and professional diplomatic corps that enjoys unlimited resources, legal immunity, and total secrecy at home, and that can cultivate relationships abroad over decades (Bruno, 2014; Talbott & Brandt, 2017; Remnick, Yaffa, & Osnos, 2017; Snegovaya, 2015). At the same time, the digital elements of the Russian strategy, naturally, had little Soviet foundation to build upon. Neither, as I will show, were they developed through the clandestine efforts of Russian military strategists. Instead, their agility and effectiveness were developed through a very long—and very public (rather than secretive)—trial-and-error process. Moreover, if Russia has an edge in digital propaganda, it comes from the most unlikely of places in Putin's Russia: market and political competition. This might have implications for the type of response best suited to effectively counter this type of Russian propaganda.

First, I discuss how the political competition in Putin's Russia created the demand for online propaganda tools, and how market competition in the Russian tech sector was allowed to efficiently meet this demand and create tools that were later deployed in foreign operations. I then discuss some of these tools in detail and describe, with empirical examples, how they could be studied and exposed.

The Domestic Origins of Russian Foreign Digital Propaganda

The Atlantic Council's Digital Forensic Research Lab provides well-documented examples of recent Russian misinformation campaigns, targeting a range of countries from Armenia to France and from Germany to the United States.[5] On the one hand, the ability of Russian propaganda to infiltrate dark corners of social media platforms—from alt-right subreddits to far-left Twitter threads—with self-serving narratives should not come as a surprise: this is Russian modus operandi in more traditional media, too. Expanding on the far-right Cold War tradition of promoting disaffected leftists, RT and Sputnik are skillfully capitalizing on existing divisions and frustrations in Western societies (Bertrand, 2016; Gorenberg, 2016; Michel, 2017; Michel & Pottier, 2017; Saletan & Carter, 2017; Yablokov, 2015). However, the audience of Russian TV and radio content abroad remains limited (Erickson, 2017) and is probably larger online than offline (Nelson, Orttung, & Livshen 2015), despite significant investments in high-quality production and English-speaking anchors.[6] In terms of audience, RT is certainly no match for CNN International or BBC World. Information campaigns online, particularly in social media, appear to be much more successful. Why?

One reason could have its origins in the differences in the domestic media environment faced by Russian TV broadcasters and social media editors. The Russian government has virtually monopolized news coverage on all major television channels[7] and, free from any competition, Russian domestic TV has descended into increasingly crude, evidence-free, often provocative political posturing (Kovalev, 2017). RT, operating in a much more competitive environment, of course, has to adopt a more nuanced approach than its sister channels inside Russia, but this is not what its executives are used to when it comes to broadcasting news on the air.

The Russian social media environment always was—and to a large degree, remains—qualitatively different from the rest of Russian media. Even the people who appear on Russian state-run TV know that they will face much more scrutiny on Twitter and will have to be much more persuasive to gain traction there (those who are not prepared to face this level of scrutiny simply avoid social media, as they believe that it will be hostile toward them).

This uniquely large difference between media freedom online and offline distinguishes Russia from countries with universally free media and from others, such as China, where both offline and online media have been put under tight government control. In Russian domestic politics, this disjointed media environment has had important implications for the evolution of Putin's coalition and his relationship with the Russian middle class (Oates & Lokot, 2013). It also prompted the Russian government to adopt bots and trolls as key propaganda tools early on, and to gain considerable expertise in deploying them in times of crisis (Chen, 2015).

Vladimir Putin had a chance to appreciate the power of the media to change public opinion and reverse political fortunes at an early stage. The rise to power of a hitherto publicly unknown former KGB lieutenant colonel turned mid-level bureaucrat by the end of the so-called war for Yeltsin's succession was, in large part, the result of a successful media campaign fought on his behalf by a group of Russian oligarchs (Tregubova, 2003, Chapter 10; Gessen, 2012, Chapter 2; Gel'man, Travin, & Marganiya, 2014, pp. 104–108). Putin's media policy over the next 15 years demonstrates that he took this lesson extremely seriously, and he worked tirelessly to place the media under his control (Burrett, 2010; Lipman, 2009).

Total control of the national TV channels and increasingly tight restrictions put on radio and the print media by the government pushed most serious reporting as well as interested readers to the only area that was left free from interference: the Internet. The reasons why Putin treated online media so differently are still unclear. Among the most popular hypotheses are that he hoped to develop an economically profitable tech sector; that he was concerned about Russia's image abroad, particularly in comparison to that of China (Nossik, 2014); that he wanted to exploit opportunities for online surveillance (Soldatov & Borogan, 2013); and that he viewed it as politically insignificant because of the low Internet penetration rate. Indeed, even three years after Putin came to power, in 2002, Russia had only 2.1 million people (two percent of the adult population) who used the Internet daily. By 2008 (the end of Putin's second term) this share had increased to 14 million (16 percent of the adult population).[8] This laissez-faire approach led to a remarkable contrast between traditional and on-line media. While Freedom House had already downgraded Russia from "Partly Free" to "Not Free" in its annual Freedom of the Press ranking by 2003 (Freedom House, 2003), a monitoring project set up by the Berkman Center for Internet & Society at Harvard noted as late as 2010 that "the Russian blogosphere is a space that appears to be largely free of government control" (Etling et al., 2010, p. 33).

This contrast produced a flourishing online media and tech sector. Their success not only shined against the bleak background of the offline Russian media, but in many respects put it ahead of the curve internationally. In stark contrast with most other countries, Russia's most popular online news media did not represent offline outlets such as newspapers, radio, and TV broadcasters. Instead, Gazeta.Ru, Lenta.Ru, NewsRu.com, Polit.ru and the like were built from scratch and became major news producers in their own right. For instance, their staff did original reporting, often as eyewitnesses, instead of simply digitizing content created by others. Russia is one of the few countries where Google is not the most popular search engine and Facebook is not the most popular social networking website. Remarkably, this occurred without restrictions on American competitors. Unlike the Chinese Baidu and Weibo, the Russian search engine Yandex and the Russian social media networks Odnoklassniki and Vkontakte won out against their American counterparts in a virtually fair competition.[9] In a perfect match, a relatively large Russian audience, which quickly regained its economic solvency but remained highly specific about its content preferences (first and foremost, from the language perspective), was well served by a large pool of well-trained IT professionals, led by a small group of visionary entrepreneurs who decided to seize on the freedoms they gained after the collapse of the Soviet Union.

Successful development of local services did not mean that foreign ones were not actively used by Russians. LiveJournal, the most popular Russian social network between 2001 and 2011, despite originally being American and being used predominantly by English speakers, developed a Russian community so large that it was eventually overtaken by a Russian media holding company and became dominated by the Russian users (Greenall 2012).

An ample and easily available infrastructure for online communication, in Russian and tailored to local preferences, produced vibrant online news media and a blogosphere that by the end of the 2000s had almost completely supplanted TV and newspapers as the main source of information and platforms for discussing them, at least for educated Russians (Clover 2011). Importantly, the Russian blogosphere set a high bar for the quality of discussions, often featuring original reporting or careful examination of the evidence in the reporting from elsewhere, and it produced many successful opinion leaders (Alexanyan et al., 2012; Etling, Roberts, & Faris, 2014). The impact of the Russian blogosphere was further amplified by the Yandex.Blogs service that featured top blog posts of the day on the main page of the most popular Russian search engine.

While the scale of this activity was still relatively small at the time, the initial decision not to pursue the same strategy of hostile takeover that had already been applied to offline media was a political one, and had to do with the power struggle that was taking place within the government rather than with any particular assessment of government as a whole regarding the risks of having a free online press or the challenges in censoring it. Dmitry Medvedev—freshly installed as the third Russian president in May 2008—lacked the power base in the security services that helped Putin so much in entrenching his own power. Neither did he directly control the largest money pools of the government, as these are officially under the jurisdiction of the Council of Ministers, and the new prime minister—Putin himself—was, of course, much more independent than any Russian prime minister before or since. This also diverted the lobbying efforts of large businesses from the Kremlin to the prime minister's office. Finally, Medvedev lacked the personal appeal and "street cred" of Putin. In his search for a power base, he identified the emerging Russian middle class— educated professionals, many of them active consumers if not participants in the Russian blogosphere—as the most promising pool of supporters for his reelection (Black, 2014; Black & Johns, 2013; Sakwa, 2014, Chapters 3–5). Largely ignored by the blatant Soviet-style TV propaganda, the middle class appeared to be ripe for more intelligent engagement by a team of enlightened bureaucrats assembled by Medvedev.

Less than a year after assuming office, in early 2009 Medvedev started a video blog which quickly moved to LiveJournal—Russia's main social network and blogging platform at the time. In 2010 he visited Silicon Valley, met Steve Jobs, and opened a Twitter account at Twitter headquarters in San Francisco. Notably, his account began to follow (in addition to foreign heads of states and Russian officials) several bloggers known for their criticism of the government and the newsfeed of the radio station Echo of Moscow—perhaps the most critical of government, among all the major media outlets, in Russia. Finally, in 2011 he started his Facebook page, which he occasionally used to communicate with his readers on matters not covered or covered badly by the official media (such as the 2011 protests), using a franker tone than in his TV interviews. In all these social networks he built up a large readership, which is typical for heads of states, but still notable since the environment was completely different from the general media environment Medvedev was used to: here he could not get his message across simply by eliminating competition and controlling the platform and the agenda (Yagodin, 2012). On a rare occasion in 2011 he visited a small private TV channel, Rain, which at the time was mainly accessible via cable networks and online. As a result, Medvedev became permanently associated with blogging and social networks and was even called, both in Russia and abroad, "Blogger-in-Chief" (West, 2010). Following Medvedev's example, several of his aides established a significant presence on social media. In particular, his close aide and economic adviser, Arkady Dvorkovich, maintains one of the most popular Russian Twitter accounts, with more than 700,000 followers; he also has a Facebook page, as does Medvedev's press secretary Natalya Timakova (who, as a former journalist with an independent politics and business daily, Kommersant, is the Facebook friend of many prominent liberal reporters).

The first known large-scale deployment of pro-government bots and trolls in Russia was carried out in support of this engagement strategy of President Medvedev (Barash & Kelly, 2012; Kelly et al., 2012). The troll contingent was, for the most part, recruited by repurposing pro-Kremlin youth movements, which had been created to combat color revolutions on Moscow's streets and squares (Hale, 2006). Their job focused primarily on the activities of typical "50-cent-ers"[10]—that is, posting diversionary comments in high-profile opposition blogs (Ananyev & Sobolev, 2017), and retweeting and reposting pro-government messages.

However, using human trolls for retweeting and reposting is inefficient given that these tasks could easily be automated. Fortunately, by the mid-2000s Russia had a well-established and innovative industry of spam and search optimization.[11] Thus technology that was originally commercial—another child of the flourishing online media and tech industry that developed in Russia without much government interference in the 1990s and 2000s—became a key advantage that the Russian government was able to leverage in its nascent online propaganda strategy.

Meanwhile, trolls, as well as more serious pro-government users, focused on generating content to spread. Following the high bar set by the Russian blogosphere, their posts often featured extensive proofs of their claims. The low-trust environment of Russian society inhibited reputation building and instead asked any user to prove their point right away, preferably with detailed, often highly technical, reports on the matter. If the point was false or half true, the proof had to be completely or partially faked, but it also had to look plausible to have a chance of succeeding. From taming down local property disputes (Balmforth, 2016) to bolstering the incumbent's popularity before a mayoral campaign in Moscow (Suleymanov, 2013), all the way to ensuring the legitimacy of presidential elections (Asmolov, 2014), the ultimate, indisputable proof was needed to win the argument. This rule applied even to pro-government trolls.

Notably, in the search for convincing evidence of wrongdoing by the leaders of the opposition and by independent journalists, the weapon of choice was hacking their emails. A hacker with a fitting nickname, "Torquemada Hell" (later identified as Sergei Maksimov and located and convicted in Germany for his activities), terrorized prominent Russian bloggers with email hacks for years (Tselikov, 2012; Gorbachev, 2015). The information he dug up was weaponized and spread by bots, trolls, and others, with the dual goal of compromising victims in the eyes of the general public and sowing discord within the opposition ranks by publicly airing their private, personal grievances against each other. Clearly, if the email accounts of the Democratic National Committee or John Podesta were indeed hacked by the Russian government, no additional training was needed to make the best of them.

The trolls' roots in the search optimization industry ensured that early on the focus was not simply on the number of retweets and reposts, but on manipulating search results and the rankings of popular posts, thereby targeting engagement not just views. Moreover, even content production was guided by search optimization algorithms. Analysis by Fedor and Fredheim (2017) of documents leaked by the chief communications manager of pro-Kremlin youth groups reveals her constant obsession with producing content that could climb to the top of LiveJournal, YouTube, and Yandex. The attention paid to the "virality" of the imagery was no less serious than to the political message it carried. Given that LiveJournal and Yandex at the time were virtually free from government control and dominated by users inclined to support the opposition, government propaganda was put to a rigorous test—which certainly helped improve its quality, particularly compared with similar content broadcast on TV. A similar approach, but one that was carried out in a more systematic fashion, was utilized by RT, when it climbed in the YouTube ratings. As Nelson et al. (2015) show, their channels in all regions and languages contain a significant amount of viral but nonpolitical content (including cat videos, of course) in order to draw audiences to their political stories.

The opportunity to use existing technologies and independent mechanisms that measure success to achieve government propaganda targets was particularly exciting for the Kremlin officials in charge. Compared to expensive state television, online propaganda was available at a bargain price and allowed verification of the amount of content produced (by counting, say, the number of retweets) and estimates of its impact (by tracking how long pro-government posts stayed at the top of LiveJournal or the Russian segment of Twitter). While it has not eliminated misreporting and embezzlement completely (Chen, 2015; Elder, 2012a, 2012b, 2012c), it has probably reduced them in absolute terms—simply because including propaganda in social media is cheaper than using the traditional media—as well as per ruble spent, through feedback and verification mechanisms that are absent offline.

At first, bots were used as a supplementary tool: they were supposed to spread the content produced by trolls and even some genuine pro-government users, who during Medvedev's presidency were (occasionally) willing to engage in discussions with the opposition supporters. When the political environment changed after Putin returned to the Kremlin in 2012—which was accompanied by the largest and longest wave of protests in Russia in two decades (Sakwa, 2014, Chapter 6)—the strategy of engaging with the educated public on social media was deemed a failure, along with many other components of Medvedev's presidency (2014, Chapters 7–9). Government propaganda grew cruder and gained clear nationalistic overtones (Laruelle, 2013; Smyth & Soboleva, 2014). Bots proved to be a reliable tool in this new environment, often supplanting trolls and genuine users: when the goal is simply to block alternative opinions, rather than to engage them in a discussion, easily scalable bot attacks have a natural advantage.

Of course, bots and trolls don't exhaust the menu of options available to a government interested in suppressing alternative views online (for a detailed discussion of the "menu" in general and Russian government choices in particular, see Sanovich, Stukal, & Tucker 2016). For example, the government could simply filter any outlets and platforms it considered to be threatening. This heavy-handed approach, however, could create significant negative economic consequences, impede the government's own operations, and hurt politically neutral and even friendly users, leading to a backlash. Alternatively, the government could try to use its legal and market power to influence what kind of media content is created. For example, news websites and blog platforms could be threatened with sizable fines or even shut down if the user-generated content they hosted were deemed "extremist" by the authorities. This would prompt them to police their content themselves or refrain from hosting it altogether. The government can also prosecute individual bloggers using legal and extra-legal means, as well as take over independent news media and dismiss disloyal editors.

Putin's new government was no longer hesitant about coercing platforms and content producers as well as using technical filtering and distributed denial of service attacks to silence the opposition. Persecution of opposition leaders and even ordinary activists increased significantly and became more systematic. New laws were quickly adopted to expand the definition of "extremist views" and to toughen punishment for spreading them (Sakwa, 2014, Chapter 8). However, as with any other authoritarian government (Howard & Hussain, 2013), it faced the problem of some social media platforms and media outlets being out of reach to both Russian legal regulations and Russian money by virtue of being located outside of Russia. This left Putin with the unenviable choice of either shutting them down within Russia completely and bearing the negative consequences, or letting them remain free so that they provided a powerful platform for alternative opinions. Bots and trolls came in handy in resolving this dilemma, and were deployed to deal with Web resources that could neither be coerced into policing content on the government's behalf, nor bought off. A comparison between the domestic Yandex and Vkontakte, on the one hand, and the foreign Facebook and Twitter, on the other, illustrates the differential government strategy.

By 2009 the state-owned banking giant Sberbank had already bought the "golden share" of Yandex, the most popular Russian search engine and information portal.[12] The influence that Sberbank had on the company's decision making (coupled with the threat of legal prosecution) paid off when at the height of the Ukrainian crisis Yandex had to close its highly popular ranking service for blogs (Smirnova, 2014).[13] The most popular Russian social network, Vkontakte (often called the "Russian Facebook"), initially resisted government pressure. When requests to remove pro-Navalny groups came in the wake of large-scale protests after the Duma elections in 2011, Vkontakte owner and CEO, libertarian Internet guru Pavel Durov, refused to comply (Razumovskaya, 2011).[14] However, when in early 2014 Vkontakte was served with a request to disclose personal data of the administrators of Euromaidan-related pages on Vkontakte, the government did not take no for an answer. Durov had to sell what was left of his share; he then resigned and left the country (Kononov, 2014; Lunden, 2014, Ries, 2014). Around the same time, right in the middle of the crisis in Crimea, LiveJournal (a Russian company since 2006) had to comply with the government order to permanently ban Alexey Navalny's blog—one of the most popular on the platform.

While domestic providers were relatively easily coerced into enforcing government censorship, global social media platforms proved much more capable of resisting the pressure. For example, in December 2014 the authorities requested that Facebook and Vkontakte block access to pages that allowed supporters of Alexey Navalny to register for a rally protesting against his looming criminal conviction, and to receive updates about the place and time of the event. Vkontakte blocked the page and all subsequent attempts to create a copy, posting a warning saying, "This page is blocked upon receiving a Roskomnadzor notification of restricting access to information, which contains calls to participate in mass public events, which fail to follow appropriate regulations, as per the request of the Office of the Prosecutor General of Russia."[15] Facebook also blocked access to a similar page inside Russia, but after a huge outcry in the Western media, refused to block new copies. Moreover, some Russian media outlets, which were afraid to report the scheduling of the event itself, covered the Roskomnadzor order and the social networks' response. As a result, more people learned about the event, and the new event page that had been started on Facebook attracted even more people.

The Russian authorities had been unable to achieve compliance with selective censorship requests, yet were hesitant to prevent access to platforms like Twitter and Facebook completely. Instead, they deployed bots and trolls to alter the balance of opinions in their favor (for example, by artificially pushing friendly content and directing users to the readily accessible "trending" lists) and to prevent the use of these platforms for coordination purposes (for example, by flooding the hashtags used by opposition rally organizers with gibberish or counter-propaganda). In the next section I will discuss the preliminary results of our work to identify one particular tool—fully automated bots—on one particular platform, Twitter.

Identifying Russian Bots on Twitter

Focusing on bots in the study of government digital propaganda might not seem very interesting as a scholarly goal: after all, bots by definition do not produce original content, lifting it instead from elsewhere. But this is exactly what has drawn our attention to them: they provide a more direct and clear connection to the owner's intent. Trolls might tweet based on instructions only some of the time, and provide their own opinions in other tweets. Moreover, drawing the line between a paid troll and a genuine supporter is challenging, and ultimately runs into the question of whether somebody who is not genuinely sympathetic to the government's cause would do this job. Bots, on the other hand, take all their content from a particular source, and if its content is political, the choice of the source becomes a political decision. It does not mean, of course, that every tweet reflects the political agenda of the owner. On the contrary, as we discovered, many bots post a lot of rather mundane content, such as the entire feeds of major news agencies, which necessarily feature many routine reports that do not have any partisan slant to them. However, the choice of one rather than the other news agency—RT instead of Radio Liberty, for example—is clearly a political choice. Given the amount of data bots can produce, such decisions by a few owners of large bot factories could overshadow the individual choices made by ordinary users, thus heavily distorting any impression we might get of what—and who—is popular on Twitter.

In order to distinguish between genuine and automated content generation, together with Denis Stukal and Joshua Tucker we at the Social Media and Political Participation Lab at New York University started collecting Twitter data related to Russian politics in early 2014, when the crisis over Crimea was just starting. The content was automatically downloaded using the Twitter API, based on a set of keywords related to Russian politics. The preliminary results presented here are based on more than 14 million tweets posted between February 2014 and December 2015 by more than 1.3 million accounts. Updated results are forthcoming (Stukal, Sanovich, Bonneau, & Tucker, 2016).

Initially, we worried about our ability to find any bots and to come up with a clear definition distinguishing between bots and humans. However, soon after looking into the data we realized that bots are ubiquitous on Russian political

Twitter, and are easily identifiable on cursory glance: they produce a vast number of very similar tweets (for example, post only retweets, or only pictures, or only news headlines) but lack many of the common attributes of human users such as a name, bio, profile picture, location, and replies to and from other users, and often (though not always) have no followers. Based on these findings we came up with a simple taxonomy of Twitter accounts (described, with the rest of the methodology, in Sanovich et al. (2016) and Stukal et al. (2016)) and charged a team of human coders to create a training dataset of labeled bots and humans using a very conservative definition of a bot that left any accounts that could possibly belong to a human being or a legitimate organization outside of the bot category. We then used this dataset to train a machine learning algorithm to predict the likelihood of any account being a bot, based on a large number of attributes, from the aforementioned number of followers, to the frequency of tweeting, to the number of hashtags used per tweet (Stukal et al., 2016).

Based on a number of performance metrics, our machine learning algorithm demonstrated very high accuracy in bot identification. Applying it to our data yielded a truly staggering result: among accounts with more than 10 tweets in our dataset, around 45 percent are bots.

We also registered a sharp increase in the number of bots (and the amount of content they produce) around the most acute moment in the conflict in Ukraine: in the late summer of 2014, after the downing of the Malaysian Flight 17 and before the new round of fighting (Stukal et al., 2016, Figure 2). This suggests that the bots' deployment follows a clear strategy and is well coordinated.

While our analysis of the characteristics and behavior of these bots is still underway, one fact is particularly illuminating in the context of the discussion of the evolution of the Russian Government's strategy. While our collection covers an important and consequential moment in recent Russian history—during the conflict with Ukraine and the subsequent period of tumultuous relationships with Western countries—and while the bots' patterns of activity clearly responded to the conflict dynamics, many of the bot accounts used in this conflict were created years before. While we don't have data from that time, it is likely that these accounts were used for purely domestic purposes (for example, against the Russian opposition, on behalf of Putin or even Medvedev) before they were deployed to wage a Russian propaganda war in Ukraine and beyond.

Conclusion

Russia could be on a mission to restore its Soviet or imperial glory and to prevent liberal democratic values from taking root in the Russian political system.

Yet the tools used are precisely the ones developed in the most internationally competitive part of the Russian economy that emerged during the liberal 1990s and that (until recently) was not subject to heavy-handed intervention by the government: the online media and tech sector.

Moreover, tools like bots and trolls were developed for rare cases when the government either wanted to engage the opposition in a relatively meaningful discussion online (under Medvedev), or when it wanted to curb it (after Putin returned to the Kremlin in 2012), but was neither able to coerce the foreign platforms hosting the unfriendly discussions to selectively censor them nor prepared to ban these platforms outright.

These external limitations, coupled with the vibrancy and tightness of (and the emphasis on the burden of proof in) the Russian blogosphere, required the government to build sophisticated tools of online propaganda and counter-propaganda. They combined the ability of bots to jam unfriendly and amplify friendly content, and the inconspicuousness of trolls posing as real people and providing elaborate proof of even their most patently false and outlandish claims. The government also utilized existing, independent online tracking and measurement tools to make sure that the content it pays for reaches and engages the target audiences. Last but not least, it invested in the hacking capabilities that allowed for the quick production of compromising material against the targets of its smear campaigns.

The latter suggests that building up cyber defense capabilities is certainly warranted for electoral campaigns and other entities (including inside Russia) that might become a target of Russian government digital propaganda campaigns. However, the former—the fact that bots and trolls thrive in the low-trust, anything goes, prove-it-on-the-spot environment—also means that building up the reputation of mainstream media, and ensuring that their objectivity, fairness, and professional integrity are trusted by the public, would do more than anything else to deny Russian digital propaganda the power it currently wields. Beyond that, exposing trolls and bots as well as the nuts and bolts of their campaigns could help both to educate the public in how to avoid falling for the misinformation they spread and to find technological means of disrupting their activity.

Acknowledgments

The data presented here were collected by the Social Media and Political Participation (SMaPP) Laboratory at New York University (https://wp.nyu.edu/smapp/). SMaPP is led by Professors Joshua Tucker, Richard Bonneau,

John T. Jost, and Jonathan Nagler, and is supported by the INSPIRE program of the National Science Foundation (Award SES-1248077), the New York University Global Institute for Advanced Study, the Moore–Sloan Data Science Environment, and Dean Thomas Carew's Research Investment Fund at New York University.

Notes

1. Russian state-owned global TV news network broadcasting in multiple languages, formerly known as Russia Today.
2. Russian state-owned international news agency and family of news websites and radio stations, succeeding foreign broadcasting of RIA Novosti and the Voice of Russia, respectively.
3. This passage is also quoted in the recent House of Commons report on the United Kingdom's relations with Russia, see: https://www.publications.parliament.uk/pa/cm201617/cmselect/cmfaff/ 120/120.pdf.
4. The countries of origin of the bots that concerned DARPA are not disclosed in publicly available documents, but the report summarizing the results of the competition mentions Russian bots' activity in Ukraine as a case where the developed methods would be applicable (Subrahmanian et al., 2016, p. 38).
5. "Three Thousand Fake Tanks" (2017), "Fakes, Bots, and Blockings in Armenia" (2017), "Hashtag Campaign" (2017), "Russian and French Twitter Mobs in Election Push" (2017), "The Kremlin's Audience in France" (2017), "How the Alt-Right Brought #SyriaHoax to America" (2017), "Portrait of a Botnet" (2017), "Spread it on Reddit" (2017), "Russian Internet" (2017). See also Broderick (2017).
6. "Kremlin Boosts Budget for TV Channel RT" (2016).
7. While all major broadcasters were taken over in the early 2000s, the three smaller and regional independent TV channels, Ren TV, TV Rain (Dozhd), and Tomsk TV2 were put under government control or taken off the air in 2014.
8. See http://bd.fom.ru/report/map/projects/internet/ internet1133/vesna2011.
9. Still, Vkontakte (but not Yandex or Odnoklassniki) had significantly benefited from the lax enforcement of the property rights. However, this does not make comparison with China less impressive, given that China is also famous for widespread piracy.
10. Chinese Internet trolls, who are allegedly paid small sums of money for every pro-government post they publish. Recent research suggests that most of them are, instead, permanently on the government payroll, working for various propaganda departments (Miller, 2016). In the Russian case, however, the work was mostly outsourced and the workers were indeed paid per post (Nossik, 2013).
11. One of the early leaders of this industry, German Klimenko, who made a fortune from blog platforms and data analytics, was ultimately appointed Putin's "Internet adviser" (Turovsky, 2016).
12. The sale, allegedly, took place after negotiations with Dmitry Medvedev and multiple threats to designate companies such as Yandex as "strategic," which would require them to re-register in Russia and hence severely diminish their appeal on the international capital markets. Yandex is incorporated in the Netherlands as Yandex N.V.—a fact that in 2014 was publicly condemned by Vladimir Putin at his meeting with People's Front for Russia (Brennan, 2014).
13. At about the same time, Yandex founder Arkady Volozh had to resign as Yandex's Russian CEO. (He kept the executive position in the international operations, though; see Beard, 2014.)

14. Alexey Navalny is the leading Russian opposition politician. He is subject to multiple on-going criminal investigations and has spent many months under house arrest. Amnesty International and the Russian human rights group Memorial designated him a prisoner of conscience and a political prisoner, respectively.

15. According to those regulations, authorities could not be notified about the upcoming rally earlier than 15 days in advance. The page was blocked 26 days before the event announced on it was scheduled to take place.

References

Alexanyan, K., Barash, V., Etling, B., Faris, R., Gasser, U., Kelly, J., Palfrey, J., Roberts. H. (2012). Exploring Russian Cyberspace: Digitally-Mediated Collective Action and the Networked Public Sphere. Berkman Center Research Publication No. 2012-2. Retrieved from http://papers.ssrn.com/abstract=2014998.

Ananyev, M., & Sobolev, A. (2017, April). Fantastic Beasts and Whether They Matter: Do Internet "Trolls" Influence Political Conversations in Russia? Paper presented at the meeting of the Midwest Political Science Association. Chicago, IL.

Applebaum, A. (2016a, December 12). Russia's Next Election Operation: Germany. *The Washington Post*. Retrieved from https://www.washingtonpost.com/news/global-opinions/wp/2016/12/12/russias-next-election-operation-germany/.

Applebaum, A. (2016b, April 8). The Dutch Just Showed the World How Russia Influences Western European Elections. *The Washington Post*. Retrieved from https://www.washingtonpost.com/opinions/russias-influence-in-western-elections/2016/04/08/b427602a-fcf1-11e5-886f-a037dba38301_story.html?utm_term=.b4dc47e046b8.

Applebaum, A., & Lucas, E. (2016, May 6). The Danger of Russian Disinformation. *The Washington Post*. Retrieved from https://www.washingtonpost.com/opinions/the-danger-of-russian-disinformation/2016/05/06/b31d9718-12d5-11e6-8967-7ac733c56f12_story.html.

Asmolov, G. (2014). Kremlin's Cameras and Virtual Potemkin Villages: ICT and the Construction of Statehood. In S. Livingstone & G. Walter-Drop (Eds.), *Bits and Atoms: Information and Communication Technology in Areas of Limited Statehood* (pp. 30–46). doi: 10.1093/acprof:oso/9780199941599.001.0001.

Balmforth, T. (2016, February 16). Praise Our Campaign to Destroy the Moscow Kiosks and We Will Reward You. Radio Free Europe/Radio Liberty. Retrieved from https://www.rferl.org/a/russia-kiosks-destruction-army-of-bots-activists-rewarded/27555171.html.

Barash, V., & Kelly, J. (2012). Salience vs. Commitment: Dynamics of Political Hashtags in Russian Twitter. Berkman Center Research Publication No. 2012-9. Retrieved from http://papers.ssrn.com/abstract=2034506.

Bartles, C. K. (2016). Getting Gerasimov right. *Military Review, 96*(1), 30–38.

Beard, N. (2014, August 26). Founder and CEO of Yandex, Arkady Volozh, Resigns. *Calvert Journal*. Retrieved from http://calvertjournal.com/news/show/3035/founder-of-yandex-resigns-amid-controversy-arkady-volozh.

Bertrand, N. (2016, December 10). "A Model for Civilization": Putin's Russia Has Emerged as "A Beacon for Nationalists" and the American Alt-Right. *Business Insider*. Retrieved from http://www.businessinsider.com/russia-connections-to-the-alt-right-2016-11

Bialik, C., & Arthur, R. (2016, November 23). Demographics, Not Hacking, Explain the Election Results. *FiveThirtyEight*. Retrieved from https://fivethirtyeight.com/features/demographics-not-hacking-explain-the-election-results/.

Black, J. L. (2014). *The Russian Presidency of Dimitri Medvedev, 2008–2012: The Next Step Forward or Merely a Time Out?* New York: Routledge.

Black, J. L., & Johns, M. (2013). *Russia after 2012: From Putin to Medvedev to Putin—Continuity, Change, or Revolution?* London: Routledge.

Brennan, C. (2014, April 24). Putin Says CIA Created the Internet, Cites Foreign Influence at Yandex. *The Moscow Times*. Retrieved from http://www.themoscowtimes.com/news/article/putin-says-cia-created-the-internet-cites-foreign-influence-at-yandex/498903.html.

Broderick, R. (2017, April 25). Here's How Far-Right Trolls Are Spreading Hoaxes about French Presidential Candidate Emmanuel Macron. *BuzzFeed*. Retrieved from https://www.buzzfeed.com/ryanhatesthis/heres-how-far-right-trolls-are-spreading-hoaxes-about.

Bruno, J. (2014, April 16). Russian Diplomats Are Eating America's Lunch. *POLITICO Magazine*. Retrieved from http://www.politico.com/magazine/story/2014/04/russias-diplomats-are-better-than-ours-105773.

Burrett, T. (2010). *Television and Presidential Power in Putin's Russia*. London: Routledge.

Chen, A. (2015, June 2). The Agency. *The New York Times*. Retrieved from http://www.nytimes.com/2015/06/07/magazine/the-agency.html.

Clover, C. (2011, December 1). Internet Subverts Russian TV's Message. *The Financial Times*. Retrieved from https://www.ft.com/content/85dd8e96-1c2d-11e1-9631-00144feabdc0.

Conley, H., Stefanov, R., Vladimirov, M., & Mina, J. (2016). *The Kremlin Playbook: Understanding Russian influence in Central and Eastern Europe*. Washington DC: Center for Strategic/International Studies.

Connell, M., & Evans, R. (2015). Russia's Ambiguous Warfare and Implications for the U.S. Marine Corps. Retrieved from Center for Naval Analyses website: http://www.dtic.mil/cgibin/GetTRDoc?Location=U2&doc=GetTRDoc.pdf&AD=ADA618343.

Dickey, J., Everett, T., Galvach, Z., Mesko, M., & Soltis, A. (2015). Russian Political Warfare: Origin, Evolution, and Application. Retrieved from the Naval Postgraduate School website: https://calhoun.nps.edu/handle/10945/45838.

Elder, M. (2012a, February 7). Emails Give Insight into Kremlin Youth Group's Priorities, Means and Concerns. *The Guardian*. Retrieved from http://www.theguardian.com/world/2012/feb/07/nashi-emails-insight-kremlin-groups-priorities.

Elder, M. (2012b, February 7). Hacked Emails Allege Russian Youth Group Nashi Paying Bloggers. *The Guardian*. Retrieved from http://www.theguardian.com/world/2012/feb/07/hacked-emails-nashi-putin-bloggers.

Elder, M. (2012c, February 7). Polishing Putin: Hacked Emails Suggest Dirty Tricks by Russian Youth Group. *The Guardian*. Retrieved from http://www.theguardian.com/world/2012/feb/07/putin-hacked-emails-russian-nashi.

Enten, H. (2016, December 23). How Much Did Wikileaks Hurt Hillary Clinton? *FiveThirtyEight*. Retrieved from https://fivethirtyeight.com/features/wikileaks-hillary-clinton/

Erickson, A. (2017, January 12). If Russia Today is Moscow's Propaganda Arm, It's Not Very Good at its Job. *The Washington Post*. Retrieved from https://www.washingtonpost.com/news/worldviews/wp/2017/01/12/if-russia-today-is-moscows-propaganda-arm-its-not-very-good-at-its-job/.

Etling, B., Alexanyan, K., Kelly, J., Faris, R., Palfrey, J. G., & Gasser, U. (2010). Public Discourse in the Russian Blogosphere: Mapping RuNet Politics and Mobilization. Berkman Center Research Publication No. 2010-11. Retrieved from http://papers.ssrn.com/abstract=1698344.

Etling, B., Roberts, H., & Faris, F. (2014). Blogs as an Alternative Public Sphere: The Role of Blogs, Mainstream Media, and TV in Russia's Media Ecology. Berkman Center Research Publication No. 2014-8. Retrieved from http://papers.ssrn.com/abstract=2430786.

European Parliament. (2016). EU Strategic Communication to Counteract anti-EU Propaganda by Third Parties. Resolution, November 23. Retrieved from http://www.europarl.europa.eu/sides/getDoc.do?pubRef=-//EP//NONSGML+TA+P8-TA-2016-0441+0+DOC+PDF+V0//EN.

European Union Institute for Security Studies. (2016). EU Strategic Communications with a View to Counteracting Propaganda. European Parliament. Retrieved from http://www.europarl.europa.eu/thinktank/en/document.html?reference=EXPO_IDA(2016)578008.

Fakes, Bots, and Blockings in Armenia. (2017). *DFRLab*. Retrieved from https://medium.com/dfrlab/fakes-bots-and-blockings-in-armenia-44a4c87ebc46.

Fedor, J., & Fredheim, R. (2017). "We need more clips about Putin, and lots of them:" Russia's State-Commissioned Online Visual Culture. *Nationalities Papers, 45*(2), 161–181.

Freedom House. (2009). *Freedom of the Press 2003: A Global Survey of Media Independence*. New York: Rowman & Littlefield Publishers.

Gel'man, V., Travin, D., & Marganiya, O. (2014). *Reexamining Economic and Political Reforms in Russia, 1985–2000: Generations, Ideas, and Changes*. Lanham, Maryland: Lexington Books.

Gessen, M. (2012). *The Man without a Face: The Unlikely Rise of Vladimir Putin*. New York: Penguin.

Gorbachev, A. (2015, July 9). Meet the Hacker Who Terrorized the Russian Blogosphere. *Newsweek*. Retrieved from http://www.newsweek.com/2015/07/17/gospel-according-hell-351544.html.

Gorenberg, G. (2016, October 14). The Strange Sympathy of the Far Left for Putin. *The American Prospect*. Retrieved from http://prospect.org/article/strange-sympathy-far-left-putin.

Gramer, R. (2017, January 10). Wary of Russian Cyber Threat, France Plans to Bolster Its Army of "Digital Soldiers." *Foreign Policy*. Retrieved from https://foreignpolicy.com/2017/01/10/wary-of-the-russian-cyber-threat-france-plans-to-bolster-its-army-of-digital-soldiers-cyber-attack-europe-elections-hack/.

Greenall, R. (2012, February 29). LiveJournal: Russia's Unlikely Internet Giant. *BBC News*. Retrieved from http://www.bbc.co.uk/news/magazine-17177053.

Groves, S. (2007). Advancing Freedom in Russia. Backgrounder No. 2088. Retrieved from The Heritage Foundation website: http://www.heritage.org/europe/report/advancing-freedom-russia.

Hale, H. (2006). Democracy or Autocracy on the March? The Colored Revolutions as Normal Dynamics of Patronal Presidentialism. *Communist and Post-Communist Studies, 39*(3), 305–329.

Hashtag campaign: #MacronLeaks. (2017, May 5). *DFRLab*. Retrieved from https://medium.com/dfrlab/hashtag-campaign-macronleaks-4a3fb870c4e8.

Hopkins, D. (2016, December 20). Voters Really Did Switch to Trump at the Last Minute. *FiveThirtyEight*. Retrieved from https://fivethirtyeight.com/features/voters-really-did-switch-to-trump-at-the-last-minute/.

How the Alt-Right Brought #SyriaHoax to America. (2017, April 7). *DFRLab*. Retrieved from https://medium.com/dfrlab/how-the-alt-right-brought-syriahoax-to-america-47745118d1c9.

Howard, P., & Hussain, M. (2013). *Democracy's Fourth Wave? Digital Media and the Arab Spring*. Oxford: Oxford University Press.

Kelly, J., Barash, V., Alexanyan, K., Etling B., Faris, R., Gasser, U., & Palfrey, J. G. (2012). Mapping Russian Twitter. Berkman Center Research Publication No. 2012-3. Retrieved from http://papers.ssrn.com/abstract=2028158.

King, G., Pan, J., & Roberts, M. (2013). How Censorship in China Allows Government Criticism but Silences Collective Expression. *American Political Science Review, 107*(2), 326–343.

Kofman, M. (2017, January 17). The Moscow School of Hard Knocks: Key Pillars of Russian Strategy. *War on the Rocks*. Retrieved from https://warontherocks.com/2017/01/the-moscow-school-of-hard-knocks-key-pillars-of-russian-strategy/.

Kononov, N. (2014, March 10). The Kremlin's Social Media Takeover. *The New York Times*. Retrieved from http://www.nytimes.com/2014/03/11/opinion/the-kremlins-social-media-takeover.html.

Kovalev, A. (2010, September 24). Russia's Blogging Revolution. *The Guardian*. Retrieved from https://www.theguardian.com/commentisfree/2010/sep/24/russia-blogging-revolution.

Kovalev, A. (2017, March 29). Crippled by the Kremlin, Russia's State Media No Longer Competes. *The Moscow Times*. Retrieved from https://themoscowtimes.com/articles/crippled-by-the-kremlin-russias-state-media-cant-even-compete-anymore-57577.

Kremlin Boosts Budget for TV Channel RT. (2016, December 1). *The Moscow Times*. Retrieved from https://themoscowtimes.com/news/rt-channel-gets-additional-12-bln-rubles-56375.

Laruelle, M. (2013). Conservatism as the Kremlin's New Toolkit: An Ideology at the Lowest Cost. *Russian Analytical Digest, 138*, (8), 2–4.

Lipman, M. (2009). Media Manipulation and Political Control in Russia. Retrieved from Chatham House website: https://www.chathamhouse.org/sites/default/files/public/Research/Russia%20and%20Eurasia/300109lipman.pdf.

Lunden, I. (2014, April 22). Durov, Out For Good from VK.com, Plans a Mobile Social Network outside Russia. *TechCrunch*. Retrieved from http://techcrunch.com/2014/04/22/durov-out-for-good-from-vk-com-plans-a-mobile-social-network-outside-russia/.

MacKinnon, R. (2011). China's "Networked Authoritarianism." *Journal of Democracy*, 22(2), 32–46.

Marusic, D. (2016, December 13). What Does Russia Really Want? *The American Interest*. Retrieved from http://www.the-american-interest.com/2016/12/13/what-does-russia-want/.

McDermott, R. N. (2016). Does Russia Have a Gerasimov Doctrine? *Parameters*, 46(1), 97–105.

Michel, C. (2017, January 13). How Putin Played the Far Left. *The Daily Beast*. Retrieved from http://www.thedailybeast.com/articles/2017/01/13/how-putin-played-the-far-left.html.

Michel, C., & Pottier, J.-M. (2017, May 4). The Kremlin's California Dream. *Slate*. Retrieved from http://www.slate.com/articles/news_and_politics/foreigners/2017/05/why_russia_cultivates_fringe_groups_on_the_far_right_and_far_left.html.

Miller, B. A. P. (2016). Automated Detection of Chinese Government Astroturfers Using Network and Social Metadata. Manuscript in preparation. Retrieved from https://papers.ssrn.com/abstract=2738325.

Musgrave, P. (2016, November 28). If You're Even Asking if Russia Hacked the Election, Russia Got What It Wanted. *The Washington Post*. Retrieved from https://www.washingtonpost.com/posteverything/wp/2016/11/28/whether-or-not-russians-hacked-the-election-they-messed-with-our-democracy/.

National Intelligence Council. (2017). Assessing Russian Activities and Intentions in Recent US Elections. Retrieved from https://www.dni.gov/files/documents/ICA_2017_01.pdf.

Nelson, E., Orttung, R., & Livshen, A. (2015). Measuring RT Impact on YouTube. *Russian Analytical Digest*, 177(8), 2–9.

Nossik, A. (2013, September 10). 11 Rubles and 80 Kopecks per Comment. *Echo of Moscow*. Retrieved from http://www.echo.msk.ru/blog/nossik/1154616-echo/.

Nossik. A. (2014, May 15). I Helped Build Russia's Internet. Now Putin Wants to Destroy It. *The New Republic*. Retrieved from http://www.newrepublic.com/article/117771/putins-internet-crackdown-russias-first-blogger-reacts.

Oates, S., & Lokot, T. (2013). Twilight of the Gods?: How the Internet Challenged Russian Television News Frames in the Winter Protests of 2011–12. Manuscript in preparation. Retrieved from http://papers.ssrn.com/abstract=2286727.

Pomerantsev, P., & Lucas, E. (2016). *Winning the Information War*. Center for European Policy Analysis. London: Legatum Institute.

Portrait of a Botnet. (2017, February 21). *DFRLab*. Retrieved from https://medium.com/dfrlab/portrait-of-a-botnet-12fa9d5d6b3.

Razumovskaya, O. (2011, December 8). Russian Social Network: FSB Asked It to Block Kremlin Protesters. *The Wall Street Journal*. Retrieved from http://blogs.wsj.com/emergingeurope/2011/12/08/russian-social-network-fsb-asked-it-to-block-kremlin-protesters/.

Remnick, D., Yaffa, J., & Osnos, E. (2017, March 6). Trump, Putin, and the New Cold War. Annals of Diplomacy, *The New Yorker*, 40–55.

Reuters. (2017, January 9). Germany Investigating Unprecedented Spread of Fake News Online. *The Guardian*. Retrieved from https://www.theguardian.com/world/2017/jan/09/germany-investigating-spread-fake-news-online-russia-election.

Ries, B. (2014, April 16). Founder of "Russia's Facebook" Says Government Demanded Ukraine Protestors' Data. *Mashable*. Retrieved from http://mashable.com/2014/04/16/vkontakte-founder-fsb-euromaidan/.

Russell, M. (2016, October). Russia's Information War: Propaganda or Counter-Propaganda? European Parliamentary Research Service Briefing, European Parliament. Retrieved from http://www.europarl.europa.eu/thinktank/en/document.html?reference=EPRS_ BRI(2016)589810.

Russian and French Twitter Mobs in Election Push. (2017, April 21). *DFRLab.* Retrieved from https://medium.com/dfrlab/russian-and-french-twitter-mobs-in-election-push-bca327aa41a5.

Russian Internet: Fake News Haven? (2017, January 28). *DFRLab.* Retrieved from https://medium.com/@DFRLab/russian-internet-fake-news-haven-b5acd9ebd06a.

Sakwa, R. (2014). *Putin Redux: Power and Contradiction in Contemporary Russia.* London: Routledge.

Saletan, W., & Carter, P. (2017, March 31). Hate Makes Us Weak. *Slate.* Retrieved from http://www.slate.com/articles/news_and_politics/politica/2017/03/how_russia_capitalizes_on_american_racism_and_xenophobia.html.

Sanovich, S., Stukal, D., & Tucker, J. (2016). Turning the Virtual Tables: Government Strategies for Addressing Online Opposition with an Application to Russia. Manuscript submitted for publication. Retrieved from NYU website: https://18798-presscdn-pagely.netdna-ssl.com/smapp/wp-content/uploads/sites/1693/2017/06/Online_Opposition.pdf.

Smirnova, A. (2014, April 18). Yandex.Blogs to Partially Shut Down. *Look At Me.* Retrieved from http://www.lookatme.ru/mag/live/experience-news/203183-rip-yandex-blogs.

Smyth, R., & Soboleva, I. (2014). Looking Beyond the Economy: Pussy Riot and the Kremlin's Voting Coalition. *Post-Soviet Affairs, 30*(4), 257–275.

Snegovaya, M. (2015). Putin's Information Warfare in Ukraine: Soviet Origins of Russia's Hybrid Warfare. Retrieved from http://understandingwar.org/report/putins-information-warfare-ukraine-soviet-origins-russias-hybrid-warfare.

Soldatov, A., & Borogan, I. (2013). Russia's Surveillance State. *World Policy Journal, 30*(3), 23–30.

Spread it on Reddit. (2017, February 10). *DFRLab.* Retrieved from https://medium.com/dfrlab/spread-it-on-reddit-3170a463e787.

Stukal, D., Sanovich, S., Bonneau, R., & Tucker, J. (2016). Detecting Bots on Russian Political Twitter. Manuscript submitted for publication.

Subrahmanian, V. S., Azaria, A., Durst, S., Kagan, V., Galstyan, A., Lerman, K., . . . Menczer, F. (2016). The DARPA Twitter Bot Challenge. *Computer, 49*(6), 38–46.

Suleymanov, S. How the Moscow Mayoral Candidates are Winning the Internet. (2013, August 30). *The Interpreter.* Retrieved from http://www.interpretermag.com/how-the-moscow-mayoral-candidates-are-winning-the-internet/.

Talbott, S., & Brandt, J. (2017, March 2). What Putin Is Up To. *The Atlantic.* Retrieved from https://www.theatlantic.com/international/archive/2017/03/putin-trump-russia-flynn-sessions-hack-kremlin/518412/.

The Kremlin's Audience in France. (2017, April 14). *DFRLab.* Retrieved from https://medium.com/dfrlab/the-kremlins-audience-in-france-884a80515f8b.

Three Thousand Fake Tanks. (2017, January 12). *DFRLab.* Retrieved from https://medium.com/@DFRLab/three-thousand-fake-tanks-575410c4f64d.

Timberg, C. (2016, November 30). Effort to Combat Foreign Propaganda Advances in Congress. *The Washington Post.* Retrieved from https://www.washingtonpost.com/business/economy/effort-to-combat-foreign-propaganda-advances-in-congress/2016/11/30/9147e1ac-e221-47be-ab92-9f2f7e69d452_story.html.

Tregubova, Y. (2003). *The Tales of a Kremlin Digger.* Moscow: Ad Marginem.

Tselikov, A. (2012, July 23). Russia: Hacker Hell, Scourge of the RuNet. *Global Voices.* Retrieved from https://globalvoices.org/2012/07/23/russia-hacker-hell-scourge-of-the-runet.

Turovsky, D. (2016, February 26). Putin's Internet Guy: Who is German Klimenko, and How Will He Advise Russia's President? *Meduza.* Retrieved from https://meduza.io/en/feature/2016/02/26/putin-s-internet-guy.

West, D. (2010). President Dmitry Medvedev: Russia's Blogger-in-Chief. Retrieved from The Brookings Institution website: http://www.brookings.edu/research/opinions/2010/04/14-medvedev-west.

Yablokov, I. (2015). Conspiracy Theories as a Russian Public Diplomacy Tool: The Case of Russia Today (RT). *Politics*, 35(3), 301–315.

Yagodin, D. (2012). Blog Medvedev: Aiming for Public Consent. *Europe-Asia Studies*, 64(8), 1415–1434.

2

Ukraine

External Threats and Internal Challenges

MARIIA ZHDANOVA AND DARIYA ORLOVA

Introduction

Oxford Dictionaries named the term *post-truth* the word of 2016. Since then, public attention to the concept has been increasing exponentially. While the term became popular in Western public discourse just recently, the case of Ukraine, an Eastern European country sandwiched between Russia and the European Union (EU), represents a vivid example of how "post-truth" circumstances have shaped developments in an entire country for the past three years.

Since the EuroMaidan revolution and Russia's annexation of Crimea, Ukraine has turned into the frontline of numerous disinformation campaigns in Europe. Many such campaigns have had a significant Internet component, involving social media to spread and promote a certain narrative. Some of the disseminated fake stories—such as the tale of a "crucified boy" (StopFake, 2014a; Nemtsova, 2014) or the story about Ukrainian soldiers being paid with "two slaves and a piece of land" (StopFake, 2014c)—have turned into textbook examples of how propaganda works. Other stories conveying peculiar narratives such as "weakness of the EU" or "migrants destroying Europe" have been circulated all over Europe.

As one of the first countries to face a serious disinformation crisis in the present day, Ukraine represents a curious case for study, with a combination of factors for exploration that is quite unique. Over the past three years, the country has lived through a massive uprising against a corrupt and authoritarian regime, annexation of part of its territory by a neighboring country, the eruption of armed conflict in the eastern provinces instigated by external forces, severe economic crisis, political turmoil, ongoing transition, and painful reforms. All these challenges have been accompanied by the rapid development of information technologies and growing Internet use, which has significantly contributed to the shaping of developments in the country.

Past Research and Previous Understandings

Given the scale of the conflict between Ukraine and Russia, and the salience of the information struggle dimension therein, the issue of propaganda and disinformation campaigns has attracted a lot of attention from the media and scholars alike. Lucas and Nimmo (2015) explored general tactics used by the Russian state-controlled TV channel RT and the news agency Sputnik in conveying the Kremlin's narrative, while Meister (2016) analyzed their influence on Western audiences. Lucas and Pomerantsev (2016) described a variety of techniques used by the Kremlin in disinformation campaigns. Hoskins and O'Loughlin (2015, p. 1320) used the case to discuss the nature of new types of present-day conflicts that are "characterized by the appropriation and control of previously chaotic dynamics by mainstream media and, at a slower pace, government and military policy-makers."

Less effort, however, has been made to analyze the technological tools employed to erode public discourse. Kelly et al. (2012) suggested that most actors were using the tactics of online marketers and PR specialists to spread their messages, while content analysis of tweets from Russian Channel One about Ukraine concluded that the aim was to blur the border between lies and reality (Khaldarova & Pantti, 2016). Bērziņš et al. (2014) suggested that the Russian government's established control over media outlets has slowly turned to social media in the form of government-controlled Internet "trolling," which remains a largely under-researched phenomenon.

The issue of computational propaganda in the Ukraine–Russia conflict has been predominantly addressed by journalists. Reports suggested that large troll factories have been actively used to create blogs, social media posts, and comments to spread certain narratives. In September 2013, a Russian journalist from Novaya Gazeta started working at the Russian troll factory in Olgino to investigate the daily operations of the company (Garmazhapova, 2013). In October 2014, the St. Petersburg-based online magazine Dp.ru suggested that the same agency employing around 250 people was actively engaged in online discussions about the Ukraine crisis with the goal of undermining the authority of Ukrainian politicians and posting hate speech and fake stories, thus shifting attention from the real events (Butsenko, 2014). Finally, in 2015, the *New York Times* proved that the Russian Internet Research Agency (the same infamous

Olgino factory) was also producing fake clones of news sites, fabricating videos, and attempting to influence US politics through disinformation (Chen, 2015). In March 2017, journalists from RBC company described a new phenomenon, the "Russian media factory," which combined 16 websites licensed by Roskomnadzor (the federal executive body overseeing media in Russia), with a total audience of over 36 million unique users, creating stories on current events and political figures such as Trump, Putin, and Poroshenko (Zakharov & Rusyaeva, 2017).

Less research has focused on computational propaganda within Ukraine, the country's counter-propaganda attempts, or the issue of internal manipulation of public opinion. Several media reports have concluded that numerous political actors in Ukraine utilize different online means to attack opponents and promote their own agenda (Ivantsova, 2015; Kriukova & Pasiutina, 2016). It is noteworthy, however, that there is significant confusion in terminology around computational propaganda in Ukraine. It is quite common to see the terms bots, political bots, trolls, and fake accounts used interchangeably in media reports, and even in the discourse of professionals who are directly engaged in providing social media management services. Thus, this chapter will start with a definition of the key terms.

Explanation of Terms and Variables

In this chapter, we consider computational propaganda to be the "assemblage of social media platforms, autonomous agents, and big data tasked with the manipulation of public opinion" (Woolley and Howard, 2016, p. 4886). One example of such agents is bots—automated software operating online. Depending on their functions, bots may be categorized into general, social, and political. The purpose of general bots (also referred to as "crawlers") is to gather information, while social bots operate on social media platforms and can interact with real users by sharing messages and engaging in comments, and so forth. Political bots, per Woolley and Howard (2016, p. 4885), are the "algorithms that operate over social media, written to learn from and mimic real people so as to manipulate public opinion across a diverse range of social media and device networks." When discussing bots in this chapter, we will use the definition of political bots operating online (through social media, blogs, in the commentary sections of popular websites, etc.). Hiding their bot identity, automated systems can promote certain ideas to create heated debates online and, according to Hegelich and Janetszko (2016), may be considered a new political actor in the Russia–Ukraine conflict. Thus, it is important to examine not only the ways bots can engage in political conversations and the scale of such activities, but the potential impact on policymaking.

Methodology

This chapter explores the peculiarities of computational propaganda in Ukraine through interviews with experts and actors involved in the online communication industry, as well as through analysis of secondary data. Examination of the context and existing literature on the use of bots and other digital tools in Ukraine prompted the following research questions to be addressed by this study—first: "How are bots and other tools used for online political communication in Ukraine?" and second: "How has Ukraine dealt with Russian online propaganda against a backdrop of ongoing conflict?"

In order to understand how computational propaganda works in Ukraine, face-to-face interviews with 10 experts (including digital and social media specialists, academics, journalists, and activists) and a number of informal conversations were conducted in Ukraine. Background research on the issue helped identify the major platforms, tools, and strategies for political communication on the Web. Quantitative data were also analyzed, namely a number of bots and fake accounts in the Twitter audience of popular Ukrainian news websites.

The chapter begins with an overview of the general context of the case study, explaining the major transformations in Ukrainian society and outlining the key political actors, media ownership structure, and the history of computational propaganda in Ukraine. This contextual overview of computational propaganda is then followed by detailed analysis of distinctive examples of its use.

Case Context

Ukraine's recent history has been characterized by dramatic events, crucial challenges, and dynamic changes across political and social landscapes. The EuroMaidan revolution that swept across Ukraine between November 2013 and February 2014 dramatically changed the Ukrainian political and social landscape and triggered crucial transformations in the country. The three-month standoff between protesters and government forces left over 100 people dead, most of them pro-Maidan protesters. Then-president Viktor Yanukovych, whose last-moment decision to suspend the signing of an association agreement with the EU prompted the initial EuroMaidan rallies, fled the country; the Ukrainian parliament created a new coalition, appointed a new government, and called for presidential and parliamentary elections that eventually took place in May and October 2014, respectively.

Right after Yanukovych's escape, pro-Russian militants seized the key buildings and parliament of Crimea, a Ukrainian peninsula in the Black Sea inhabited by a Russian-speaking majority. Military personnel without insignia occupied Crimea, a dubious and internationally unrecognized public vote was held in March 2014, bringing pro-secession results, and this was followed by Russia's formal annexation of Crimea. The situation was exacerbated in other parts of the country, especially in the industrial region of Donbas, when Russia-supported militants seized government buildings in some oblasts of Donetsk and Luhansk, following the "Crimean scenario," and created the so-called Donetsk and Luhansk People's Republics in May 2014. The conflict turned into a fully fledged war involving the Ukrainian army, separatist forces, and Russian troops, as numerous reports show. While ceasefire agreements were signed in Minsk in September 2014 and February 2015 and the situation stabilized some-what, minor skirmishes continue in the conflict area. Part of Ukraine's territory remains under the control of pro-Russian separatist forces, and Crimea has been annexed by Russia.

The conflict between Ukraine and Russia has been characterized by a fierce standoff in the realm of information. Following EuroMaidan and throughout the conflict, Ukraine has been targeted by numerous disinformation campaigns and propaganda efforts, predominantly from Russia (Snegovaya, 2015; Khaldarova & Pantti, 2016; Nygren et al., 2016). The post-Maidan internal transition of Ukraine has been marked by political instability, a high level of political competitiveness (Way, 2015), dynamic development of civil society (Solonenko, 2015), and "democratization" of communication between political elites, civil society, and citizens. In this context, the significance of political communication online has been increasing in Ukraine, giving way to new approaches and tools (Novoye Vremya, 2016).

POLITICAL ACTORS

The presidential and parliamentary elections that followed the victory of EuroMaidan brought a new reconfiguration of political elites in power. Petro Poroshenko, a rich Ukrainian oligarch with multiple businesses, including his most famous confectionery company Roshen, was elected as president of Ukraine. His election agenda emphasized pro-European aspirations and promises of reforms. Poroshenko's political force, Petro Poroshenko Bloc, also gained many seats in the Ukrainian parliament, 132 out of 450. The second-largest faction of parliament is represented by the Narodny Front party. The two forces made up the core of the post-Maidan parliamentary coalition and formed the government. The other parliamentary factions are represented by the Samopomich party, headed by the mayor of Lviv city, Andriy Sadovy; Opposition Bloc, a rebranded Party of Regions that had been a ruling party during the Yanukovych presidency; and Yuliya Tymoshenko's Batkivshchyna and Radical Party of Ukraine. While the political environment remains highly competitive and unstable in Ukraine, President Poroshenko is believed to have quite strong control over the government and a parliamentary majority, although even his own faction has several informal groups with opposing standpoints on many crucial issues.

It is also important to note that the Ukrainian political landscape has long been dominated by the oligarchs and financial and industrial groups. While this pattern has been broadly criticized as being an obstacle to Ukraine's transition to democracy, free market, and rule of law, it has also secured the so-called pluralism by default in Ukraine (Way, 2015). Oligarchs have largely kept their leverage in post-Maidan Ukraine, although the dynamic political situation is characterized by occasional reconfiguration of powers and loyalties in the political establishment. Consequently, major political players have been plowing money into all sorts of self-promotion campaigns, including "black" PR campaigns against opponents as they search for a stronger standing for themselves.

MEDIA OWNERSHIP AND STRUCTURE

Much like the political landscape, Ukraine's media market has long been dominated by the oligarchs. Over three-quarters of the television market is divided between four media groups owned by the oligarchs (KAS, 2015), a striking figure given that television remains the number one media outlet for the majority of Ukrainians (Internews, 2016). Inter Media group, which comprises the popular INTER TV channel and a number of smaller TV stations, is reportedly controlled by oligarch Dmytro Firtash and a former head of Yanukovych's presidential administration, Serhiy Lyovochkin. Another popular TV channel, 1 + 1, is owned by oligarch Ihor Kolomoysky, who also controls several smaller channels, UNIAN news agency, and a few online outlets. Viktor Pinchuk, a businessman and son-in-law of ex-president Leonid Kuchma, owns a set of TV channels (STB, ICTV and Novyi). The country's richest man and a close ally of ex-president Yanukovych controls a number of national and regional media, including the popular nationwide TRK Ukrayina TV channel and a Segodnya daily. The current president himself owns a smaller TV station, 5th Channel.

The Ukrainian media market has seen a critical lack of foreign investors, especially after the financial crisis of 2008 when a number of foreign publishers left the press industry. While the mainstream media remain under the control of oligarchs, smaller independent media outlets have been contributing to media pluralism in Ukraine. Some of those media have been profitable as businesses, like one of the most popular news websites, Ukrayinska Pravda; others have relied on crowdfunding and grant support, like Hromadske TV.

Ukrainian TV and radio channels are regulated by the National Council for TV and Radio Broadcasting. In March 2014, due to the conflict with Russia, the council advised all cable operators to stop transmitting a number of Russian channels (Ennis, 2014). The number of Russian channels that have the right to broadcast in Ukraine has consequently decreased from 72 in 2014 to 14 in 2016 (Dzerkalo Tyzhnia, 2016). The Ukrainian regulator later issued a recommendation to ban Russian-made content that praised "special forces" and symbols of the "aggressor state," which included many films and TV series (BBC, 2016a).

SOCIAL MEDIA AND INTERNET PENETRATION

EuroMaidan marked a milestone in the use of social media and information technologies for the purposes of political activism, and contributed to the rapid rise of the significance of social network sites in the country at large, which has been examined by scholars (Bohdanova 2014; Dickinson 2014; Onuch, 2015; Gruzd & Tsyganova 2015).

According to the Factum Group Ukraine (Factum Group Ukraine, 2017), 63 percent of the adult Ukrainian population today are considered active Internet users. In addition to information sharing, social networks in Ukraine are being actively used for fundraising, e-commerce, and data gathering. However, social media have also become platforms for disinformation campaigns and efforts to manipulate public opinion.

The most recent survey data suggests that almost 21 percent of Ukrainians use social media as their main source of news (Detector Media, 2017). The most popular social media networks in Ukraine are VKontakte, or VK, (11.9 million users), Facebook (over 8 million users), Odnoklassniki (5.7 million users), and Twitter (2.5 million users). Since two of the networks (VK and Odnoklassniki) are owned by Russian companies, it is important to underline the Russian desire to influence and control social media in relation to the crisis in Ukraine. StratCom's March 2015 report documents vivid examples of such attempts: from blocking of pro-Ukrainian groups on social networks, requesting personal information of activists, and government-initiated Internet trolling to the recruitment of the volunteer fighters for Donbas online.

BOT-PROOF MEDIUMS?

All popular social networking sites in Ukraine can be used to deploy bots. The difference is in the cost of production and the popularity of such services. The easiest and the cheapest platform for the creation of bots is VK, since it does not have strict security measures, allowing for easy registration of mass accounts. In addition, VK is considered to be focused around groups and close communities, celebrities, and entertainment, so the phenomenon of political bots on this platform in Ukraine is not that visible.

Twitter takes second place in this rating, being open for bot creation and not very effective at banning suspicious activity, according to a software developer working with the platform. Unsurprisingly, a significant amount of the overall activities on Twitter are generated by bots, with about 48 million accounts (15 percent of all users) being bots rather than people (Varol, Ferrara, Davis, Menczer, & Flammini, 2017).

Facebook, on the other hand, proves to be the most efficient in terms of protecting its API and user data, making it the most challenging environment for bot creators. Since this network is also the most popular among social and political elites in Ukraine (Orlova & Taradai, 2016), bots on Facebook are the most expensive to create, and demand for them is growing. The bot developers we talked to as part of this research managed to create a large bot farm using a script that not only registers accounts but can automatically fill in profile information and create posts. It is easier to register female bot accounts on Facebook using pictures of models and good-looking girls from the social network VK, since they will get an organic following as well. The program also allows the creation of bot accounts to like posts of certain people or groups or on specific topics. One way to detect these bots on Facebook is to check whether they have liked or reacted to the comments left under the posts, our informant revealed.

Messengers are being called "the new social media" and their use in Ukraine is also growing. The most popular are Skype (94 percent) and Viber (84 percent), while 69 percent of all messenger users still use ICQ (the name of which is derived from the English phrase "I seek you). Numbers for WhatsApp and Telegram are considerably lower, with 46 percent and 24 percent of users, respectively (IVOX, 2016). This is an important observation, as both technical and marketing specialists view them as platforms for personalized communication where the efficiency of bots would be minimal, since the architecture of the platform does not create a fruitful environment for bots to operate in. The only exceptions are chatbots that can simulate human conversations and are marked as robots from the beginning of their existence.

A number of companies in Ukraine provide social media monitoring services that can potentially be used for computational propaganda prevention. The market is evolving, with key players being the YouScan.io, ContextMedia, NoksFishes, SemanticForce, and InfoStream agencies. They can measure the online presence of people and brands, track negative feedback, and drive brand conversation online. The ability of such services to track bots and fake accounts, however, is very limited, and it seems that there is currently no demand for such identification.

Bots, Trolls, and Fake Accounts as Instruments of Online Manipulation of Public Opinion in Ukraine

While the information struggle has been extremely fierce externally, with numerous aggressive media campaigns generated against Ukraine (Khaldarova & Pantti, 2016), the internal information sphere has also seen the increased use of social media as a platform for attempts to manipulate public opinion.

In January 2015, the Ukrainian website dedicated to media and technology news, AIN.UA, published an interview (AIN.UA, 2015) with the so-called former Akhmetov's bot, a young man who claimed to have worked for the company that managed the online presence for one of Ukraine's biggest oligarchs, Rinat Akhmetov. In the interview, which became one of the first stories presenting first-hand evidence on organized trolling online in Ukraine, the self-confessed "troll" told of the daily instructions he and his colleagues received on what kinds of comments to make and where they had to publish them. Although the outlet and the hero of the story himself frequently used the term *bot* to describe their activities, in reality these "bots" turned out to be fake accounts managed by paid-for people.

The experts interviewed admitted that there have been multiple such cases in Ukraine, with an entire industry of various services developed for the purposes of political communication. However, contrary to common belief, the use of bots and trolls in Ukrainian sociopolitical life is not a recent phenomenon. An industry of computational propaganda in the country emerged in the early 2000s with the rise of Internet use. Marketing and PR professionals were the first to start employing such services, the interviewed experts noted. As soon as Ukrainian customers turned to the Internet for recommendations and product reviews, agencies started hiring people to create fake accounts and write fake positive comments. One particularly notable segment for such campaigns, one of the interviewed experts observed, was young mothers, as they not only were interested in participating in online conversations but also wanted to earn money while looking after their children at home.

Later on, the concept of paid comments through fake accounts was adopted by political technologists. They operated on the forums or in the comments sections of popular news websites, the most popular being Ukrainska Pravda. Similar activities have also been registered on LiveJournal—a popular blogging platform in Russia and Ukraine with a strong political content. In the popular slang, those paid commentators are widely referred to as "trolls" in Ukraine. Nowadays, social media have become the primary platforms for such campaigns.

TYPICAL COMMUNICATION CAMPAIGNS ONLINE

Interviews with experts suggest that bots and fake accounts constitute an essential element of online communication campaigns in Ukraine, but that these also involve some other crucial components. Our analysis shows that a typical campaign used for the purposes of self-promotion, discrediting of opponents, and promotion of certain issues/decisions has several stages. It usually begins with the initial publication of the key message packaged into a story in some online outlet as an entrance point for the campaign. It is made possible because a large number of Ukrainian online media that deal with news and politics publish stories for money. In some cases, such initial messages are posted on social media platforms or blogs. After that, the topic is picked up by opinion leaders with a large number of followers on social media and boosted through fake manual or automated accounts. Usually, all these stages are cash-driven. Once the issue gets significant publicity online, it is very likely to be picked up by mainstream media, including major TV channels. It is thus possible to conclude that bots and fake accounts are part of a broader network of media tools employed by political actors.

INSIDE THE INDUSTRY

Stakeholders interviewed for this chapter acknowledged the large scale of employment of bots and fake accounts to manipulate public opinion online in Ukraine. The market for such services seems to be particularly driven by political actors. Interviewed experts noted that the market is diverse and horizontal in Ukraine, in contrast to the Russian one. While the market is quite big given the high demand for such services, it is also quite disguised.

As part of the project we managed to establish contact with several market insiders, but they refused to identify their companies due to sensitivity of the issue. According to the information obtained, a large part of the market is represented by small and medium-sized companies without a public profile. Some interviewees suggested that digital agencies also provide services related to political social media management that involve paid-for commenting and audience boosting through bots and the like. However, established agencies do not openly promote their expertise in such services.

One of the interviewed stakeholders who owns a small company of his own noted he usually gets political clients from intermediaries. Typical tasks involve promotion of a politician or political force online, distribution of certain messages, neutralization of negative information, or an attack on clients' rivals. Many projects are related to election campaigns; sometimes the company provides a "package" of services, or deals only with specific cases, for example a scandal. Once there is a project, the owner of the company hires a team, usually targeting students. The team receives guidelines on what they are supposed to do, for example boost certain posts by reposting with the help of the established database of fake accounts. If needed, they also get engaged in commenting (spreading certain messages or neutralizing others). Such commentators are usually expected to post up to 200 comments each day, the informant said. During the 2012 parliamentary election campaign they received about US$100 per week. All the discussed activities are conducted with the help of fake accounts that are manually maintained. According to the owner of this small company, his database of fake accounts, which includes several hundred "advanced" accounts on Facebook and VKontakte (meaning accounts that have up to 5,000 friends), is an asset in its own right and can be sold any time.

The interviews conducted, as well as media reports, suggest that major political parties have created internal divisions within their offices/headquarters that deal directly with social media (Ivantsova, 2015). Such divisions are led by political consultants/advisors who develop key messages and a plan for their distribution across different communication channels. Sometimes in-house SMM departments also outsource some of their projects to independent companies, like the one described earlier. This happens, for instance, if they need some extra capacity in times of crisis.

Analysis shows that manually maintained fake accounts are one of the most popular instruments for online campaigns due to their relatively small cost and flexibility, since they can be used for boosting pages, posts, and links through likes and rigorous commenting. Automated bots seem to be less widespread in Ukraine, although our study identified several market players who developed technological solutions for bots. An informant asserted that there is a leading company in Ukraine that creates bots and sells them across the world, but did not specify which one.

POPULAR MYTHS

As mentioned earlier, despite there being quite a developed market, there is significant confusion regarding bots, trolls, and other instruments of computational propaganda in public discourse, as well as myths about the industry. Firstly, the terms are often confused, which reveals a lack of understanding. Many people believe computational propaganda is either fully manual or completely automated, while in reality it can be a mixture of both. The second myth suggests that bots used for political purposes are cheap, while PR services are more expensive. In fact, correct and effective automation is time- and resource-consuming, and hiring a software developer is much pricier than using paid-for commentators. The final popular assumption among the public concerns the inability of bots to influence public opinion. While there may not be direct impact, bots constitute a big threat to those working with big data (Hegelich, 2016). Since most PR, marketing, and political campaigns rely on primary research and market data, it is often hard to assess quality, as analysis of social media narratives, audience reach of certain pages, and influence of various people becomes inaccurate due to the increased volumes of fake and automated accounts.

FAKE ACCOUNTS

Out of the variety of tools, manually maintained fake accounts seem to be the most widely used in Ukraine. Fake accounts play a critical part in the chain of tools used to boost attention to certain topics or messages in social media. Hundreds of such accounts are easily bought online. The price of Facebook accounts in Ukraine varies from US$0.90 to US$200 depending on the year of registration, previous activities, and level of profile completeness (bio, pictures, friends, etc.). Twitter accounts cost US$0.40 to $90, and VK accounts are the lowest at US$0.40 to US$1.50. Popular websites for such services are https:// buyaccs.com/, http://darkstore.biz/, and others. However, these services do not provide a guarantee, and purchased accounts can be easily blocked by the social media platforms themselves due to suspicious behavior; for example, an account on Facebook registered in the United States and reactivated in Ukraine will require a security check that can only be tricked with certain computer expertise, which buyers of such fake accounts do not always have. In addition, fake accounts are most often used for manual commenting and are not likely to be turned into automated bots. Therefore, it is plausible to conclude that fake accounts are predominantly used to promote certain messages or trivialize or hijack the debate online.

BOTS

Automation of media, political communication, and propaganda also takes place in Ukraine. However, this tool is rather under-researched compared with paid commentators and fake accounts. Interviews and secondary data suggest the following types of bots can be distinguished.

Impact bots. These are used to create a mass following for certain pages or persons and to establish a bigger presence online. Most popular on Twitter, they are usually inactive and easily detained by programs such as BotOrNot, StatusPeople, TwitterAudit, and so forth. We analyzed five of the most popular accounts on Ukrainian Twitter according to SocialBakers stats. The percentage of bot accounts in their audience varies from 1 to 14 percent according to StatusPeople, and up to 72 percent of the audience consists of inactive accounts; thus it is difficult to determine their bot identity. The high percentage of bots can be explained by the periods of active bot registration on Twitter after the start of the EuroMaidan protests in 2013 and the armed conflict in eastern Ukraine in early spring 2014 (Alexander, 2015b).

Amplifiers. These are used for liking, sharing, and promoting certain content. These operate on all social platforms in Ukraine. Journalists from the online outlet Texty.org.ua conducted an investigation and uncovered an organized network of bots on Facebook operated from Russia that pretended to be Ukrainian patriots, and spread information calling for the third Maidan, an uprising against the government (Romanenko, Mykhaylyshyn, Solodko, & Zog, 2016). Examples of automated accounts for promotional and quite probably propaganda purposes on Twitter include @schancellery, @laraz1377, and @IvanPetrov_34.

Complainers. Some clients of Ukrainian bot developers also request blocking of certain accounts with the help of complaints lodged by bots. Even though Facebook itself does not allow banning of a user without giving reasons, complainers may monitor the posts of other accounts for certain terms that do not comply with Facebook policy and send ban requests.

Trackers. These are used for detection and driving attention toward certain behaviors online. As an example, in July 2014, Twitter bots were launched to track anonymous edits in Wikipedia from Russian (@RuGovEdits) and Ukrainian (@UAGovEdits) government IP addresses. Among others, the bots helped track attempts to rewrite an article on MH17 in the German version of Wikipedia (Rothrock, 2014).

Service Bots. These are often defined as software or scripts that can help automate the process of bot account registration, for instance by automatically generating names or email addresses, or reading CAPTCHAs. Together with external services for obtaining virtual cell phone numbers in order to receive an SMS for account creation, service bots may help create a bot account on Facebook within four minutes, our informant revealed. More advanced versions of such software may even automate creation of fake photos of ID documents that can be sent to Facebook as proof of user authenticity if the bot user is blocked.

The use of amplifier bots for content promotion purposes creates a misleading narrative for the users, who will only see a certain part of the story or a particular angle. For instance, the message "I think big war is coming" was widely shared at the time of active military action by Russian-backed rebels in the cities of Schastya and Artemivsk in eastern Ukraine (Alexander, 2015c).

A study by Alexander (2015a) revealed an average retweet rate for Russian media by bot accounts on Twitter is 20 percent. Some commentators claim impact bots are used for search engine optimization (SEO) purposes only—a claim that is debatable because tweets produced/retweeted by bots do not always contain links to any articles (which would be necessary for SEO). It is more likely that they are used to abuse the trending topics section on Twitter. The official policy of the social network does not allow this, discouraging the following: "Repeatedly Tweeting the same topic or hashtag without adding value to the conversation in an attempt to get the topic trending or trending higher; Tweeting about each trend in order to drive traffic to your profile or website, especially when mixed with advertising."

Impact and amplifier bots on Facebook are much more difficult to create, and therefore they are more valuable. According to one of our informants, Facebook bots are in large demand for the purposes of PR and political communication in Ukraine. One automated account can reach a target of gaining the maximum 5,000 friends limit within a three-month period. Facebook itself promotes such accounts through its "You may also know" section. Therefore, 100 bots in the audience of a certain person can achieve access to hundreds of thousands of new users. When bots suggest liking this or that page to their "friends," conversion is quite high, which makes the use efficient. Most pages of Ukrainian politicians on Facebook have seen a suspicious boost in the audience numbers, according to the Ukrainian monitoring resource Zmiya. However, it remains unclear whether the politicians themselves are ordering such boosts, or whether it is an initiative of their advisors, digital agencies providing social media management services, or external forces such as opponents trying to manipulate the numbers of real followers.

One industry insider provided an interesting scenario of how Ukrainian PR consultants would use the information conflict with Russia to pursue their own agendas. For instance, if there is an unpopular decision that needs to be made by an MP or a new bill, they could use paid commentators or automated bots to spread negative messages about this MP and the project. Screenshots with often identical messages would then be sent to the press saying this MP is a target of Russian propaganda and the infamous Olgino trolls. Such publicity would thus work in favor of a "victim of Russian disinformation games" and his or her ideas, according to the industry insider.

THE COMPLEXITY OF THE ISSUE: THE CASE OF MH17

A remarkable example of computational propaganda operations is the notorious case of the MH17 tragedy. On 17 July 2014, a Malaysian Airlines Boeing 777 crashed into fields in Donbas in an area not under the control of the Ukrainian government, causing the deaths of all 298 people on board (BBC, 2016b). In September 2016, a joint investigation team presented their first results, concluding that MH17 was shot down by a BUK surface-to-air missile fired from Russian-backed, separatist-controlled territory in eastern Ukraine (JIT, 2016). Prior to release of the official version, the case was subject to many conspiracy theories (Shandra, 2015), such as one claiming that a military jet downed the passenger Boeing (Higgins, 2015).

This theory was initiated by tweets of an alleged Spanish air traffic controller named Carlos (@spainbuca) working in the Kyiv Boryspil Airport, who claimed to have seen a military aircraft in the area of the catastrophe.

The story was quickly picked up by the Russian channel RT, as well as many other news outlets such as RIA Novosti, Tass, and others. On July 21, 2014, Russia's Ministry of Defense held a press conference presenting a statement (Ministry of Defense, 2014) and a fake satellite image suggesting an Su-25 fighter jet had been spotted near the Boeing (Kivimäki, 2014). An investigation conducted by the fact-checking website StopFake later proved that the account of the so-called Carlos was fake, because non-Ukrainian citizens are not allowed to work as flight operations officers in Ukraine (StopFake, 2014b). Soon the @ spainbuca account was blocked, but it reappeared in late 2014 under the name of Lyudmila Lopatyshkina (The Insider, 2016).

Many assumed this account to be a bot tweeting out anti-Ukrainian messages and images, which caused its complete suspension later on.

Research by the Ukrainian deputy minister of information policy shows an account of the so-called Carlos was registered during the active phase of the EuroMaidan revolution in February 2014, and actively retweeted pro-Russian messages. This was most active on May 2, 2014, almost two months in advance of the MH17 case. On May 8, 2014, a person calling himself Carlos gave an interview to the Spanish version of RT, accusing Ukraine of aggression and hatred, but his face was covered up and no proof of the existence of such a person has been found (RT, 2014). This fake account became active once again in July 2014 to produce one of the strongest fake theories of what had happened to the MH17 flight.

Bots were also actively used to help block Facebook accounts of journalists posting about the MH17 case. One such incident happened with a journalist called Sergey Parkhomenko, whose account was temporarily suspended. Comments from the experts suggest bots have been used to send thousands of complaints to Facebook's abuse team to cause blocking of certain opinions online (Novaya Gazeta, 2015).

In September 2016, when the official results of the MH17 investigation were presented, a Twitter user named @TimurKhorev spotted a second increase in bot activity. He noticed a certain pattern: each time somebody used the #MH17 hashtag in tweets in Russian, a bot would join the conversation and reply with a link to a fake article questioning the results of the investigation. A number of users have proved the theory to be correct and demonstrated how the bot reacted to messages that had nothing to do with the context but simply contained the #MH17 tag (Online.ua, 2016). Automated accounts were also actively promoting certain messages related to the story (such as this one). Media expert and director of Mohyla School of Journalism Yevhen Fedchenko suggests the case of MH17 illustrates how tools of computational propaganda become powerful and effective when supported by other actors—journalists and government officials.

Ukraine's Response to Computational Propaganda

EXTERNAL RESPONSE

Analysis suggests that the Ukrainian government's response to the external threats of propaganda within the context of the Ukraine–Russia conflict has been quite sporadic and weak. Representatives of and advisors to the Ukrainian government claim they do not have the necessary funds to conduct comprehensive monitoring of the online sphere, develop appropriate software, or create and manage accounts that could "fight" with Russian bots online. In January 2015, the Ukrainian Ministry of Information announced its "Internet Army" project—a voluntary initiative aimed at "fighting back Russian occupants in the information war" (Yarovaya, 2015). Media reports suggested that almost 40,000 people registered as "information soldiers" with the ministry. However, our interviewees indicated the "Army" did not exist in the first place, since the volunteers did not receive any particular tasks. The effectiveness of the project is therefore quite dubious.

RESPONSE FROM THE MEDIA AND CIVIL SOCIETY

More rigorous attempts to respond to Russian computational propaganda have been undertaken by civil society and media initiatives. For instance, the StopFake.org project—a website launched by students, professors, and alumni of the Kyiv Mohyla School of Journalism in March 2014—has debunked over 1,000 fake stories produced mainly by the Russian media. Activists of the project have been relying on fact-checking and news verification to deal with news content in the mainstream media, but they have also tackled disinformation in social media.

The issue of Russia's disinformation campaigns against Ukraine has received significant public attention in Ukraine, even resulting in private initiatives aimed at fighting propaganda. For instance, a Ukrainian software developer nicknamed Alex Novodvorski developed an extension for the Chrome browser that allowed automatic blocking of thousands of Russian websites (Forpost, 2017).

Ukrainian media have also been trying to investigate computational propaganda, with Texty.org.ua producing the most impressive example. This analyzed the network of accounts that purposefully disseminated messages to instigate public unrest, the so-called third Maidan.

All in all, Ukraine's response to Russian computational propaganda has been decentralized and largely driven by civil society, whereas investigations from St. Petersburg's troll HQ suggest a high level of organization and vertical structures.

It is not only external threats of computational propaganda that have attracted the attention of Ukrainian civil society and media. Increasing attempts to manipulate and erode public discourse online through organized communication campaigns have not gone unnoticed. Ukrainian journalists and experts have been acknowledging the toxic influence of paid commentators from fake accounts on public discourse. Thus, a recent survey of media professionals showed that 56 percent of respondents believe there is pro-government manipulation in online debate (Internews, 2017).

One of the most notorious cases occurred in July 2016. It began with a post on the Facebook page of the press service of Ukraine's anti-terror operation, which accused journalists from Hromadske TV of smuggling a Russian journalist to the frontline in eastern Ukraine and exposing the position of Ukraine's troops. The journalists denied both claims and provided evidence of their innocence. However, they faced an avalanche of attacks from Facebook users. In her op-ed piece published in *The Guardian*, Katya Gorchinskaya (2016), an executive director of Hromadske TV, noted that, "As soon as the statement on their Facebook page appeared, something strange started to happen. In the first five minutes, the statement was shared more than 360 times. Within an hour, it became the most popular post on the joint staff's press page," adding that a typical post on the page received a few dozen likes and shares, whereas that post "spread like a forest fire." "Reposts trashed our journalists, attacking their reputations and slamming their work," Gorchinskaya wrote, suggesting that Hromadske TV was hit by pro-government commentators due to the independence of the medium and its frequent criticism of the government.

Even though this story was much discussed in the media, there was no factual evidence of the involvement of bots, and no particular countermeasures have been taken. However, a number of Ukrainian journalists have experienced attacks via comments, especially under posts criticizing various political actors. One of the interviewed experts, the former deputy minister of information policy, Tetyana Popova, also said she was targeted by pro-Russian bots and even received death threats on Facebook. She reported the incident to cyberpolice, but they do not deal with such complaints.

The most recent countermeasure taken by the Ukrainian government involved a ban on Russian Web services and social media networks in Ukraine, for example VK, Odnoklassniki, mail.ru, and Yandex (BBC, 2017). Similar to the blocking of Russian TV channels in the country, the legislation comes as part of Ukraine's sanctions against Russia. President Poroshenko admitted the government's attempt to use social networks to fight Russia's "hybrid war," but "the time has come to act differently and more decisively" (Luhn, 2017).

Conclusion

Analysis of Ukrainian cases revealed a number of curious trends in the use of computational propaganda. Given a complex political context, both external and internal, the study focused on two major dimensions: the use of bots in political communication inside the country, and Ukraine's response to the challenges of computational propaganda caused by the Ukraine–Russia conflict.

Our findings suggest the internal market of online political communication in Ukraine is quite diverse and horizontal, with many players, but mostly hidden. Evidence of the variety of tools used for online information campaigns has been obtained. The main purposes of the utilization of computational propaganda tools include not only manipulation of public opinion but often discrediting opponents and defending the interests of different business and political groups. Many still rely on manually maintained fake accounts due to their relatively cheap cost and flexibility, but automated political bots are gaining popularity as more technological solutions appear.

Our study suggests the following classification of bots: impact bots, amplifiers, service bots, trackers, and complainers, depending on their functions. The technical capacity of Ukrainian software developers is quite significant, but most innovative tools seem to be developed for foreign countries and out of commercial interest. The effectiveness of tools such as bots and fake accounts remains to be explored, but the widespread use that we witnessed in Ukraine definitely undermines the credibility of public debate and requires a more rigorous reaction.

Analysis of the external dimension of computational propaganda has disclosed the complexity of challenges it brings for countries engaged in this information standoff, especially under conditions of unequal resources. Past research, as well as a variety of media reports, show the Russian government has created a strong network of online actors and tools such as bloggers, trolls, and automated bots in order to spread misinformation online, promote the official narrative, and attack opponents.

One of the strongest examples of such disinformation attacks is the case of MH17. It illustrates the complexity of the computational propaganda phenomenon and suggests it can have a visible influence on the international political domain. Russia actively used the Twitter accounts of mass media and bots to disseminate fake information about the tragedy, and the followers of these accounts, including mass media, used this information in further references. Moreover, this fake evidence was used by the Russian Ministry of Defense and other officials to build a case against Ukraine, blaming it for the catastrophe and complicating the official investigations.

Our findings suggest that the response of the Ukrainian government to these challenges has been rather weak and sporadic. It has lacked a comprehensive strategy and responsiveness to the immediate challenges created by the growing influence of social media. Nevertheless, a lot of effort to tackle computational propaganda has been made by activists and volunteers. This indicates the potential of civil society to address the challenges of computational propaganda in the digitized world.

References

AIN.UA. (2015, January 31). Kak rabotayut internet-trolli i kak ikh raspoznat: intervyu s byvshim "akhmetovskim botom" (How Internet trolls work and how one can recognize them: an interview with a former "Akhmetov's bot"). *AIN.UA*. Retrieved from https://ain.ua/2015/01/31/kak-rabotayut-internet-trolli-i-kak-ix-raspoznat-intervyu-s-byvshim-axmetovskim-botom.

Alexander, L. (2015a). Are Russian News Media Getting a Boost from Retweet Bots on Twitter? *Global Voices*. Retrieved from https://globalvoices.org/2015/11/27/are-russian-news-media-getting-a-boost-from-retweet-bots-on-twitter/.

Alexander, L. (2015b). The Curious Chronology of Russian Twitter Bots. *Global Voices*. Retrieved from https://globalvoices.org/2015/04/27/the-curious-chronology-of-russian-twitter-bots/.

Alexander, L. (2015c). Social Network Analysis Reveals Full Scale of Kremlin's Twitter Bot Campaign. *Global Voices*. Retrieved from https://globalvoices.org/2015/04/02/analyzing-kremlin-twitter-bots/.

BBC. (2016a, April 21). Ukraine Bans Russian Films in Media War. *BBC News*. Retrieved from http://www.bbc.com/news/world-europe-36099885.

BBC. (2016b, September 28). MH17 Ukraine Plane Crash: What We Know. *BBC News*. Retrieved from http://www.bbc.com/news/world-europe-28357880.

BBC. (2017, May 16). Ukraine's Poroshenko to Block Russian Social Networks. Retrieved from http://www.bbc.com/news/world-europe-39934666.

Bērziņš, J., Jaeski, A., Laity, M., Maliukevicius, N., Navys, A., Osborne, G., . . . Tatham, S. (2014). Analysis of Russia's Information Campaign against Ukraine. NATO StratCom Report.

Bohdanova, T. (2014). Unexpected Revolution: The Role of Social Media in Ukraine's Euromaidan Uprising. *European View*, 13(1), 133–142.

Butsenko, A. (2014, October 28). Trolli iz Olgino pereehali v novyy chetyrekhetazhnyy ofis na Savushkina (Trolls from Olgino moved into a new four-storey office on Savushkina). *Dp.ru*. Retrieved from https://www.dp.ru/a/2014/10/27/Borotsja_s_omerzeniem_mo/.

Chen, A. (2015, June 2). The Agency. *The New York Times*. Retrieved from https://www.nytimes.com/2015/06/07/magazine/the-agency.html?_r=1.

Detector Media. (2017). Yak rosiyska propaganda vplyvae na suspilnu dumku v Ukrayini (doslidzhennia) (How Russian propaganda influences public opinion in Ukraine [research findings]). Retrieved from http://osvita.mediasapiens.ua/mediaprosvita/research/yak_rosiyska_propaganda_vplivae_na_suspilnu_dumku_v_ukraini_doslidzhennya/.

Dickinson, J. (2014). Prosymo maksymal'nyi perepost! (Tactical and discursive uses of social media in Ukraine's EuroMaidan). *Ab Imperio*, 2014(3), 75–93.

Dzerkalo Tyzhnia. (2016, September 20). Ukrayina zaminyt rosiyski telekanaly na koreyski (Ukraine will substitute Russian TV channels with Korean ones). Dzerkalo Tyzhnia. Retrieved from http://dt.ua/UKRAINE/ukrayina-zaminit-rosiyski-telekanali-na-koreyski-219354_.html.

Ennis, S. (2014, March 12). Ukraine Hits Back at Russian TV Onslaught. *BBC Monitoring*. Retrieved from http://www.bbc.com/news/world-europe-26546083.

Factum Group Ukraine. (2017). Proniknovenie Interneta v Ukraine (Internet Penetration in Ukraine). Internet Association of Ukraine. Retrieved from http://inau.ua/sites/default/files/file/1701/iv_kvartal_2016.pptx.

Forpost. (2017, April 18). Stop Propaganda: Ukrayintsi mozhut vstanovyty sobi dodatok, yakyi blokuye rosiysku propagandu (Stop Propaganda: Ukrainians can install an extension that allows blocking Russian propaganda). *Forpost*. Retrieved from http://forpost.lviv.ua/novyny/2815-stop-propaganda-ukraintsi-mozhut-vstanovyty-sobi-dodatok-iakyi-blokuie-rosiisku-propahandu.

Garmazhapova, A. (2013, September 9). Gde zhivut trolli. I kto ikh kormit (Where do trolls live. And who feeds them). *Novaya Gazeta*. Retrieved from https://www.novayagazeta.ru/articles/2013/09/07/56253-gde-zhivut-trolli-i-kto-ih-kormit.

Gorchinskaya, K. (2016, July 27). The rise of Kremlin-style Trolling in Ukraine Must End. *The Guardian*. Retrieved from https://www.theguardian.com/world/2016/jul/27/kremlin-style-troll-attacks-are-on-the-rise-in-ukraine-hromadske.

Gruzd, A., & Tsyganova, K. (2015). Information Wars and Online Activism during the 2013/2014 Crisis in Ukraine: Examining the Social Structures of Pro- and Anti-Maidan Groups. *Policy & Internet*, 7(2), 121–158.

Hegelich, S. (2016). Invasion of the Social Bots. Policy Paper. Konrad Adenauer Stiftung. Retrieved from http://www.kas.de/wf/doc/kas_46486-544-2-30.pdf?161007093837, September, no.221.

Hegelich, S., & Janetszko, D. (2016). Are Social Bots on Twitter Political Actors? Empirical Evidence from a Ukrainian Social Botnet. International AAAI Conference on Web and Social Media. Retrieved from http://www.aaai.org/ocs/index.php/ICWSM/ICWSM16/paper/view/13015/12793.

Higgins, E. (2015, January 10). SU-25, MH17 and the Problems with Keeping a Story Straight. *Bellingcat.* Retrieved from https://www.bellingcat.com/news/uk-and-europe/2015/01/10/su-25-mh17-and-the-problems-with-keeping-a-story-straight/.

Hoskins, A., & O'Loughlin, B. (2015). Arrested War: The Third Phase of Mediatization. *Information, Communication & Society, 18*(11), 1320–1338.

Internews. (2016). Media Consumption Survey—Ukraine 2016. *Internews Network.* Retrieved from https://www.internews.org/sites/default/files/resources/Media_Consumption_Survey_2016-09_Eng_Internews.pdf.

Internews. (2017). Results of the Survey about the Risks of Internet Freedom in Ukraine. *Internews Ukraine.* Retrieved from http://internews.ua/2017/01/netfreedom-survey/.

Ivantsova, A. (2015, May 29). Internet-troli na sluzhbi v oligarkhiv i politykiv (Internet trolls servicing oligarchs and politicians). Radio Free Europe/Radio Liberty. Retrieved from http://www.radiosvoboda.org/a/27042051.html.

IVOX. (2016, January 20). Samye populiarnye messendzhery v Ukraine i Rossii—infografika (The most popular messengers in Ukraine and Russia—infographics). *Tehnot.* Retrieved from http://tehnot.com/samye-populyarnye-messendzhery-v-ukraine-i-rossii-infografika/.

JIT. (2016). Criminal Investigation MH17. Joint Investigation Team. Retrieved from https://www.om.nl/onderwerpen/mh17-crash/.

KAS. (2015). Ukrainian Media Landscape—2015. Policy Paper. Konrad Adenauer Stiftung. Retrieved from http://www.kas.de/wf/doc/kas_43639-1522-13-30.pdf?15120916112727, March 2016.

Kelly, J., Barash, V., Alexanyan, K., Etling, B., Faris, R., Gasser, U., & Palfrey, J.G. (2012). *Mapping Russian Twitter.* The Berkman Center for Internet & Society.

Khaldarova, I., & Pantti, M. (2016). Fake News: The Narrative Battle over the Ukrainian Conflict. *Journalism Practice, 10*(7), 891–901.

Kivimäki, V.-P. (2014, November 14). Russian State Television Shares Fake Images of MH17 Being Attacked. *Bellingcat.* Retrieved from https://www.bellingcat.com/news/2014/11/14/russian-state-television-shares-fake-images-of-mh17-being-attacked/.

Kriukova, S., & Pasiutina, A. (2016, June 2). Territoriya botov. Kto i kak sozdaet parallelnuyu realnost v ukrainskikh socsetiakh (Bots' territory. Who and who creates a parallel reality in Ukrainian social networks). *Strana.ua.* Retrieved from http://longread.strana.ua/territoriya_botov.

Lucas, E., & Nimmo, B. (2015). Information Warfare: What Is It and How to Win It? Policy Paper. CEPA Infowar Paper No.1. Retrieved from http://cepa.org/files/?id_plik=1896.

Lucas, E., & Pomerantsev, P. (2016). Winning the Information War: Techniques and Counter-Strategies to Russian Propaganda in Central and Eastern Europe. *CEPA Report.* Legatum Institute. Retrieved from http://cepa.org/reports/winning-the-Information-War.

Luhn, A. (2017). Ukraine Blocks Popular Social Networks as Part of Sanctions on Russia. *The Guardian.* Retrieved from https://www.theguardian.com/world/2017/may/16/ukraine-blocks-popular-russian-websites-kremlin-role-war.

Meister, S. (2016). Isolation and Propaganda. The Roots and Instruments of Russia's Disinformation Campaign. Transatlantic Academy Paper Series. April 2016. Retrieved from https://dgap.org/en/article/getFullPDF/28043.

Ministry of Defence. (2014, July 21). Materialy Ministerstva oborony Rossiyskoy Federatsii k brifingu po obstoyatelstva katastrofy samoleta "Boing-777" aviakompanii "Malaziyskie avialinii" (Materials of the Ministry of Defence of Russian Federation for the briefing on the circumstances of Boeing-777 crash of Malaysian Airlines). Ministry of Defence of

Russian Federation. Retrieved from http://function.mil.ru/news_page/country/more. htm?id=11970771@egNews.

Nemtsova, A. (2014, July 15). There's No Evidence the Ukrainian Army Crucified a Child in Slovyansk. *The Daily Beast*. Retrieved from http://www.thedailybeast.com/articles/2014/07/15/there-s-no-evidence-the-ukrainian-army-crucified-a-child-in-slovyansk.

Novaya Gazeta. (2015, May 7). Facebook zablokiroval Sergeya Parkhomenko za kommentariy doklada o sbitom "Boinge" (Facebook blocked Sergey Parkhomenko for a commentary on report about shutdown Boeing). *Novaya Gazeta*. Retrieved from https://www. novayagazeta.ru/news/2015/05/07/112052-facebook-zablokiroval-sergeya-parhomenko-za-kommentariy-doklada-o-sbitom-171-boinge-187.

Novoye Vremya. (2016). Geroi Feisbuka: Novoye Vremya predstavliaet ezhegodnyi reyting liderov mneniy v socsetiakh (Facebook heroes: Novoye Vremya presents the annual ranking of opinion leaders in social networks). *Novoye Vremya*. Retrieved from http://nv.ua/ukraine/events/geroi-fejsbuka-novoe-vremja-predstavljaet-ezhegodnyj-rejting-liderov-mnenij-v-sotssetjah-276466.html.

Nygren, G., Glowacki, M., Hök, J., Kiria, I., Orlova, D., & Taradai, D. (2016). Journalism in the Crossfire: Media Coverage of the War in Ukraine in 2014. *Journalism Studies*, 1–20.

Online.ua. (2016, September 24). V socsetiakh na paltsakh pokazali, kak rabotayut boty Kremlia: opublikovany foto (Social media users showed how Kremlin's bots work: photo published). *Online.ua*. Retrieved from https://news.online.ua/754036/v-sotssetyah-na-paltsah-pokazali-kak-rabotayut-boty-kremlya-opublikovany-foto/.

Onuch, O. (2015). EuroMaidan protests in Ukraine: Social Media Versus Social Networks. *Problems of Post-Communism, 62*(4), 217–235.

Orlova, D., & Taradai, D. (2016). Facebook as an alternative public space: The use of Facebook by Ukrainian journalists during the 2012 parliamentary election. *Central European Journal of Communication, 9*(16), 37–56.

Romanenko, N., Mykhaylyshyn, Y., Solodko, P., & Zog, O. (2016, October 4). Trolesfera (Trolls sphere). *Texty.org.ua*. Retrieved from http://texty.org.ua/d/fb-trolls/.

Rothrock, K., (2014, July 29). The Russian Government's 7,000 Wikipedia Edits. *Global Voices*. Retrieved from http://www.globalvoicesonline.org/2014/07/20/the-russian-governments-7000-wikipedia-edits/.

RT. (2014, May 9). Ispanskiy bloger o situatsii na Ukraine: liudi perepolneny nenavistiu (Spanish blogger about situation in Ukraine: people are overwhelmed with hatred). *RT*. Retrieved from https://russian.rt.com/article/31215.

Shandra, A. (2015). The Most Comprehensive Guide Ever to MH17 Conspiracies. *Euromaidan Press*. Retrieved from http://euromaidanpress.com/2015/10/14/confuse-and-obfuscate-the-most-comprehensive-guide-ever-to-mh17-conspiracies/#arvlbdata.

Snegovaya, M. (2015). Putin's Information Warfare in Ukraine. Soviet Origins of Russia's Hybrid Warfare. Russia Report, 1. Institute of the Study of War. Retrieved from http://understandingwar.org/sites/default/files/Russian%20Report%201%20Putin's%20Information%20Warfare%20in%20Ukraine-%20Soviet%20Origins%20of%20Russias%20Hybrid%20Warfare.pdf.

Solonenko, I. (2015). Ukrainian Civil Society from the Orange Revolution to Euromaidan: Striving for a New Social Contract. In *OSCE Yearbook 2014*, 219–236. Nomos Verlagsgesellschaft mbH & Co. KG, 2015. doi: 10.5771/9783845260945-219.

StopFake. (2014a, July 15). Fake: Crucifixion in Slovyansk. *StopFake*. Retrieved from http://www.stopfake.org/en/lies-crucifixion-on-channel-one/.

StopFake. (2014b, July 18). Lies: Spanish Flight Operations Officer from Kiev Informed about Ukrainian Planes Involved in Boeing Tragedy. *StopFake*. Retrieved from http://www.stopfake.org/en/lies-spanish-flight-operations-officer-from-kiev-informed-about-ukrainian-planes-involved-in-boeing-tragedy/.

StopFake. (2014c, November 3). Fake: Ukrainian Militaries are Promised "a parcel of land and two slaves." *StopFake*. Retrieved from http://www.stopfake.org/en/fake-ukrainian-militaries-are-promised-a-parcel-of-land-and-two-slaves/.

The Insider. (2016, August 4). Ispanskiy dispetcher, videvshiy kak ukraintsy sbili MH17, prevratilsia v Liudmilu Lopatyshkinu (Spanish flight operations officer who saw how Ukrainians shot down MH17 turned into Liudmila Lopatyshkina). *The Insider*. Retrieved from http://theins.ru/antifake/27246.

Varol, O., Ferrara, E., Davis, C.A., Menczer, F., & Flammini, A. (2017). Online Human-Bot Interactions: Detection, Estimation, and Characterization. arXiv preprint arXiv:1703.03107. https://arxiv.org/pdf/1703.03107.pdf.

Way, L. (2015). *Pluralism by Default: Weak Autocrats and the Rise of Competitive Politics*. Baltimore, US: JHU Press.

Woolley, S., & Howard, P.H. (2016). Political Communication, Computational Propaganda, and Autonomous Agents. *International Journal of Communication, 10*, 4882–4890.

Yarovaya, M. (2015, February 23). "Minstets" zapustil i-army.org i ischet dobrovoltsev "Internet-voiska Ukrainy" ("Minstets" launched i-army.org and looks for volunteers to join "Ukraine's internet army") *AIN*. Retrieved from https://ain.ua/2015/02/23/minstec-zapustil-i-army-org-i-ishhet-dobrovolcev-v-internet-vojska-ukrainy.

Zakharov, A., & Rusyaeva, P. (23 March 2017). V nedrakh "fabriki trollei" vyros krupneishiy v Rossii mediaholdin (The biggest media holding in Russia grew out of "troll factory"). *RBC*. Retrieved from http://www.rbc.ru/technology_and._media/23/03/2017/58d2c2df9a79 47273ccb28e5?from=main.

3

Canada

Building Bot Typologies

ELIZABETH DUBOIS AND FENWICK MCKELVEY

Introduction

Evil AI watching voters online? Secret voter suppression over social media? Armies of automated accounts spreading misinformation? The scene in Canada seems pretty tame compared to such reports of political bots elsewhere. Canadian media coverage expresses worries about these bots coming to Canada, not the fact that they're already here. We find that bots have, so far, had limited influence on Canadian politics. That news alone offers a corrective to deeper international fears about a public sphere that has failed the Turing test. When Canadians discuss bots, they are largely treated as a novelty: a journalistic experiment, a one-off hack, or a blip on the electoral radar. But Canadians risk trivializing an important debate about the future of its democracy. The limited influence of bots is probably a temporary phenomenon.

Political bots are automated software programs that are "written to learn from and mimic real people so as to manipulate public opinion across a diverse range of platforms and device networks" (Woolley & Howard, 2016, p. 4885). Political bots have been deployed to artificially boost the perceived popularity of politicians, to crowd out legitimate contributors to online political discussion, and, more broadly, as a tool for propaganda. There are many "bad" or nefarious uses of bots around the world. But there are also "good" uses, such as chat bots that provide basic information about elections and transparency bots that aim to make information about government spending (among other issues) more accessible to the wider public.

There has been limited academic work on political bots in Canada. One published journal article examined the @gccaedits bot in particular. This bot tweets whenever an anonymous edit to Wikipedia is made from a Government of Canada IP address. Ford, Dubois, and Puschmann (2016) compare the quality and quantity of Wikipedia edits flagged by the bot with mentions of that bot in news media. They find that news reports focus on sensational stories about partisan editing, vandalism, and frivolous editing by bureaucrats, while most of the edits are themselves simple but useful edits. They also discover a chilling effect wherein the number of edits over time has decreased despite the growing popularity of Wikipedia as a key source of information for citizens. In mapping the relationship between bot creators, bots, journalists, and Wikipedia editors, the authors show that this Wikipedia edits bot is not necessarily good or bad for Canadian democracy. Amanda Clarke (2016) wrote a brief discussion of this bot as well, which pointed to the potential drawbacks of @gccaedits and more specifically to the way journalists report on the bot. While this detailed investigation is interesting, it examines only one bot that has been promoted by its creator as a bot.

To that end, this chapter aims to map out the wider landscape of political bots in Canada. Our guiding research questions are: What kinds of bots exist in Canada? What organizations use them? What is the impact of political bots on public life in Canada? And do bots fit within Canada's legal and policy frameworks? We have analyzed political coverage of bots in Canada, identified bots used in social media discourse during the 2015 federal election, and reviewed government records discussing the presence of bots in Canada. We conclude with a discussion of the legal and policy frameworks that are likely to capture bots in Canada.

The Canadian Context

Canada is a weak federation of 10 provinces and three territories. Provincial and federal government is modeled after the Westminster system of representative democracy and has three major national political parties: the Liberal Party, the Conservative Party, and the New Democratic Party (NDP). Candidates compete in a first-past-the-post voting system every four years. Canada has a total of 338 electoral districts representing somewhere between approximately 60,000 to 120,000 voters each. With two official languages and large geographic dispersion, Canada has a hybrid media system composed of old and new, local, national and international, public and private, and French and English outlets. Much of its hybridity stems from variations in the level of media regulation per sector.

No matter the channel, ownership largely remains highly concentrated in domestic conglomerates or international players entering the Canadian market

(Winseck, 2016). The five largest players—Bell, Telus, Rogers, Shaw, and Quebecor—control 72 percent of the total media economy (Winseck, 2016). These companies own most of the major television channels, newspapers, and magazines in the French and the English markets. Canada also has a multi-media public broadcaster, the CBC/Radio-Canada, that operates in both the French and the English markets. After years of chronic underfunding, the 2016 federal budget restored $150 million to the annual budget of the public broad-caster (CBC), which has committed to using the extra funding to reposition its digital presence (Bradshaw, 2013). More recently, major international outlets like the *New York Times*, the BBC, Buzzfeed, and the repatriated Vice Canada have expanded their online presence in Canada. By comparison with the large incumbents, these players remain small, as do the many new digital entrants—such as the National Observer, the Rebel, Canadaland, and iPolitics—that are testing the viability of the Canadian market (where nine percent of the popula-tion pays for online news) (Brin, 2017).

The Canadian news industry is at a crossroads and many predict a bumpy path forward. Journalism, whether online, on television, or in print, increasingly seems financially unviable (Canadian Radio-television and Telecommunications Commission, 2016a; Public Policy Forum, 2017; Winseck, 2017). Canada, like the rest of the world, is also coping with the growing influence of online platforms (Bell & Owen, 2017; Kleis Nielsen & Ganter, 2017; Poell & van Dijck, 2014). While there is little debate about whether journalism in Canada is declining, there is wide disagreement about the cause. Recently, the Canadian government commissioned the Public Policy Forum to write a report on the state of Canadian journalism. *The Shattered Mirror* argues that journalism is becoming less prof-itable in Canada due to a decline in classified advertising revenues and firms shifting their advertising budgets from newspapers to Facebook and Google, as well as a news ecosystem that is less receptive to traditional journalism standards (Public Policy Forum, 2017). By contrast, the decline has more to do with the growing concentration of media firms that have, furthermore, mismanaged their journalistic operations, as well as a loss of revenue caused by the 2008 financial crisis and an increase in public relations jobs (Winseck, 2017).

Canadians rely on the Internet for news (though estimates vary). A ma-jority of Canadians (55 percent), according to the 2016 CIRA State of the Internet report, use the Internet for news and current events (Canadian Internet Registration Authority, 2016). That is lower than figures revealed in the *2016 Reuters Digital News Report*, which found that 75 percent of Canadians access news online (of which 48 percent get their news from social media). Facebook is the top platform from which to access news (46 percent), followed by YouTube (17 percent) and Twitter (12 percent). As a hybrid system, the online news eco-system exists in tandem with a traditional broadcasting environment. Canadians continue to watch television news (71 percent), listen to radio (27 percent), and read newspapers (36 percent) to access their news (Brin, 2017).

Canadians, in general, have embraced the Internet and digital life. The national regulator, as of December 2015, reports that 96 percent of Canadians have access to broadband equal or greater than 5 mbps (Canadian Radio-television and Telecommunications Commission, 2016b). Availability and affordability, however, vary greatly, with rural, remote, and northern communities still underserved in Canada.

Canadians actively use social media. In 2015, 59 percent of Canadians used Facebook, 30 percent used LinkedIn, 25 percent used Twitter, and 16 percent used Instagram (Forum Research Inc., 2015). Of these platforms, Facebook is the most globally significant. More recent numbers for 2016 suggest that 62 percent of Canadians use Facebook, making Canada the country with the most users per capita, ahead of even the United States at 60 percent.

Canadians, from what little data exist, seem less interested in the Internet as a means to engage in politics. A study from 2014 found that just under half of Canadians (50 percent) have visited a federal government website. Even fewer have friended or followed a political actor on Facebook (six percent) or Twitter (four percent). Not only do Canadians avoid politicians online, they avoid politics of all sorts. Only 18 percent of Canadians have signed a petition, posted a political message on Facebook (14 percent), or retweeted political content (three percent) (Small, Jansen, Bastien, Giasson, & Koop, 2014).

Politicians and political parties have embraced the Internet as part of their election campaigns and everyday political activities. In the 2015 election, political campaigns also relied more on Internet advertising, with 40 percent of Canadians reporting seeing at least one advertisement for a political party on social media. That said, Canadians received most of their direct campaign messages via mail or telephone, while only about 17 percent of Canadians report receiving an email from a campaign and nine percent through Facebook.

Not all social media platforms are equal. Twitter, according to our interviews and data, is an elite medium in Canada, as elsewhere in the world. Indeed, out of 338 federal Members of Parliament, 267 have a Twitter account (79 percent). Twitter is also popular among the press. One prominent journalist, David Akin, has identified 126 Twitter accounts for the 332 active members of the press gallery (39 percent)—a number that probably conservatively describes the popularity of Twitter among Canadian political journalists, since many press gallery members are video and sound crew rather than being in publicly visible roles (Akin, n.d.).

There have been some notable examples of Twitter use by government. Former minister of what is now called Innovation, Science and Economic Development, Tony Clement, used Twitter to announce policy positions and interact with journalists (Chase, 2011). His activity, as well as its adoption on the Hill, suggests that Twitter remains an influential medium in politics, more so than other platforms. While there has not been a recent comparison, Steve Patten (2013) found that more parliamentarians had Twitter (80 percent) than Facebook (75 percent) accounts, in contrast to the greater popularity of Facebook than Twitter among Canadians—evidence of what Anders Olof Larsson and Bente Kalsnes (2014) call a communication mismatch.

Our interviewees noticed a negative turn in the tone of Canada's social media, with growing partisanship, polarization and hostility. One interviewee familiar with large-scale social media analytics put it bluntly: "Canadians are increasingly vitriolic in their discussions regarding politics in Canada" (Longhorn, personal communication, March 10, 2017), with increasing use of hate speech, intolerant language, and misogyny. While a negative tone is seen on both sides, right-wing groups appear more willing to make extreme statements. They continued, "[I]t is a red-pill world, right-wing ideology and white nationalism is running rampart in North American and Canadian online discussions." Much of this vitriol has targeted female politicians and journalists, who disproportionately receive online abuse. Sandra Jansen, a Member of the Legislative Assembly in Alberta, read messages targeted at her in the provincial legislature to document the abusive statements she received online (McConnell, 2016). By contrast, the former Conservative leadership candidate Maxime Bernier tweeted an image comparing a vote for "Mad Max" with taking the "red pill"—either a covert endorsement of the "red pill" community or a message worryingly oblivious to the harassment faced by female politicians online.

Bots in Canada

In this section, we describe four types of bots present in the Canadian political ecosystem and their use by political actors such as political parties, journalists, government, and civil society.

DAMPENERS: CROWDING OUT AND REDUCING ACCESSIBILITY

Dampeners are bots that suppress certain messages, channels, or voices. Their goal is to discourage or drown out information or people. Dampeners have actively targeted a number of Canadian political websites and institutions. A cyberattack prevented access to online voting for the NDP during its 2012 leadership race (Payton, 2012, 2014). Dr. Benjamin Perrin, a law professor at the University of British Columbia, reported being harassed by dampeners after commenting about the trending hashtag #GoodRiddanceHarper, which celebrated the resignation of Prime Minister Stephen Harper. His tweet received one negative reply around noon. By mid-afternoon, that negative reply had over 1,000 likes and retweets. Dr. Perrin discovered that bots had amplified this negative tweet to discourage him from tweeting. Writing about the incident in Canada's leading national newspaper, Dr. Perrin warned that such automated bots could become a tool for cyberbullying in the future (Perrin, 2016).

Dampeners have been popularized in Canada by factions of the online hacker collective Anonymous. Anonymous has been a fixture in Canadian politics since at least 2008, when Toronto was the site of the group's global protest against the Church of Scientology (Coleman, 2013). Anonymous has aided the aboriginal #IdleNoMore movement (Callison & Hermida, 2015) as well as investigated the sexual assault of Rehtaeh Parsons (McGuire, 2013; Omand, 2015).

Anonymous uses bots—or rather botnets—to launch forms of distributed denial of service attacks (DDoS) to knock websites offline. Prior to the 2015 election, Anonymous used a DDoS attack against government websites as well as the website of then-Liberal leader Justin Trudeau to protest against a recent government bill expanding surveillance powers (Bill C-51) (Boutilier & Desson, 2015). Anonymous probably used a botnet to shut down the site, according to sources familiar with the story. These attacks use bots to mimic online collective action like virtual sit-ins. In the past, Anonymous required supporters to use a tool called the Low Orbital Ion Cannon to collectively shut down a website. By contrast, exploits and botnets achieve a similar goal (Huang, 2013; O'Neill, 2015). One source compared these botnet DDoS attacks to tearing down a poster from a lamp post.

Botnet attacks can be a paradigmatic dampener. As one source put it, DDoS attacks can muzzle free speech on the Internet (if their purpose is indeed to knock resources offline rather than act as a virtual protest). Dampeners have targeted civil society groups such as Black Lives Matter in the United States as well as organizations in Canada (Tuohy, 2016).

Dampeners can have a paradoxical relationship with publicity, amplifying the attacker's voice while suppressing their target. In the case of OpAnonDown, although their attack only slightly dampened the government of Canada's message, it significantly raised OpAnonDown's profile as press covered the attack and their motivation. This press attention might actually be a key feature of a DDoS attack. One source suggested that DDoS attacks make enticing headlines, though for how long is not clear.

AMPLIFIERS: INFLATING POPULARITY DURING ELECTIONS

Where dampener bots have an indirect effect of amplification, other bots deliberately seek to increase the number of voices or attention paid to particular voices and messages. We call these bots *amplifiers*. For both benign and controversial reasons, these bots increase the popularity, visibility, and reach of certain accounts and/or messages online.

In our study of 3,001,493 tweets collected during the 2015 federal election we found some evidence of amplifier bots. We collected tweets using the Netlytic tool, looking for tweets using #cdnpoli or #elxn42 hashtags from September 1 to October 19, 2015. Out of the accounts that tweeted more than 10 times per day, we manually found at least five accounts that resembled amplifier bots (see Table 3.1). These accounts are suspicious because of their current status (suspended or deleted), their ratio of tweets to retweets, and the sources they retweeted. Flagged accounts averaged 131 tweets per day, mostly retweets, as seen in Table 3.1. None of these bots had an explicitly traceable effect on the election, but they do help explicate amplifier bots. It is also worth noting that at least three bots (@StopHarperToday, @MapleLeaks and @BeenHarperized) directly targeted the incumbent Conservative Prime Minister Stephen Harper. This suggests that some bots did try to amplify negative messages against one candidate in the 2015 election.

Canadian political norms largely dictate which amplifiers are perceived to benefit conversations on social media, which amplifiers hinder it, and which are just ignored. The account @hashtag_cdnpoli seems to be an acceptable amplifier. It is still active and simply retweets Canadian political news with the #cdnpoli hashtag. Similar amplifiers are common in other areas, such as city-based accounts that retweet any time a given city is mentioned (for example, @ hashtagTOpoli). As of May 2017, it had only 292 followers even though it has

Table 3.1 **Suspected Bots on Twitter during the 2015 Canadian Federal Election**

Account	Total Tweets	Retweets	Mentions	Still Active?
StopHarperToday	9,822	7,040	518	Deleted
MapleLeaks	7,704	4,645	330	Deleted
hashtag_cdnpoli	5,263	3,259	261	Yes
FireDragonTroll	4,789	3,336	244	Suspended
BeenHarperized	4,551	2,724	226	Yes

26,000 tweets. That it is still active suggests that it has not been flagged as a nuisance on Twitter. Perhaps followers of the hashtag appreciate the bot-assisted dose of articles from Canadian newspapers. By contrast, the second most active account, @MapleLeaks, has been deleted. According to our sample, tweets by @MapleLeaks largely promoted its affiliated website, MapleLeaks.com (490 tweets), and its Facebook page (621 tweets). Mentions of the account before it was deleted complained that it was a bot, repetitive and overly self-promoting. @MapleLeaks appeared to have violated political norms by being too self-interested, as opposed to the arguably public mindedness of the #cdnpoli community. While being a nuisance can lead to being suspended on Twitter, as in the case of @FireDragonTroll, amplifier accounts might just be ignored. @BeenHarperized, now focused on tweeting pro-marijuana information, seems just as much an unwanted amplifier as @MapleLeaks, linking to its own website. Stories posted were copied and pasted from other sites and the bot was probably intended to increase Google ad revenues by driving traffic to the site (compare Langlois & Elmer, 2009).

Amplifiers were active in Canadian politics well before the 2015 federal election. During the 2012 Quebec election, a supporter of the provincial Coalition Avenir Québec party in Quebec created a bot to broadcast party messages at a rate of 150 per day, influencing coverage of the election on social media (Normandin, 2012). During the 2013 Nova Scotia provincial election, a faction of Anonymous alleged that the incumbent New Democratic Party had hired bots to amplify its messages on Twitter. These allegations were later dismissed by all parties as well as researchers studying social media during the election (Payton, 2012). In 2015, two-thirds of Montreal mayor Denis Coderre's followers were fake, according to an analysis by social media analytics firm Nexalogy (Gyulai, 2015). The Conservative Party of Canada was also accused of buying Facebook likes during the 2015 federal election (Sherren, 2015). Neither of these cases seems to have impacted the political discourse, at most being reported as a political novelty.

Amplifier bots continue to be active. During the 2017 provincial election in British Columbia, the social media analytics firm MentionMapp found an active account on the #BCPoli hashtag, @ReverendSM. The firm suspected the account hired a commercial botnet to amplify its tweets, with most of the posts targeting the incumbent Christy Clark of the Liberal Party with accusations of corruption. MentionMapp analyzed a sample of 15 tweets collected over 11 days from the account. Bots retweeted all of the disgruntled Conservative's tweets, probably with the aim of amplifying them so that humans would interact. MentionMapp only found one tweet when someone other than a bot retweeted @ReverendSM. The investigation also revealed some of the inner workings of an amplifier botnet: MentionMapp identified 280 distinct bots that retweeted

@ReverendSM, with none retweeting more than once. Instead, @ReverendSM's tweets were part of a bot's random stream of retweets and other posts that were probably part of a coordinated network.

TRANSPARENCY BOTS: MAKING DATA ACCESSIBLE AND HOLDING GOVERNMENT TO ACCOUNT

A key role of journalism is to hold government to account, something many have claimed the Internet should enable through both professional journalistic innovation and citizen journalism (Dubois & Dutton, 2012). Most of the bots observed in Canadian journalism try do this. Transparency bots are described, in one of the only academic articles about bots in Canada (Ford et al., 2016, p. 4892), as "automated agents that use social media to draw attention to the behavior of particular [political] actors" (Leghorn, personal communication, April 6, 2017). For example, @StruckTOBot tweets whenever the police report a pedestrian or cyclist has been hit by a vehicle in Toronto (Simcoe, 2016). It had 345 followers as of March 19, 2017.

One of the most popular transparency bots in Canada is @gccaedits, mentioned earlier, that tweets whenever an Internet address associated with government departments, the House of Commons, the Senate, and government agencies edits Wikipedia. Inspired by similar accounts in the United Kingdom, United States, and other countries, the account, which states clearly "I am a bot," has been active since 2014, has tweeted 8,879 times, and has 8,145 followers as of 31 May 2017. The creator, Nick Ruest, explained that the bot is intended to be used by anyone, including journalists, who can find important edits and discuss them in a public forum (Ford et al., 2016).

For whatever reason—lack of support, time, or investment—we only encountered a few transparency bots explicitly linked to journalism. The *Globe and Mail* has experimented with much more public bots. It created Facebook chat bots to give readers a different way to access its reporting during the 2016 US election and also to provide advice on buying gifts during the Christmas season (Busta, 2016; Busta & Pereira, 2016). J-Source, a leading website of journalism studies in Canada, now offers a guide to coding chat bots (Shiab, 2015; Watson, 2017). DiffEngine bots, which tweet every time news organizations make corrections, have also been established internationally. In Canada there are at least five Twitter accounts, one for each of Canadaland, CBC, the *Globe and Mail*, the *Toronto Star*, and the *Calgary Herald* (Summers, 2017). Notably, there are also instances of Twitter accounts that are not bots but serve a similar function, such as the hand-curated account @OttawaSpends that journalist David Akin maintains.

SERVANT BOTS: AUTOMATING TASKS

Journalists also code another kind of bot—servants, or butlers. These bots automate simple tasks, help maintain data, or simplify data analysis. Journalists use these bots to monitor governmental websites and report any updates or changes. The hope, according to one source, is to better automate information gathering so journalists can focus on analysis and writing. As one developer explained, journalists can focus on "telling the human story because [bots] can automate the basic data collection for them." Although the public might never see the work of these servant bots, journalists have experimented with creating servant bots for their readers.

Additionally, parts of the Canadian government have experimented with servant bots to automate data analysis. Since at least 2014, some branches of the Canadian federal government have been evaluating potential applications of big data in the health, legal, and finance sectors. These initiatives include using software automation—or bot-like activity—to ease decision making ("Big Data @ SSC," 2015). Canada's National Research Council, for instance, partnered with the Thales Group, MediaMiser, and an undisclosed intelligence agency to build, collect, and analyze social media activity. Though only a prototype, the system opens up the possibility for big data projects to leverage bots to comb through and analyze the volumes of data being collected by these crawlers (Ling, 2017).

Servants also help political parties and politicians manage social media content. The Communications Office of Ontario Premier Kathleen Wynne manages her Facebook page so that it automatically removes posts that contain any word from a list of banned words. This is just one example of how automation might allow politicians to stay connected online without having to suffer constant abuse (Delacourt, n.d.).

Canada hosts an innovative use of a bot to manage the problem of online child exploitation. The Canadian Centre for Child Protection is a leading Canadian nonprofit organization confronting child sexual exploitation. Launched in 2017, Project Arachnid is a Web-crawling bot that traverses public websites and sites on the Deep Web searching for pornographic images of children. The automated crawlers use a database of hashed images to identify other images. Most of these hashes come from the center itself, which uses a team of three analysts to confirm the content of the image. Once flagged, the image is cryptographically hashed using seven different functions, including Microsoft's PhotoDNA, which enables the bot to detect likely images of child exploitation. A positive identification triggers the bot to automatically file a take-down notice if the content matches a known image. If the image is suspicious, the bot flags it for review by the analysts. In the past few months, the center has also developed and deployed a deep-learning algorithm that uses machine vision to prioritize images. Although the center does not intend the deep-learning algorithm to entirely replace human judgment, it hopes to find ways for it to cut down on the fatigue experienced by its analysts. The center's use of bots demonstrates a novel application for bots to handle difficult, disturbing, and high-volume data analysis.

Could Project Arachnid be a sign of a next generation of bots for use by the Canadian government? Without taking away from the bot's important mission, these types of crawler and analysis bots might find applications in the Canadian government as a way to keep up with the volume of big data as well as the increasing sophistication of cyberattacks. Will these bots be a benefit or a problem (that is, Jarvis or an Ultron, to recall the robot protagonist and villain of the last Avengers blockbuster)? One source familiar with cybersecurity speculated that next-generation cyberattacks will only be identified and mitigated through machine learning and automated countermeasures. More critically, if government agencies have outsourced social media monitoring, will these third parties begin developing and using bots in their big data analysis? We return to these concerns in our section on bots and law in Canada.

BOTS IN PUBLIC DISCOURSE

Bots have had little impact in the public discourse. We conducted a scan of news coverage about bots in Canada looking for the four types of bots we identified: dampeners, amplifier, transparency, and servant.[1] In total, we identified 207 newspaper articles that discussed bot-related subjects during 2016. Of them, only 29 articles discussed political bots, most of which are servant bots. There was some discussion of transparency bots (in three articles), and in nonpolitical contexts, two articles each discussed dampener and amplifier bots. Notably, the term *bot* is inconsistently used, and often specific names are used rather than the general term "bot," which makes it difficult to reliably collect news articles. Nevertheless, the coverage suggests that to date, bots have not had a strong impact on the Canadian political information cycle. Furthermore, this analysis points to a lack of public discussion about the various roles bots can play in the Canadian political system, which is problematic for developing appropriate media literacy, policy, and law.

Please Do Not Build SkyNet: Bot Law in Canada

Political bots are potentially implicated in issues governed by the Criminal Code, spam legislation, election regulation, privacy law, and charter rights. It is a tall order to say exactly where and how a political bot will fit into this legal nexus. For the most part, bots are secondary—either as a tool or an outcome—rather than the principle focus of any law. This overall orientation might align with what Neff and Nagy call "symbiotic agency." Our reading of bots in Canadian law tries then to remember that agency can "be thought of not as universal, generalizable, and autonomous, but as particular, contextual, and dialogic" (Neff & Nagy, 2016, p. 4925). With this emphasis on content, we recognize there is no one path through the intersection of Canadian law and bots. Instead, here we are guided by the bots we have encountered so far. We begin with the proviso that we are not lawyers but merely interpreters of the law.

DAMPENERS

Dampeners might in special cases be considered tools of libel, criminal harassment, or hate speech. Dampeners could be programmed to spread messages that violate libel law. The test would be whether the bot published messages that damaged an individual's reputation by intentionally making false or unqualified statements to the public. Simply retweeting a story or sharing a hyperlink likely would not count as publishing, and thereby not be considered libel. If found to be guilty of committing libel, a bot's creator could be forced to pay damages and, in some contexts, to remove the offending content or even the offending bot (Canadian Journalists for Free Expression, 2015). In more exceptional circumstances, courts could link a bot to a human campaign of criminal harassment of a person (s 264) or view it as a tool of hate propaganda under the Criminal Code (s 320). To violate the latter section, bots would have to be part of an intentional plan to make statements advocating genocide or inciting hatred toward an identifiable group (Department of Justice, 2012).

What happens if someone's computer or account is hacked and turned into a bot? The Criminal Code also addresses occasions when technologies are the target of criminal activity, not the instrument. The Criminal Code includes provisions against unauthorized use of computer services (s 342.1) and what it calls "mischief in relation to computer data" (s 430). A botnet might violate the law if its creation and use required unauthorized access to a computer or service to carry out its tasks. A programmer engages in data mischief if the bot "obstructs, interrupts or interferes with the lawful use of computer data." Though we found no such bots, a dampener might violate this section if its coordinated attack interferes with an online poll to suppress certain choices or otherwise interferes with online data (Royal Canadian Mounted Police, 2014).

Attempts to stop dampeners must consider the legitimate political uses of DDoS attacks (Sauter, 2014; Wray, 1998). There is considerable debate about whether DDoS attacks stifle or support free speech. The work of Anonymous that we observed certainly had a political intent. Still, botnet DDoS attacks differ from the mass virtual sit-ins that defined early electronic disobedience. The former only appears to be a mass protest, whereas the latter is a mass public participation online. Future bot law, then, has to consider whether bots should be protected by an individual's charter rights to free expression, or if a bot's activity substantively alters its political meaning or intent. Bots, to be clear, can operate at a scale beyond humans, even though they share the same channels.

AMPLIFIERS

Given that amplifier and dampener bots respectively raise and lower the volume of messages online, both violate the same types of law. Amplifier bots might be treated as a tool of harassment, propaganda, or libel, just like dampener bots. However, an amplifier bot's promotional nature raises another set of questions. Amplifier bots might break the law if they ramp up commercial or political messages. The former act chiefly concerns the Canadian Anti-Spam Law (CASL), whereas the latter might violate the Elections Act.

Amplifiers and other political bots might violate CASL in very specific circumstances. CASL prohibits sending commercial messages directly targeting individuals or electronic addresses without consent. Commercial messages, according to CASL, are messages that encourage participation in commercial activities or messages on websites that encourage commercial activities. An amplifier might violate CASL if its messages appear commercial *enough*. However, CASL only applies to messages sent to an electronic address campaign, not a hashtag or public group (Canadian Radio-television and Telecommunications Commission, 2014). All these stipulations mean that amplifier bots probably only rarely violate CASL law since their messages are political not commercial, and the bots we have seen tend to target public channels not individual addresses.

Canada's Elections Act might apply to amplifier bots if they seem to be advertising for or against a political party. The Act broadly interprets advertising online as messages that have a placement cost. If an amplifier bot sold its services to post or promote messages, then the placement costs would probably qualify the bot as advertising. Political parties or registered third parties would then have to disclose their expenses for using the bot, and the message would have to include the name of the organization that paid for the placement or authorized it (Elections Canada, 2017). Most of our amplifiers did not appear to be advertising, raising the possibility that bots might circumvent advertising rules in the future by broadcasting a message without any accountability.

The Elections Act also addresses who or what can advertise during an election. Though we did not observe any bot activity by foreign parties in the Canadian

2015 federal election, despite what appeared in some recent press coverage, they are prohibited from doing so. The Elections Act prohibits foreigners from using advertising or influencing voting. US comedian Sarah Silverman might have broken this law during the 2015 election when she tweeted to encouraged Canadians to vote NDP (Yeung, 2015). Press coverage questioned whether her endorsement counted as foreign influence, but in the end, Elections Canada did not intervene, and the NDP candidate endorsed by Silverman did not win her seat. But Silverman unwittingly raised a question likely to vex Elections Canada for years to come: how can free speech be weighed against foreign interference?

Beyond celebrity endorsements, bots are part of the challenge that an accessible and global communication system poses to domestic elections. There have already been concerns that Canadian elections might become targets for hackers, global political movements, and foreign governments, as seen in the United States and France (Van Praet, 2017), and the Canadian security establishment has begun a risk assessment of possible foreign interference in the 2019 election (Boutilier, 2017). With these larger concerns, the Elections Act faces a major challenge to attribute and stop bot activity in the future. How can Elections Canada be sure a party paid for a commercial botnet's services? What if a partisan supporter paid for a botnet to promote a party without its consent? What if a foreign party paid to amplify a national party's message? Attribution is a major issue in cybersecurity, and Elections Canada will have to face it, too. Attribution might also be the lesser problem faced by Elections Canada. The law might eventually bring a bot's creators to justice without stopping a bot from being influential during the election. Elections Canada then has to judiciously consider how to prevent malicious bots from interfering in an election.

The regulatory response to the 2011 Robocalling Scandal provides one possible foundation for proactive bot legislation. The scandal and subsequent scrutiny led the government to establish the Voter Contact Registry. Managed by the Canadian Radio-television and Telecommunications Commission, the registry governs both callers and calling services. Political entities—a broad term capturing both candidates and citizens as well as parties, unions, and corporations—have to register before they contact voters using robocalling services. Companies that provide robocalling services also need to register. Failure to register means that any robocalls would be in violation of the Elections Act and be subject to fines.

Commercial bot services have enough of a passing resemblance to robocallers that we wonder if current laws around automated voter contact might someday apply to bots. Extending the Voter Contact Registry to bot services might legitimate their work during elections while establishing accountability practices and codes of conduct. If a bot registry sounds ambitious, then at least closer cooperation between platform providers and Elections Canada might lead to better recognition of the importance of elections amid our status updates. The challenge of monitoring the VCR will also inform the feasibility of any bot law in Canada. Not unlike the challenge of bots, the VCR has to manage cheap, automated voter contact services operating globally. How well the VCR tracks and stops rogue operations should inform any legislative solutions to bot services.

TRANSPARENCY BOTS

Copyright laws probably cover the work of transparency bots. These bots might infringe copyright by reproducing copyrighted information. Canada, however, has liberal user rights that enable reuse for certain purposes. Canada's highest court has recognized that user rights are as integral to the broader copyright scheme as are those of copyright owners. Canadian user rights include as fair dealing copying for the purpose of "research, private study, education, parody or satire" as well as criticism, review, or news reporting. These fair dealing provisions lay ample ground for justification of bot activity on the basis of research, education, or reporting.

Beyond stopping bad bots, could Canadian regulation do more to promote the public good generated by transparency bots? We found transparency bots had a clear public benefit. Interviewees especially appreciated the @gccaedits transparency bot, which reports edits to Wikipedia made from Internet domains associated with the Government of Canada. Where open data is generally associated with public transparency, it might also be an instrument to encourage more transparency bots. Canada already has a good foundation to encourage these types of bots. The Canadian government already has a portal with many open data sources. Better data that is properly maintained and updated could incentivize more transparency bots. Further, initiatives for proactive disclosure—releasing information before it is requested—might also incentivize better bots.

SERVANTS

Servant bots are perhaps the biggest category, as well as the most difficult to fit into any one law. However, they might be subject to Canadian privacy law. Commercial servant bots would have to respect the federal Personal Information Protection and Electronic Documents Act (PIPEDA), unless they operated in provinces with comparable privacy laws. Bots used in governments would have to abide by provincial or the federal Privacy Act. Any bot programmed to collect or analyze personal information should have to comply with these laws. *Personal information* is an inclusive term in Canada that can mean the obviously personal, such as a person's photograph, as well as social media metadata such as likes, dislikes, comments, and ratings.

Bots raise privacy concerns, but the links remain speculative. Bots could violate principles of informed consent if they autonomously collect personal information on social media without obtaining consent. And as bots become more intelligent, their decisions might complicate an organization's responsibility to disclose how it uses personal information. In any case, bots should be considered during the ongoing reviews of the Privacy Act and PIPEDA, especially in relation to machine learning and artificial intelligence.

Bots used by the government would fall under the jurisdiction of the Canadian Charter of Rights and Freedoms as well as the Privacy Act. The Canadian charter guarantees a right to freedom of expression as well as a right "to be secure against unreasonable search or seizure." Canadians also have protection of the use of their personal information under the Privacy Act. The Privacy Act requires government institutions to only use data "for the purpose for which the information was obtained or compiled by the institution or for a use consistent with that purpose." Some exceptions apply. Bill C-51 controversially increased data sharing between 17 federal agencies for national security reasons (Office of the Privacy Commissioner of Canada, 2016). National security and terrorism might create the exemptions necessary for more elaborate uses of bots in government.

All examples so far assume a link between human intent and a bot's actions. Already, that link seems tenuous at best. We already had difficulty discerning whether dampener or amplifier bots acted intentionally or coincidentally. So, we are not sure if @ReverendSM actually paid to be amplified or whether it was a glitch in the botnet. Broader regulatory responses to bots might also have to learn how to address bots as central rather than peripheral to the law. As Neff and Nagy write, "Tay shows that people may no longer treat or view smart agents as mere tools. Such objects have technical agency that have a unique participation status in interaction" (Neff & Nagy, 2016). In doing so, the law might have to consider rules for the bot alone. Apart from new laws targeting scalper bots that buy tickets before humans do, most laws focus on the creator not the bot, and tend to treat bots as just another technology (Leslie, 2014). IRC channels and Reddit, by comparison, have a "robot etiquette" that stipulates that bots must be identifiable and support community standards (Latzko-Toth, 2017, pp. 56–57; Massanari, 2017, p. 118). While we have listed a few ways to promote good bots implicitly through open data or the Voter Contact Registry, a broader public conversation should continue to discuss the democratic goals of an election and perhaps develop an etiquette for bots in this context.

Conclusion

Amplifiers, dampeners, transparency, and servant bots (see Table 3.2) are an active part of Canada's political landscape. Though they have not had as great an influence on Canadian politics as their international counterparts, they will probably become even more established in Canada. To understand this trend, we should focus more on *what is said* than *who is speaking.*

Amplifiers and dampeners may just find legitimate political uses, but only if their activity receives public scrutiny. Just as easily, they could blend into the cycles of clickbait, sponsored content, and influencer marketing. These bots would just be another tool of media manipulation to game public opinion. It remains to be seen if these bots will cause a re-evaluation of the use of social media analytics in journalism. Certainly, social media trends can no longer be assumed to be an indicator of public opinion. Such conditions would encourage bot innovation from partisan or public relations firms capable of subsidizing development as a cheap way to manipulate public perception of issues and candidates.

The use of bots also reiterates a need to review the digital campaigning by parties and political third parties. Facebook advertising has reportedly been used by political campaigns to target and suppress certain voters in recent elections in the United States and the United Kingdom (Cadwalladr, 2017; Winston, 2016). Read alongside reports about a lack of oversight about what ads can be placed online (Angwin & Parris Jr., 2016), there is legitimate concern that the Internet might be creating the conditions for a voter suppression campaign resembling the Robocalling Scandal. Bots would probably be a key player in such an event.

Table 3.2 **Types of Political Bots Active in Canada**

Type of Bot	Definition	Example
Dampener	Stifles a particular voice or message	DDoS attacks
Amplifier	Promotes a particular voice or message	@MapleLeaks, tweeted own website repeatedly
Transparency	Collects and makes available information for the purpose of holding other actors to account	@gccaedits, tweets anonymous Wikipedia edits from government IP addresses
Servant	Preforms mundane or repetitive tasks for another actor	Project Arachnid, automatically identifies child pornography

Steps should be taken to ensure that online advertisers and platforms respect election advertising rules and oversight. Elections Canada might also require political campaigns to better report their online campaigning and submit a record of their messages and targets. This could expose the dark arts of online campaigning to the public.

Good bots should be encouraged in Canada. The neutral or positive impacts of transparency and servant bots provide a good foundation for future bots to build on. Chat bots, crawlers, and automated journalists have made thoughtful contributions to Canadian politics. Mindful public discourse aided by some bots might be an antidote to mindless automation. Strong privacy laws, generative open data policies, and journalists working in the public interest are also key parts of building good bots in Canada.

For all these important pieces, one part is still missing. Media literacy and debate about bots seems to be completely outside public awareness and media coverage. As Canada tries to become a hub of research into artificial intelligence, a gap persists between research funding and support to consider its ethical and political consequences (Owen & Ananny, 2017). The same could be said for bots. Bots—good and bad—lack sufficient attention as a sign of a changed political media environment. Canada's political discourse largely ignores bots (see Greenspon & Owen, 2017 for a notable exception). For all the discussion of bots in Canadian law, better education about artificial intelligence, privacy, and social media might be the most proactive response to the bots to come. Media literacy, in short, remains as crucial as ever.

Note

1. New sources collected from Canadian News Source in the Factiva database. We queried the database for news stories including "bot" or "spam." We excluded articles labeled as Arts and Entertainment or as News Releases.

References

Akin, D. (n.d.). Canadian Political Twits: Federal Liberals on Twitter. Retrieved May 25, 2017, from http://www.davidakin.com/politicaltwits/.

Angwin, J., & Parris Jr., T. (2016, October 28). Facebook Lets Advertisers Exclude Users by Race. Retrieved June 5, 2017, from https://www.propublica.org/article/facebook-lets-advertisers-exclude-users-by-race.

Bell, E., & Owen, T. (2017). *The Platform Press: How Silicon Valley Reengineered Journalism.* New York: Tow Center for Digital Journalism. Retrieved from https://www.cjr.org/tow_center_reports/platform-press-how-silicon-valley-reengineered-journalism.php.

Big Data @ SSC. (2015, June 18). Retrieved May 2, 2017, from http://www.ssc-spc.gc.ca/pages/itir-triti/itir-triti-afac-030615-pres1-eng.html.

Boutilier, A. (2017, May 12). Canada's Spies Examining "Vulnerabilities" in Election System. *Toronto Star*. Retrieved from https://www.thestar.com/news/canada/2017/05/12/canadas-spies-examining-vulnerabilities-in-election-system.html.

Boutilier, A., & Desson, C. (2015, June 17). Cyberattack Knocks Canadian Government Websites Offline. *Toronto Star*. Retrieved from https://www.thestar.com/news/canada/2015/06/17/canadian-government-websites-hit-with-massive-outage.html.

Bradshaw, T. (2013, March 21). YouTube Reaches Billion Users Milestone. *Financial Times*. Retrieved from http://www.ft.com/intl/cms/s/0/8f06331a-91ca-11e2-b4c9-00144feabdc0.html.

Brin, C. (2017). *Digital News Report 2016: Canada*. Retrieved May 2, 2017, from http://www.digitalnewsreport.org/survey/2016/canada-2016/.

Busta, S. (2016, December 1). Need Last-Minutes Gift Tips? Let the Globe Elf Help. *The Globe and Mail*. Retrieved from http://www.theglobeandmail.com/life/holiday-guide/holiday-survival-guide/globe-elf-the-globe-and-mail-advent-calendar-chatbot/article33088499/.

Busta, S., & Pereira, M. (2016, October 4). Introducing "GloBot," The Globe and Mail's New Facebook Messenger Chatbot. *The Globe and Mail*. Retrieved from http://www.theglobeandmail.com/community/digital-lab/introducing-globot-the-globe-and-mails-new-facebook-messenger-chatbot/article32239050/.

Cadwalladr, C. (2017, May 27). Revealed: Tory "Dark" Ads Targeted Voters' Facebook Feeds in Welsh Marginal Seat. *The Guardian*. Retrieved from https://www.theguardian.com/politics/2017/may/27/conservatives-facebook-dark-ads-data-protection-election.

Callison, C., & Hermida, A. (2015). Dissent and Resonance: #Idlenomore as an Emergent Middle Ground. *Canadian Journal of Communication, 40*(4), 695–716.

Canadian Internet Registration Authority. (2016, November 24). *CIRA Internet Factbook 2016*. Retrieved May 25, 2017, from https://cira.ca/factbook/domain-industry-data-and-canadian-Internet-trends.

Canadian Journalists for Free Expression. (2015, June 15). Defamation, Libel and Slander: What Are My Rights to Free Expression? Retrieved May 25, 2017, from http://www.cjfe.org/defamation_libel_and_slander_what_are_my_rights_to_free_expression.

Canadian Radio-television and Telecommunications Commission. (2014, June 13). Frequently Asked Questions about Canada's Anti-Spam Legislation. Retrieved May 25, 2017, from http://crtc.gc.ca/eng/com500/faq500.htm.

Canadian Radio-television and Telecommunications Commission. (2016a, January 12). Local and Community TV [Consumer information]. Retrieved May 25, 2017, from http://www.crtc.gc.ca/eng/television/services/local.htm.

Canadian Radio-television and Telecommunications Commission. (2016b, December 21). CRTC Submission to the Government of Canada's Innovation Agenda [Reports]. Retrieved June 1, 2017, from http://www.crtc.gc.ca/eng/publications/reports/rp161221/rp161221.htm.

Chase, S. (2011, February 3). Government Policy Decisions, in 140 Characters or Less. *The Globe and Mail*. Retrieved from http://www.theglobeandmail.com/news/politics/government-policy-decisions-in-140-characters-or-less/article564885/.

Clarke, A. (2016, May 13). Outrage over Government Wikipedia Edits Wrong Message. Retrieved August 1, 2016, from http://policyoptions.irpp.org/2016/05/13/outrage-over-government-wikipedia-edits-wrong-message/.

Coleman, G. (2013). *Anonymous in Context: The Politics and Power behind the Mask* (Internet Governance Paper Series No. 3). Waterloo: The Centre for International Governance Innovation. Retrieved from http://www.cigionline.org/sites/default/files/no3_7.pdf.

Delacourt, S. (n.d.). *More than Mean Tweets*. Retrieved from https://www.blubrry.com/briefremarks/21665701/episode-15-more-than-mean-tweets.

Department of Justice. (2012). *A Handbook for Police and Crown Prosecutors on Criminal Harassment.* Ottawa: Communications and Executive Services Branch, Dept. of Justice Canada. Retrieved from http://publications.gc.ca/collections/collection_2013/jus/J2-166-2012-eng.pdf.

Dubois, E., & Dutton, W. (2012). The Fifth Estate in Internet Governance: Collective Accountability of a Canadian Policy Initiative. *Revue Francaise D'Etudies Americaines, 2012*(4), 134.

Elections Canada. (2017, April). Election Advertising Handbook for Third Parties, Financial Agents and Auditors. Retrieved May 25, 2017, from http://www.elections.ca/content.aspx?section=pol&dir=thi/ec20227&document=p2&lang=e#2.1e.

Ford, H., Puschmann, C., & Dubois, D. (2016). Keeping Ottawa Honest, One Tweet at a Time? Politicians, Journalists, Wikipedians and Their Twitter Bots. *International Journal of Communication, 10*(Special Issue), 20.

Forum Research Inc. (2015, January 6). Federal Social Media News Release: Poll - Instagram Tops in User Satisfaction [News Release]. Retrieved from http://poll.forumresearch.com/data/Federal%20Social%20Media%20News%20Release%20(2015%2001%2006)%20Forum%20Research.pdf.

Greenspon, E., & Owen, T. (2017, May 28). "Fake News 2.0": A Threat to Canada's Democracy. *The Globe and Mail.* Retrieved from https://www.theglobeandmail.com/opinion/fake-news-20-a-threat-to-canadas-democracy/article35138104/.

Gyulai, L. (2015, October 27). Who's Really Following Mayor Coderre on Twitter? Retrieved January 16, 2017, from http://montrealgazette.com/news/local-news/whos-really-following-mayor-coderre-on-twitter.

Huang, C. (2013, April 16). Botnets Involved in Anonymous DDoS Attacks. Retrieved April 27, 2017, from http://blog.trendmicro.com/trendlabs-security-intelligence/botnets-involved-in-anonymous-ddos-attacks/

Kleis Nielsen, R., & Ganter, S. A. (2017). Dealing with Digital Intermediaries: A Case Study of the Relations between Publishers and Platforms. *New Media & Society,* 1461444817701318. https://doi.org/10.1177/1461444817701318.

Langlois, G., & Elmer, G. (2009). Wikipedia Leeches? The Promotion of Traffic through a Collaborative Web Format. *New Media & Society, 11*(5), 773–794.

Larsson, A. O., & Kalsnes, B. (2014). "Of Course We Are on Facebook": Use and Non-Use of Social Media among Swedish and Norwegian Politicians. *European Journal of Communication, 29*(6), 653–667.

Latzko-Toth, G. (2017). The Socialization of Early Internet Bots: IRC and the Ecology of Human-Robot Interactions Online. In R. W. Gehl & M. Bakardjieva (Eds.), *Socialbots and Their Friends: Digital Media and the Automation of Sociality* (pp. 47–68). New York: Routledge.

Leghorn. (2017, April 6). Phone interview with F. McKelvey.

Leslie, K. (2014, April 4). Ontario to Outlaw "Scalper Bots" that Scoop Up Concert Tickets. Retrieved July 15, 2018, from https://www.theglobeandmail.com/news/national/ontario-to-outlaw-scalper-bots-that-scoop-up-concert-tickets/article32452803/.

Longhorn, (2017, March 10). Phone interview with F. McKelvey.

Ling, J. (2017, March 9). The Canadian Government Developed Software to Monitor Your Social Media for Threats. Retrieved April 28, 2017, from https://news.vice.com/story/the-canadian-government-developed-software-to-monitor-your-social-media-for-threats.

Massanari, A. L. (2017). Contested Play: The Culture and Politics of Reddit Bots. In R. W. Gehl & M. Bakardjieva (Eds.), *Socialbots and Their Friends: Digital Media and the Automation of Sociality* (pp. 110–127). New York: Routledge.

McConnell, R. (2016, November 22). "Don't Ignore It": Alberta MLA Calls on Legislature to Stand against Misogyny. Retrieved May 2, 2017, from http://www.cbc.ca/news/canada/edmonton/impassioned-sandra-jansen-calls-on-legislature-to-stand-against-misogyny-1.3863097.

McGuire, P. (2013, April 12). Inside Anonymous's Operation to Out Rehtaeh Parsons's Rapists. Retrieved April 27, 2017, from https://www.vice.com/en_ca/article/inside-anonymouss-operation-to-out-rehtaeh-parsonss-rapists.

Neff, G., & Nagy, P. (2016). Talking to Bots: Symbiotic Agency and the Case of Tay. *International Journal of Communication, 10*(Special Issue), 20.

Normandin, P.-A. (2012, August 6). Un robot au service de la CAQ. *La Presse.* Retrieved from http://www.lapresse.ca/actualites/elections-quebec-2014/201208/06/01-4562707-un-robot-au-service-de-la-caq.php.

Office of the Privacy Commissioner of Canada. (2016, November 22). Appearance before the Standing Committee on Access to Information, Privacy and Ethics (ETHI) on the study of the Security of Canada Information Sharing Act (SCISA)—Office of the Privacy Commissioner of Canada. Retrieved May 25, 2017, from https://www.priv.gc.ca/en/opc-actions-and-decisions/advice-to-parliament/2016/parl_20161122/.

Omand, G. (2015, August 3). Anonymous Vigilantism Fills Hole in Traditional Justice System, Says Beneficiary. Retrieved April 27, 2017, from http://www.cbc.ca/news/canada/nova-scotia/rehtaeh-parsons-s-father-credits-anonymous-for-reopening-investigation-1.3177605.

O'Neill, P. H. (2015, May 12). Anonymous Botnet Runs on Hacked Routers Using Default Logins. Retrieved April 27, 2017, from https://www.dailydot.com/layer8/botnet-incapsula-research-report-default/.

Owen, T., & Ananny, M. (2017, March 30). Ethics and Governance are Getting Lost in the AI Frenzy. *The Globe and Mail.* Retrieved from https://www.theglobeandmail.com/opinion/ethics-and-governance-are-getting-lost-in-the-ai-frenzy/article34504510/.

Patten, S. (2013). Assessing the Potential of New Social Media. *Canadian Parliamentary Review, 36*(2), 21–26.

Payton, L. (2012, March 27). NDP Voting Disruption Deliberate, Hard to Track. Retrieved January 16, 2017, from http://www.cbc.ca/news/politics/ndp-voting-disruption-deliberate-hard-to-track-1.1204246.

Payton, L. (2014, March 4). Online Attack on 2012 NDP Leadership Vote Targeted Party's Site. Retrieved January 16, 2017, from http://www.cbc.ca/news/politics/ndp-site-the-weak-link-in-online-attack-during-2012-leadership-vote-1.2557861.

Perrin, B. (2016, August 29). I Tweeted about Harper. Then the Twitter Bots Attacked. Retrieved January 16, 2017, from http://www.theglobeandmail.com/opinion/i-tweeted-about-harper-then-the-twitter-bots-attacked/article31591910/.

Poell, T., & van Dijck, J. (2014). Social Media and Journalistic Independence. In J. Bennett & N. Strange (Eds.), *Media Independence: Working with Freedom or Working for Free?* (1st edition, pp. 181–201). New York ; London: Routledge.

Public Policy Forum. (2017). *The Shattered Mirror: News, Democracy and Trust in the Digital Age.* Retrieved from https://shatteredmirror.ca/wp-content/uploads/theShatteredMirror.pdf.

Royal Canadian Mounted Police. (2014). *Cybercrime: An Overview of Incidents and Issues in Canada.* Retrieved from http://epe.lac-bac.gc.ca/100/201/301/weekly_checklist/2014/internet/w14-25-U-E.html/collections/collection_2014/grc-rcmp/PS64-116-2014-eng.pdf.

Sauter, M. (2014). *The Coming Swarm: DDoS Actions, Hacktivism, and Civil Disobedience on the Internet.* New York: Bloomsbury Academic.

Sherren, R. (2015, September 15). How I Ended Up "Liking" the Conservative Party on Facebook without Knowing It. Retrieved January 16, 2017, from http://www.cbc.ca/news/politics/canada-election-2015-like-jacking-facebook-1.3229622.

Shiab, N. (2015, June 22). On the Ethics of Web Scraping and Data Journalism. Retrieved June 2, 2017, from http://www.j-source.ca/article/ethics-web-scraping-and-data-journalism.

Simcoe, L. (2016, March 26). Toronto Twitter Bot Tracks Pedestrian and Cyclist Collisions. Retrieved January 16, 2017, from http://www.metronews.ca/news/toronto/2016/05/26/toronto-twitter-bot-tracks-pedestrian-and-cyclist-collisions.html.

Small, T. A., Jansen, H., Bastien, F., Giasson, T., & Koop, R. (2014). Online Political Activity in Canada: The Hype and the Facts. *Canadian Parliamentary Review*, 9–16.

Summers, E. (2017). *diffengine: track changes to the news, where news is anything with an RSS feed.* Python, Documenting the Now. Retrieved from https://github.com/DocNow/diffengine (Original work published January 3, 2017)

Tuohy, S. (2016, December 14). Botnet Attack Analysis of Deflect Protected Website blacklivesmatter. com. Retrieved April 27, 2017, from https://equalit.ie/deflect-labs-report-3/.

Van Praet, N. (2017, January 15). Hacking Likely in Canadian Politics, Former Spy Chief Richard Fadden Says. *The Globe and Mail.* Retrieved from https://www.theglobeandmail.com/news/national/hacking-likely-in-canadian-politics-former-spy-chief-richard-fadden-says/article33630088/.

Watson, H. G. (2017, May 5). We Built a Chatbot, and You Can Too. Retrieved June 1, 2017, from http://www.j-source.ca/article/we-built-our-own-chatbot-and-you-can-too.

Winseck, D. (2016, November 22). Media and Internet Concentration in Canada Report 1984–2015. Retrieved May 2, 2017, from http://www.cmcrp.org/media-and-internet-concentration-in-canada-report-1984-2015/.

Winseck, D. (2017, February 9). Shattered Mirror, Stunted Vision and Squandered Opportunities. Retrieved May 2, 2017, from https://dwmw.wordpress.com/2017/02/09/shattered-mirror-stunted-vision-and-a-squandered-opportunities/.

Winston, J. (2016, November 18). How the Trump Campaign Built an Identity Database and Used Facebook Ads to Win the Election. Retrieved June 1, 2017, from https://medium.com/startup-grind/how-the-trump-campaign-built-an-identity-database-and-used-facebook-ads-to-win-the-election-4ff7d24269ac#.9r6w8gkhp.

Woolley, S. C., & Howard, P. N. (2016). Political Communication, Computational Propaganda, and Autonomous Agents—Introduction. *International Journal of Communication, 10,* 4882–4890.

Wray, S. (1998). Electronic Civil Disobedience and the World Wide Web of Hacktivism: A Mapping of Extraparliamentarian Direct Action Net Politics. *Switch, 4*(2). Retrieved from http://switch.sjsu.edu/web/v4n2/stefan/.

Yeung, L. (2015, October 4). Sarah Silverman Endorses Tom Mulcair and NDP candidate in Vancouver. Retrieved July, 5 2018, from https://www.cbc.ca/news/canada/british-columbia/sarah-silverman-endorses-tom-mulcair-and-ndp-candidate-in-vancouver-1.3256425

4

Poland

Unpacking the Ecosystem of Social Media Manipulation

ROBERT GORWA

Introduction

Since the 2016 US election, an increasing amount of public attention has been paid to the effect that digital disinformation is having on democracy and political life in the West. Leading newspapers, captivated by the apparent influx of "fake news" and the various online influence operations that seem to have targeted political campaigns in countries such as France and the United States, have in recent months covered bots, trolls, and various other, previously esoteric aspects of the digital public sphere. In a sense, this was to be expected: as the online dimension of politics became more prominent, so did the likelihood that efforts to shape online media ecosystems and manipulate public opinion on social networks would emerge (Woolley & Howard, 2016). A recent body of scholarship has begun to engage with the various new forms of "computational propaganda," such as automated social media bots, organized networks of fake online identities, and coordinated trolling campaigns that have become increasingly prevalent and are rapidly being established as an important aspect of contemporary digital politics (Woolley, 2016). However, scholarly understanding of these developments remains limited, especially in countries outside of Western Europe and North America. For all the talk of bots, trolls, and "fake news" in the United States and United Kingdom, it is not entirely clear if they pose an issue elsewhere. Have these phenomena spread? And if so, how are they understood and perceived in other countries?

Poland provides a fascinating case study for a variety of reasons. First, despite the numerous cases of alleged political trolling and online manipulation by foreign actors that have been covered in the Polish media, as well as a highly adversarial domestic political climate and accusations that certain Polish political parties are using paid commentators and fake accounts on a variety of social networks, there have been no comprehensive efforts to assess these developments in the country. Second, Poles have in recent years eagerly embraced multiple online platforms, and today the Internet has become very important for political life in the country. In particular, Facebook has emerged as a major source of political information and news, especially among younger demographics. Finally, Poland's complex history and current political climate combine to yield a challenging yet unique environment for any study.

This chapter aims to provide an initial exploration of computational propaganda and media manipulation in Poland and, in the process, gain further insight into the general operation and effects of bots, fake accounts, and other false amplifiers.

It proceeds in five parts. In the section that follows, key terms are defined and the chapter's methodology is discussed. In the third section, background for the case study is provided, and various recent developments in Polish digital politics are discussed. The fourth section discusses the various sources of apparent Russian disinformation to which Poles are regularly exposed, as well as what is believed to be Russian-linked activity on Polish social networks that has persisted since the onset of the 2013 Ukraine crisis. The final section explores the production and management of artificial identities on Facebook by Polish political consultancies and social media marketing firms, and assesses how they can be deployed for both political and commercial purposes.

Definitions and Methods

Setting baseline definitions for the processes being observed allows one to better understand how the observations from our study adhere to, or deviate from, the commonly held conceptions of these phenomena. As we will see, these definitions can be flexible and are often contested.

Howard and Woolley have theorized that three main elements—political bots, organized trolling campaigns of hate and harassment, and the online dissemination of "fake news" and disinformation—form a broader system of *computational propaganda,* an "assemblage of social media platforms, autonomous agents, and big data tasked with the manipulation of public opinion" (Woolley & Howard, 2016, p. 4887). These are explored in turn.

BOTS

Shortly following the emergence of Twitter as a major microblogging service in the late 2000s, certain computer scientists began to express interest in *social bots*, automated accounts that mimic users on social media platforms (Lee et al., 2011). Scholars noted that Twitter's fairly open API was conducive to its flexible integration with many apps and third-party services, but also made it quite easy for bots to proliferate, leading some to suggest that this increase in automation could create a "double edged sword" for the platform, as benevolent bots would inflate Twitter's user numbers and "generate large numbers of benign tweets" while also allowing for the possibility that more malicious bots could manipulate hashtags and spread spam (Chu et al., 2010, p. 21).

Most recently, social scientists have become concerned about the influence of partisan *political bots*, especially in the run-up to major elections (Howard & Kollanyi, 2016; Woolley, 2016). In the simplest sense, these are bots that serve some political function, and political bots are generally, but not always, *social media bots* (bots that operate on social media). There are many different types of bots, performing a variety of tasks online. For example, Tsvetkova and colleagues outline the many different types of bots that tend to perform one or more of four broad functions: they can collect information, execute actions, generate content, and emulate humans (Tsvetkova et al., 2017). These bots can be benign—for example, there have been several examples of Twitter bots that attempt to foster positive online discourse—but more malevolent bots also exist, spreading spam and malicious links (Murthy et al., 2016; Ferrera et al., 2016). Exactly how much automation is required for an account to be properly considered a bot is still an open question, but for the purposes of this chapter, *bot* simply refers to an automated account on an online platform. A full overview and literature review on bots is provided in Gorwa & Guilbeault (2018).

TROLLING AND FAKE ACCOUNTS

Another increasingly important element of political life online is *trolling*. Trolling is difficult to define and has its roots in the early days of bulletin boards such as Usenet (Coleman, 2012). As Marwick and Lewis (2017, p. 4) note, the term initially "described those who deliberately baited people to elicit an emotional response." But since the early 2000s, scholars have demonstrated how playful trolling emerged on certain online forums but eventually would become more synonymous with hate and harassment as demonstrated on message boards such as 4Chan's /b/ (Herring et al., 2002; Marwick & Lewis, 2017). While key questions about trolling today remain unanswered, elements of trolling have been established as an important aspect of twenty-first century online political mobilization (Beyer, 2014).

In the past few years, investigative journalists have shed light on different forms of government-sponsored or organized activity on a variety of social networks, with Adrian Chen most notably investigating a Russian operation in St. Petersburg that was allegedly home to hundreds of employees paid to post comments on articles, write blog posts, and attempt to influence political debates on social media in a variety of ways (Chen, 2015). This kind of operation is commonly called a "troll-farm" or "troll-army" by commentators, although it does not ascribe to traditionally held definitions of what constitutes trolling and possibly should not be classified as such. Others have called these sorts of users *sock puppets* (Woolley, 2016, p. 4), but for the sake of clarity, this chapter will refer to fake accounts on Facebook or other platforms simply as "fake accounts."

"FAKE NEWS"

Finally, "fake news" has become an especially popular term in recent months (Allcott & Gentzkow, 2017). However, as it has come to mean everything from tabloid "clickbait" content to overt misinformation—and seems to have been recently subverted by Donald Trump and the American alt-right media—it is a particularly difficult concept for researchers to operationalize (Starbird, 2017). For the purposes of this chapter, "fake news" will generally be referred to as meaning intentionally incorrect or misleading information spread by a news organization (real or not) for political purposes.

Methodology

This study was conducted using a mix of qualitative and quantitative methods. The qualitative portion consisted of 10 semi-structured and anonymous interviews conducted in Poland. Interviews were selected with a hybrid purposive/snowball sampling strategy, where potentially interesting political campaign managers, journalists, activists, employees of social media marketing firms, and digitally minded civil society members were sought out and asked to recommend further interviewees. Interviewing has been shown to be one of the best currently known methods for understanding computational propaganda, given the difficulties inherent in studying processes which often occur behind the scenes on social media platforms that do not share data with researchers (Woolley & Howard, 2016). These interviews were further informed by approximately two dozen informal and off-the-record conversations with a variety of Polish experts.

Background: The Emergence of Polish Online Politics

In 1991, the first Polish Internet connection was established between the University of Copenhagen and the University of Warsaw (Trammell et al., 2006). After dial-up Internet access became widely available in the country in 1996, various forms of online communication, such as bulletin boards, emerged and would grow steadily, eventually being supplanted by early blogging platforms (Trammell et al., 2006). These set the stage for the first Polish social network, *NaszaKlasa* ("Our Class"), which was launched in 2006 by a group of university students from Warsaw. Designed as a method for classmates to stay in touch after graduation, it became a popular platform and experienced impressive growth in the late 2000s. In the past few years, however, Poles have increasingly shifted toward a variety of next-generation online platforms and forums (Koc-Michalska et al., 2014). In 2011, the overall Internet penetration rate was around 59 percent, and there were only 5.5 million Polish Facebook users, but in the past six years, household Internet penetration is said to have increased substantially to 80 percent, representing approximately 30.4 million Internet users (Eurobarometer, 2016). According to the most recent data available, more than three quarters of those online are now on Facebook, which now has approximately 22.6 million users in the country (Gemius/PBI, 2017).

As these numbers continue to rise, Polish academics have begun to engage with the ways the Internet and social media platforms are affecting political communication in the country. Specifically, scholars have noted the steadily increasing importance of the Internet as a vehicle for political marketing in Poland (Baranowski, 2015). Since the 2011 Federal election—held up as the first time that the Internet was used broadly by candidates from multiple parties—campaigns have been using an increasingly professionalized set of tools to manage their online self-presentation and to mobilize supporters (Koc-Michalska et al., 2014). These include various social networks and the online marketing tools that can be deployed on them. Many politicians now have a visible Twitter presence, although Twitter is still widely seen as an "elite" platform for journalists and politicians (Baranowski, 2015). As of 2015, there were four million Polish Twitter users (Sotrender, 2016b).

Factoring into these shifts is Poland's unique political situation. Only a few years ago, Poland was being praised as the premier example of a thriving post-Soviet democracy (Simons, 2008). In the past several years, however, the political climate has changed substantially, with the governing Law and Justice (*Prawo i Sprawiedliwość*, abbreviated as PiS) party having set off a series of constitutional crises after its rise to power in the 2015 federal elections. Poland's new government has drawn international condemnation for measures said to limit freedom of expression, and triggered a series of highly publicized mass protests on multiple political and social issues (Kublik, 2015; Rankin & Traynor, 2016).

Since the 2015 election, journalists and commentators have reflected on whether PiS "won the Internet" during its successful campaign (Głowacki, 2015). The broad consensus seems to be that PiS managed to mobilize their supporters and control media narratives far more effectively than its opponents, the Civic Platform party (*Platforma Obywatelska*, abbreviated as PO). This is surprising because PiS's traditional demographic base is generally older and more rural than its competitors' (and is not traditionally conceived as a particularly Internet savvy audience). Some have gone as far as to suggest that PiS's ability to successfully engage and convert young people was a key, if not the key, factor for its success (Dubiński, 2015). As younger Poles rely on digital news sources and social networks for their political information, the various forces shaping online politics in the country have become increasingly important. Some of these phenomena (such as trolling, "fake news," Russian disinformation, fake accounts, and social media bots) are briefly explored in the following three sections.

TROLLING, ACTIVISTS, AND CIVIL SOCIETY

Facebook is the most important social network and, by extension, the most popular online space for online political debate and discussion. It has in recent years become a highly energetic political forum, and at least as early as 2014, networks of Antifa (meaning anti-fascist) groups have clashed with far-right groups on Facebook, using mass flagging and reporting to pull down their Facebook pages and ban users. According to one interviewee, a political activist, the golden era of these flagging wars (or "troll wars") was in late 2014 and early 2015, when left-wing groups were successful in blocking the pages of many right-wing groups. In late 2016, this issue once again came to the fore when the Facebook pages of several prominent Polish nationalist groups were blocked, some of which had hundreds of thousands of likes (Sotrender, 2016a). This seems to have been part of a massive flagging campaign organized by several left-wing Facebook groups a few weeks before a controversial nationalist parade in Warsaw.

One such group, with a Facebook page titled the "Organization for Monitoring Racist and Xenophobic Behavior" proclaimed its victory, claiming responsibility for the bans and saying that these bans were important because they would cut off the Facebook advertising revenue stream for these pages before signing off with "good night white pride". Facebook reinstated the pages after government pressure, but the incident has sparked conversations about freedom of speech online, and demonstrates the ways in which groups of online users have organized online to successfully make high-profile political statements (Urbanek, 2016).

Another major source of political, commercial, and social information for Poles are online-only news portals such as ONET (onet.pl), and Virtual Poland (wirtualnapolska.pl). These are basically online news sites, but feature cross-platform integration and sections for comments and discussion, and are by some measures the most popular news websites in the country (Alexa, 2017). Portals and the online websites of conventional news organizations have increasingly become inundated with political gamesmanship, and the problem of political trolling and spam on comment sections has become so pervasive that several news sites, most notably the premier Polish weekly, *Gazeta Wyborcza*, have modified their comment sections to make it more difficult for users to reply to each other (Sobkowicz & Sobkowicz, 2012).

Activists and journalists in Poland have suggested that Polish right-wing and nationalist groups were mobilizing online in a highly effective way, one that seems to combine new and traditional modes of organization. By leveraging traditional mobilization networks, such as the youth organizations that have been long associated with various political parties, as well as emailing lists, closed Facebook groups, and group WhatsApp chats, a group can issue specific instructions to its supporters as to what content they should share, where they should comment, and how they can best steer online discussion on key issues. The general lack of neutral online platforms for debate on Polish politics (Sobkowicz & Sobkowicz, 2012) has allowed energetic groups of supporters to infiltrate and spam the comment sections and forums occupied by their clearly defined political opposites. Activists are particularly likely to be caught in the crossfire, especially those that become visible in the public media. "Trolling is an everyday thing," said one digital rights advocate, "All activists know it is a part of their life now" (personal interview, 02/14/2017).

Even in Poland, the emerging forces of politically motivated hate speech are interacting with an online experience that is increasingly governed by algorithms, with various interesting and troubling effects. In one notable example, a journalist writing in a prominent publication was "outed" by mocking users posting in the comment section. Although these comments were promptly deleted by moderators, they were online long enough to be picked up by Google's indexing algorithm, and searches of the journalist's name would suggest embarrassing autocomplete results that were supposed to be private (e.g., those searching for "John Doe" would see "John Doe is homosexual" as the top suggestion).

With the help of a Polish digital rights NGO, the journalist complained to Google, which initially argued that it could not affect the autocomplete results as they were algorithmically generated, but eventually agreed to change them (Głowacka et al., 2016). This presented itself as a fascinating "Right to be Forgotten" case, as the central issue was not with online content itself, but rather with algorithmically generated tags that were automatically attached to this content. In the words of one interviewee, this example shows that in the age of algorithms, "trolling and hate can generate lasting effects" that may not be immediately apparent (personal interview, 2017).

DIS- AND MIS-INFORMATION

Much like the rest of the world, Poland has recently been seized with the apparent emergence of "fake news." As elsewhere, the phenomenon is still not particularly well understood, although commentators and even major Polish television shows have run exposés touching on this issue. In a few cases, hoaxes and unsubstantiated information spread online in other countries have made it into Poland. For example, the Polish Ministry of Education recently sent out a letter to all schools warning of a social media–based suicide game called "Blue Whale" (*Niebieski Wieloryb*) that had apparently already led to the death of dozens of teenagers in Eastern Europe. However, the story was shortly thereafter revealed to be a hoax, originating on a Russian news site before being reprinted by the English *Sun* newspaper and getting picked up by Polish outlets (Napiórkowski, 2017). There have yet to be explicit examples of political hoaxes and fake news that attain this same level of reach, but the propagation of *fejki* (fakes) and other forms of disinformation has become a prominent concern for many Polish commentators.

It is important to note that Poland has long had a complex media climate, one that may be unique among former Warsaw Pact countries (Pfetsch & Voltmer, 2012). Even during the Communist days, a strong civil society and widespread *samizdat* (underground press) literature spread independent and opposing ideas, factors which led scholars to predict that Poland's diverse media climate would prove highly resistant to political maneuvering (Pfetsch & Voltmer, 2012). However, this narrative has been challenged in recent years, as political parties have in the past decade done their best to exert their influence over the general media climate. The Law and Justice party (PiS) drew widespread condemnation in both Poland and the West after passing controversial media reform laws that give it more influence over the state-backed broadcaster, TVP, which is now widely seen on the left as an official channel for PiS propaganda. However, it has been pointed out that the previous governments, including the Civic Platform government that was in power earlier, similarly passed policies that intensified the polarization of the Polish traditional media. This underlies the difficulties of understanding disinformation in a country like Poland: one research subject, an academic who studies Polish social media, stated that it is incredibly challenging to meaningfully study "fake news" when the state-backed television channel, TVP, has repeatedly been shown to itself be propagating objectively false information, and when the channels for information dissemination are widely viewed as inherently partisan in some way or another (personal interview, 2017).

In sum, the networked public sphere in Poland has grown considerably in the past decade, and a variety of political forces have combined to make Polish online politics energetic, partisan, and often controversial.

Russian Disinformation and Fake Accounts

Along with these domestic forces, Polish online politics have unquestionably been affected by recent events in Ukraine and the complicated Polish–Russian and Polish–Ukrainian relationships. As Polish officials had spent more than two years pushing for deeper ties with Ukraine and were supporting Ukraine's European aspirations, they were troubled when the Ukrainian President, Viktor Yanukovych, chose not to sign the Ukraine–European Union Association Agreement in November of 2013, sparking massive protests and the Ukraine crisis (Przełomiec, 2014). This moment has been widely pointed to as the beginning of what is often perceived to be an active campaign of Russian disinformation propagated via Polish social networks.

As Russia is rumored to be actively funding nationalist groups, spreading propaganda online, and using other indirect means to destabilize the Polish state, the notion that Russia is engaging in "information operations" or an "information war" in Poland has become quite popular among Polish scholars and commentators, and has come to dominate recent work on propaganda in Poland (Nimmo, 2016; Ostrowki & Woycicki, 2016). A recent report published by the Warsaw-based foreign policy think tank, the Centre for International Relations (*Centrum Stosunków Międzynarodowych*), titled "Exposing and Countering pro-Kremlin Disinformation in the Central and Eastern European Countries," provides a series of typical examples. It argues that a variety of dubious outlets spread false information in an effort to undermine the NATO Summit held in Warsaw in the summer of 2016 (Wierzejski, 2016). From fabricated interviews with high-ranking Polish military leaders to sensational attempts to stir up Polish–Ukrainian tensions, the report cites multiple cases in which anonymous "journalists" and bloggers, believed to be linked to Russia, published dubious information that was spread on Facebook and Twitter.

The report notes that this information has occasionally trickled into the mainstream press and has been picked up by large Polish news organizations (an example being when TVP reported a false story about Egypt selling Russian warships that had been originally shared by a questionable Russian news site). Furthermore, the report claims that "Russian trolls are very active in Poland," and relies on manual heuristics (such as poor Polish grammar and the use of Russian idioms) to claim that Russian fake accounts are common on the biggest Polish news portals (Wierzejski, 2016, p. 3). However, as concrete attribution of certain accounts and stories directly to Russian agents is usually impossible, the report is not able to truly provide conclusive evidence for its claims. In a bizarre twist that illustrates the complexities of today's online disinformation ecosystem, Sputnik.pl, the Polish branch of Russia's controversial Sputnik News Agency, critiqued and mocked the report's methods in a satirical Polish-language article titled "How to Spot a Russian Troll" (Sputnik Polska, 2017).

Despite the protestations of Sputnik, there is considerable circumstantial evidence that indicates that a few days after the Euromaidan protests broke out in Kiev, large numbers of fake accounts flooded Polish Facebook and news portals to weigh in on debates related to Ukraine (Savytsky, 2016; Szczepaniak & Szczygieł, 2017). According to one interviewee, a journalist working on the Caucasus and Eastern European issues, most online discussions touching on Russia held in an open online forum or public Facebook group would quickly be targeted by accounts that spammed comment sections and insulted or harassed commentators.

Those brave enough to engage in discussion on the topic of Russian–Ukrainian–Polish relations under their real name would face the threat of targeted hate and harassment (personal interview, 2017). This seems to have become particularly common for journalists and other civil society members, with one interviewee noting that although he had become used to the spam and harassment that he would receive after he published articles critical of Russia, it became particularly worrisome when he began receiving private Facebook messages from anonymous accounts that threatened his wife and children by name. Journalists who attempt to engage with these commentators on the portals themselves (or expose them as potentially fake accounts) are especially likely to receive threats and insults.

A 2015 report published by the Polish Government's Computer Emergency Response Team noted Russian influence in Polish cyberspace, and especially on Polish social networks, as a prominent concern (CERT Poland, 2015). However, determining what precisely constitutes Russian influence (or Russian trolling) is a difficult matter: when it comes to conventional cyber activity, attribution is difficult, but governments maintain various investigative options (Rid & Buchanan, 2015). However, the nature of modern disinformation campaigns, especially those conducted via fake accounts, is that they are extremely difficult to conclusively attribute to a certain actor.

While it may have once been possible to identify suspect accounts via certain manual heuristics (for example: the number of friends, choice of profile picture, the use of Russian figures of speech or spelling), evidence suggests that in the past few years it has become significantly more difficult to do so, especially on non-transparent platforms such as Facebook. As one interviewee (a researcher working at a think tank that deals with cyber issues and attempts to map and track fake Russian accounts) noted, suspected Russian accounts on Facebook have been steadily increasing in their sophistication, and now seem to feature more believable profile photos and larger networks of friends. While everyone seems to suspect that Russian-linked organizations or actors are using large numbers of fake accounts on Polish social media platforms, nobody has managed to find evidence or concrete data at a broader level.

Many have attempted to infer the broader goal or motive behind these apparent Russian campaigns. Some have speculated that the goal is to undermine a population's trust in institutions, spread conspiracy theories, and discredit the idea of truth itself (Pomarantsev & Weiss, 2014). In Poland specifically, others have argued that, "Kremlin narratives seek, paradoxically, to promote extreme Polish nationalism—even anti-Russian nationalism—with the goal of making Poland seem unreliable and 'hysterical' to its Western allies" (Ostrowki & Woycicki, 2016). The combination of fake accounts, fake news sources, and targeted narratives propagated via social media is increasingly being portrayed as a new form of digital propaganda. But Polish researchers face two problems: the first is with determining what exactly should be considered propaganda, as it is a politicized term and carries an inherent value judgment. Should pro-government propaganda be treated the same as propaganda that is apparently foreign in origin? The second is with attributing this propaganda to a specific actor, and trying to meaningfully assess its effects. In the short, medium, and long term, do users really have their opinions changed when repeatedly exposed to these narratives online? Research is sorely needed into this matter.

At a certain point, one might argue that political discourse becomes saturated to the point that determining true causation may be less important. One research subject memorably noted that "it does not matter if the Russians are actually using fake accounts or bots" to influence online debate in Poland, "as either way, they have succeeded in poisoning the political discourse" (personal interview, 2017). They suggested that calling someone a "Russian bot" was rapidly becoming a new slur, deployed to discredit any opinion that was not completely hawkish on Russian affairs. If Poles have begun to constantly accuse each other of being Russian agents if they express unpopular opinions, this is a significant development, and one that does not bode well for the health of online political discourse in the country.

The New Age of Political Marketing: An Insider View

It is interesting to note that the term *bot* seems to have a different connotation in Poland than in the United States or United Kingdom. As opposed to having a conception of a bot as some kind of script or automated agent, interviewees seemed to broadly view bots as synonymous with "trolls" (manually operated false accounts). From this perspective, an account would be a bot in the sense that they are seen to be a cog in the Russian propaganda machine (a Russian "bot"), regardless of whether they are operated by a human user or a simple algorithm.

This may be because fully automated social bots, as commonly seen Twitter in the United States, were perceived by the interviewees as relatively uncommon on Polish Twitter. The bigger concern seemed to be with what are often termed "troll farms," networks of fake accounts on social media platforms that are manual (and still predominantly backed by a human user). And it is not just foreign fake accounts (be they real or perceived) that are a source of public concern, as Polish political parties are rumored to be active in this space as well. Multiple journalists and politicians have accused PiS of using paid "haters" or "trolls" on social media platforms and news portals as part of their extraordinarily effective online resurgence (Głowacki, 2015).

On Twitter, suspicious accounts with no profile photos that engage with other users on political issues have been termed "Szefernaker's Eggs" after Paweł Szefernaker, a Secretary of State in the Chancellery of the Polish Prime Minister who has been referred to as PiS's "Internet genius" and is widely believed to be the mastermind behind its successful online efforts (Krzymowski, 2016). While journalists and commentators have investigated some of these operations with varying degrees of success, and there is a great deal of speculation as to how these sorts of operations work, relatively little is known about how these techniques work in practice.

Valuable insight into the nebulous underground ecosystem of false amplifiers was provided on the condition of anonymity by a research subject who is a political consultant and marketer, and works for a communications firm that has experience in using fake identities on Polish social media platforms. Over the past 10 years, his company (which we'll refer to here as "The Firm") created more than 40,000 unique identities, each with multiple accounts on various social media platforms and portals, a unique IP address, and even its own personality, forming a universe of several hundred thousand specific fake accounts that have been used in Polish politics and multiple elections (personal interview, 2017).

The process begins with a client: a company in the private sector (pharmaceuticals, natural resources), or a political party/campaign. A strategic objective is outlined and a contract is written up that includes "word of mouth" or "guerrilla" marketing services. An employee of The Firm then starts by creating an email address via a large provider (such as Gmail). Using this email and an invented name, they create accounts on multiple platforms and portals. A suitable profile photo is found via an image search and modified in Photoshop so that it will not appear in a Google image search, and the employee begins posting on various platforms and building a comment history. Each employee manages multiple identities at a time, with each having a coherent writing style, interests, and personality. They use a VPN to spoof IP addresses so that their accounts will have a series of associated addresses, allowing them to post from multiple locations in a predictable way (as would befit a normal user using a mobile phone and traveling around a city, or using their laptop from home/work/elsewhere).

When these accounts are ready to begin posting on comment sections and Facebook groups or pages, the employee uses only unique content (each account never copies or repopulates posts) as to make it unsearchable and difficult to link to other accounts. All steps are taken so that these accounts are very difficult (in the words of the research subject, "completely impossible") to conclusively identify as fake.

This all provides a level of deniability for the client, who may not even know exactly (and probably does not want to know) what techniques are being used by their marketing consultants. Furthermore, this is a low-risk endeavor: while these processes violate the terms of service for platforms, they exist in a legal grey area. If a firm takes the basic precautions described above, it is highly unlikely that this activity will ever be exposed, and if it is, it is not clear how either the firm or their clients would be held legally accountable.

These steps are largely performed manually, although the firm has experimented with automating various steps of the account creation process. While past research on automated social bots has demonstrated the ways in which bots are used amplify certain content by gaming platform algorithms and piggybacking on strategic hashtags (Woolley, 2016; Murthy et al., 2016), the goal of these types of accounts is to persuade in a subtler manner. Outlining his firm's broader strategy, the research subject argued that their trolls/bots/influencers cannot, and do not attempt to influence public opinion directly. Rather, the firm's strategy is to target "opinion leaders," including journalists, politicians, bloggers, and key activists. By infiltrating influential Facebook groups, mining comment sections, and directly striking up conversations with these opinion leaders, the goal is to try to convince the target that their followers sincerely believe a certain argument and to provide long-term nudges toward certain strategically devised positions.

The amount of work that goes into these efforts is staggering, and the most involved campaigns will include multiple employees bringing their networks of accounts together to stage threads on discussion boards and steer conversations on forums. An entire thread on such a platform can feature dozens of fake accounts all posing as users, down-voting unsympathetic points of view, and generally steering a conversation in a form of what is often termed "astroturfing" (Woolley, 2016). All this occurs invisibly and behind the scenes, and the ordinary person that logs onto these forums may believe that they are receiving a legitimate signal for public opinion on a topic when they are in effect being fed a narrative by a secret marketing campaign.

While the current academic discussion predominantly focuses on automated bots, The Firm believes that their uses are limited because they are not able to interact with real users in a sophisticated manner. According to the research subject, political bots that try to directly impact discussion are highly inelegant and will almost certainly be discovered. Because a client must never be linked to these fake accounts, their company only uses truly automated bots for spam and hate, or as a red herring designed to discredit another actor. In the first case, the accounts used need not be highly sophisticated as they are not designed to persuade but rather to spam and to perhaps influence platform algorithms (bots that retweet a negative story about a political figure, for example, can spread it widely by helping it "trend" on Twitter). In the second scenario, they would try to discredit another candidate by building a network of obvious bots that would pose as that candidate's followers, spamming forums and harassing others in the name of another candidate, making it seem as if the rival candidate was employing bots and trolls.

A recent Facebook report, titled "Information Operations and Facebook," corroborates some of the information provided by The Firm's employees. The paper, authored by members of Facebook's security team, provides the first public acknowledgment that state and nonstate actors have been using a variety of "false amplifiers," such as fake accounts, bots, and astroturf groups filled with fake users, to influence political debate on the platform.

The authors suggest that Facebook's sophisticated anti-spam mechanisms are effective at thwarting most methods of automation, and instead argue that Facebook is more concerned by manually controlled and created fake accounts (Weedon et al., 2017). They note that much of this activity, such as the targeted infiltration of influential Facebook groups and pages, "could only be performed by people with language skills and a basic knowledge of the political situation in the target countries, suggesting a higher level of coordination and forethought" akin to that displayed by the firm's employees. These types of manual influence efforts pose a particularly difficult problem for Facebook, as for privacy reasons it must find ways to find ways to flag fake accounts without directly screening content *en masse*. A new push on this front has yielded some success, with Facebook apparently removing some 30,000 fake accounts in the context of the 2017 presidential election in France (Weedon et al., 2017). While platforms are beginning to crack down on fake accounts, their prevalence on Polish social networks is likely to remain an issue in the foreseeable future.

Conclusion

The Internet's architecture and affordances of anonymity not only make it very difficult to impede the various mechanisms of computational propaganda, but also to simply gain an understanding of their scope and scale. From detailed efforts to influence via meticulously crafted fake accounts on Facebook to networks of automated Twitter accounts that attempt to megaphone content, if these sorts of practices are happening in Poland then it seems especially likely that they are happening in other countries. But how prevalent is this activity, really? And what kinds of effect does it really have on political discourse?

First of all, one needs to reflect on the issue of automated accounts and manually coordinated astroturfing campaigns. It is likely that networks of artificial identities have been deployed on Facebook by other actors for a long period of time, despite having only become the focus of mainstream public debate and discussion in the West since the 2016 US election. These practices pose several questions and challenges for researchers. The first type of challenge is a theoretical one. These accounts are not quite bots, but not quite trolls as traditionally conceived in the online political communication literature either. In many ways, they blur the lines between political marketing and propaganda, as the same techniques could in effect be transitioned seamlessly from the commercial space (to benefit a firm or industry) to the political space (to benefit a party or candidate). The second set of challenges features various methodological problems. How should academics best study these false amplifiers, which have been confirmed by Facebook itself as having an important influence on political debate but which operate invisibly and behind the scenes on closed platforms that withhold data from researchers? Without concrete data, it becomes very difficult to measure the true scope and scale of these efforts and to empirically determine their actual effects on users.

Second, Twitter bots need to be better understood. While we know that they can have an amplifying effect on content and help game trending algorithms, to what extent do they really affect the experience of the average user, especially if they are simply engaging with content created within their potentially insular groups of friends and followers? How much do they really influence political opinions over time? What role exactly do these accounts play within the larger disinformation ecosystem, and how exactly do they coordinate to potentially spread hyper-partisan "fake news"?

These are increasingly important questions, as we rapidly seem to be entering a new golden age of propaganda, misinformation, and media manipulation, compounded by the wide-ranging political instability and electoral uncertainty that has characterized European politics of late. We must better understand these developments before we can truly begin to craft solutions.

A look at Poland provides insight into the complexities of studying computational propaganda today, and provides some new perspectives into what is rapidly becoming a global phenomenon. Overall, the findings suggest that false amplifiers are indeed prevalent on both Polish Facebook and Twitter, and that further research should be conducted in this area.

References

Alexa (2017). Top Sites in Poland. Retrieved July 5, 2018, from https://www.alexa.com/topsites/countries/PL

Allcott, H., & Gentzkow, M. (2017). *Social Media and Fake News in the 2016 Election* (National Bureau of Economic Research Working Paper). Rochester, NY. Retrieved from https://papers.ssrn.com/abstract=2903810.

Baranowski, P. (2015). Online Political Campaigning during the 2014 Regional Elections in Poland. *Media and Communication*, 3(4), 35–44.

Beyer, J. (2014). *Expect Us: Online Communities and Political Mobilization*. New York: Oxford University Press.

CERT Polska (2015). "Krajobraz bezpieczeństwa polskiego internetu." Retrieved from https://goo.gl/4MI0p3.

Chen, A. (2015, June 2). The Agency. *The New York Times*. Retrieved from https://www.nytimes.com/2015/06/07/magazine/the-agency.html.

Chu, Z., Gianvecchio, S., Wang, H., & Jajodia, S. (2010). Who is Tweeting on Twitter: Human, Bot, or Cyborg? In *Proceedings of the 26th Annual Computer Security Applications Conference* (pp. 21–30). ACM. Retrieved from http://dl.acm.org/citation.cfm?id=1920265.

Coleman, E. G. (2012). Phreaks, Hackers, and Trolls: The Politics of Transgression and Spectacle. In Mandiberg, Michael (Ed.), *The Social Media Reader*. New York: New York University Press.

Dubiński, P. (2015, October 23). Internet znów przesądzi o wyniku wyborów? Eksperci nie mają wątpliwości. Retrieved from http://wiadomosci.wp.pl/internet-znow-przesadzi-o-wyniku-wyborow-eksperci-nie-maja-watpliwosci-6027738241049217a.

Eurobarometer (2016). Internet Access and Use Statistics—Households and Individuals. Retrieved from http://ec.europa.eu/eurostat/statistics-explained/index.php/Internet_access_and_use_statistics_-_households_and_individuals#Database.

Ferrara, E., Varol, O., Davis, C., Menczer, F., & Flammini, A. (2016). The Rise of Social Bots. *Communications of the ACM*, *59*(7), 96–104.

Gemius/PBI (2017). Poland Internet Statistics. Retrieved from http://www.wirtualnemedia.pl/artykul/wyniki-badania-gemius-pbi-za-luty-2017.

Gorwa, R., & Guilbeault, D. (2018). Understanding Bots for Policy and Research: Challenges, Methods, and Solutions. *ArXiv:1801.06863 [Cs]*. http://arxiv.org/abs/1801.06863.

Głowacka, D., Ploszka, A., & Sczaniecki, M. (2016). Wiem i powiem: Ochrona sygnalistów i dziennikarskich źródeł informacji. Warsaw, Poland: Helskinki Foundation for Human Rights.

Głowacki, W. (2015, September 28). Prawo i Sprawiedliwość króluje w polskim internecie. Pomaga w tym zdyscyplinowana armia trolli. *Gazeta Krakowska*. Retrieved from http://www.gazetakrakowska.pl/artykul/8866523,prawo-i-sprawiedliwosc-kroluje-w-polskim-internecie-pomaga-w-tym-zdyscyplinowana-armia-trolli,id,t.html.

Herring, S., Job-Sluder, K., Scheckler, R., & Barab, S. (2002). Searching for Safety Online: Managing "Trolling" in a Feminist Forum. *The Information Society*, *18*(5), 371–384.

Howard, P. N., & Kollanyi, B. (2016). *Bots, #Strongerin, and #Brexit: Computational Propaganda during the UK-EU Referendum* (Working Paper No. 2016.1). Oxford, UK: Project on Computational Propaganda. Retrieved from www.comprop.oii.ox.ac.uk

Koc-Michalska, K., Lilleker, D. G., Surowiec, P., & Baranowski, P. (2014). Poland's 2011 Online Election Campaign: New Tools, New Professionalism, New Ways to Win Votes. *Journal of Information Technology & Politics*, *11*(2), 186–205.

Krzymowski, M. (2016, June 5). Ucho partii. *Newsweek Polska*. Retrieved May 30, 2017, from http://www.newsweek.pl/plus/polska/pawel-szefernaker-kim-jest-internetowy-geniusz-pis-,artykuly,386767,1,z.html.

Kublik, A. (2015, January 2). Rząd bierze media publiczne. Retrieved May 30, 2017, from http://wyborcza.pl/1,75398,19419297,rzad-bierze-media-publiczne.html?disableRedirects=true.

Lee, K., Eoff, B. D., & Caverlee, J. (2011). Seven Months with the Devils: A Long-Term Study of Content Polluters on Twitter. In *AAAI Int'l Conference on Weblogs and Social Media (ICWSM)*. Washington, DC: George Washington University.

Marwick, A., & Lewis, R. (2017). Media Manipulation and Disinformation Online. Data & Society Research Institute Report. https://datasociety.net/output/media-manipulation-and-disinfo-online/.

Murthy, D., Powell, A. B., Tinati, R., Anstead, N., Carr, L., Halford, S. J., & Weal, M. (2016). Bots and Political Influence: A Sociotechnical Investigation of Social Network Capital. *International Journal of Communication*, *10*, 20. Retrieved from http://ijoc.org/index.php/ijoc/article/view/6271.

Napiórkowski, M. (2017, March 21). Niebieski wieloryb. List z Ministerstwa Edukacji Narodowej. Retrieved May 30, 2017, from http://mitologiawspolczesna.pl/niebieski-wieloryb-list-ministerstwa-edukacji-narodowej/.

Nimmo, B. (2016). Indenifying Disinformation: An ABC. *Institute for European Studies Policy Brief*, *2016*(1). Retrieved July 5, 2018, from https://www.ies.be/files/PB%202016:01%20Ben%20Nimmo.pdf

Ostrowki, W., & Woycicki, K. (2016). Case Study: Poland. In *Winning the Information War: Techniques and Counter-strategies to Russian Propaganda in Central and Eastern Europe*. Centre for European Policy Analysis. Retrieved from http://cepa.org/reports/winning-the-Information-War.

Pfetsch, B., & Voltmer, K. (2012). Negotiating Control. *The International Journal of Press/Politics*, *17*(4), 388–406. https://doi.org/10.1177/1940161212449084.

Pomerantsev, P., & Weiss, M. (2014). The Menace of Unreality: How the Kremlin Weaponizes Information, Culture and Money. *The Interpreter*. Retrieved from http://www.interpretermag.com/the-menace-of-unreality-how-the-kremlin-weaponizes-information-culture-and-money/.

Przełomiec, M. (2014). Poland on the Euromaidan. In Bachmann, Klaus & Lyubashenko, Igor (Eds.), *The Maidan Uprising, Separatism and Foreign Intervention: Ukraine's Complex Transition* (pp. 299–314). Frankfurt: Peter Lang.

Rankin, J., & Traynor, I. (2016, January 12). European Commission to Debate Poland's Controversial New Laws. *The Guardian*. Retrieved from https://www.theguardian.com/world/2016/jan/12/european-commission-to-debate-polands-controversial-new-laws.

Rid, T., & Buchanan, B. (2015). Attributing Cyber Attacks. *Journal of Strategic Studies, 38*(1–2), 4–37. https://doi.org/10.1080/01402390.2014.977382.

Savytskyi, Y. (2016, June 20). Kremlin trolls are engaged in massive anti-Ukrainian propaganda in Poland. *Euromaidan Press*. Retrieved December 15, 2016, from http://euromaidanpress.com/2016/06/21/kremlin-trolls-are-engaged-in-massive-anti-ukrainian-propaganda-in-poland/.

Simons, T. W. (2008). *Eurasia's New Frontiers: Young States, Old Societies, Open Futures*. Ithaca, NY: Cornell University Press.

Sobkowicz, P., & Sobkowicz, A. (2012). Two-Year Study of Emotion and Communication Patterns in a Highly Polarized Political Discussion Forum. *Social Science Computer Review, 30*(4), 448–469.

Sotrender. (2016a, January 28). Facebook w Polsce—podsumowanie 2015. Retrieved May 30, 2017, from https://www.sotrender.com/blog/pl/2016/01/facebook-w-polsce-podsumowanie-2015-r-infografika/.

Sotrender. (2016b, January 27). Twitter w Polsce—podsumowanie. Retrieved May 30, 2017, from https://www.sotrender.com/blog/pl/2016/01/twitter-w-polsce-podsumowanie-2015-r-infografika/.

Sputnik Polska. (2017, February 20). Jak rozpoznać rosyjskiego trolla? Retrieved February 23, 2017, from https://pl.sputniknews.com/polityka/201702204869717-Sputnik-Rosja-trolling/.

Starbird, K. (2017). Examining the Alternative Media Ecosystem through the Production of Alternative Narratives of Mass Shooting Events on Twitter. In *11th International AAAI Conference on Web and Social Media (ICWSM)*. Washington, DC: George Washington University.

Szczepaniak, P., & Szczygieł, K. (2017, March 5). Polskie fejki, rosyjska dezinformacja. OKO. press tropi tych, którzy je produkują. Niektórzy z nich nie istnieją. *OKO Press*. Retrieved from https://oko.press/wszystkie-media-popelniaja-bledy-niektore-robia-celowo/.

Trammell, K. D., Tarkowski, A., Hofmokl, J., & Sapp, A. M. (2006). Rzeczpospolita blogów [Republic of Blog]: Examining Polish Bloggers through Content Analysis. *Journal of Computer-Mediated Communication, 11*(3), 702–722.

Tsvetkova, M., García-Gavilanes, R., Floridi, L., & Yasseri, T. (2017). Even good bots fight: The case of Wikipedia. *PLOS ONE, 12*(2). https://doi.org/10.1371/journal.pone.0171774.

Urbanek, G. (2016, November 3). Facebook odblokowuje konta. Narodowcy nie składają broni—Kraj. *Rzeczpospolita*. Retrieved from http://www.rp.pl/Kraj/311039855-Facebook-odblokowuje-konta-Narodowcy-nie-skladaja-broni.html.

Weedon, J., Nuland, W., & Stamos, A. (2017). *Information Operations and Facebook*. Facebook Security. Retrieved from https://fbnewsroomus.files.wordpress.com/2017/04/facebook-and-information-operations-v1.pdf.

Wierzejski, A. (2016). *Information Warfare in the Internet: Exposing and Countering Pro-Kremlin Disinformation in the CEEC*. Centre for International Relations. Retrieved from http://csm.org.pl/en/publications.

Woolley, S. C. (2016). Automating power: Social bot interference in global politics. *First Monday, 21*(4).

Woolley, S. C., & Howard, P. N. (2016). Political Communication, Computational Propaganda, and Autonomous Agents—Introduction. *International Journal of Communication, 10*, 9.

5

Taiwan

Digital Democracy Meets Automated Autocracy

NICHOLAS J. MONACO

Introduction

Taiwan is one of Asia's greatest success stories. From its bloody authoritarian beginnings, it has grown into a robust, healthy democracy and one of Asia's least corrupt and most free societies (Freedom House, 2017; Transparency International, n.d.). A few facts quickly illustrate this—within South East Asia, only Singapore, Bhutan, Japan, and Hong Kong scored higher than Taiwan on Transparency International's Corruption Perceptions Index 2016. Similarly, in April 2017, Reporters Without Borders (RSF) announced Taiwan as the location of its headquarters in Asia—RSF Secretary General Christophe Deloire noted, "The choice of Taiwan was made [. . .] considering its status of being the freest place in Asia in our annual Press Freedom Index ranking" (Reporters Without Borders, 2017).

Taiwan's future, however, is both bright and precarious. Whether Taiwan will be allowed to continue on its current progressive path and eventually gain full diplomatic recognition as a country in its own right depends in large part on a number of unpredictable factors, including tensions with its neighbor across the Taiwan Strait—mainland China—and its relations with the United States of America. Taiwan's future, however, is a reliable bellwether for the future of the world. Whether societies will remain open to the international influence of liberal democracy or succumb to darker atavistic, authoritarian impulses is one of the most important questions of the current age, and Taiwan will be one of the main arenas in which this battle plays out. Taiwan is culturally, linguistically, and increasingly economically linked to a growing authoritarian hegemon, mainland China, while being supported in funds, arms, and ideology by the United States of America.

It is against this backdrop that we approach the digital sphere in Taiwan. The successful 2014 digital campaign of Ko Wen-je for mayor of Taipei, the capital of Taiwan, was a watershed in the nation's politics. Politicians can no longer ignore the central role of digital media in campaigning, messaging, and mobilizing. A natural consequence of this is that the central questions of the republic—international issues such as the extent of Taiwan's strategic cooperation with the mainland, as well as issues of domestic concern—will ever increasingly be discussed and fought over in the digital sphere. The role of computational propaganda is therefore central to the nation's present and future.

In this chapter, references to "computational propaganda" will assume the definition provided by Howard and Woolley (2016), namely "the assemblage of social media platforms, autonomous agents, and big data tasked with the manipulation of public opinion." There has been minimal work on computational propaganda in Taiwan, and no research has been able to conclusively point toward evidence of automation in this regard. Ko and Chen (2015) explored the possible existence of a small cyber army supporting the Kuomintang (KMT) candidate in the Taipei mayoral election of 2014, and King, Pan, and Roberts (2017) recently shed light on the internal workings of mainland propaganda online.

This chapter will explore three main questions:

1. Is computational propaganda present in Taiwanese society?
2. What is the composition of computational propaganda in Taiwan (manual vs. automated)?
3. Where are campaigns most likely to come from?

While few Taiwanese experts have carried out conclusive research on bot usage or have firm evidence about it, the ground is fertile for the use of automated propaganda. While one must still speculate on the existence of malicious political bots in Taiwan, manual computational propaganda is alive and thriving on the island. The existence of cyber armies—網軍 (wǎng jūn) in Chinese—has been covered in the Taiwanese media and formally explored in at least one academic paper (Ko & Chen, 2015). Social media campaigns from the mainland targeting prominent Taiwanese figures have also been covered in the Taiwanese and international media.

When we were searching for evidence of bots and computational propaganda in Taiwan, two particular areas of interest emerged: (1) mainland campaigns—online agitprop with the intent to smear Taiwan's pro-independence figures and vaunt the mainland's superiority, and (2) internal campaigns—propaganda launched with the intent to influence Taiwan's national politics. These campaigns could be on behalf of a party (such as the KMT, the Democratic Progressive Party [DPP], or the New Power Party [NPP]) or could be propagandizing for or against a given national political issue in Taiwan, such as legalizing gay marriage.

Case Study

Taiwan's history and diplomatic status are labyrinthine in their complexity. Be that as it may, a cursory understanding is necessary to understand where potential hotspots for computational propaganda may lie online. The next section will therefore proceed in three parts: First, we will examine relevant details of Taiwan's history and current media structure; next, we will proceed to an overview of computational propaganda in Taiwan, examining both Taiwan-internal and cross-Strait propaganda; and finally, we will conduct a thorough analysis of the 2016 Diba campaign on Tsai Ing-wen's Facebook page.

THE MEDIA AND SOCIAL MEDIA LANDSCAPE IN TAIWAN

Even with 1949 as a starting point, Taiwan is an island with an incredibly complex history. That year, General Chiang Kai-Shek defected to the island after being defeated by Mao Zedong and the communist army in the Chinese civil war, and the country has existed as a de facto independent nation ever since.

The rub lies in the words *de facto*—there is no more central issue to Taiwanese politics than the country's strange diplomatic quandary. The debate stems from the fact that, since 1949, both mainland China (whose formal name is the People's Republic of China, PRC) and Taiwan (the Republic of China) have claimed to be the one true China, each claiming dominion over the other. This predicament has undergone various official incarnations in the one-China policy and the two nations' 1992 Consensus—which states that the two states recognize that there is only one China, but disagree about what that means. *The Economist* has aptly characterized this history as "not so much fraught with ambiguities as composed of them" (The Economist, 2017). Taiwan currently maintains official diplomatic ties with only 21 countries, a number that has steadily dwindled as the mainland's wealth and global influence has grown (Huang & Steger, 2016).

However, there are stark differences in the two countries that stand out to any observer—in governance, daily life, and the media. Freedom House's 2017 *Freedom in the World* report drove the point home—in this most recent report, mainland China scored lower than Iran, and Taiwan garnered a rating higher than the United States.

In addition to changes in international affairs, domestic politics in Taiwan has also undergone significant change in the past three years. In 2014, the Sunflower Movement, a series of largely student-organized protests, successfully derailed a bill to establish closer financial ties between Taiwan and the mainland (Ramzy, 2014). A new left-wing party, NPP (時代力量) emerged from this movement, and even won five seats in the Taiwanese Legislative Yuan in 2016 (van der Horst, 2016). Historically, Taiwan has predominantly been ruled by the Chinese Nationalist Party (KMT / 國民黨). In January 2016, the country elected its second president from the pro-independence DPP (民進黨) and its first female president, Tsai Ing-wen (蔡英文) (Hsu, 2016).

This is the context behind the political digital sphere in Taiwan. Given Taiwan's history and mainland China's prolific expertise in propaganda, two vectors are of particular interest for computational propaganda research: Taiwan-internal campaigns, namely propaganda campaigns for domestic political issues; and cross-Strait campaigns, or propaganda campaigns targeting high-profile Taiwanese politicians from the mainland and/or promoting unification of China and Taiwan.

In relation to the latter, mainland China has a twofold interest in Taiwan—promoting pro-unification politicians (most of whom belong to the KMT) and smearing pro-independence politicians (who belong to the DPP or the NPP). President Tsai Ing-wen, Taipei's mayor, Ko Wen-je (柯文哲), and Huang Kuo-chang (黃國昌, head of the NPP) would fit this profile.

Equally probable, however, is the use of computation to spread messages about domestic issues. In conversation with the author, one expert journalist in particular thought it likely that high-volume messaging campaigns may have been used around the issue of gay marriage. Though this area is a promising area of research, efforts in this chapter, discussed below, have thus far focused on cross-Strait attacks.

In its 2016 Freedom of the Press report on Taiwan, Freedom House stated: "Taiwan's media environment is one of the freest in Asia, and the vigorous and diverse press reports aggressively on government policies and alleged official wrongdoing." However, this is not to say that these outlets are immune to untoward influence—many media owners in the country have significant ties to the mainland and rely on Chinese companies for advertising. Taiwan's social media landscape is somewhat different from that in countries covered in previous research by the Computational Propaganda Project at the University of Oxford. Although Twitter is available on the island, it is substantially less popular than other social media, notably Facebook and LINE, which interview subjects unanimously agree are the two most popular social media platforms in Taiwan.

It has been claimed that LINE had reached 75 percent of Taiwan's population by late 2015 (LINE platform, 2015), and the company itself verified that over

70 percent had been reached in early 2014 ("World's First," 2014). LINE is a messaging app, similar in functionality to WeChat, Viber, or WhatsApp, originally released in Japan. Since its early days as a smartphone-based application, it has grown to become available on other devices, including tablets and desktops.

A rich facet of the social media landscape in Taiwan is the existence of several relatively popular domestic services on the island. The most popular of these is PTT (批踢踢), a bulletin-board service system similar to Reddit. The platform was developed in 1995 and originally only available to college students, and although it is now available to anyone, it remains most popular among current and former college students. Users can post on "boards" (板) if they are searching for jobs or apartments or can simply chat on different boards, such as the gossip board (八卦板). According to Dr. Strangelove, an interviewee who researches natural language processing, this remains one of the most popular parts of the service, and political discussion is common on these gossip boards (Dr. Strangelove, personal communication, March 7, 2017). Once a comment is posted, other users have the ability to upvote (推) or downvote (噓) it, which has an influence on its overall visibility.

In conversation with the author, Q Continuum (hereafter referred to as Q) also mentioned several Taiwanese social media platforms that are popular only on the island—among these are Dcard, a social media platform available only to high school and college students, and Plurk, a Twitter-like platform that preceded the tech giant's arrival on the island but still enjoys modest popularity (Q Continuum, personal communication, March 7, 2017; "Tai da," 2012).

OVERVIEW OF COMPUTATIONAL PROPAGANDA IN TAIWAN

As already mentioned, this analysis of computational propaganda in Taiwan will be divided into two parts: Taiwan-internal and cross-Strait propaganda. This section will explore the details and potential areas of interest in both arenas.

TAIWAN-INTERNAL: MANUAL PROPAGANDA, OR "CYBER ARMY" TACTICS

One theme that threaded itself through all interviews herein was manual propaganda—online messaging campaigns carried out by humans for a political cause or person. All subjects unequivocally agreed that manual propaganda is alive and thriving in Taiwan. The term "cyber army" (網軍) is often used to describe this phenomenon in Taiwan.

"Certainly there are some candidates/politicians/parties who hire 'real persons' to post opinions, comment," said Cortisol, an interview subject who does quantitative political science research in Taiwan. Cortisol also mentioned knowing people who worked as cyber army propagandists on election campaigns:

> I do have some friends; they [were] working for candidates or parties to do that. And they got paid. Not well paid, but still, since they are students it's [an] okay [amount] for them. So, they spend online every day about like one or two hours [posting] news or messages or they attack the other candidates or parties [. . .] [E]specially during the elections, they just mentioned what they [had] done recently. Most of the time they just tell me how they tried to promote the reputation of their candidates online, but I know under the table, they [. . .] tried to attack other candidates. Negative campaigning is very popular in Taiwan. (Cortisol, personal communication, March 9, 2017)

Another interview subject, Wizard, gave additional context on the use of the term *cyber army* in Taiwan:

> Before the 2014 election, it [was] mostly used [to mean] people who disrupt security infrastructures and so on, which is much more serious. It's like the cyber-arming kind of stuff. During 2014 [Taipei mayoral campaign] [. . .] Sean Lien and Ko Wen-je both accused each other of additional propaganda; they brought up this term "網軍". Then afterwards, it lost any meaning whatsoever. Normal astroturfing is sometimes described as 網軍 as well [. . .] All they have to do is [craft] some memetic device, and then the viral nature of social media will take care of the rest. The people who then spread this news are incidentally 網軍, but they are largely unpaid. (Wizard, personal communication, March 16, 2017)

TAIWAN-INTERNAL: PRO-SEAN LIEN CYBER ARMY TACTICS IN THE 2014 TAIPEI MAYORAL RACE

Ko and Chen (2015) explored data showing that manual propagandists had been used as a cyber army on Taiwan's PTT platform during the 2014 mayoral race. Sean Lien (KMT) and Ko Wen-je (Independent, supported by the DPP) were the two main candidates in this race.

Savvy users on the platform retrieved the IP address of an official representative of KMT, mayoral candidate Sean Lien (連勝文). They found an additional 20 accounts using this same IP address, of which 14 posted an unusual number of articles on PTT just a few months before the election. These tended to post articles giving a favorable view of Lien, or giving a negative view of his opponent, Ko Wen-je, who later won the election (Y. Huang, 2017).

AUTOMATION AND PROPAGANDA

Taiwan is no stranger to Distributed Denial of Service (DDoS) attacks. From January to March 2017 alone, the private sector experienced large numbers of DDoS attacks (J. Lin, 2017; Wu & Wagstaff, 2017). Indeed, 2017 has seen an un-paralleled increase in the number of DDoS attacks being carried out on the island.

According to Akamai Technologies, in the month from mid-February to mid-March 2017, technology, manufacturing, and financial industries were all victims of DDoS attacks. A subset of these attacks were Bitcoin ransomware attacks, in which brokerage firms received threats saying that they would be shut down by DDoS attacks unless they paid a ransom in Bitcoins to a designated account (Y. Huang, 2017). By the beginning of March, over 46 companies in Taiwan had received similar threats (Li, 2017). The origin of these attacks varies—Bitcoin ransom threats have used numerous different foreign IP addresses, but many private sector attacks on other industries in early 2017 originated from within Taiwan (J. Lin, 2017).

There have also been DDoS attacks on governmental sites. Notably, 2015 saw attacks on several governmental websites from "Anonymous Asia" (匿名者亞洲), including the website for the Office of the President (Guo, 2015). The May 2017 global WannaCry ransomware attacks also ended up infecting at least 226 governmental computers in Taiwan (F. Su, 2017; "WannaCry," 2017).

CRAWLER BOTS—INTELLIGENCE GATHERING FOR KO WEN-JE'S MAYORAL CAMPAIGN OF 2014

As briefly mentioned above, the Taipei mayoral race of 2014 was a watershed for digital politics in Taiwan. The two main candidates were the independent Ko Wen-je, a doctor at National Taiwan University backed by the DPP, and Sean Lien, a more seasoned KMT politician.

Many interview subjects mentioned the edge that Ko Wen-je gained by using technology to campaign successfully in 2014. Interview subject Q, who was in-volved in several technical aspects of the campaign, reported that Ko "trusted numbers" and had faith in a technical approach to campaigning. Moonbeam, an-other technical expert involved in Ko's campaign, corroborated this view: "[Ko Wen-je] is a doctor, so he really believes numbers." Moonbeam also described the way that technology helped to make up for Ko's lack of experience as a poli-tician prior to the 2014 campaign.

A journalist, Quinine, mentioned in conversation with the author that it was quite probable that political parties were using bots for "intelligence" purposes, gathering information on opposition parties (Quinine, personal communication, February 10, 2017). I was unable to find any more details about this usage of bots until my conversation with Moonbeam. Moonbeam was part of a team that used data science to help strategize and reach out to different demographic groups. As part of this effort, Moonbeam built an impressive crawler bot for Ko's campaign. This bot would crawl public pages on Facebook and collect all the data it could—how many likes or shares each post got and how many people liked or followed the page, etc. According to Moonbeam, "We collect[ed] lots of pages from Facebook [. . .] We at least have more than 300+ [Taiwanese] pages in our crawling pool. We updated the data every two hours [during the campaign]."

This bot respected Facebook's privacy terms and only crawled public pages, not individual user profiles. The crawler bot was still able to generate data on individual users, however, given that any Facebook user's activity on a public page is also public.

Moonbeam described the data they would gather from the pages:

> Not only the content; we also crawled the like list. We can [find out] who liked this post: [like] lists are public. The people who like these posts also engage with this kind of content. So that's quite interesting— we can know how many people like the content of Ko Wen-je's fan-page and how many like [Sean] Lien's page [too]. After this, we can know what kind of content can touch the fans' hearts, what kind of audience really cares about this content. (Moonbeam, personal communication, April 6, 2017)

With this data, Moonbeam could classify users into interest groups, such as people who care about wildlife preservation, or avid board game players. Using this information, the team Moonbeam worked on could tailor a message to the group, emphasizing how voting for Ko Wen-je would benefit them. Moonbeam mentioned that "like lists" of users could be used to determine who should be contacted or targeted for advertising. Days before the election, Moonbeam used their data to send tailored messages to over 10 groups, encouraging them to vote for Ko Wen-je and emphasizing the main issue of the groups they belonged to. "On the Facebook ads system, we can have precise targeting," Moonbeam told me.

Apart from targeting users with tailored messages, the intelligence gathered by this bot was also useful to gauge voters' reactions to real-time events, such as mistakes Ko Wen-je made, or campaign strategies. For instance, if Ko Wen-je made a controversial mistake in a speech, Moonbeam's team would be able to generate a list of how many users removed their "like" from Ko Wen-je's fan page and then "liked" the fan page of his opponent, Sean Lien. Moonbeam highlighted that this approach ended up being a useful kind of ad hoc, heuristic political training for Ko, who was not experienced as a politician and had never previously run for office.

Overall, Moonbeam estimated that the team generated data on 11–14 million Taiwanese users on Facebook. This is astounding given that the island's population is only around 23 million (Central Intelligence Agency, 2016). This is also a very powerful tool insofar as Facebook is the most popular social media platform online—an ideal place to collect real-time data on users' political musings and feelings. Though Moonbeam did not mention aggregating public records data or building comprehensive profiles on Facebook users, this method was still somewhat redolent of Cambridge Analytica's microtargeting methods in the Brexit referendum and the 2016 US presidential election (Grassegger & Krogerus, 2017).

Fake News

Taiwan has not been immune to the fake news epidemic plaguing societies around the world recently. As mentioned above, LINE is one of the most popular social media platforms in Taiwan, and fake news stories have recently been spreading on the platform prolifically. In conversation with the author, a web developer, Surefire, mentioned that fake news in Taiwan has been both political and apolitical. While there have been stories smearing gay rights activists that have spread, there have also been many apolitical stories relating to health that have spread virally. The insidious nature of false information is compounded by the fact that many LINE users are not experienced Internet users. Surefire mentioned that, given that one only needs a smartphone and an Internet connection to use LINE, many users are not very savvy and may not know how to fact-check an article or use Google.

Leading researchers have highlighted that solutions to misinformation online cannot be purely technological—social solutions are also crucial. In this vein, danah boyd of Data & Society recently wrote: "Addressing so-called fake news is going to require a lot more than labeling. It's going to require a cultural change about how we make sense of information, whom we trust, and how we understand our own role in grappling with information" (boyd, 2017). In Taiwan, both social and computational responses to the problem are currently under way.

SOCIAL RESPONSES TO FAKE NEWS

Taiwan's digital minister, Audrey Tang, recently revealed that there is a plan to address the problem of rumors and fake news online through public education, such as teaching students to identify a fake domain online. Nicola Smith interviewed the digital minister, who unveiled in April 2017 that "media literacy" will be on the curriculum in Taiwanese schools in the next year. In conversation with Smith, Tang said, "I would say that we take freedom of speech much more seriously than most of the other Asian countries. Many other Asian countries see it as a utilitarian value that could be traded somehow, if some other value of higher utility, like national security, is at risk. But for many Taiwanese it's a core value [. . .] and I think we're unique in that" (Smith, 2017).

COMPUTATIONAL RESPONSE TO FAKE NEWS—THE FAKE NEWS FIGHTING LINE BOT

In addition to the social response, a computational solution to the problem is also currently under development. Johnson Liang, an engineer working in Taiwan, decided in late 2016 to build a LINE bot to combat fake news (H. Huang, 2017). The Taiwanese civic technology collective g0v.tw (read as "gov zero"; Chinese: 零時政府) decided to lend additional funding to the project in early 2017 because of the promise it showed (g0v.tw, 2017).

To combat this problem, a team of developers with funding from g0v.tw have decided to build a LINE bot called 真的假的—which roughly translates as "Are you kidding me?!" or "For real!?" The idea behind the bot is simple—after a user adds the LINE bot as a friend, the user can send suspicious links to potentially fake news articles to the bot. The bot will then report back on whether the article is false and will provide relevant facts on the issue.

This bot was created in late 2016. Although it is still under active development, media and popular interest in the bot have exceeded expectations. A developer who works on the project, Surefire, talked with the author about the goals of the project:

> The ultimate goal of this LINE bot—I hope that not only the rumors can get a response. Any article that has an opinion [. . .] We can attach replies that will provide an opposite opinion or different views to those messages. The platform can become something greater—currently [it] is about rumors and rumor busters. Later we can use it to link articles to each other. It's not only about web development [. . .] it's also about

building a community of editors. (Surefire, personal communication, March 27, 2017)

Currently, an article that has been reported by someone is posted to a board of articles that are to be reviewed. Then, editors (小編) are invited to contribute from their respective areas of knowledge about what is problematic about the article. A standard response, with links to supporting evidence, is crafted from this crowdsourced knowledge and saved. If new users report the article, they will automatically receive the standardized response. Surefire reported that in the first three months of LINEbot, over 5,000 stories were reported to the bot. This bot represents a novel use of bots that does not fit cleanly into previous typologies of political bots' behavior (Woolley, 2017). It uses human contributions to build its databank of answers, but functions on its own after this stage. It shows promise in its transparency and its use of both social and computational methods to address a complex problem (Hwang & Woolley, 2016).

CROSS-STRAIT PROPAGANDA

As already discussed, one type of international propaganda is particularly relevant in Taiwan—messaging coming from the mainland, generally promoting reunification of Taiwan and China and discouraging liberal democratic polity. There is currently no research to suggest that this phenomenon is anything but unidirectional: it would seem that China's efforts to spread propaganda in Taiwan are not being mimicked from Taiwan to China.

NOTES ON MAINLAND CHINA'S PROPAGANDA EFFORTS

Taiwan is unique insofar as it exists on the peripheries of one of the most prolific propaganda-filled regimes on earth—mainland China. Although the country functions as an independent political entity, it is nevertheless a satellite target for China's propaganda efforts, given the two countries' complex relationship. A brief examination of propaganda efforts on the mainland will help contextualize cross-Strait propaganda efforts from China to Taiwan.

China is a country notorious for its censorship and propaganda efforts online (He, 2008; Ng, 2013). The government drives its own propaganda efforts, of course, both through official means such as governmental units, the *People's Daily*, and the Communist Youth Party, but also through more insidious methods such as the 50-cent Party (五毛黨) (McGregor, 2010; Weiwei, 2012). The last was believed until recently to consist of private citizens paid to post pro-government content and argue online in favor of the Party. Recent research has suggested that the 50-cent Party is more likely to be composed of public employees—not private citizens—who tend to post "cheerleading" content but do not engage in acrimonious debate.

Researchers Gary King, Jennifer Pan, and Margaret E. Roberts recently published a thorough analysis of a trove of leaked emails to and from the Zhanggong district Internet Propaganda Office (章貢區網宣辦), in the province of Ganzhou, China. The conclusions of this research shed light on the nature and internal workings of the 50-cent Party, a faction within China thought to be paid by the government to promote the Party's views online. King, Pan, and Roberts (in press) mention finding "a massive government effort, where every year the 50c party writes approximately 448 million social media posts nationwide." The team's research also indicates that

> the purpose of 50c activity is (a) to stop arguments [. . .] and (b) to divert public attention from actual or potential collective action on the ground [. . .] that the 50c party engages in almost no argument of any kind and is instead devoted primarily to cheerleading for the state [. . .] It also appears that the 50c party is mostly composed of government employees contributing part time outside their regular jobs, not, as has been claimed, ordinary citizens paid piecemeal for their works. (p. 29)

The researchers also found no evidence of automated propaganda efforts: "We also looked extensively for evidence that 50c posts were created by automated means such as bots, but the evidence strongly indicates [. . .] that each was written by a specific, often identifiable, human being under direction from the government" (p. 11). Overall, this research indicates that 50-cent propagandists tend to be cheerleaders rather than arguers, and "promoting unity" is an explicit goal in leaked directives (p. 14).

It would not be unreasonable to think Taiwan could be a rare exception: a country where unity could be promoted through more acrimonious attacks. Quinine and other interview subjects noted the deep conviction the average mainlander feels about the Taiwan issue—Taiwan may represent a rare area where allowing acrimony may serve to unify mainlanders.

Of course, in addition to official, state-directed propaganda, there are also online harassment and trolling campaigns organized by what seem to be ordinary citizens. We will explore such campaigns below.

ONLINE CAMPAIGN AGAINST LEON DAI (戴立忍)

Chinese netizens on Weibo mobilized against a popular Taiwanese actor, Leon Dai, when it was announced that he would be starring in a popular Chinese director's new film, *No Other Love*. After Zhao Wei, the director, made the announcement on Weibo, articles appeared on Weibo and in the *China Military* online newspaper (中國軍網), an outlet that is officially sponsored by the Chinese People's Liberation Army, expressing outrage about the Taiwanese actor's involvement ("Xuan jiao shang hai min zu gan qing," n.d.). These articles demonized Leon Dai for his involvement in Taiwan's Sunflower movement and claimed he supported Falun Gong—a persecuted religious group in China. After weeks of online fury, Zhao Wei announced online that Dai would be replaced in the film. Dai, Zhao, and the film's producer apologized online for the incident (L. Lin, 2016).

It is also relevant to note that "hurting the feelings of the Chinese people" ("傷害中國人民的感情") was an accusation leveled at Dai in this campaign. Many targets of trolling or political frustration have been accused of this, such as Ursula Gauthier, a French journalist who, after significant online trolling and official persecution, was eventually ousted from China for her reporting questioning the Party's official narrative on the fractious Xinjiang province (Forsythe, 2015; RFI, 2015; J. Su, 2016). Joel Martinsen of Danwei, a website that covers Chinese media, found that an astonishing 19 countries and organizations had been accused of "hurting the feelings of the Chinese people" in the pages of the *People's Daily* between 1946 and 2008 (Martinsen, 2008).

Though there is no evidence that there was governmental involvement in this event, it is important to note that governments have been involved in similar incidents before. This was notably the case with Indian movie star Aamir Khan. After Khan made statements about feeling unsafe as a Muslim in Prime Minister Narendra Modi's India, an online petition began that eventually successfully convinced the company Snapdeal to terminate its business ties with Khan (Safi, 2016). In her book *I Am a Troll*, Swati Chaturvedi recently revealed that members of the government's IT cell had received orders to promote this petition online (2016). The Chinese government could easily espouse similar tactics in the future.

SUSPICIOUS CHINESE ACCOUNTS IN THE TWITTERSPHERE

As mentioned above, Twitter does not enjoy a prominent status in Taiwan—all interview subjects firmly agreed that Facebook, LINE, and PTT have substantially more activity on the island. Nevertheless, the oddity of Chinese netizens hopping over the Great Firewall for the Diba Facebook campaign (explored in the next section) made me curious about whether similar coordinated mainland messaging campaigns were occurring on Twitter.

We attempted to find similar evidence of a coordinated campaign on Twitter during the observation period (roughly January–April 2017), but were ultimately unable to find any evidence of a large-scale automated effort. Be that as it may, there are still a large number of suspicious accounts on the platform that deserve to be considered in future research. By "suspicious," we mean accounts displaying signs that typify political bots, and/or acerbic accounts abusing President Tsai Ing-wen online, or generally promoting pro-unification views on Twitter. While the latter is not necessarily indicative of governmental involvement, it is a topic that would be expected to appear in organized propaganda efforts.

The abuse hurled at Taiwan and Taiwan's president online had a few motifs in common: intentional misspelling of Tsai's name (using the homonymous character 菜, meaning vegetable), using insults with the word "dog" in them, calling Tsai the "head of Taiwan county"—implying that Taiwan is a province belonging to the mainland—and accusing Tsai of being Japan's and America's lapdog, to name a few. Abuse also ranged from the trivial and puerile to the acrimonious and obscene.

In the preliminary stage of our collection, we selected over 50 accounts that displayed signs of being propaganda accounts on a qualitative basis. A few such qualitative criteria, and screenshots of suspicious accounts, are detailed below (see also Figures 5.1 and 5.2):

1. Recent date of creation, for example many accounts attacking President Tsai in March 2017 were created in February or January 2017;
2. No profile picture (until recently, Twitter displayed a white oval over a colored background for such accounts, colloquially known as a "Twitter egg");
3. Long or maximum-length handles (15 characters is the current maximum length for a Twitter handle);
4. Twitter handle resembling a randomly generated string of numbers and letters;
5. Tweets in simplified Chinese;
6. Lack of followers, higher number of following.

After this first step of manually culling suspicious accounts, we used Twitter's streaming API to track the @mentions for President Tsai Ing-wen (@iingwen) and followed her Tweet ID. This allowed us to capture tweets mentioning her username, as well as capture her own tweets. We collected this data from April 23 to 29, 2017. Overall, we captured 1,396 tweets from 596 unique users during this week. These tweets included six tweets from her own account. We also captured 347 retweets of the president's recently posted tweets.

The most active user in this time frame was @UFsh1rxk2IVOgAd, an account that was almost certainly automated. The account had no profile picture; a maximum-length, seemingly random handle; tweeted in simplified Chinese (the mainland writing system); and sent nearly all its tweets in fours within the

Figure 5.1 Screenshots of Tsai Ing-wen's First Party Meeting Facebook Post After Being Elected President in 2016. Source: Author's screenshot, June 16, 2017. Note: This post was the target of a coordinated messaging campaign from the Chinese members of the Baidu forum Diba (帝吧), which has been involved in several trolling incidents (Z. Huang, 2017).

Figure 5.2 Screenshot of Suspicious Accounts on Twitter. Source: Author's screenshots, June 16, 2017. Note: Signs include having a handle of maximum length that seems randomly generated, lacking a profile photo or follower base, and exclusively tweeting abusively at Taiwan's President Tsai Ing-wen. These and many other suspicious accounts tweeting abusive messages at President Tsai had also joined only a few weeks before engaging in abusive behavior on Twitter.

span of a minute. It only joined Twitter in January 2017, and tweeted 52 of its 123 total tweets at President Tsai Ing-wen. This account's abusive tweets ranged from the puerile and innocuous to extremely obscene and misogynist. While we were preparing this chapter, this account also disappeared from the platform entirely.

While we are quite certain that this account was a bot, we were unable to find many others so obviously automated, or evidence of large-scale automation. Our hopes were that tracking the interactions of these accounts and analyzing their networks and metadata would yield evidence of automation or coordination, but unfortunately we were unable to find any signs of mass automation in the data. Again, this was to be expected in light of the fact that Twitter is a banned platform in China and is not particularly popular in Taiwan. It further supports the findings of King et al. (2017) that no evidence of automation could be found in the 50-cent Party leak from the Zhanggong Propaganda Office from 2013 to 2014.

Furthermore, in discussion with the author, an interview subject named Quinine highlighted an important fact in this regard. Taiwan is a subject about which nearly all mainland Chinese feel an ardent, sometimes jingoistic, sense of conviction. Quinine highlighted that, given China's huge population and the passion mainlanders feel about Taiwan, it is conceivable that the Party has no need to automate cross-Strait propaganda efforts. This tallies with our current findings and previous research. Two alternatives to automating cross-Strait propaganda therefore exist for the mainland: the laissez-faire approach of letting normal citizens air their opinions online; and paying or otherwise incentivizing public employees or private citizens to promote the regime's views on Taiwan online. Of course, these two approaches aren't mutually exclusive. Engaging in either may well be enough to accomplish the Party's goals.

The 2016 Diba Facebook Expedition

Our foray into Twitter described above was inspired by an incident that occurred in early 2016, shortly after Tsai Ing-wen was elected as president of Taiwan (Figure 5.3). Sia, Woolley, Monaco, and Howard (2016) carried out in-depth computational analysis of this campaign—the "Facebook expedition" carried out by the Chinese netizens from the popular online forum Diba (帝吧fb出征). Though this analysis did point to coordination, it did not conclusively prove that there was automation in the campaign. Our full-length article on this topic is forthcoming; a brief description of our work follows below.

Diba is an online forum, one of the many hosted on China's Baidu Tieba (百度貼吧), which is similar to Reddit. Diba has been described by *Quartz*'s Nikhail Sonnad as "the largest group [on Tieba] of all, with a staggering 20.6 million users [. . .] like 4chan, but for Chinese patriots" (Sonnad, 2016).

Figure 5.3 Political Abuse on Twitter Aimed at President Tsai Ing-wen. Source: Author's screenshot, June 16, 2017. Note: The first tweet reads "County head Tsai, Taiwan's people need you to step down, learn from others like Hung Hsiu-chu"—a KMT politician who was ousted from the 2016 presidential race for explicitly supporting unification with the mainland. The second tweet reads "actually there's no need, Tsai Ing-wen is bad. We mainlanders will hop over the wall and come over there no problem and show you what we're made of. Tsai Ing-wen will be toppled one day soon enough."

Diba has been involved in several coordinated trolling incidents since 2016 (Horwitz, 2016).

The Diba Facebook campaign of 2016 was a coordinated grassroots messaging campaign on President Tsai Ing-wen's Facebook page shortly after her election in January 2016. The goal of this mass messaging was to show the reaction of Chinese citizens to Taiwan's election of Tsai Ing-wen, who is a member of the pro-independence DPP in Taiwan. This event was covered in Taiwanese media, the *China Digital Times,* and also in a select few Western outlets such as *Quartz* and the *Wall Street Journal* (Henochowicz, 2016; M. Huang, 2016; Z. Huang, 2017).

For this particular campaign, Diba members organized what was referred to as "Diba's Facebook Expedition." The attackers posted pro-mainland comments on President Tsai's Facebook post from January 20, 2016, on Tsai Ing-wen's Web page (Tsai, 2016). Tsai had been elected four days earlier on January 16. The members of the forum also attacked the official fan pages of a popular Taiwanese newspaper, *Apple Daily* (蘋果日報), and of a famous singer from Hong Kong, Ho Wan-see (何韻詩) ("Zhongguo di ba," 2016).

The targeted post garnered 49,541 total comments and replies from January 20 to April 4, which was a disproportionate number in comparison with all other posts on her wall. An interesting point to note is that this organized effort would have had to use techniques to circumvent the Great Firewall, since Facebook is banned in the People's Republic ("Chinese society: Looking ahead," 2016; Horwitz, 2016). Most of these posts expressed opposition to Taiwanese independence and extolled the Communist Party's rule in mainland China. One phrase in particular was repeatedly used among pro-China commenters, 八榮八恥—"Eight Honors and Eight Shames." These eight principles of morality were penned by former president of China Hu Jintao, and were part of his Socialist Conception of Honors and Shames (社會主義榮辱觀), a document meant to be a moral guide for citizens of China, released in 2006 ("Hu Jintao ba rong," 2006). Many commenters typed out the full eight lines of these principles in their comments on Tsai Ing-wen's post.

Our team explored this post further. Though ultimately we did not find clear evidence of entirely automated accounts, we did find signs that there was heavy coordination and overlap between messages being posted promoting the PRC. As an initial step, we crawled all comments and responses on the post using the Facebook Graph API. We then automatically separated users into Chinese and Taiwanese sets, based on their predominant writing system. It is important to note that mainland China and Taiwan use two slightly different orthographic systems to write Mandarin Chinese. Mainland China uses simplified characters, which Mao Zedong made the official writing of the mainland in 1956. Taiwan still uses the traditional writing system ("Chinese, Mandarin," n.d.). This is briefly illustrated in Table 5.1.

This was a useful heuristic for separating users into Chinese and Taiwanese accounts. Chinese users are of course able to type in traditional, Taiwan-style characters, just as Taiwanese users can type in simplified characters, but it is reasonable to assume most type using their native writing system, in keeping with the linguistic principle of least effort (Zipf, 1949). We classified accounts according to whether their writing favored one system over the other with a ratio of at least 6:5. Accounts that didn't meet this threshold were classified as "unknown."

After this step, our team ran various computational analyses on the users in question. We analyzed accounts according to temporal, semantic, and network characteristics. For the temporal dimension, we analyzed the coordination between accounts posting in the first 24 hours through Euclidian and Dynamic Time Warping distance. For semantic analyses, we used a Latent Dirichlet

Table 5.1 **Traditional vs. Simplified Chinese**

Traditional (used in Taiwan)	龍	葉	龜	人
Simplified (used in China)	龙	叶	龟	人
Pronunciation	lóng	yè	guī	rén
Meaning	dragon	leaf	turtle	person

Source: Authors

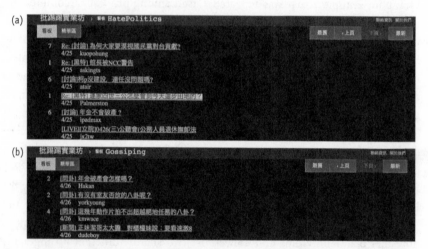

Figure 5.4 Screenshots of Two Popular Boards on PTT (批踢踢), HatePolitics (黑特), and Gossiping (八卦). Source: Author's screen capture taken June 16, 2017. Note: Interview subject Wizard described PTT as "the main" area for political discussion and propaganda in Taiwan: "Facebook is the peripheral." These two boards in particular were mentioned by Wizard as being hotspots for political discussion on PTT.

Allocation algorithm to explore overlap of messaging between accounts. We also analyzed the entropy of accounts' messages in attempts to find signs of automation. Finally, for the network dimension, we observed connections between accounts using identical posts as edges linking users (nodes). For the latter, we observed a much higher network connectivity among Chinese accounts than among Taiwanese ones.

Our full results are forthcoming. Overall, a few conclusions can be drawn from this incident:

1. Though we attempted to find signs of automation in the data, we did not find any accounts that were fully automated. We did, however, find evidence of heavy coordination for mainland accounts. This could be indicative of

a cyborg approach, in which some automation was used in tandem with human intervention (Ferrara, Varol, Davis, Menczer, & Flammini, n.d.).

2. In the 24 hours following the original post, the highest rate of posting by a single user was 2.3 posts per minute. The user with the greatest number of contributions posted 825 times within the observed period, but also had diverse content (with an entropy measure of 0.94 on a scale of 0–1). Both of these statistics, while on the upper bound of human activity, have not quite reached infeasible levels. All the same, they represent extraordinary engagement and may lend more credence to the cyborg theory.

3. For the most part, the content posted was not extremely acrimonious or invidious in nature. The messages mainly expressed a desire to reunify China and Taiwan and extolled the Eight Honors and Shames.

4. Although there is no reason to believe that the 50-cent Party was involved in this incident, these findings tally with the research discussed above from King et al. (in press), in that there is little evidence of automation, little to no acrimony in messaging, and messages seem to have the ultimate goal of distracting or stifling discussion, rather than arguing.

Conclusion

This chapter has aimed to explore three questions: First, is computational propaganda present in Taiwanese society? Second, what is the composition of computational propaganda in Taiwan? And finally, where are campaigns most likely to come from?

After reviewing the data, we can be sure that computational propaganda is heavily present in Taiwan. Domestic campaigns take the form of manual propaganda through the use of cyber army tactics and automated intelligence-gathering techniques. Many subjects also expressed confidence that political bots are being used on PTT, a domestic bulletin-board system, but no research has proven this conclusively. Benevolent political bots are also being used to combat fake news on LINE, a popular messaging app and social media platform in Taiwan.

In addition to domestic campaigns, cross-Strait propaganda is also present. We have seen that bots do not thus far seem to be present in official Chinese government propaganda techniques, nor have we seen them in civilian propaganda campaigns (such as the many Diba trolling/mass-messaging incidents that have taken place in recent years). Our analysis of Twitter accounts in the Taiwanese Twittersphere, Facebook accounts from the 2016 Diba Facebook expedition, and the research on domestic Chinese propaganda leads us to believe that automation does not yet figure heavily in Chinese propaganda efforts, nor even across the Taiwan Strait. Furthermore, the PRC benefits from immense reserves of human capital—legions of citizens who feel a sense of personal mission when it comes to the Taiwan issue, and who in so doing become megaphones for the official party line of the Chinese Communist Party. These facts do not preclude use of malicious political bots in future Chinese propaganda efforts, but they lead to the conclusion that bots do not currently play a central role in China's official propaganda apparatus.

The digital sphere will occupy an ever more important role in Taiwanese politics in the years to come. Ko Wen-je's digital campaign in the Taipei mayoral election of 2014 was successful and transformative, heralding a new era for politics on the island.

References

boyd, danah. (2017, January 5). Did Media Literacy Backfire? Retrieved from https://points.datasociety.net/did-media-literacy-backfire-7418c084d88d.

Central Intelligence Agency. (2016). Taiwan. Retrieved from https://www.cia.gov/library/publications/the-world-factbook/geos/tw.html.

Chaturvedi, S. (2016). *I Am a Troll: Inside the Secret World of the BJP's Digital Army*. New Delhi: Juggernaut.

Chinese, Mandarin. (n.d.). Retrieved from https://www.ethnologue.com/language/cmn.

Chinese Society. Looking Ahead: The Writing on the Wall. (2016, July 7). Retrieved from http://www.economist.com/news/special-report/21701647-communist-partys-policy-balancing-freedom-expression-repression-not.

Cortisol. (2017). Personal interview.

Dr. Strangelove. (2017). Personal interview.

Economist (2017, March 11). The Great Obfuscation of China. Retrieved July 5, 2018, from https://www.economist.com/briefing/2017/03/11/the-great-obfuscation-of-one-china

Ferrara, E., Varol, O., Davis, C., Menczer, F., & Flammini, A. (n.d.). The Rise of Social Bots. *Communications of the ACM, 59*(7), 96–104. https://doi.org/10.1145/2818717.

Forsythe, M. (2015, December 26). China Says It Will Expel French Journalist. *The New York Times*. Retrieved from https://www.nytimes.com/2015/12/27/world/asia/china-says-it-will-expel-french-journalist.html.

Freedom House. (2016). Taiwan | Country Report | Freedom of the Press | 2016. Retrieved from https://freedomhouse.org/report/freedom-press/2016/taiwan.

Freedom House. (2017). Freedom in the World 2017 | Freedom House. Retrieved from https://freedomhouse.org/report/freedom-world/freedom-world-2017.

g0v.tw. (2017). g0v gong min ke ji chuang xin jiang xue jin [g0v civic tech innovation stipend]. Retrieved April 30, 2017, from https://grants.g0v.tw.

Grassegger, H., & Krogerus, M. (2017, January 28). The Data that Turned the World Upside Down. Retrieved from https://motherboard.vice.com/en_us/article/how-our-likes-helped-trump-win.

Guo, Z. (2015, August 4). Zhengfu wang zhan zao yu DDoS gong ji xiong shou zai na zhua de dao ma [Government Website Suffers DDoS Attacks—Can the Perpetrators Be Found Somewhere?]. Retrieved from https://www.bnext.com.tw/article/36928/BN-2015-08-04-173401-44.

He, Q. (2008). *The Fog of Censorship: Media Control in China*. New York: Human Rights in China.

Henochowicz, A. (2016, January 22). Minitrue: Trolling Tsai Ing-wen Beyond the Great Firewall. *China Digital Times* (CDT). Retrieved from http://chinadigitaltimes.net/2016/01/minitrue-trolling-tsai-ing-wen-beyond-great-firewall/.

Horwitz, J. (2016, August 15). China's Internet Users Are Increasingly Jumping the Great Firewall—To Launch Epic Trolling Campaigns. Retrieved from https://qz.com/757996/chinas-internet-users-are-increasingly-jumping-the-great-firewall-to-launch-epic-trolling-campaigns/.

Howard, P. N., & Woolley, S. (2016). Political Communication, Computational Propaganda, and Autonomous Agents. *International Journal of Communication, 10*(Special Issue), 20.

Hsu, H. (2016, January 20). Twenty-Somethings in Taiwan and the Country's First Female President. Retrieved from http://www.newyorker.com/news/news-desk/twenty-somethings-in-taiwan-and-the-countrys-first-female-president.

Hu Jintao ba rong ba chi jiang hua yin qi qiang lie fan xiang [Hu Jintao's speech on eight honors and eight shames draws a strong reaction]. (2006, March 8). Retrieved from http://news.xinhuanet.com/misc/2006-03/08/content_4276314.htm.

Huang, H. (2017, January 22). Yaoyan zhen jia nan bian? zhen de jiad de LINE ji qi ren bang ni cha [Hard to tell if rumors are true or false? LINE's "zhende jiade" bot will help you look into it]. Retrieved from http://www.chinatimes.com/realtimenews/20170122000004-260412.

Huang, M. (2016, January 21). Chinese Netizens Flood Tsai Ing-Wen's Facebook Page with Anti-Taiwan Independence Posts. Retrieved from https://blogs.wsj.com/chinarealtime/2016/01/21/chinese-netizens-flood-tsai-ing-wens-facebook-page-with-anti-taiwan-independence-posts/.

Huang, Y. (2017, February 16). Zi jia xia dan ping tai zao DDoS gong ji fang hu fei yong jing yao quan min mai dan [When private companies run into DDoS attacks, should the people foot the bill for preventative measures?]. Retrieved from http://www.ithome.com.tw/news/111998.

Huang, Z. (2017, January 3). Chinese Trolls Jumped the Firewall to Attack Taiwan's President and Military on Facebook. Retrieved from https://qz.com/876614/chinese-trolls-jumped-the-firewall-to-attack-taiwans-military-and-president-tsai-ing-wen-on-facebook/.

Huang, Z., & Steger, I. (2016, December 21). And Then There Were 21: Taiwan Loses Another Diplomatic Ally to Beijing. Retrieved from https://qz.com/868794/taiwan-loses-another-diplomatic-ally-as-tiny-sao-tome-and-principe-switches-allegiance-to-beijing/.

Hwang, T., & Woolley, S. (2016, March 8). How Politicians Should and Shouldn't Use Twitter Bots. *Slate*. Retrieved from http://www.slate.com/articles/technology/future_tense/2016/03/how_politicians_should_use_twitter_bots.html.

King, G., Pan, J., & Roberts, M. E. (2017). How the Chinese Government Fabricates Social Media Posts for Strategic Distraction, Not Engaged Argument. *American Political Science Review*. Retrieved from http://j.mp/2ovks0q.

Ko, M.-C., & Chen, H.-H. (2015). Analysis of Cyber Army's Behaviours on Web Forum for Elect Campaign. In *Proceedings of the Asia Information Retrieval Societies Conference*. Brisbane, Australia.

Li, Y. X. (2017, March 1). Lesuo bi te bi guo ji hai ke da ju qin tai [Blackmailing Bitcoin International Hackers Invade Taiwan]. Retrieved from https://udn.com/news/story/7321/2312590.

Lin, J. (2017, March 15). Taiwan High-Tech Industry Hardest Hit by DDoS Attacks in Last 30 Days. Retrieved from http://www.taiwannews.com.tw/en/news/3117326.

Lin, L. (2016, July 18). Taiwanese Actor Leon Dai Loses Part in Zhao Wei Film After Political Pressure in China. Retrieved from https://blogs.wsj.com/chinarealtime/2016/07/18/taiwanese-actor-leon-dai-loses-part-in-zhao-wei-film-after-political-pressure-in-china/.

LINE Platform Reaches Nearly 75% of Taiwan Population, Dominates App Charts. (2015, January 13). Retrieved from http://www.metaps.com/press/en/blog/194-0113taiwan.

Martinsen, J. (2008, December 11). Mapping the Hurt Feelings of the Chinese People. Retrieved from http://www.danwei.org/foreign_affairs/a_map_of_hurt_feelings.php.

McGregor, R. (2010). The Party: The Secret World of China's Communist Rulers. *HarperCollins*. Retrieved from https://books.google.se/books?id=TxchbfKHfhsC.

Moonbeam. (2017). Personal interview.

Ng, J. Q. (2013). *Blocked on Weibo : What Gets Suppressed on China's Version of Twitter (and why)*. New York: The New Press.

Q. Continuum. (2017). Personal interview.

Quinine. (2017). Personal interview.

Ramzy, A. (2014, April 4). Students End Occupation of Taiwan's Legislature. Retrieved from https://sinosphere.blogs.nytimes.com/2014/04/10/students-prepare-to-end-occupation-of-taiwans-legislature/.

Reporters Without Borders (RSF) Opens Its First Asia Bureau in Taipei | Reporters Without Borders. (2017, April 6). Retrieved from https://rsf.org/en/news/reporters-without-borders-rsf-opens-its-first-asia-bureau-taipei.

RFI. (2015, December 24). Chine: la journaliste Ursula Gauthier menacée d'expulsion. Retrieved from http://www.rfi.fr/asie-pacifique/20151224-chine-ursula-gauthier-lobs-journaliste-francaise-menacee-expulsion.

Safi, M. (2016, December 27). India's Ruling Party Ordered Online Abuse of Opponents, Claims Book. *The Guardian*. Retrieved from https://www.theguardian.com/world/2016/dec/27/india-bjp-party-ordering-online-abuse-opponents-actors-modi-claims-book.

Sia, S., Woolley, S., Monaco, N., & Howard, P. (Forthcoming). *A Comparative Study of Chinese Online Agents on Facebook—an Anti-Taiwan Independence Expedition*.

Smith, N. (2017, April 6). Schoolkids in Taiwan Will Now Be Taught How to Identify Fake News. Retrieved from http://time.com/4730440/taiwan-fake-news-education/.

Sonnad, N. (2016, January 20). An Army of Chinese Trolls Has Jumped the Great Firewall to Attack Taiwanese Independence on Facebook. Retrieved from https://qz.com/598812/an-army-of-chinese-trolls-has-jumped-the-great-firewall-to-attack-taiwanese-independence-on-facebook/.

Su, F. (2017, May 17). Le suo ruan ti si nüe quan tai 226 zheng fu wu dian nao zhong biao [In Taiwan 226 governmental computers are devastated by ransomware]. Retrieved from http://news.ltn.com.tw/news/politics/breakingnews/2070547.

Su, J. (2016, March 11). Zao beijing qu zhu hou zhe ming fa guo nv ji zhe gen wo men tan le tan [After being deported by Beijing, this French reporter talked with us]. Retrieved from https://theinitium.com/article/20160311-international-francereporter/.

Surefire. (2017). Personal interview.

Tai da nan chuang da xue sheng zhuan shu jiao you wang [Student from National Taiwan University Creates Exclusive Social Network for College Students]. (2012, September 30). Retrieved from http://www.appledaily.com.tw/appledaily/article/headline/20120930/34542701/.

Transparency International. (n.d.). *Corruption Perceptions Index 2016*. Retrieved April 18, 2017, from https://www.transparency.org/news/feature/corruption_perceptions_index_2016.

Tsai, I. (2016, January 20). 蔡英文 Tsai Ing-wen. Retrieved May 29, 2017, from https://www.facebook.com/tsaiingwen/posts/10153130814816065.

van der Horst, L. (2016, February 24). Taiwan's "Third Force" Makes Its Presence Known in Legislature. Retrieved from http://thediplomat.com/2016/02/taiwans-third-force-makes-its-presence-known-in-legislature/.

WannaCry Should Make People Treat Cyber-Crime Seriously. (2017, May 20). Retrieved from http://www.economist.com/news/science-and-technology/21722158-it-has-been-neglected-too-long-wannacry-should-make-people-treat-cyber-crime.

Weiwei, A. (2012, October 17). China's Paid Trolls: Meet the 50-Cent Party. Retrieved from http://www.newstatesman.com/politics/politics/2012/10/china%E2%80%99s-paid-trolls-meet-50-cent-party.

Wizard. (2017). Personal interview.

Woolley, S. C. (2017). Computational Propaganda and Political Bots: An Overview. *Can Public Diplomacy Survive the Internet?* U.S. Department of State, Washington: D.C.

World's First LINE Theme Park Opens in Taiwan, Featuring the Beloved LINE Characters. (2014, February 7). Retrieved from http://official-blog.line.me/en/archives/36922370.html.

Wu, J. R., & Wagstaff, J. (2017, February 7). Five Taiwan Brokerages Report Cyber Attack Threats, Regulator Says. Reuters. Retrieved from http://www.reuters.com/article/us-taiwan-cyber-idUSKBN15L128.

Xuan jiao shang hai min zu gan qing wang you fa sheng di zhi ying pian [Choice of role hurts the people's feelings—netizens speak out and boycott movie]. (n.d.). Retrieved April 28, 2017, from http://www.81.cn/gfbmap/content/2016-07/14/content_150503.htm.

Zhongguo di ba wang you fa qi jin wan gong tai mei ti fen si tuan [China's Diba Netizens launch tonight's attack on Taiwan Media Fangroups]. (2016, January 20). Retrieved from http://www.appledaily.com.tw/realtimenews/article/new/20160120/779720/.

Zipf, G. K. (1949). *Human Behavior and the Principle of Least Effort: An Introduction to Human Ecology.* Cambridge, MA: Addison-Wesley Press.

6

Brazil

Political Bot Intervention During Pivotal Events

DAN ARNAUDO

Introduction

As the Internet grows exponentially in size and scope, so does its impact on our everyday activities, from our communications to market exchange to participation in political systems. It is changing political discourse throughout the world, while simultaneously the computational systems and the networks that connect them are playing an integral role in shaping elections and debates. The 2016 presidential elections in the United States (Kollanyi, Howard, & Woolley, 2016) and the United Kingdom's vote to leave the European Union (Howard & Kollanyi, 2016) offer two prime examples. In both cases, evidence shows that computer-controlled accounts, or bots, often promoted false or inaccurate information and played an integral part in propagating information about candidates and campaigns online.

The US government found that Russian state-sponsored computational propaganda played an instrumental role in the 2016 presidential election (U.S. Office of the Director of National Intelligence, 2017), a conclusion that Facebook said its data did not contradict (Weedon, Nuland, & Stamos, 2017). Massive networks of automated accounts, also known as botnets, can be built to manipulate algorithms in major social networks such as Facebook, Twitter, and YouTube, and can drive users to content supporting or attacking candidates and issues.

However, while these examples provide the most well-known, globally influential accounts of how computational propaganda operates in the twenty-first century, they are not the only types of situations where these techniques are being used. Across the developing world and the Global South, political actors are operating using the same kind of botnets and a wide range of propagandistic tactics online, from the use of large datasets of information about voters to algorithmic manipulation. As the largest national economy, population, and territory in Latin America, Brazil is a critical case that can be used to study how these systems and actors operate in a relatively young, developing democracy.

The world's fifth largest populace also dominates the Internet in the western hemisphere in a way only surpassed by the United States. It controls much of the backbone network infrastructure of South America, including transatlantic fiber optic cables, international interconnections, Internet Exchange Points, and data centers (Arnaudo, 2017). This extends to critical Internet resources such as Domain Name Systems, IP addresses, Autonomous System Numbers, and other measures of online influence (DeNardis, 2013). It also wields considerable international influence in virtual and physical space as a member of the BRICS group of developing nations and a leader in the Global South. The company that used big data and the manipulation of social network algorithms to promote the Trump (Cadwalladr, 2017a) and Brexit (Cadwalladr, 2017b) campaigns, Cambridge Analytica, has recently bet on Brazil by opening an office in São Paulo (Brigatto, 2017). Clearly, Latin America's biggest democracy is a huge growth market for international political consultancy.

However, it is also mired in long-standing, deeply intertwined political and economic crises. Years of a sprawling corruption scandal known as Car Wash (*Lava Jato* in Portuguese) has hobbled the political class, leading to many arrests, investigations, and resignations throughout the government. Consecutive years of recession have tarnished the legacy of the Workers' Party (*Partido dos Trabaladores*, or PT) that ruled the country from 2002 to 2016 under former presidents Lula Ignacio de Silva (Lula) and Dilma Rousseff (Dilma). Lula is under investigation for corruption as part of the Lava Jato scheme. While his successor Dilma is not, she was impeached in 2016 and removed from office for supposedly manipulating government accounts in the run-up to her 2014 re-election. She and her supporters have suggested that her former allies in coalition, now opposition, impeached her because they wanted to stymie the Lava Jato investigation and take power for themselves.

The new government, led by Dilma's former vice president and erstwhile ally Michel Temer, has not stopped the disastrous economic decline or the Lava Jato investigation, which has claimed several of his ministers, allies in Congress, and bureaucrats throughout the government. President Temer ran as Dilma's vice president in the 2014 election when his Partido Movimento Democratico Brasileiro (PMDB, or Brazilian Democratic Movement Party) aligned with her Workers' Party in a coalition. This coalition broke up soon after the election, and Temer and his party were thereafter instrumental in her impeachment.

This volatile political environment provides a large, rich, and dynamic field for the study of computational propaganda. Parties to various electoral contests in recent years have made increasing use of social networks and the Internet in general to organize campaigns and promote their candidates or any given issue, while attacking others (Buckstegge & Stabile, 2016). Simultaneously, in this period Brazil has rapidly adopted social networks as the existing media environment has rapidly shifted. John Perry Barlow, a founder of the Electronic Frontier Foundation, described the situation as follows: "Brazil is an enormous inside joke, and the Internet is a mass conversation. Brazil was the Internet before the Internet existed." Barlow distributed all 100 of his early invitations to Google's pioneering social network Orkut to Brazilians, leading to rapid adoption and the largest user base in the world. It remained the largest social network in Brazil until it was overtaken by Facebook in 2014 (Ruvolo, 2014).

This widespread, intense online participation extends to the democratic process itself. The Internet and social networks have become instrumental in spreading information about candidates, following news and debates, and tracking issues ranging from corruption to pension reform. This same energy contributed to the creation of a digital bill of rights within the country's constitution that now forms the core of laws governing Brazilian cyberspace, created through an open source, online, creative commons system that crowdsourced the process of drafting the text of the bill. This law, known as the *Marco Civil da Internet*, or the Internet Bill of Rights, became a model for Internet governance for countries around the world (O'Maley, 2015). It provides strong privacy guarantees for all citizens and situates principles such as network neutrality, universal Internet access, and freedom of expression online in the constitution.

Simultaneously, this vibrancy is overshadowed by instability in the economy, corruption, and deep political uncertainty. Computational propaganda in forms such as bot networks, fake news, and algorithmic manipulation play key roles in the political system in Latin America's largest democracy. But what role did computational propaganda play in the elections that have shaped modern Brazil, particularly the presidential election of 2014 and the local elections in 2016? How did its users attempt to shape discourse during the impeachment process that ended over a decade of control by the Workers' Party? Does this form of propaganda play any role in shaping ongoing debates about corruption investigations, social reforms, and other issues that transcend singular events? How does the legal system, buttressed by the Marco Civil, respond to this kind of propaganda? Are the laws, the media, and other actors structured in a way that can monitor these challenges to open, democratic discourse in the networked public sphere (Benkler, 2006) and respond to them?

To begin to answer these questions, this chapter will examine computational propaganda found during three specific political events that engendered intense political debate: the presidential election in 2014, the local elections in 2016, and the impeachment of former president Rousseff in the same year. Second, it will attempt to examine underlying, ongoing political issues that have been consistently debated and discussed in society and online throughout this period: corruption in the form of the Lava Jato investigation, social change in terms of the reform of the pension and education systems, and the economic system at the heart of many of these debates. Besides evaluating the academic literature tracking these events and issues, it will examine the media systems in which they are situated and how they portray the role of this kind of computational propaganda in society, as well as the laws that attempt to govern virtual space.

Interviews with political consultants, academics, journalists, and technologists will provide further background information on aspects of how bots and other forms of manipulation work online. Datasets of tweets linked to underlying political issues provide examples of how computers, individually and collectively, are contributing to online discourse. Bots that are identified in the collection will be examined in terms of their content, links, followers, and network to show examples of how these autonomous agents operate online. Finally, this chapter will offer some thoughts on how this propaganda could shape the political debates of Brazil's future, based on this discussion and data.

Setting the Scene: A Turbulent but Vibrant Political System Reflected Online

As described earlier, Brazil is a center of raging political debates about the best way forward for a rapidly developing society as its economy sags under the strain of a deep recession. As the country hosted the World Cup in 2014 and the Olympics in 2016, the economy stalled and shrank, leading to rising unemployment and attacks on the leading Workers' Party, which had held power under Presidents Lula and Rousseff since 2002 ("GDP per capita growth (annual %)," 2017). In over a decade in power, the center-left party had pushed for policies that supported large-scale social programs such as the Bolsa Familia, which provided subsidies to poor families to buy food and other necessities. It was generally supported by an upswing in economic fortunes, which was bolstered by a commodity boom that fed markets across Latin America, Africa, and Asia.

The political system is fragmented. In 2014, the number of political parties in Congress grew from 23 to 28, one of the highest numbers in the world. Governments must work in a coalition of many, which has always made for an unstable political environment. Besides Lula and Dilma's PT, and Temer's PMDB, there are also the Social Democracy Party of Brazil (PSDB), the Party of the Republic, and the Progressive Party that now rule in coalition (de Melo, 2015). Altogether, at the time of writing in May 2017, there are 20 parties in the alliance of the current government in the lower Chamber of Deputies, another measure of the diverse factions within the political system. In the upper house, 17 parties are represented in the Senate. Coalition governments are the norm, but they also lead to situations such as in 2014, when the president recruited a vice president from another party which later became the opposition.

Before this rupture, the PT had held power since 2003 in coalition with other left- to center-left parties, and oversaw a rapidly growing economy that contributed to its success. After President Lula ended his second term under term limits, his successor President Rousseff served from 2011 and stood for re-election in 2014 against candidates including Aécio Neves of the PSDB and Marina Silva of the smaller Brazilian Socialist Party. Despite winning the election, increasing protests fueled by online campaigns for her impeachment alongside the deteriorating economic situation and increasing opposition from Rousseff's coalition partners ensured that opposition continued to grow. This combination of factors led to her suspension from office in May 2016 and full impeachment in August, when she was replaced by her vice president, Temer (Romero, 2016).

The debate over the reasons for impeachment amplified major fault lines in society over the future direction of the country. There is ample evidence in terms of recorded conversations between Temer and his allies in Congress and the government, many of whom became ministers, which shows that they conspired to take down President Rousseff to thwart the Lava Jato corruption investigation that increasingly touches all the major players in government (Greenwald, 2016). The sprawling investigation focuses on payments made to fund political campaigns and secure contracts, particularly for major infrastructure projects.

During the early part of the twenty-first century, Brazil's economy represented a major success, creating growth and lifting many people out of poverty. However, it also created huge new opportunities for investment, from oil exploration by the state firm Petrobras to massive infrastructure projects supporting the 2014 World Cup and the 2016 Olympic Games. It is increasingly evident that to secure the contracts to build, service, and profit from projects such as these, massive payments were made at all levels and branches of government ("Irredeemable?," 2016). The investigation began by examining a small money-laundering operation at a petrol station, but has grown to touch many of the political and corporate elite, including the head of the largest construction firm in Latin America, former president Lula, Congressional and Senate leadership, and now President Temer himself (Padgett, 2017).

These political actors are operating in a corporate media market dominated by large monopolies. The Globo Network, a media group with properties in television, radio, print, and online, dominates almost all sectors. Its television station is the highest rated in the country and controls most advertising revenue, with 122 affiliates, an international version, and the ability to export its productions worldwide (Mango, 2014). It also controls the Brazilian newspapers with the second and eighth highest circulation, *O Globo* and *Extra*, respectively ("Maiores jornais do Brasil," 2015), and a large network of radio affiliates throughout the country. Its online portal, G1, bolsters this network, reporting over 50 billion page views since its inception and 46.3 million unique visitors per month in July 2016 ("G1 completa 10 anos com pioneirismo entre os sites de notícias," 2016).

Its major rivals are the UOL network, supported by the *Folha de São Paulo*, the third largest newspaper in the country, and smaller television and radio networks such as Bandeirantes, Record, Rede and SBT, which are all family owned. However, no other network plays such a central role in print, television, radio, and online as Globo, itself a family business since its founding by Robert Mourinho in 1963 (Mango, 2014). Media devoted to politics is small and targeted at an elite readership, with online portals such as Intercept Brazil, Jota, and Nexo alongside corporate magazines such as *Istóe, Veja, CartaCapital* and *Piauí*. The international press has Portuguese versions with Brazilian correspondents and some local bureaus, including the BBC, *El País*, DeutcheWelle, TV5, Buzzfeed and *Vice*.

As in almost every other country in the world, traditional corporate media networks are being overtaken by the Internet, and more informal, alternative information sources spread through social networks, email, personal messaging systems, or other online means. Facebook is by far the dominant social network, followed by WhatsApp, Google+, Instagram, Skype, Twitter, and LinkedIn. YouTube is almost as popular as Facebook as a social network, but in terms of time spent, Facebook is the overwhelming favorite (We are social Singapore, 2017). One estimate by ComScore, a global marketing and data analysis firm, suggests that Brazilian users spend over 95 percent of their social media time on Facebook (Banks & Yuki, 2014).

Political parties have made use of modern campaign strategies and taken to social networks, using them to promote their messages and attack opponents. Since at least the 2010 presidential elections, companies have made use of modern online propaganda campaigns driven by big data, often in concert with automated systems, to promote content (Rebello, 2014). A political scientist interviewed commented that in his view, US President Barack Obama's campaign in 2008 demonstrated how these techniques could be used, and were widely replicated. Regarding the use of automated accounts or bots, he noted:

> The use of bots is not something that just came about, they have been working for at least six years here in Brazil, and now it is becoming more

common. Now the bots are becoming more sophisticated, the technology is becoming more sophisticated, such as cyborgs that are a mixture of human and bot, something more efficient than bots.

Driven by major protests in 2013, new alternative media sources have sprung
up, most notably Midia Ninja, which spread videos and other information about
the opposition to the government. These protests started in response to rising
bus fares in Rio and São Paulo but quickly grew to encompass anger at the rising
costs of public services, corruption, and a host of other issues. In contrast to the
narrative created by traditional media such as Globo that these were protests
led by a minority of anarchists, Midia Ninja and other alternative media groups
exposed police brutality and the true breadth and nature of public support at
the time. These protests grew to include millions, numbers that were unprecedented in Brazil since before the advent of the commercial Internet, and the
groups spread viral videos and messages on Facebook, YouTube, WhatsApp,
Twitter, and several other social networks with methods that set a pattern for the
large-scale protests that were to follow (Santoro, 2017).

Internet penetration, while uneven and broadly confined to mobile access,
has supported this movement, increasing rapidly in the past two decades. The
International Telecommunications Union reported that 59 percent of Brazilians
used the Internet in 2015 ("Percentage of individuals using the Internet," 2016).
Only 26 million broadband subscriptions for a population of roughly 200 million suggests that there is still a gap in fixed line, computer-based access, but
250 million cellular subscriptions demonstrate how almost every citizen is increasingly online through mobile access (International Telecommunications
Union, 2016). This follows a global pattern, suggesting that almost everyone will
be connected to the Internet by 2020 (Woolley & Howard, 2016).

The country is also confronting a deep legacy of dictatorship. Brazil is a relatively young democracy, having only emerged in 1985 from decades of military-
backed authoritarian rule. Surveillance infrastructure and methods online are
not well documented, but the government maintains aspects of its dictatorial
legacy, including federal and state military police that have a history of working
in direct cooperation with the armed forces, and a Brazilian Intelligence Agency
(ABIN) that remains under the direct control of the military (Figueiredo, 2016).

The government also created a Cyber Defense Center (CDCiber) in 2012
to unify the command and control systems of various government agencies
with responsibilities for security in cyberspace under the authority of the military (Bernardo, 2014). It inaugurated this system with the special aim of co-
ordinating responses to large-scale events such as the United Nations summit
in 2012, the Pope's visit in 2013, the World Cup in 2014, and the Olympics
in 2016 (Canabarro & Borne, 2013). The CDCiber group has been tracking

protests online in various forms and has led various commentators to question its role in tracking online debates and those involved in protests (Muggah & Thompson, 2016).

Cybercrime is a major issue in the country. In 2016, Symantec, a major multinational cybersecurity firm, reported that Brazil hosted the eighth highest number of bots in the world, according to data collected from its systems ("2016 Symantec internet security threat report," 2016). The Spamhaus Project, a consortium that monitors networks worldwide, says it found 485,133 bots on the networks it monitored on May 17, 2017, third in number and in company with other BRICS countries China, India and Russia, and South Africa (the other BRICS; "The top 10 worst botnet countries," 2017). The Brazilian Computer Emergency Response Team (CERT) network of private and public entities responsible for security online throughout the country reported over 700,000 attacks in 2015 and over 1,000,000 in 2014, the year of the World Cup ("Estatísticas do CERT.br—Incidentes," 2017). Besides the sheer scale of Brazil's virtual space, large-scale piracy of operating systems and server software, and organized criminal groups contribute to the creation of fertile ground for botnets and other forms of criminality online.

Bots Enter a Presidential Debate

Events surrounding the 2014 presidential elections provide some of the earliest and well-documented cases of how botnets play a role in the political system. President Rousseff was up for re-election after her first five-year term, and after failing to win 50 percent of the vote in the first round, faced off in a second-round run-off against center-right candidate Aécio Neves. Earlier reports showed that candidates in the first round, including a senator who later died in a plane crash, were supported by botnets. Various articles at the time, backed by research done by the Federal University of Espírito Santo, showed that bots were operating to promote both candidates. This activity spiked particularly during debates between the two run-off candidates, Rousseff and Neves. Reporting done by *Folha de São Paulo* and backed by a research group from the university showed that within 15 minutes of the start of the television debate, tweets with hashtags related to Neves and the debate tripled in number (Aragão, 2014).

This kind of abnormally rapid rise in support is a strong indication that bots were being used, especially when rival hashtags supporting President Rousseff did not increase at anywhere near an equivalent rate. Shortly after, in October 2014, her online supporters group Muda Mais reported a list of over 60 accounts it said were automated to retweet Neves' account over 180 times each (Liberato,

2014). Her party documented various acts of accounts that appeared to be automated on Twitter, Facebook, and other social networks, attacking Dilma and supporting Neves, including the cases documented by the *Folha de São Paulo* and Muda Mais. They were linked to a businessman who received $R130,000 (Brazilian reals) to support the campaign. The campaign sought fines under the electoral law of between $R5,000 and $R30,000 (Umpierre, 2014).

Campaigns are prohibited from paying for the propagation of campaign materials on social media during an election, but private companies or individuals can still operate in this fashion if they are not directly connected to a campaign. A "mini reform" of the electoral law in 2015 ensured that restrictions on this form of "electoral propaganda" was prohibited on the Internet and specifically on social networks ("Altera as Leis do Código Eleitoral," 2015). Even in 2014, the law said that campaigns cannot pay to promote their causes directly on the Internet during the election, nor can they promote them through social networks. It also said that any accounts promoting messages within a campaign must be operated by "natural persons" (Toffoli, 2014). However, a political consultant we interviewed suggested that the law is inadequate to the task of monitoring infractions because it is restricted by the limitations of private parties operating on behalf of campaigns, and ultimately is behind the pace of technological development. An interviewee who is a political scientist studying the use of bots in campaigns commented:

> One always has to run ahead of these innovations in communications that are evolving, faster all the time. Each election you have a new law about campaigns (…) It is very dynamic, you make a new regulation, and new law, six months later a new technology is developed which can frustrate the system. (…) There is also the problem of private networks such as WhatsApp, where there is no way to monitor them.

Rousseff's campaign also used bots, but not on the scale used by Neves, as was later confirmed by leaked internal party memoranda published in the *Estadão de São Paulo* after the election (Filho & Galhardo, 2015). The memoranda covered the use of bots during the campaign, stating that Neves' operation used them not only on Twitter and Facebook but also on WhatsApp, and that it spent an estimated $R10 million in purchasing and deploying these.

The political consultant with experience of the campaign who was interviewed confirmed that WhatsApp was indeed a popular messaging system for pushing political messages. She described how a campaign would develop identities in private groups to push automated political messages or articles generated on public networks such as Twitter and Facebook. In her campaign, one person would operate roughly 250 accounts to push the same messages throughout these networks; much of the automation was internal. Conversely, these accounts were also used to measure the impact of communication campaigns and capture the "mood" of the network, such as topics frequently discussed and positions adopted.

A public company known as "Brasil Liker" sells likes that come from Facebook accounts registered in Brazil. Likes for Facebook pages cost R$4.99 for 50 and R$200 for 3000, while for posts, clients could gain 10,000 for only R$90 ("Brasil Liker," n.d.). These figures give an idea of how inexpensive these services can be, especially when automated or even outsourced to other countries, such as China or India.

The 2014 memo reported that this spending continued after the campaign had ended, to support groups on networks such as Facebook that opposed President Rousseff. It estimated that 16 million joined Revoltados ONLINE (Revolted Online), one opposition Facebook group, and another four million joined another known as Vem Pra Rua (Go to the Street). The site of the ruling Workers' Party had only three million engaged in a similar period, and the memo noted this discrepancy, stating that this investment "got a result," with content from these opposition sites reaching roughly 80 million people while sites related to the ruling party and the presidency reached only around 22 million. "If it was a football match we are entering the field losing 8 to 2," the report concluded gloomily (Filho & Galhardo, 2015).

This was partly because the Workers' Party bots were now part of the presidency. A Brazilian researcher who has worked in online democratic campaigns described what happened after election as follows:

> After the election, all the servers and bots of Dilma's campaign were turned off or they went to work for the presidency, which means that they had rules to follow, because they were working for the president's cabinet, and the other bots didn't have rules to follow.

In the view of the ruling party, the Neves campaign and its allies never disconnected many of the key components of the online campaign machinery, the raw materials of computational propaganda, and this had a major effect on the strength of the social movement that was then driven to oppose the president, her party, and their agenda. The online electoral campaign never ended, and these networks became key tools for generating support for impeachment.

The case of the 2014 Brazilian presidential election generates several interesting and important findings for the study of computational propaganda. It shows the weakness of electoral and other cybercriminal laws in combating the use of this technology online, as well as the inability of parties to understand and combat botnet activity that is not necessarily explicitly connected to the opposition. It also demonstrates how modern campaigns link together various social networks in a coherent strategy, using WhatsApp groups to drive people to more public forums on places like Facebook and Twitter. The campaign memo indicates that the amount of money required to create large social groups and massive streams of content while engaging users across platforms is quite small relative to the size of the return.

Finally, this election demonstrates the ability of campaigns to persist beyond the formal limits of the election, in contravention of the intent if not the actual language of the electoral law, and after the end marker of the election day itself. Just as the Internet allows campaigns to reach people in more personal ways than candidates and parties were able to in an age of mass media governed by television, newspapers, and radio, it also allows political actors to continue to pursue their political objectives through computational or traditional propaganda beyond conventional limits.

On one level, these groups target people using vast troves of data they have collected about what they like, who they follow, demographic information, and information about their group of friends and acquaintances and their family. On another, the campaign machinery can use personal connections of associates to gain access to voters, often through social networks such as WhatsApp or Facebook, which are—without such connections—designed to be closed to circles of people that are not directly connected to users in some way. During the presidential election in 2014, this created a powerful mechanism whose power, visibility, and range were boosted by botnets in various ways that were well documented both during the election and after it.

This system, honed during the campaign, coupled with a lack of any limitations to obstructing the ruling party's objectives, also helped lay the groundwork for the impeachment campaign that followed shortly after President Rousseff's second electoral victory in October 2014. Indeed, this online energy grew directly from a movement funded during an election by donors that were now able to channel these resources and throw new ones into the next phase of propaganda. This second phase proved the campaign had never completely paused online once the election was over. In reality, the opposition to the ruling party and its government was only getting started.

Impeachment and the Electronic Campaign that Never Ended

Modern, large-scale protests had already become an entrenched part of Brazilian political culture since the events of June 2013. In contrast to earlier manifestations, such as those that preceded the impeachment of President Fernando Collor de Mello in 1992, these protests were also the first on a national scale to make use of the Internet and social networks (Waldram, 2013). It is also notable that they were not backed by any political party or trade union, as all major political manifestations had been since the return of democracy in 1985 (Santoro, 2017).

At that time, protests against rising bus fares exploded into widespread, multifarious political manifestations of millions of people country-wide. These protests were partly linked to the Confederations Cup and the exorbitant amounts being spent to support the construction of stadiums and infrastructure for the World Cup in 2014 and the Olympics in 2016. Many felt that this expenditure was made without consideration for the real needs of the population, lining the pockets of politicians at the same time. The protests that arose were massive but also unconnected to any party, or ultimately any singular issue, spanning corruption to include health, safety, and education reform, as shown by analysis of hashtags on Twitter at the time (Cardoso, Lapa, & Fátima, 2016).

This movement provided the template for what was to come, including sporadic political protests during the election process in 2014. However, these generally fell within the scope of the traditional political manifestations, party rallies, and meetings. After the elections, as catalogued by the PT memo and confirmed by interviews, the machinery of the opposition remained in place and was connected to two Facebook groups, Revoltados ONLINE earlier and Vem Pra Rua. A communications professor studying social networks indicated that based on data he had collected, the calls began for impeachment immediately following the election, in November 2014:

> Many of these activities, actors and pages on Facebook also have Twitter and vice versa. So, it's very interesting that there is this historical connection, this continual line between impeachment and the post electoral movement in 2014; it is concrete.

They were joined by other groups such as Movimento Brasil Livre (Free Brazil Movement) and Endireita Brasil (Righting Brazil) in calling for organized opposition, which began to coalesce. The same group of researchers from the Federal University of Espírito Santo that had identified bot activity during the television debate and the campaigns in 2014 reported botnet activity in early March 2015. This called for protests against the president, and even for impeachment. The researchers collected images published on Twitter related to the hashtag #VaiaDilma (Scream Dilma) (Goveia, 2015).

In their analysis, the researchers found evidence of bots both calling for opposition to President Rousseff and supporting her. Protests reflected activity on social media, the motivation of the opposition to Rousseff, and the much weaker position of her supporters. A protest in support of the president on March 13, 2015, was said to consist of anywhere from 33,000 to 175,000 supporters, depending on organizer or police estimates respectively ("Más de un millón de brasileros protestaron contra la presidenta Rousseff," 2015). Either way, these numbers were exceeded by a protest of over a million people in São Paulo and thousands in other cities two days later. Another data collection completed at the same time for hashtags related to the impeachment protests showed that the most retweeted messages were generated by bots (Oliveira, França, Goya, & Penteado, 2016). Interestingly, in an analysis comparing the networks of images formed in 2013 and 2015, researchers found such clusters to be much more defined in that the interconnections and related groups were demarcated in support of or in opposition to the president. The communications expert interviewed specializing in social network research commented on how both bots and real partisans could heighten this dynamic:

> There exists a kind of human character in robots and a kind of robotic character in humans; there is a mono-thematization of their timeline. If you enter into the timeline of a bot, it will be speaking within a defined context. For example, yesterday there were protests in Brasilia, [but] it will be speaking continually of information such as Lula in Jail, vandalism, etc.; they are speaking only of one theme. This is not the style of a real user who doesn't participate in political topics, that will speak of various subjects. [...] However, a partisan political supporter or militant, will also have mono-thematic timeline, talking continually around the same subject over a large volume of tweets.

In 2013, the hashtags suggested the disorganized, multifarious nature of the issues that brought people onto the streets. In 2015, the battle lines had been drawn, partly with robotic help, and these trends would increase for the rest of the year (Côrtes, Ziigoni, Cancian, & Malini, 2016).

Successive protests followed in April, August, and December 2015, when largely antigovernment protestors again brought millions onto the streets (Sulleiro, 2015). These continued in 2016, especially in March and April, when protests faced off on successive days, sometimes even on the same day. A major protest occurred on March 18, 2016, this time in support of President Rousseff. A data collection at the time of tweets with the hashtag #VEMPRADEMOCRACIA (Come for Democracy) showed significant bot activity in favor of Rousseff as well as against her. They also observed that a significant amount of organization occurred on other networks, particularly private ones that could not be easily monitored (Bainbridge, 2014). The popularity and overwhelming use of Facebook is confirmed by various subjects interviewed for this chapter, and social networking surveys of Brazilians (Banks & Yuki, 2014).

The information environment had become particularly polarized, mirroring events that were happening in places like the United States and Europe at the same time. Researchers at the University of São Paulo surveyed the attitudes of 571 protestors at the April 2015 protests and found that they did not trust any of the major political parties, or trusted them very little (Ortellado & Soltano, 2016). The effects of fake news were also detected: 64 percent of respondents thought the PT wanted to create a communist regime and 53 percent that a drug gang represented the armed wing of the party. Mirroring Donald Trump's accusations about fake voting in the United States, 43 percent believed that the party had brought 50,000 illegal Haitian immigrants into the country to vote in the 2014 elections. Months later, at a protest supporting Rousseff in 2016, the researchers found that 57 percent believed that the United States had fomented protests against corruption to get at Brazil's oil, and 56 percent believed that the judge leading the Lava Jato case, Sergio Moro, had a connection with the PSDB (Albuquerque, 2016). These facts were demonstrably false but were widely shared on social media (Desidério, 2015).

Rousseff's government ended on May 12, 2016, when she was suspended by the lower House of Deputies and replaced by her vice president, and now enemy, Michel Temer. Ultimately, several factors, ranging from the struggling economy to widespread corruption to souring public opinion against all politicians, had helped to end her administration early. There is no doubt that social networks played a key role in developing this narrative and organizing the protests. Within the online landscape, bots had played a role from the beginning, and never stopped in their electronic opposition to her administration, possibly a key factor in the speed of her unseating.

The 2016 Rio de Janeiro Municipal Elections

Municipal and state elections are often harbingers of what is to come on a national scale. They are where political campaigns test out new tactics in local environments: there is less scrutiny and they are often able to get away with more. A campaign consultant interviewed for this chapter commented that in 2016, a kind of hybrid, cyborg automation became popular in her campaigns. What was known as "doe um like" (donate one like) was a feature in which a candidate's official campaign asked for supporters to "donate" the capacity of liking and sharing content from their personal profiles on Facebook for a three-month window. Once the supporter clicked on a link and agreed to make this "donation," the tool captured their profile's ID and password. Profiles of real people started to follow automated tasks and joined the candidate's army, a kind of cyborg botnet. She suggested that this tool was often only offered to one side, and argued this was decisive in the result of the elections in many municipalities.

In the elections for mayor of Rio de Janeiro in 2016, botnets appeared to be particularly active in the campaign. Marcelo Crivella, the right-wing leader of an evangelical mega-church, and Marcelo Freixo, a state representative, professor, and member of the left-wing Socialism and Liberty Party, faced off in the final round. Both candidates accused each other of spreading online rumors and complained to elections authorities and in public debates about rampant fake news. Stories shared included one claiming that Crivella would privatize and charge for access to public parks, and another that stated that Freixo would legalize marijuana and abortion. Both candidates created websites to denounce these rumors, and Freixo entered a legal action against Crivella (Schmidt, 2017). They also used WhatsApp, particularly Freixo, who had less exposure on television, but legal scholars criticized the anonymity of the network and the lack of specific laws addressing its use in the spread of false information (Couto, 2016).

Researchers at the Federal University of Espírito Santo found a botnet of 3,500 accounts on Twitter attacking Freixo with repeated messages with the same phrase, often posting 100 or more times per hour. They used the hashtags #freixista (Freixo supporter), and according to the research group this is more likely to have been to create trending topics against the candidate (Albuquerque, 2016). Ultimately, Crivella won the campaign, denying any connection to the botnets or the spread of rumors. As in the cases found in the presidential campaign, while such activities are prohibited by the electoral law, it is very difficult to prove automation or, when found, to make connections between actual bots and the campaigns. Much of this activity again centered on private or semi-private networks such as Facebook, WhatsApp, and YouTube, which are much more difficult to track, monitor, and report than open networks like Twitter. As on a national level, fake news, automation, and other computational propaganda tactics used by the presidential campaigns can be identified.

BRAZILIAN COMPUTATIONAL PROPAGANDA IN ONGOING DEBATES

Underlying these distinct political events are ongoing debates, particularly ones centered around corruption in government and reform. These proposed reforms are linked not only to the political system but also to education, pensions, and other publicly funded goods. Citizens are justifiably angry that the entire political class appears to be caught up in a consistent pattern of bribes for access to public contracts in exchange for campaign funding, among other schemes, while the government remains unable to balance the budget and support basic public services. These issues are reflected in conversations in social networks, especially when these issues come to a head in the form of events such as strikes, public protests, investigations, or political scandals. Interestingly, bots are playing roles in these thematic debates as well, often going undetected for long periods of time.

BRAZILIAN EXPERIMENTS IN AUTOMATING SOCIAL NETWORK INFLUENCE

In order to understand how bots could infiltrate social networks, gain followers, spread messages, and interact with real people, researchers at the Federal University of Minas Gerais created two fake accounts (Messias, Schmidt, Oliveira, & Benevenuto, 2013).

The experiment began in 2011, and one bot is still active at the time of writing in May 2017, with nearly 2,000 followers (@scarina91). The first account, now deactivated, only followed users and did not interact, but did gain some followers, tweets, messages, and interaction. The second bot tweeted and retweeted based on a predetermined algorithm and gained many followers, nearly 2,000 of which persist in May 2017, although the account stopped tweeting on June 25, 2016, when the research group announced its paper with a tweet. The account is not based on a real person, but posed as a young Globo journalist disseminating news articles and other tweets. It also reacted to others automatically, gaining responses from celebrities and other popular accounts, including a football announcer, a host of *The Voice Brasil*, and a mixed martial arts fighter (Messias, Schmidt, Oliveira, & Benevenuto, 2015). This research suggests the ease with which bots can fool and engage people of all kinds in Brazilian society, multiplying their ability to reach large audiences through influential followers and automated messaging.

A STUDY OF TWEETS ON CORRUPTION, "CAR WASH," PENSION REFORM, AND STRIKES

For this study, two collections were made of hashtags related to ongoing political themes including corruption, reform, political protest, and economic issues. The first collection was made from February 27 to March 27, 2017, and 281,441 tweets were collected from 82,575 users. The hashtags, noted in Table 6.1 with translations in parentheses, were generally associated with the themes of corruption, the Lava Jato investigation, and protests around those issues.

The second collection was more targeted and lasted for two weeks from May 1 until May 14, 2017. It collected 80,691 tweets from 33,046 users focused on a strike that was called on April 30 and generated major public attention, as well as on the May 1 "May Day" protests and events celebrating the "Day of the Worker" in Brazil (Table 6.2). The strike attracted peculiar, possibly automated support from an unlikely place after a Portuguese hashtag related to the opposition to the strike (#AGreveFracassou, or the weakened strike) began trending in India ("Como #AGreveFracassou chegou aos trending topics na Índia?," 2017). Simultaneously, Congress debated a major reform of the pension system that would raise the age of retirement and allow companies to hire people with much less onerous unemployment, pension, healthcare, and other benefit requirements. The strike had been called in response to these reforms, while various protests in the streets and online focused on them. As a result, the general protest terms were included again.

From these collections, six accounts were chosen as likely bots based on the high frequency of their tweets in the selected data-capture periods, the type of system they used to tweet, the content of the tweets and their score in an application called "Bot or Not" developed by the University of Indiana to test for bot activity. Table 6.1 shows basic information related to the collected accounts.

The top two accounts, @LavaJatoNews and @br45ilnocorrupt, generated the most tweets in the collection from February 27 to March 27, 2017, and have the highest number of tweets captured, partly because of the longer period. The other four accounts were principally collected during the period from May 1 to 14, 2017. Four of the six accounts were found in both collections, either because they contained the hashtags associated with general protest or because they posted ones related to both captures. All the accounts focus on corruption in different forms; three have names or account images related to the subject, while others mention it in different hashtags or tweets.

The @ktrem10 and @stelles_13 accounts generally post information protesting about the current government of President Temer, with hashtags such

Table 6.1 **Hashtags Collected from February 27 to March 27, 2017**

General Corruption: #corrupção, #corrupcao, #corruptos, (corruption, corrupted)
Lava Jato Hashtags: #Lavajato, #Lava_jato, #lavajatointocavel, #operação_lava_jato, #somostodosmoro, #moro, #LavaJatoEuApoio, #Odebrecht, #delação, #SergioMoro, (Car Wash, Car Wash untouchable, operation Car Wash, we are all Moro, Moro, I support Lava Jato, Odebrecht, accusation/censure, Sergio Moro)
General Protest: #vemprarua, #VemPraRuaBrasil, #acordabrasil, #nasruas (come to the street, Come to the street Brazil, wake up Brazil, in the streets)

Table 6.2 **Hashtags Collected from May 1 to May 14, 2017**

General Protest Terms: #vemprarua, #VemPraRuaBrasil, #acordabrasil, #nasruas #foratemer
(come to the street, Come to the street Brazil, wake up Brazil, in the streets, get out temer)

Strike Terms: #BrasilemGreve #greve #grevegeral #BrasilEmGreve #AGreveFracassou, #euvoutrabalhar #GreveNao
(Brazil on strike, strike, general strike, Brazil on strike, The weakened strike, I will work, No strike)

Reforma da Previdencia/May Day: #DiadoTrabalhador #DiadoTrabalho #reformaprevidencia #reformadaprevidência #reformatrabalhista #Previdencia #PrevidênciaSocial #Terceirização #NenhumDireitoaMenos #Reformas #PEC287 #TerceirizaçãoNÃO #TerceirizaçãoSIM #NãoÀReformaTrabalhista #NãoÀReformaDaPrevidência #SimÀReformaTrabalhista #SimÀReformaDaPrevidência
(Day of the worker, Day of work, pension reform, worker reform, pension, social pension, Outsourcing, Outsourcing Yes, Outsourcing No, No to the worker reform, No to the pension reform, Yes to the Worker Reform, Yes to the Pension Reform)

---

as #ForaTemer (Get out Temer), while @br45ilnocorrupt's name suggests that it is against former president Rousseff. The number 45 symbolizes the 45th president, Rousseff, and the integration with the words *Brazil* and *corrupt* emphasizes the blog's support of right-wing parties and opposition to her. Interestingly, this account tweeted many times in both data collections, over 3,000 in the first and almost 600 in the second, suggesting the wide range of topics it connects to, from the general strike of April 8 (#GreveGeral) in the second capture, to the Lava Jato investigation (#LavaJatoEuApoio) in the first.

The account that is most likely to be a bot is @2374Costa, which is the same text, composed of hashtags (#RT #QuintaDetremuraSDV Índia #GostoDe #NaoTemCoisaMelhorQ #GreveNAO #PuniçãoParaVitoria #MeOdeiaMas) followed by a link to a "like factory" website where users can purchase bots to like or follow their accounts on Twitter and Facebook. It has a 67 percent Bot or Not score, the highest of the set. This is probably a commercial service making use of popular tags to drive traffic to its product.

Two accounts are focused more pointedly on corruption, @LavaJatoNews and @Wudson_, and both use automatic posting systems, Auto Post Viper IT and dlvr.it. They are also both rated highly (55 percent and 60 percent, respectively) as likely bots. However, they both use the accounts in different ways. @LavaJatoNews mostly retweets or sometimes quotes a retweet based on hashtags such as #Odebrecht, the largest Brazilian construction firm currently at the center of the Lava Jato scandal concerning payoffs to politicians. @Wudson_ generates only original tweets and does not interact with others through retweets. The account parses the source, hashtags, and headlines related to corruption and creates a link it can track through dlvr.it.

The two left-leaning bots also take different approaches. @stelles_13 is a more standard automated system. It is rated to be 50 percent bot and uses If That Then This, a popular applet that automates programmed actions across platforms. For instance, if a Gmail or a Google news alert is received by a user, then a tweet is sent out. This is probably the type of command that is scripted; tweets are original but consist mostly of a link, the headline text, and two or three tags related to opposition to President Temer. The second (@ktrem10) is more complex, being a mix of retweets, quoted tweets, and some original content. Many tweets have the same string: "#MafiaGolpistaðŸ?€@RedeGlobo @UOL @abraji @Globonews @Bandtv @sbtonline @recordtvoficial #JG @ g1 #Previdencia" followed by a link to an article, or a retweet, or the quote of another tweet. The hashtag #MafiaGolpista signifies "the coup mafia" and the accounts are all media organizations, followed by the "pension system" hashtag.

Sometimes, there are different original texts, such as on May 2, 2017, when it tweeted "@CFOAB se posiciona oficialmente contra a reforma da #Previdencia #sbtbrasil #jornaldaband @jornaldarecord #JN @g1" (the Federal Council of the Brazilian Bar Association positions itself officially against the reform of the pension system) followed by hashtags related to the reform and major media organizations, followed by a link. This is a phrase that does not appear to have been repeated in the dataset. One reason for this could be that this tweet was generated from a story appearing elsewhere, but another could be that an actual user generated this text, which would make this a kind of cyborg account using both automatically generated and human-generated content. The account always uses the traditional Twitter Web Client rather than automating applications, and has a 27 percent Bot or Not score, suggesting some level of human intervention or an algorithm that successfully masks its robotic nature.

These accounts demonstrate the wide range of tactics used to promote different political topics, some for over seven years, some for less than a month, generally to drive traffic to articles and issues but sometimes for purely commercial reasons. All of them, apart from the commercial bot (@2374Costa), are relatively popular, with thousands of followers each, although many of these followers may themselves be bots. @br45ilnocorrupt is especially suspect, attracting almost 30,000 followers in less than two months of existence. Overall, they demonstrate several different tactics for driving traffic and gaining followers, from retweeting repeatedly to using specialized automation software and spreading articles from a wide range of news sites. Harnessed collectively in botnets, these kinds of techniques could gain significant followers and create large-scale support or opposition for a wide range of issues.

Conclusion: Responses and Emerging Trends

As shown in these cases, the legal system has struggled to keep up with the use of computational propaganda in Brazil. Interviews with campaign consultants and case studies show that while the law prohibits any electoral propaganda within three months of the election, this is extremely difficult to control. Private individuals can always offer their support for campaigns, spreading rumors or other kinds of fake news, and these accounts are often automated using bots at local and national levels, despite the requirement that all accounts related to the campaign be associated with "natural persons" (Toffoli, 2014).

The computational propaganda tactics used during the 2014 election did not stop after the election of former president Rousseff. These methods were used to drive people to groups opposing her and her party's agenda, which in turn led to calls for her impeachment, ultimately achieved in October 2016.

Proposals for laws currently germinating in Congress could provide responses to the use of bots. One proposal, known by its nickname "PL Espião" (the Big Spy Bill), would require all Internet companies that wish to operate in Brazil to collect data about users, including their name, email, address, and national identity number. It is difficult to imagine how this system would be developed or enforced, but if this law were implemented it would have major implications for the privacy sections of the Marco Civil and would make more user data at risk of exposure. However, it could also have the effect of making it much more difficult to operate bots, as each Brazilian account would require a real, identifiable person associated with it. Accounts that do not abide by these terms could be more quickly removed. There is also the need for stronger data protection law, which would provide regulations for private and public entities that store vast quantities of voter data as part of their core functions.

The Lava Jato investigations illuminating corruption at the heart of the political system remain a potent focus of bots throughout Twitter, as evidenced by the bots discovered in the data collections. Interestingly, one response developed by researchers comes in the form of a bot that tracks spending by Congressional leadership. Named Rosie after the robot housekeeper in the cartoon *The Jetsons*, this bot is operated by a project known as "Operation Serenade of Love," which is a reference to a 1990s case that caused the resignation of Sweden's deputy prime minister for using a state credit card for private expenses (Kinzer, 1995). Rosie tracks the deputies' requests for reimbursements of expenses and automatically checks the prices and accounts, formulating applications for investigation if there are suspicious data (Mendonça, 2017).

Rosie has a Twitter account (@RosieDaSerenata) that reports her activity, alongside a project website (https://serenatadeamor.org/) and a Facebook page (operacaoSerenataDeAmor) to encourage transparency in its operation. This is a notable example of how Brazilians are attempting to use bots to fight corruption and change political norms; already it has found egregious examples such as a deputy filling up his car 30 times a month on average, another requesting a meal costing R$6205, and that 219 deputies simply request the maximum amount every day. Such initiatives promoting transparency, when coupled with a new freedom of information law that mandates publicly accessible data, could drive further anti-corruption initiatives (Lei de Acesso à Informação, LAI, 2011).

Certainly, after years of scandal, Brazilian society is taking a hard look at a complete reform of its political system. In May 2017, with the Lava Jato scandal widening, police released a recording of President Temer organizing bribes for the imprisoned former head of the Senate with the head of the largest meatpacking companies in the world (Greenwald, 2017). The tapes have led to calls for a new impeachment process after he refused to resign, markets crashed, and Brazil again seems on the verge of a political cataclysm. The government's fate is unclear, but this chapter certainly demonstrates that rapidly developing computational propaganda will play a growing role in the upcoming national elections in 2018, potential impeachment, and the deeper political processes that have yet to be revealed.

References

Albuquerque, A. L. (2016, October 18). Eleição no Rio tem tática "antiboato" e suspeita de uso de robôs. *Folha de São Paulo*. Retrieved from http://www1.folha.uol.com.br/poder/eleicoes-2016/2016/10/1823713-eleicao-no-rio-tem-tatica-antiboato-e-suspeita-de-uso-de-robos.shtml.

Altera as Leis do Código Eleitoral, Pub. L. No. 13.165/15 (2015) (enacted). Retrieved from http://www.planalto.gov.br/ccivil_03/_ato2015-2018/2015/lei/l13165.htm.

Aragão, A. (2014, September 30). Eu, robô. *Folha de São Paulo*. Retrieved from https://web-beta.archive.org/web/20150121042218/http://www1.folha.uol.com.br:80/fsp/especial/188299-eu-robo.shtml.

Arnaudo, D. (2017). *Brazil, the Internet and the Digital Bill of Rights* (Strategic Papers No. 25). Retrieved from the Igarapé Institute website: https://igarape.org.br/marcocivil/en.

Bainbridge, L. (2014, April 26). How Social Media Gives New Voice to Brazil's Protests. Retrieved from https://www.theguardian.com/world/2014/apr/27/social-media-gives-new-voice-to-brazil-protests

Banks, A., & Yuki, T. (2014, August). O cenário das redes sociais e métricas que realmente importam. Retrieved from https://www.comscore.com/por/Insights/Presentations-and-Whitepapers/2014/The-State-of-Social-Media-in-Brazil-and-the-Metrics-that-Really-Matter.

Benkler, Y. (2006). *The Wealth of Networks: How Social Production Transforms Markets and Freedom.* New Haven, CT: Yale University Press.

Bernardo, K. B. (2014, December 1). Por dentro do CDCiber, o Centro de Defesa Cibernética do exército Brasileiro. Retrieved from https://medium.com/brasil/por-dentro-do-cdciber-o-centro-de-defesa-cibernetica-do-exercito-brasileiro-40ce637d119.

Brasil Liker. (n.d.). Retrieved from http://brasilliker.com.br/.

Brigatto, G. (2017, March 13). Após Trump e Brexit, Cambridge Analytica vai operar no Brasil. *Valor Econômico.* Retrieved from https://www.pressreader.com/brazil/valor-econ%C3%B4mico/20170313/281883003145524.

Buckstegge, J., & Stabile, M. (2016). Campanhas eleitorais. In T. Silva & M. Stabile (Eds.), *Monitoramento e pesquisa em mídias sociais: Metodologias, aplicações e inovações* (pp. 301–316). Retrieved from http://www.ibpad.com.br/o-que-fazemos/publicacoes/monitoramento-e-pesquisa-em-midias-sociais-metodologias-aplicacoes-e-inovacoes/.

Cadwalladr, C. (2017a, February 26). Robert Mercer: The Big Data Billionaire Waging War on Mainstream Media. *The Guardian.* Retrieved from https://www.theguardian.com/politics/2017/feb/26/robert-mercer-breitbart-war-on-media-steve-bannon-donald-trump-nigel-farage.

Cadwalladr, C. (2017b, May 7). The great British Brexit Robbery: How Our Democracy Was Hijacked. *The Guardian.* Retrieved from https://www.theguardian.com/technology/2017/may/07/the-great-british-brexit-robbery-hijacked-democracy?CMP=share_btn_tw.

Canabarro, D. R., & Borne, T. (2013). *Brazil and the Fog of (Cyber)War.* NCDG Policy Working Paper, No. 13-002. Retrieved from https://pdfs.semanticscholar.org/902c/aae6fa4a3f1fea5d0625364dcaaf5dd5f26e.pdf.

Cardoso, G., Lapa, T., & Fátima, B. D. (2016). People Are the Message? Social Mobilization and Social Media in Brazil. *International Journal of Communication, 10*(0), 3909–3930.

Como #AGreveFracassou chegou aos trending topics na Índia? (2017, April 29). Retrieved from https://www.cartacapital.com.br/politica/como-agrevefracassou-chegou-aos-trending-topics-na-india.

Côrtes, T. G., Ziigoni, L. P., Cancian, A. M., & Malini, F. L. L. (2016). O #VemPraRua em dois ciclos: análise e comparação das manifestações no Brasil em 2013 e 2015. In *Intercom— sociedade Brasileira de estudos interdisciplinares da comunicação.* Retrieved from http://portalintercom.org.br/anais/nacional2016/resumos/R11-1938-1.pdf.

Couto, M. (2016, August 15). Estratégico na disputa eleitoral, WhatsApp deve ter efeito inesperado. *O Globo.* Retrieved from https://oglobo.globo.com/brasil/estrategico-na-disputa-eleitoral-whatsapp-deve-ter-efeito-inesperado-19923064.

de Melo, P. O. S. V. (2015). How Many Political Parties Should Brazil Have? A Data-Driven Method to Assess and Reduce Fragmentation in Multi-Party Political Systems. *PLOS ONE, 10*(10), e0140217. doi:org/10.1371/journal.pone.0140217.

DeNardis, L. (2013). *The Global War for Internet Governance.* New Haven, CT: Yale University Press.

Desidério, M. (2015, June 23). 7 boatos da política brasileira que podem ter enganado você. *Exame.* Retrieved from http://exame.abril.com.br/brasil/7-boatos-da-politica-brasileira-que-podem-ter-enganado-voce/.

Estatísticas do CERT.br—Incidentes. (2017, February 13). Retrieved May 26, 2017, from https://www.cert.br/stats/incidentes/.

Figueiredo (2016, August 16). Brazilian Intelligence Service Stokes Olympic Terrorism Fear for its Own Benefit. Retrieved July 5, 2018, from https://theintercept.com/2016/08/16/brazilian-intelligence-service-stokes-olympic-terrorism-fear-for-its-own-benefit/

Filho, V.H., & Galhardo, R. (2015, March 17). Governo cita uso de robôs nas redes sociais em campanha eleitoral. *Estadão de São Paulo*. Retrieved from http://politica.estadao.com.br/noticias/geral,governo-cita-uso-de-robos-nas-redes-sociais-em-campanha-eleitoral,1652771.

G1 completa 10 anos com pioneirismo entre os sites de notícias. (2016, September 26). Retrieved from http://www.inteligemcia.com.br/g1-completa-10-anos-com-pioneirismo-entre-os-sites-de-noticias/.

Goveia, F. (2015, May 13). As imagens da #vaiadilma: rede relacional. Retrieved from http://www.labic.net/cartografia/a-rede-das-imagens-da-vaiadilma-novas-relacoes/.

Greenwald, G. (2016, June 30). Major New Brazil Events Expose the Fraud of Dilma's Impeachment—and Temer's Corruption. *The Intercept*. Retrieved from https://theintercept.com/2016/06/30/major-new-brazil-events-expose-the-fraud-of-dilmas-impeachment-and-temers-corruption/.

Greenwald, G. (2017, May 18). After Latest Bombshells, Only Michel Temer's Removal and New Elections Can Save Brazil's Democracy. *The Intercept*. Retrieved from https://theintercept.com/2017/05/18/after-latest-bombshells-only-michel-temers-removal-and-new-elections-can-save-brazils-democracy/.

Howard, P. N., & Kollanyi, B. (2016). Bots, #StrongerIn, and #Brexit: Computational Propaganda during the UK-EU Referendum. *arXiv:1606.06356 [Physics]*. Retrieved from http://arxiv.org/abs/1606.06356.

International Telecommunications Union. (2016). *ITU Mobile Cellular Subscriptions by Country*. Retrieved from http://www.itu.int/en/ITU-D/Statistics/Documents/statistics/2016/Mobile_cellular_2000-2015.xls.

International Telecommunications Union. (2016, December). Percentage of Individuals Using the Internet. Retrieved from http://www.itu.int/en/ITU-D/Statistics/Documents/statistics/2016/Individuals_Internet_2000-2015.xls.

Irredeemable? (2016, January 2). *The Economist*. Retrieved from http://www.economist.com/news/briefing/21684778-former-star-emerging-world-faces-lost-decade-irredeemable.

Kinzer, S. (1995, November 14). The Shame of a Swedish Shopper (A Morality Tale). *The New York Times*. Retrieved from http://www.nytimes.com/1995/11/14/world/stockholm-journal-the-shame-of-a-swedish-shopper-a-morality-tale.html.

Kollanyi, B., Howard, P. N., & Woolley, S. C. (2016). *Bots and Automation over Twitter during the U.S. Election* (Data Memo). Oxford: Project on Computational Propaganda. Retrieved from http://comprop.oii.ox.ac.uk/2016/11/17/bots-and-automation-over-twitter-during-the-u-s-election/.

Lei de Acesso à Informação (LAI), Pub. L. No. L12527/2011 (2011) (enacted). Retrieved from http://www.planalto.gov.br/ccivil_03/_ato2011-2014/2011/lei/l12527.htm.

Liberato, W. (2014, October 5). Blog do Liberato: No dia da democracia, Aécio Neves continua usando robôs no Twitter #Dilma13PraVencer [Blog post]. Retrieved from https://blogdoliberato.blogspot.com.br/2014/10/no-dia-da-democracia-aecio-neves.html.

Maiores jornais do Brasil. (2015). Retrieved May 26, 2017, from http://www.anj.org.br/maiores-jornais-do-brasil/.

Mango, A. (2014, July 30). TV Globo CEO Roberto Irineu Marinho to Receive International Emmy Directorate Award. *The Hollywood Reporter*. Retrieved from http://www.hollywoodreporter.com/news/tv-globo-ceo-roberto-irineu-722247.

Más de un millón de brasileros protestaron contra la presidenta Rousseff. (2015, March 15). *El País*. Retrieved from http://www.elpais.com.co/mundo/mas-de-un-millon-de-brasileros-protestaron-contra-la-presidenta-rousseff.html.

Mendonça, H. (2017, January 24). Rosie, a robô que detecta quando deputados usam mal o dinheiro público. *El País*. Retrieved from http://brasil.elpais.com/brasil/2017/01/23/politica/1485199109_260961.html.

Messias, J., Schmidt, L., Oliveira, R., & Benevenuto, F. (2013). You Followed My Bot! Transforming Robots into Influential Users in Twitter. *First Monday, 18*(7). Retrieved from http://firstmonday.org/ojs/index.php/fm/article/view/4217.

Messias, J., Schmidt, L., Oliveira, R., & Benevenuto, F. (2015). Bots socais: Como robôs podem se tornar influentes no Twitter. *Revista Eletrônica de Sistemas de Informação ISSN 1677-3071 doi:10.21529/RESI, 14*(2). doi:org/10.5329/1564.

Muggah, R., & Thompson, N. B. (2016, January 13). A balcanização da internet pode começar no Brasil. *El País*. Retrieved from http://brasil.elpais.com/brasil/2016/01/12/opinion/1452609555_927730.html.

Oliveira, É. T. C., de França, F. O. D., Goya, D. H., & Penteado, C. L. de Camargo. (2016). The Influence of Retweeting Robots during Brazilian Protests. Paper presented at the 2016 *49th Hawaii International Conference on System Sciences* (HICSS), Koloa. Retrieved from https://www.researchgate.net/publication/300415619_The_Influence_of_Retweeting_Robots_During_Brazilian_Protests.

O'Maley, D. (2015, December). *Networking Democracy: Brazilian Internet Freedom Activism and the Influence of Participatory Democracy*. Nashville: Vanderbilt University. Retrieved from http://www.academia.edu/17053807/Networking_Democracy_Brazilian_Internet_Freedom_Activism_and_the_Influence_of_Participatory_Democracy.

Ortellado, P., & Soltano, E. (2016). Nova direita nas ruas? Uma análise do descompasso entre manifestantes e convocantes dos protestos antigoverno de 2015. In *História, memória e política* (Vol. 11, pp. 169–181). São Paulo: Perseu.

Padgett, T. (2017, May 25). Brazil's Car Wash Scandal Reveals a Country Soaked in Corruption. *Bloomberg*. Retrieved from https://www.bloomberg.com/news/articles/2017-05-25/brazil-s-car-wash-scandal-reveals-a-country-soaked-in-corruption.

Rebello, A. (2014). Guerra pelo voto. *UOL*. Retrieved from https://www.uol/eleicoes/especiais/a-campanha-por-tras-das-timelines.htm.

Romero, S. (2016, August 31). Dilma Rousseff Is Ousted as Brazil's President in Impeachment Vote. *The New York Times*. Retrieved from https://www.nytimes.com/2016/09/01/world/americas/brazil-dilma-rousseff-impeached-removed-president.html.

Ruvolo, J. (2014, June 29). Why Brazil is Actually Winning the Internet. Retrieved from http://www.buzzfeed.com/jruv/why-brazil-is-actually-winning-the-internet.

Santoro, M. (2017, May 19). Brazil's Year of Living Dangerously. *Americas Quarterly*. Retrieved from http://www.americasquarterly.org/content/brazils-year-living-dangerously.

Schmidt, S. (2017, April 9). Estudo mostra que menções a Crivella nas redes sociais caiu em três meses. *O Globo*. Retrieved from http://oglobo.globo.com/rio/estudo-mostra-que-mencoes-crivella-nas-redes-sociais-caiu-em-tres-meses-21180048.

Sulleiro, R. (2015, December 14). Brazil Impeachment Protests Downsized but Still Determined. *AFP*. Retrieved from http://news.yahoo.com/weak-turnout-brazil-impeachment-protests-180205914.html.

Symantec. (2016, April). *Symantec Internet Security Threat Report*. Retrieved from https://www.symantec.com/content/dam/symantec/docs/reports/istr-21-2016-en.pdf.

The Top 10 worst Botnet Countries. (2017, May 17). Retrieved from https://www.spamhaus.org/statistics/botnet-cc/.

Toffoli, D. (2014). Dispõe sobre propaganda eleitoral e condutas ilícitas em campanha eleitoral nas Eleições de 2014. Pub. L. No. 23404, 127-41.2014.6.00.0000. Retrieved from http://www.tse.jus.br/eleicoes/eleicoes-anteriores/eleicoes-2014/normas-e-documentacoes/resolucao-no-23.404.

Umpierre, F. (2014, October 10). Dilma vai à Justiça contra os robôs de Aécio. Retrieved from http://www.pt.org.br/dilma-vai-a-justica-contra-os-robos-de-aecio/.

U.S. Office of the Director of National Intelligence. (2017, January 6). *Background to "Assessing Russian Activities and Intentions in Recent US Elections": The Analytic Process and Cyber Incident Attribution*. Retrieved from https://web-beta.archive.org/web/20170421222356/https:/www.dni.gov/files/documents/ICA_2017_01.pdf.

Waldram, H. (2013). Brazil Protests Continue as Story Develops Over Social Media. Retrieved from https://www.theguardian.com/world/2013/jun/21/brazil-protest-social-media

We Are Social Singapore. (2017, January). Digital in 2017: South America. Retrieved from https://www.slideshare.net/wearesocialsg/digital-in-2017-south-america.

Weedon, J., Nuland, W., & Stamos, A. (2017, April 27). *Information Operations and Facebook.* (Report by Facebook). Retrieved from https://fbnewsroomus.files.wordpress.com/2017/04/facebook-and-information-operations-v1.pdf.

Woolley, S. C., & Howard, P. N. (2016). Political Communication, Computational Propaganda, and Autonomous Agents—Introduction. *International Journal of Communication, 10*(0), 4882–4890.

7

Germany

A Cautionary Tale

LISA-MARIA N. NEUDERT

Preface

The strategic manipulation of public opinion over social media has emerged as a critical threat to democracy in the twenty-first century. During the 2016 US presidential election, Russian state actors leveraged fake accounts and commercial data targeting tools to orchestrate disinformation campaigns. UK Prime Minister Theresa May and French President Emanuel Macron both publicly accused Russia of interfering with democratic processes, launching information operations designed to undermine trust in public institutions. In Europe, groups at the fringe of the political spectrum successfully used fabricated falsehoods, conspiracy theories, and hate speech to mobilize voters and sow public discontent with political systems. Increasingly, political parties around the globe rely on data-driven advertising solutions to target individual citizens with political messages in ways that cloud the transparency of political campaigning. Mainstream political actors amalgamate fact and fiction to boost their agendas to public attention, eroding public trust in the truthfulness of public actors. A small circle of giant technology companies controls and directs the flow of information through profit-driven algorithms, diminishing regulatory and public concerns just as much as competition.

The viral spread of junk news, coordinated misinformation campaigns and tactical leaks, automated political bots that distort public discourse online, and algorithmically afforded micro-targeting of susceptible individuals with manipulative messages are all instruments of a novel form of twenty-first century propaganda. "Computational propaganda" is the use of algorithms and automation tasked with the manipulation of public opinion online. Equipped with big data, both state and nonstate actors leverage technological infrastructures and information networks to propagate propaganda online with the objective of sowing discontent, fomenting uncertainty, and silencing opposition (Woolley & Howard, 2016). Political, commercial, and private actors have used computational propaganda to manipulate conversations, demobilize opposition, and generate false support. Providing a central networked sphere for public discourse and information seeking, social media platforms serve as an arena for these informational attacks on democracy.

As reports about computational propaganda rose to prominence in Germany, they inspired a wave of public scrutiny manifesting in numerous media reports, and civic and governmental countermeasures. In light of the German elections of 2017, politicians and the media scrambled to come up with overblown proposals to secure the German cyberspace from threats of computational propaganda, some posing substantial restrictions to the freedom and openness of public discourse online. Episodic instances of computational propaganda were repeatedly blown out of proportion in the media and served as a frame of reference for regulatory and public assessment of the threats to political stability. Misconceptions and terminological confusions were dominant, blending phenomena such as political bots, chatbots, junk news, hate speech, filter bubbles, micro-targeting, and Russian propaganda into a shadowy picture of looming interference in German democracy.

This chapter sets out to substantiate the heated public discourse with a mixed-methods analysis of computational propaganda in the German sphere, seeking to anchor the disordered public debate with conceptual clarity and empirical evidence. Originally published before the German elections of 2017, this working paper was updated for this publication. Evidence on computational propaganda over social media during the German Federal Election of 2017 was added. Despite the fact that this working paper and follow-up data memos on the German parliamentary election (Neudert, Howard, & Kollanyi, 2017a) did not find any substantial evidence of computational propaganda in Germany, the Network Enforcement Law was introduced as a strict regulatory countermeasure to tackle the spread of propaganda by holding social networks liable for content posted there. Computational propaganda has emerged on the public agenda. In light of ongoing public scrutiny, these findings have been contextualized with media, civil society, and government reports.

Introduction

Germany has fallen victim to a skeptical political zeitgeist that is suspicious of political elites and the establishment (Decker & Lewandowsky, 2017; Jessen,

2017). Suffering from the late effects of the Euro crisis and its controversial "culture of welcoming" in the European refugee crisis, increasingly wide shares of the German public have grown wary of political power. The growing skepticism has created a fertile soil for right-wing populist movements that are blossoming in Germany. Most prominently, the anti-immigration, right-wing Alternative für Deutschland (AfD) party, founded only in 2013, has been steadily growing their support. In the Federal Election in September 2017 the AfD gained 12.6 percent of votes, tripling their results from the previous election in 2013 (Bundeswahlleiter, 2017).

In addition, extremist right-wing fringe voices have repeatedly accused immigrants of committing crimes, indoctrinating citizens with harmful interpretations of Islam, and freeloading off the German welfare system— concerns that have been echoed in the political mainstream. Most prominently the Reconquista Germanica, a self-proclaimed right-wing activist group, declared a "war of memes" on the political establishment, vowing to push right-wing positions into power (Hammerstein, Höfner, & Rosenbach, 2017). In search of what motivates these outbursts of right-wing sentiments, some have suggested that eroding trust in the German media could be a factor. Indeed, *Lügenpresse*, or "lying press," was the word of the year in 2014 (Chandler, 2015). However, recent research from the University of Würzburg finds that German trust in the media is at an all-time high (University of Würzburg, 2017).

The 2017 election year marked a turning point in German politics. After months of struggles to form a coalition to govern, Angela Merkel was only confirmed as chancellor in March 2018, months after the elections. For the first time, the right-wing AfD was elected into parliament, forming the largest opposition party and therefore leading the opposition. Yet the effects of the 2017 election expanded far beyond the German sphere. As the economic powerhouse of the crumbling Eurozone, Germany's political leadership is pivotal for determining the course of European politics. And with the rise of a brand of far-right conservatism led by Donald Trump in the United States, a similar vein of nationalism highlighted by Brexit in the United Kingdom, and the possibility (though ultimately unsuccessful) of Marine Le Pen in France, Germany has been thought of as one of the "liberal West's last defenders" (Smale & Erlanger, 2016). All factors that politicians and the media feared might make interference in German democratic processes an endeavor of both foreign and internal actors, with high stakes, going into the election.

With the election of Donald Trump as President of the United States having come as a potent reminder that mobilizing the margins can decide an election outcome in favor of an unlikely candidate, Chancellor Angela Merkel took it upon herself to explicitly caution the Bundestag about the threats of computational propaganda in November 2016. Referencing the US election, Merkel pointed out that the formation of opinion worked "fundamentally different than 25 years ago," whereby "fake news sites, bots, trolls . . . self-enforcing opinion and amplification . . . through algorithms can tamper with public opinion" (Brien, 2016). Following Merkel's address, computational propaganda—and especially the role of political bots—emerged as an issue of critical public and political concern.

All of the major German parties—including the Sozialdemokratische Partei Deutschlands (SPD), Christlich Demokratische Union/Christlich-Soziale Union (CDU/CSU), Bündnis90/Die Grünen and Die Linke—publicly stated that they would refrain from using social bots in elections and strongly condemned their employment. The right-wing AfD, in contrast, stated that they would "consider the use of social bots for elections" (Stern, 2017). However, the party later distanced itself from this statement. Regulators and lawmakers started thinking about how to counter computational threats to the democracy of public discourse online. Criminalizing the use of bots or banning bots altogether (Rosenbach & Traufetter, 2017) were discussed. Governmental expert hearings and task forces were initiated, tasked with bringing the parliament up to speed on computational propaganda (Hausding, 2017). In an effort to combat the manipulation of citizens online within existing legal frameworks, a Network Enforcement Law (Net DG) was proposed for the first time, which now holds social network companies liable for illegal content posted to their platforms following its introduction in January 2018 (Strathmann, 2018). Meanwhile, influential legacy publishers like the *Süddeutsche Zeitung* (Domainko, 2016) and *Der Spiegel* (Amann et al., 2016) ran in-depth stories that extensively detailed the use of political bots to manipulate public opinion.

What remained absent from the debate was a conceptual consensus about the nature of emerging online threats. Increasingly, phenomena in relation to digital media literacy, foreign interference in elections, new media consumption patterns, and cybersecurity were fused together under the umbrella terms of *fake news* and *political bots*. With the threat of computational propaganda being very present in the media in light of the 2017 parliamentary election, the discourse became as political as it became politicized. Though the debate lacked clarity and empirical evaluation, Germany pioneered regulatory and civil society countermeasures designed to specifically tackle the spread of misinformation and hostile automation online. This chapter seeks to tackle the deficit in evidence of computational propaganda, providing a quantitative analysis of real-time social media data during critical moments of public life in Germany.

The German Political Sphere

Germany is a federal parliamentary democratic republic, with pluralist parties competing in a multiparty system that informs the formation of the division of powers. Historically, the German political landscape has been dominated by the Christlich Demokratische Union / Christlich-Soziale Union (CDU/CSU) and the Sozialdemokratische Partei Deutschlands (SPD), with government usually formed by coalitions. Germany held a national election in September 2017 in which Angela Merkel was confirmed in her role as German Chancellor. Merkel had run against SPD politician Martin Schulz, former President of the European Parliament. The Schulz campaign was off to a promising start, with his party's full support and strong results in the polls. Eventually, however, Schulz led his SPD party to a historical failure, with the lowest number of votes the party had ever seen (Kinkartz, Werkhäuser, & Hille, 2018). Yet the 2017 election also fell short of success for Merkel's party. Despite winning the largest number of votes, the results required the party to find a coalition partner in order to govern. After months of negotiations with Die Grünen / Bündnis 90 and the FDP for a so-called Jamaica coalition, the FDP announced they were pulling out, resulting in the failure to form a government. Breaking a campaign promise, the SPD ultimately agreed to form a great coalition, and Merkel was confirmed as chancellor in March 2018—with the struggles leaving a shadow over the newly formed government and Merkel's power (Tretbar et al., 2018).

Right-wing populist currents, on the other hand, were able to successfully transform their momentum into votes. The anti-immigration, right-wing AfD had already gained substantial support in European Union and state-level elections. As the topic of immigration continued to polarize the German political sphere, the AfD was able to establish itself as a nationalist party protecting German values and culture. During the 2017 German parliamentary election the AfD won 12.6 percent of the votes. This result not only won the AfD a position in the parliament for the first time in the party's history but also catapulted the party into opposition leadership. In Saxony the AfD even became the largest party (Kolb, 2017). Despite difficulties surrounding the formation of government and an increasing shift toward the right, experts agree that the German government is still stable, not least because Merkel has been reelected as chancellor for the fourth time in a row.

Next to the government, the press functions traditionally functions as the fourth estate of power in Germany. It is bound to diverse regulations and norms for both online and offline journalism executed by the state, watchdog organizations, and journalists' unions in an effort to ensure quality reporting and ethical standards. The German media system is internationally acclaimed for having "a strong track record of reliable reporting from both public service and commercial news brands" (Hölig & Hasenbrink, 2016). In recent years, however, the German media has increasingly been accused of biased, self-referential reporting (Klöckner, n.d.). The accusations peaked in relation to the debate on New Year's Eve sexual assaults in Germany in 2015/16 (Reinemann & Fawzi, 2016). Hundreds of women were sexually assaulted in various German cities, and police officials announced that the perpetrators were mostly Arab and African men, fueling much debate on Germany's refugee politics (Hill, 2016). At first, several German media outlets did not cover the incidents, but only started reporting after increasingly facing public critique in social media, prompting much disdain for the traditional media (Karnitschnig, 2016). However, communication science scholars Reinemann and Fawzi (2016) dismiss "lying press" allegations as instruments of populist and extremist politics that have found fertile soil on social media to disseminate distorted ideological and conspiracy content.

The vast majority of Germans rely on traditional media for their news consumption. Only a fifth of Germans get their news from social media, putting it far behind countries like the United States and the United Kingdom, where a majority of users get their news from social media channels (Höig & Hasenbrink, 2016).

Germany has held a central role as both an originator and a victim of propaganda throughout the twentieth century. In World War I, propaganda was employed to mobilize and motivate the public for the war and to demonize opponents. Nazi propaganda during World War II was an integral element of totalitarian, nationalist politics. The press, broadcasting, and all liberal arts media and mass events were instrumentalized for the manipulation of public opinion (bpb, 2011a). In the German Democratic Republic (GDR), widespread propaganda was used to discredit the Federal Republic of Germany and Western capitalism. The entire media ecosystem was censored and steered by the government (bpb, 2011b). The Federal Republic of Germany, too, frequently used propaganda during the Cold War, criticizing communism and the GDR (Gries, 1996). More recently, politicians and journalists have accused Russia of disseminating agitating propaganda messages directed against the German media and political sphere (Gathmann & Wittrock, 2016; Noworth, 2016), though a year-long investigation by the German intelligence service failed to reveal any "smoking guns" (Mascolo, 2017). With all this in mind, it is evident that Germany today takes much pride in freedom of expression and its liberal press system, as well as a climate of political discourse that allows for debate and diversity.

Methods

This chapter seeks to complicate simplistic narratives around computational propaganda in Germany, in an effort to address the lack of empirical evidence and conceptual clarity of the phenomenon. It makes use rigorous social science fieldwork to reflect upon three units of analysis: (1) social network sites as the sociotechnical infrastructure that affords the generation and spread of computational propaganda; (2) actors, who generate and spread computational propaganda; and (3) instances of computational propaganda in Germany. This classification of areas of interest is based on Castells' network perspective on the media ecosystem; Howard summarizes Castells' arguments to this end in saying that networked media research "must involve studying large organizations that build and manage media infrastructure (here: SNS), the individuals who produce and consume content over media (here: makers of computational propaganda), and the content that is produced and consumed over media (here: instances of computational propaganda)."[1]

The enquiry employs a mixed-methods approach that accommodates triangulation and contextualization of quantitative and qualitative data. The big data analysis of the German social media sphere during critical moments of public life in Germany provides an empirical basis to assess the scope of automation and spread of misinformation. The semi-structured interviews of the expert community of fake news experts provide access to in-depth expert knowledge on the emergent phenomenon that remained yet to be codified.

The analysis is an in-depth extension and advancement of the data memo, "Junk news and bots during the German Federal Presidency Election" (Neudert, Howard, & Kollanyi, 2017a) with the Oxford Internet Institute's Computational Propaganda Project led by Philip Howard. This study goes beyond the interim data evaluation, providing detail on the choice of methods and offering a contextualized discussion of findings.

BIG DATA ANALYSIS OF COMPUTATIONAL PROPAGANDA ON SOCIAL MEDIA

In an effort to ground phenomenological assessments of online propaganda, bots, and junk news in Germany, this quantitative big data analysis seeks to provide a conclusive representation of instances of computational propaganda in Germany.

Twitter in Germany: In 2016 for the first time Twitter announced user numbers for Germany. The network claimed to have 12 million active users in Germany—a number that experts recommend should be taken with a grain of salt (Die Zeit, 2016). Despite moderate public adoption, Twitter was selected for analysis, as it is a focal forum of political discourse in Germany. The platform serves as a central publication and networking venue, and source of information for traditional gatekeepers and opinion leaders in media and politics (Neuberger et al., 2014). In relation to sharing behavior, Neuberger et al. (2014) demonstrated that German Twitter users primarily link to well-established news sources that originate offline, suggesting an extension of media power structures into the digital sphere. Bright (2016) proposed a "social news gap" whereby social media users filter out certain types of high-quality news. Boczkowski and Mitchelstein (2012) found that during times of heightened political activity, public affairs content is shared more often.

Political Context: The enquiry focuses on the election, as recent research finds that moments of heightened public interest in political life are likely especially prone to disinformation campaigns (Woolley & Howard, 2016). The political significance of the parliamentary election is not only expressed in the election of a new chancellor, but also in the formation of a multiparty, pluralistic parliament that will steer the political course of the four years to follow. The parliamentary election analyzed in this chapter was held on September 24th of 2017.

Data Collection: Twitter provides free access to a sample of the public tweets posted on the platform through its Streaming API. Tweets were selected on the basis of 20 political keywords used as hashtags in relation to the election. This has the advantage that the data captured is most likely on the election. Three additional hashtags were added as they rose to prominence on election day. This method has proven successful in previous study of political social media discourse (Howard et al., 2017a). The streaming API yields (A) tweets that contain the keyword or hashtag; (B) tweets with a link to a Web source, where the URL or title of the Web source includes the keyword or hashtag; (C) retweets that contain a message's original text, wherein the keyword or hashtag is used either in the retweet or original tweets; (D) quote tweets of tweets containing the keyword or hashtag. Each tweet was coded and counted if it contained one of the specific keywords or hashtags. If the same hashtag was used multiple times in a tweet, the tweet was still counted only once. The dataset analyzed contained 984,713 tweets generated by 149,573 unique users that were collected between the 1st and the 10th of September 2017, using hashtags associated with the primary political parties in Germany, the major candidates, and the election itself.

INTERVIEWS WITH EXPERTS ON COMPUTATIONAL PROPAGANDA

A close-knit community of computational propaganda experts has distinguished itself in Germany. They possess unique expertise and knowledge on the emergent phenomenon, serve as informants to the media, public sector, and the government (Hausding, 2017; Kurz, 2017), and are eager to exchange opinions and engage in knowledge transfer with each other during conferences, workshops, or online. They come from multifaceted organizational and sociopolitical backgrounds and are dispersed over significant distances. To access high-level expert knowledge, semi-structured, qualitative interviews are combined with immersive observation of the multisite community in a way that underscores the relationship between both the collective of experts and the sociotechnical and political context they are located in.

Participants: The community of experts share unique knowledge about the generation and spreading mechanisms of fake news on social media that is implicit (Littig, 2008); they are an elite, in that they are the "the influential, the prominent, the well-informed" (Dexter, 2006). I targeted three networked groups.

Policy Advisors and Regulators: Seeking primarily to counter fake news and social bots, these experts are concerned with how policy and regulation can prevent and defend against computational propaganda to protect public welfare. They are politicians, government intelligence experts, policy experts at nonprofits, think tanks, and political foundations, and digital lobbyists.

Social Media Experts: These experts are acquainted with relevance algorithms, online content monetization, marketing strategies, and user behavior on social media. They are social media journalists and managers, platform moderators, software experts and engineers, digital marketers and advertisers, and publishing professionals.

Mainstream Hackers: This group of interviewees has expertise in the making, deployment, or purchasing of computational propaganda attacks, including bots, leaks, and the manipulation of social media algorithms. Coming from a hacker background, these experts have made it their mission to share their digital competencies with a broader public. They are members of organized hacker groups, IT experts, security engineers, and penetration testers.

Academics: Germany has a long tradition of research in technology and information studies, as well as communication and media science. Though academic research lacks empirical evidence in Germany, these experts are highly knowledgeable about computational propaganda techniques and how they relate to the German media and political sphere. They are professors and senior researchers at leading research institutions and universities.

Recruitment: To identify German experts on computational propaganda, participant lists of public hearings in front of the German Bundestag were used as a primary starting point. In addition, mainstream media reporting and social media discourse, as well as relevant research, watchdog, and think tank endeavors, were closely examined. Using a hybrid selective/snowballing sample, a total of 12 experts were recruited. Interviewing was stopped as emergent patterns repeated and expert knowledge was exhausted.

Research Design and Analysis: Through combination of in-depth interviews and immersive observation, a holistic understanding of expert knowledge was successfully accessed which lent credence to expert reports. Questions for the semi-structured interviews were highly individualized to address actor-specific knowledge. Each of the interviews lasted between 45–90 minutes, and participants were interviewed face-to-face. The interviews were recorded with informed consent. For analysis the interviews were selectively transcribed. All interviewees were granted the right to remain anonymous and to choose an alias, which is used in this study. A qualitative, thematic coding approach was used for analysis which uncovered rich nuance in the data.

GROUNDED TYPOLOGY OF SOURCES OF NEWS AND INFORMATION

Drawing from the big data analysis, a grounded typology of sources of political information and news emerged. This grounded typology first had been used by the researcher and the Project on Computational Propaganda during the 2016 US election (Howard et al., 2017a). For the German context, categories were refined and adapted in an iterative process, based on data from the 2016 federal presidency election and parliamentary election. To draw the distinction between junk news and quality sources of news, the professionality of the organization, their journalistic standards, accountability, practices of fact-checking, and transparency were evaluated. For this purpose, individual sources were analyzed at the level of their organization.

Findings A: Bots in Germany

It is now common for people who log on to social media sites to find themselves interacting not only with human users but also with code-driven social actors—automated bot accounts. Bots are computer scripts that automate human tasks online, deploy messages, and replicate themselves. Security experts estimate that bots generate as much as 10 percent of the content on social media websites and drive 62 percent of all Web traffic (Rosenberg, 2013). That said, bots also administer legitimate tasks on the Internet. They track and disseminate breaking news articles on behalf of media outlets, correct typos on Wikipedia, promote matches on social media, and have performed the first real census of device networks. But, they can also be deployed for commercial tasks that are rather less positive, such as spamming, carrying out distributed denial-of-service and virus attacks, email harvesting, click fraud, and content theft. Networks of such bots are referred to as *botnets*, which describes a collection of connected computer programs that communicate across multiple devices to jointly perform a task. These botnets, which can comprise hundreds and even thousands of accounts, can be controlled by a single user on a single device. Bots are cheap to produce and maintain, highly versatile, and ever evolving (Hegelich & Janetzko, 2016; Woolley & Howard, 2016; Howard & Woolley, 2016).

Political bots, frequently referred to as *social bots* in Germany, are a subcategory of bots that are active on social media. They are automated social media accounts that mimic human behavior and interact with other users on social networking sites, where they usually do not reveal their nonhuman nature. These bots are especially active on Twitter, but they are also found on other platforms such as Facebook, Instagram, or online dating services (Samuel, 2015; Guilbeault & Gorwa, 2017). Increasingly, social bots are being used go beyond the social spheres and into the political: both state and nonstate actors have used bots to manipulate public opinion, choke off political discourse, perturb conversation, and muddy the identity of political actors (Woolley & Howard, 2016). Social bots have been found to be active during important political moments worldwide: the UK Brexit referendum (Howard & Kollanyi, 2016), the 2016 US presidential election (Howard, Woolley, & Kollanyi, 2016), during the Ukraine crisis (Hegelich & Janetzko, 2016), and during protests in Syria (Qtiesh, 2011).

The prominent media discussion of computational propaganda during pivotal moments of political life in 2016 has spurred much public concern about social bots. Political scientist and bot expert Simon Hegelich predicted an "invasion of opinion robots" (2016), the Tagesschau claimed that German politicians had declared a "war on opinion machines" (Mair, 2016), and Andree Thieltges from the University of Siegen diagnosed an "exceptional multiplier potential" (Beuth, 2017) whereby German opinion leaders on Twitter are susceptible to political bots. In the run-up to the 2017 parliamentary election, all of the major German parties declared that they would refrain from using social bots for political campaigning. A data memo led by the author of this chapter at the Project on Computational Propaganda found limited activity of bots during the German federal presidency election in February 2017 (Neudert, Howard, & Kollanyi, 2017a). Overall, however, despite the highly dynamic public discourse on bots and their potential to manipulate the upcoming election, empirical evidence on the use of political bots has remained sparse—which this enquiry seeks to address.

EMPIRICAL EVIDENCE OF THE USE OF SOCIAL BOTS DURING THE PARLIAMENTARY ELECTION

To understand the scope and the strategies of social bots in Germany, a data-driven enquiry on social bot activity was conducted. Building on research results from the German federal presidency election in February 2017, which found limited bot activity across party lines, the German parliamentary election on the 14th of September 2017 was evaluated. For the German federal presidency elections, 984,713 tweets were collected that were generated by 149,573 users between the 1st and 10th of September 2017. An analysis on the levels of automation was conducted, focusing on high-frequency accounts (Table 7.1), with a high level of automation defined as accounts that post at least 50 times a day using the identified hashtags. Though this methodology fails to capture low-frequency tweeting bots, it has been proven successful at detecting bots in various political contexts (Howard et al., 2017b; Howard & Kollanyi, 2016).

Table 7.1 **Twitter Conversation about German Politics Around the Parliamentary Presidency Election, 2017**

	High-Frequency Tweeting about German Politics		
	N of Tweets	*N of Highly Automated Tweets*	*% of Total Within Party*
Neutral election-related	285,185	26,821	9.4
AfD	296,658	44,533	15.0
CDU/CSU	180,046	13,099	7.3
FDP	25,478	2,127	8.3
Bündnis90/Die Grünen	15,705	1,752	11.2
Die Linke	14,751	1,819	12.3
SPD	87,642	6,669	7.6
Total	905,465		100.0

Source: Authors' calculations from data sampled September 1–9, 2017.

Note: Neutral election-related hashtags include: #btw2017, #bundestagswahl, #wahlkampf. AfD hashtags include: #afd, #holdirdeinlandzurück, #gauland. CDU/CSU hashtags include: #angelamerkel, #fedidwgugl, #CDU. FDP hashtags include: #lindner, #denkenwirneu, #fdp. Bündnis90/Die Grünen hashtags include: #grüne, #darumgrün, #diegruenen. Die Linke hashtags include #dielinke, #linke. SPD hashtags include: #martinschulz, #SPD, #zeitfürmartin.

The traffic generated by high-frequency accounts focusing on the German election was not substantial: only 92 such highly automated accounts were identified. These accounts generated a total of 73,012 tweets, that is, about 7.4 percent of all traffic. The results conclude an overall low level of bot-driven automation. During the federal presidency election, similar levels of activity were found with 5.7 percent of all traffic.

Table 7.1 reveals that the traffic generated by high-frequency accounts for the general election–related hashtags, the CDU/CSU, FDP, and SPD, averaged between 7.3 and 9.4 percent. For the AfD-related hashtags, 15 percent of the traffic was automated this way. Bündnis90/Die Grünen and Die Linke saw 11.2 percent and 12.3 percent of automated traffic, respectively. While the right-wing party AfD leads in automated content, Die Linke and Bündnis90/Die Grünen show similar levels of automation.

Due to the low number of bots it was possible to perform a close qualitative analysis of the bot accounts, with some common patterns emerging that revealed strategies and techniques of automation in Germany. German bots were primarily active in retweeting content rather than generating original tweets themselves or engaging in conversation. It stands to reason that more sophisticated conversational bots are not yet employed in the German-language context. Bot accounts revealed curated profiles, displaying symbolic profile pictures of political cartoons, mobilizing self-descriptions, and party slogans. Several accounts were only activated in the summer 2017 prior to the September election, indicating that they were specifically launched for the elections. However, bot accounts of several years in age were also active. Among the bot accounts identified, several of the bots were retweeting and following each other, and several accounts even shared the same profile picture, which indicates some form of coordination. There were both old and new accounts, indicating that some of the accounts might have been generated specifically for the elections.

The overwhelming majority of bot-generated posts supported views on the political right and extreme right of the spectrum. Hateful comments on immigration, xenophobic conspiracy theories, and racist slurs were common themes, as well as support for the right-wing AfD. The nationalist party NPD did not gain prominence. Conversation about the two top candidates for the chancellorship, Angela Merkel and Martin Schulz, often appeared to be negative, using abusive language and hate speech toward both candidates.

MEDIA MULTIPLIERS AND UNREALIZED POTENTIAL

Confirming prior results from the federal presidency election, the empirical analysis of bots in Germany concluded no substantial activity. That is, however, not to give the all-clear on bot-driven computational propaganda. Indeed, there are several reports of targeted bot attacks during pivotal moments of public life, as well bot activity in secret social media groups. Angela Merkel was targeted with bot-generated hate speech messages in response to the 2016 German Christmas market attack (Nicola 2016). There are reports of xenophobic bots manipulating the debate on refugees on popular political Facebook pages (Schulte, 2016). Presumed bot networks have been discovered on Facebook supporting the right-wing AfD and automatically adding users to pro-AfD groups (Bender & Oppong, 2017). The German satire party Die Partei discovered networks of automated Facebook accounts that steered at least 31 pro-AfD groups (Gensing, 2017). Providing evidence from expert interviews, the following section seeks to address gaps in empirical evidence about the use and impact of bots in the German sphere.

An interviewee, who is working as a social media manager at a German legacy publisher, offered a conclusive explanation for the rather unsubstantial bot activity measured empirically. He hypothesized that rather than disseminating specific political messages and engaging in conversation, bots in Germany were mainly involved in manipulating user metrics. By driving likes, shares, and adding users to political interest groups, the pieces of content engaged with appear to gain popularity over social media. This in turn then hacks both human attention, with humans adjusting their own behavior to social information, and algorithmic attention, with algorithms rewarding popular content with increased visibility. Evidently, it seems likely that political bots have entered the German discourse on social media, both out in the open in conversations over public platforms such as Twitter, and also more clandestinely through metric manipulation and activity in secret groups.

Measuring the impacts of bots on public discourse by a quantitative evaluation of their activity over social media neglects the potential effects of follow-up communication and the human retransmission of automated messages. When multiplier figures such as influential figures in public life, like politicians, journalists, and celebrities, engage with automated content, bots are provided with an elevated platform for realizing their potential. When gatekeepers pass along bot-generated messages they not only expand the bots' reach but also provide them with credibility, multiplying their effects. Both German politicians and journalists use social media as a source of information and to detect sentiments among the public (Neuberger, Langenkohl, & Nuernbergk, 2014). German Twitter is especially populated by such opinion leaders, which might create an exceptional opportunity structure for bots to disseminate content (Beuth, 2017). One of our interviewees, who runs a distinguished digital think tank and serves as a technology advisor to the government, assessed the media literacy of German journalists as follows:

German journalists use social media as a source because it is cheap and available, but they often don't understand it. . . . Some of them [the media multipliers] take the social media agenda as reality without further reflection or awareness of manipulation or bias. (Che, personal communication, February 17, 2017)

When asked about the potential future application of bots in Germany, most interviewees highlighted the need for continued detection and vigilance. Sleeping political bot networks often exist undiscovered on social media, remaining either completely inactive or focusing on non-political issues and spamming. Theoretically, these bot networks can be activated to disseminate political content any time. In Germany, one interviewee who has been systematically tracking bots for almost two years reported a number of smaller bot networks whose activity and agendas changed over the course of the period of enquiry. The expert mentioned a network of bots tweeting on American football that later became active tweeting on German political TV debates. Similarly, Nicola (2016) observes that Twitter accounts that were almost exclusively tweeting on Donald Trump suddenly targeted Angela Merkel during the 2016 German Christmas market attacks. These observations serve as a reminder that German bots are highly adaptable. What is more, one participant also claimed to have observed that a bot network she had been tracking had adapted the frequency of their tweets to a number lower than 50 tweets per day, as this threshold was adopted in science and the media. An interviewee who is an expert on digital law and has served as a political advisor to the government on social bots summarized observations on highly flexible and adaptable bot use:

The debate on social bots is a debate about their [future] potential, not about evidence (. . .) That is not to say we shouldn't be cautious. (Azur, personal communication, March 29, 2017)

No substantial commercial market for bots seems to exist within the country, but simple software that operates social bots is readily available online. User accounts that host bot activity can also be obtained online, with 1,000 fake accounts on Twitter and Facebook being offered for between US$45 and US$150, from sellers usually located abroad (Hegelich, 2016). An interviewee who is a cybersecurity expert in academia explained that while Germans are comparatively well equipped with the technological capacities and knowledge needed to build a bot, there were few incentives for commercial bot developing, as Eastern European countries offer them very cheaply, making bots easily accessible with a Google search and a PayPal transaction.

In summary, the research conducted did not find substantial bot activity on German social media or evidence of bot making for political purposes in the run-up to the parliamentary election. While political bots have been found to be active in amplifying opinions, disseminating biased content, and targeting influential politicians with hate speech, these activities remain outliers rather than common patterns. However, targeted automation could potentially be more impactful than widespread activity, when bot-generated messages are amplified by political and journalistic influencers. Both politicians and journalists in Germany are highly reliant on social media as a source of information yet often lack digital competencies, which may make them vulnerable targets for bots.

Findings B: Misinformation and Junk News on German Social Media

Digital misinformation has become so pervasive online that the World Economic Forum already named the concern over the rapid spread of misinformation online among the top 10 perils facing society in 2014 (World Economic Forum, 2014). As junk news, conspiracy theories, and hyper-partisan propaganda left an imprint on the US election, Germany, too, has become a playing field for misinformation, with falsehoods manifesting both at the fringe of the spectrum as well as in the mainstream. High-penetration social media websites like Facebook and Twitter have become important venues for the massive diffusion and consumption of misleading and nonfactual content. They provide users with convenient tools for the creation and mass distribution of propaganda content at low or no cost. Social media content can bypass traditional information gatekeepers, fact-checking mechanisms, journalistic norms, and legal obligations. Social media favors sensationalist content irrespective of whether the content has been fact-checked or is from a reliable source (Alejandro, 2014; Anderson & Caumont, 2014). That in turn encourages less rigorous journalistic practices and the deliberate presentation of misleading or incorrect information as factual in an effort to generate attention (Silverman, 2015). Attention-grabbing presentation and selection logics are not only exploited for journalistic content strategies but also for ideological motives, with both state and nonstate political actors deliberately manipulating and amplifying nonfactual information online.

In response to prominent cases of misinformation in the US elections such as #pizzagate, fake news stories have been under much scrutiny for manipulating public opinion. Fake news websites deliberately publish misleading, deceptive, or incorrect information purporting to be real news for political, economic, or cultural reasons. When fake news content is backed by automation through opaque social media algorithms designed to maximize attention, or political bots promote content through simulating false approval, political actors have a powerful set of tools for computational propaganda (Neudert, Howard, & Kollanyi, 2017). These fake news sites often rely on social media to attract Web traffic and drive engagement, so they do not rank behind in engagement as compared with traditional major news outlets (Silverman & Nardelli, 2017). Both fake news websites and political bots are crucial tools in digital propaganda attacks in many of the same ways. They aim to influence conversations, demobilize opposition, and generate false support, and may serve as an instrument for the perpetuation and amplification of fake news content through widespread diffusion of URLs over social media. Evidently, there is much potential for the deliberate manipulation of public opinion.

EMPIRICAL EVIDENCE OF JUNK NEWS DURING THE PARLIAMENTARY ELECTION

For the tweets collected during the German parliamentary election, we conducted a content analysis of misinformation content on Twitter (Table 7.2). Of the total tweets captured in this sample (see methods section), some 115,563 tweets included links to external content. If Twitter users shared more than one URL in their tweet, only the first URL was analyzed. This approach yielded 11,646 URLs that were then analyzed. Based on a dictionary of classified sources of news and political information from our previous memo on the German federal presidency elections, we were able to automatically classify 88.9 percent of URLs. A random sample of 10 percent of the rest of the tweets containing URLs were drawn and analyzed.

Drawing from data collected during German federal presidency (Neudert, Howard, & Kollanyi, 2017a) and parliamentary elections, a grounded typology of sources of news and information was developed in an iterative process. The unit of analysis was the superordinate host page, rather than the specific content linked. In a first cycle of open coding a "categorized inventory" (Saldana, 2012, p. 12) of sources was produced as a framework. Axial coding in a second and third cycle of coding then resulted in the grounded typology of the sources presented. The method finds its strength in its ability to provide a categorization that is highly contextual and closely connected to the data. Combined with a quantitative assessment of the data, the typology pioneers the methodological assessment of the magnitude of junk news.

The evaluation of sources considered organizational and content-related factors for categorizing the type of source. The strongly institutionalized self-regulation of German media (Hallin & Mancini, 2004) was helpful in classifying

Type of Source	*German Political News and Information on Twitter*			
	N	%	N	%
Professional News Content				
Major News Brands	4,565	97.6		
Minor News Brands	114	2.4		
Subtotal	4,679	100.0	4,679	40.2
Professional Political Content				
Political Party or Candidate	1,047	85.4		
Experts	99	8.1		
Government	80	6.5		
Subtotal	1,226	100.0	1,226	10.5
Other Political News and Information				
Junk News	1,055	32.2		
Other Political	940	28.7		
Citizen or Civil Society	719	21.9		
Humor or Entertainment	378	11.5		
Russia	130	4.0		
Religion	55	1.7		
Subtotal	3,277	100.0	3,277	28.1
Relevant Content Subtotal			9,182	78.8
Other				
Social Media Platform	1,352	66.2		
Other Non-Political	691	33.8		
Subtotal	2,043	100.0	2,043	17.8
Inaccessible				
No Longer Available	294	69.8		
Language	127	30.2		
Subtotal	421	100.0	421	3.6
Total			11,646	100.0

Source: Authors' calculations from data sampled September 1–9, 2017.

Note: General election-related hashtags include: #btw2017, #bundestagswahl, #wahlkampf. AfD hashtags include: #afd, #holdirdeinlandzurück, #gauland. CDU/CSU hashtags include: #angelamerkel, #fedidwgugl, #CDU. FDP hashtags include: #lindner, #denkenwirneu, #fdp. Bündnis90/Die Grünen hashtags include: #grüne, #darumgrün, #diegruenen. Die Linke hashtags include #dielinke, #linke. SPD hashtags include: #martinschulz, #SPD, #zeitfürmartin.

professional news media. The official database of German news media curated by the Bund Deutscher Zeitungsverleger, the committee of German news publishers, was consulted as a reference (BDZV, 2017).

Professional News Content

- **Major News Brands.** This is political news and information by major outlets that display the qualities of professional journalism and commit to the German publicist code of conduct including guidelines of fact-checking and credible standards of production. They provide clear information on authors, editors, publishers, and owners, and the content is clearly produced by an organization with a reputation for professional journalism. The content comes from significant, branded news organizations, including any locally affiliated publications.
- **Minor News Brands.** As above, but this content comes from small news organizations or start-ups that typically reach a smaller audience. These outlets often target a special-interest audience.

Professional Political Content

- **Government.** These links are to websites of branches of government or public agencies.
- **Experts.** This content takes the form of white papers, policy papers, or scholarship from researchers based at universities, think tanks, or other research organizations.
- **Political Party or Candidate**. These links are to official content produced by a political party or candidate campaign.

Other Political News and Information

- **Junk News.** This category includes news publications that present verifiably false content as factual news. This content includes propagandistic, ideologically extreme, hyper-partisan, or conspiracy-oriented news and information. Frequently, attention-grabbing techniques are used, such as lots of pictures, moving images, excessive capitalization, ad hominem attacks, emotionally charged words and pictures, populist generalizations, and logical fallacies. It presents commentary as news.
- **Citizen, Civic, or Civil Society**. This category included links to content produced by independent citizens, civic groups, or civil society organizations, blogs, and websites dedicated to citizen journalism, citizen-generated

petitions, personal activisms, and other forms of civic expression that display originality and creation more than curation or aggregation. There is a clear distinction between commentary and news, and sources of information are frequently linked.

- **Humor and Entertainment.** Content that involves political jokes, sketch comedy, and political art of lifestyle- or entertainment-focused publications.
- Religion: Links to political news and information with distinctly religious themes and faith-based editorializing presented as political news or information.
- **Russia.** This content was produced by known Russian sources of political news and information.
- **Other Political Content.** Myriad of other kinds of political content, including private survey providers, political documentary, or political merchandise.

Other Political News and Information

- **Social Media Platforms.** Links that refer to other public and non-public social media platforms, such as Facebook or Instagram. Public Facebook pages were unwrapped as specified.

Inaccessible Content

- **Language.** Links that led to content in a foreign language that was neither English, German, nor French, when their affiliation could not be verified through reliable sources and databases.
- **No Longer Available.** These links were shared during the sample period, but the content being linked has since been removed. If some evidence from an author or title field, or the text used in a UR code could be attributed to a source, it is.

Table 7.2 presents the findings of this grounded catalogue of content. Overall, 40.2 percent of the political news and information being shared by Twitter users discussing the German election in Germany came from professional news organizations. Links to content produced by government agencies, political parties and candidates, or experts, altogether added up to just 7.4 percent of the total. The ratio of links to professional versus junk news is roughly four to one, which confirms previous results from the federal presidency election. The junk news sources identified can be distinguished from opinionated content in that they present incorrect information as facts, as opposed to opinion. The right-wing, anti-Islam blog Philosphia Perennis (156 shares) leads in shares, followed by the conservative, right-extremist Junge Freiheit (91).

Mirroring the findings from the enquiry on social bots, the majority of the misinformation pages identified were politically right, and xenophobic, nationalist, pro-Pegida, pro-AfD, and Islamophobic content was common. Many of the sources mixed misinformation reporting with content from news agencies such as Reuters and dpa, which were quoted as sources. Only a handful of the sites were comparable to established online media publications in their design and functionality, whereas the majority of outlets resembled blogs and newsfeeds. Emotive language, all-caps, and an emphasis on visual over textual content emerged as indicative of misinformation. The misinformation sources commonly referred to themselves as alternative, unbiased sources of information that provide news against the mainstream and that present content that media and political news elites remain silent about. This communication style, which claims to be an antagonist to elites and a member of "the people," is symptomatic of a populist communication style (Jagers & Walgrave, 2007). A substantial number of outlets displayed indicators of Russian references: the page language could be switched from German to Russian, but not to any other language, and there was Russian advertising.

"FAKEBOOK" AND RUSSIAN REVERBERANCE

With a ratio of information to misinformation of four to one in the German election, the share of misinformation was relatively low compared with findings on misinformation on Twitter during the 2016 US presidential elections, where the ratio was one to one (Howard et al., 2016). The German Twittersphere, however, is populated with politicians, journalists, and highly educated users (Neuberger, Langenkohl, & Nuernbergk, 2014), whereas US Twitter engages a broader public. During elections in the United Kingdom and in France, users shared information and misinformation with a ratio of 4:1 and 11:1, respectively (Neudert, Howard, & Kollanyi, 2017c).

With an estimated user base of more than 25 million monthly active users in Germany, Facebook is a focal point of news consumption and information sharing (Allfacebook, 2018). While communication on the social network is per default private, and Facebook is very restrictive in providing data for research, there is some evidence that misinformation has gained prominence on German Facebook. Silverman and Nardelli (2017) find that the top-performing Merkel stories on Facebook in both English and German are mainly highly critical and misleading articles from fake news and conspiracy pages. Syrian refugee Anas Modamani, who took a selfie with Angela Merkel, unsuccessfully sued Facebook for defamation after fake news stories that accused him of terrorist activities repeatedly popped up on the network and were shared hundreds of times (Eddy, 2017). An interactive map of alleged refugee crimes was circulated widely over the social network (Schöhauer, 2017).

Many of our interview participants, among them journalists and social media managers, stated that they had been subjected to junk news content that was circulated on public pages and in private groups on Facebook. One subject had collected a list of more than 400 such sources. A social media manager from a leading German newspaper observed that junk news and conspiracy content was shared frequently in comments on controversial political posts, alongside hate speech and trolling. She stated that this is a trend that emerged only around 2014, and which has forced many German publishers to disable comments on Facebook as well as on their websites. Indeed, junk news content has become so prevalent to the platform that the German media landscape frequently refers to the platform as "Fakebook" (Beuth, 2016), as interviewees pointed out.

The interviews echoed that the majority of fake news and conspiracy stories are presumed to originate from individuals who see themselves as activists and minor, semi-professional media organizations, a handful of major professional media corporations, or Russian media outlets. Given Russia's role as a global disinformation aggressor, the significant Russian–German diaspora community, and the reverberant influence of Russia from the ex-GDR, Russian influence on the German political sphere appears likely. The quantitative analysis confirmed the evaluations made by interviewees. The majority of the junk news sources identified were attributed to individuals and minor media organizations, whereas about a third of sources were major organizations. Russian content accounted for roughly four percent of all sources. Coordinated political communication from a party, nonstate commercial organization, non-Russian state actors, or military operations was suspected to play a minor role for computational propaganda, if any.

A common pattern in the interviews originated in the assumption that for individual activists and minor organizations, the online sphere serves as a public domain, where they can speak out (anonymously) and connect with like-minded supporters of unpopular, often "politically incorrect" viewpoints. Ideological and cultural motivations dominate rather than economic incentives. What is more, personal discontent and a feeling of discrimination in the overall political system were presumed to be drivers for propagating propaganda. Indeed, right-wing, nationalist content is not a novel phenomenon, but has a longstanding tradition both online and offline, with social media and easy-to-use content tools having expanded the misinformation sphere in Germany. An interview subject, who is the editor-in-chief of a leading digital politics publication and digital expert, summarized this as follows:

> They [the providers of fake news and conspiracy content] are unhappy, often unemployed or somehow excluded from benefits . . . these people see themselves as ideological activists. (Verfassungsschützer, personal communication, February 14, 2017)

Major Russian media corporations such as Russia Today and Sputnik are well established in Germany, as indicated by their significant social media following and Web traffic. They are known for heavily biased, often factually inaccurate reporting that is critical of the German government, Merkel, and the European Union (Kohrs, 2017). However, mirroring the findings of the German intelligence investigation, while this reporting is highly questionable, it is hardly illegal to an extent that would justify censorship or filtering. The most prominent example of Russian misinformation in Germany is arguably "the criminal case of Lisa," the Russian–German girl who claimed to have been kidnapped and raped by migrants in Berlin in January 2016. The German police had evidence that she had made a false statement, but the Russian media accused German officials of hushing up the case and covered the story extensively, claiming the girl had been mistreated and was being held as a sex slave. Eventually, foreign minister Sergey Lawrow repeated the accusations, whereupon the former German foreign minister Frank-Walter Steinmeier cautioned Russia not to politicize the case (McGuinness, 2016). The interviews highlighted that pro-Russian content does not exist in a political vacuum, but that there is a discernible share of the public that agrees with the views propagated. An interview subject reflected:

> In Germany a share of 10 to 15 percent of the population is pro-Russian, skeptical of the US and NATO (. . .) The most vocal, most shrill are often Russian publications (. . .) It is a business model that caters to a pro-Russian, conspiracy milieu. (Verfassungsschützer, personal communication, February 14, 2017)

Responses to Computational Propaganda

Fake news, social bots, and micro-targeting algorithms have triggered much debate on how to control propagandistic, political content and its dissemination mechanisms on the Internet. While journalistically produced content in Germany is subject to strict professional norms and a journalistic duty of care, and is regulated by the law, user-generated content and social media as content platforms largely operate in a legal vacuum, with the exception of the Network Enforcement Act. Social networking sites and search engines with opaque algorithms are thus sometimes perceived as threats to democracy in Germany (Schweiger, 2017); however, the existing framework is often not applicable to digital contexts. That said, regulatory and self-regulatory efforts are increasingly being put into motion in Germany, with three key actors emerging: government and regulators, social networking sites, and civic society.

GOVERNMENT AND REGULATORS: A POLITICIZED SPHERE

In the run-up to the German election in September 2017, social bots and misinformation gained a continuous presence on the political agenda in Germany. All of the major German parties (with the exception of the right-wing AfD) stated publicly that they would refrain from using social bots in elections and strongly condemned such instruments. The Green Party (Die Grünen/Bünndnis 90) demanded a mandatory labeling obligation for bots on social media that would apply to all kinds of Twitterbots, chatbots, and conversational assistants (Göttsche, 2017). The governing party CDU/CSU has proposed a binding obligation for users to register with their real name on social media, but this would violate German law (Braun, 2017).

Regulatory efforts proposed in Germany are increasingly directed at social networking sites, corresponding to vocal public calls for treating such platforms as media companies rather than technology companies. In early January 2017, three German states revived a legislative initiative on digital trespassing that would impose fines on users for breaking the terms and conditions of social networking sites (Reuter, 2017). This measure would effectively criminalize the use of social bots on Facebook, which bans bots in its terms and conditions.

In March 2017, Germany's judiciary minister, Heiko Maas, proposed the Enforcement Act (Netzwerkdurchsetzungsgesetz) that would impose heavy fines of up to 50m Euro on social networking sites if they failed to take down illegal hate speech and fake news content. The Enforcement Act became effective in January 2018, and ever since has been subject to ongoing criticism in politics and the media. Critics fear that the law may have a chilling effect on speech online, privatizes decisions of content deletion without legal oversight, and falls short of providing efficient mechanisms for enforcement (Amann et al., 2016).

When the act was still being debated, an alliance of leading civic society and commercial associations, including Bitkom and D64, warned that such a law would be overbearing and could negatively affect freedom of expression (Beckedahl, 2017). The policy experts we interviewed concurred with this evaluation of German digital policies, pointing out that the regulatory efforts correspond to public concerns about digital political campaigning and manipulation of opinion online, and were highly politicized rather than results-driven. Most experts considered media literacy campaigns as pivotal for countering such issues. An interview subject who is a public digital politics media figure and acclaimed expert summarized this as follows:

> This reminds me of road traffic regulations, where we (the German state) heavily invested into education (. . .) The alternative is abolishing cars. But none would get rid of cars, to prevent accidents. (Verfassungsschützer, personal communication, February 14, 2017)

This statement highlights that regulatory measures in Germany often seek to attend to symptoms rather than underlying structural conditions and fail to effectively create a regulatory framework for the interaction with new technologies.

SOCIAL NETWORKING PLATFORMS: ILL-EQUIPPED SELF-REGULATORS

Social networking platforms increasingly have begun to acknowledge responsibility for the actions on their platforms. After the United States, Germany was the first country in which Facebook rolled out fake news detection tools. During the parliamentary election the company cooperated with the independent German fact-checker *correctiv* to report and flag fake news content (Horn, 2017). In April 2017, Facebook launched a nationwide media literacy campaign on how to detect fake news content. Users were provided with 10 tips for how they could protect themselves from misinformation on the platform. Neither Twitter nor YouTube have undertaken similar efforts in Germany. Mirroring expert opinion in the press, our interviewees agreed that, while social networking platforms acknowledging responsibility was generally commendable, the measures proposed were rarely sufficient. Cutting economic incentives and changing the algorithm to down-rank fake news content lower in the newsfeed were proposed. Furthermore, the legitimacy and capability of platforms as fact-checkers was questioned. A digital policy advisor and former member of the German parliament provided the following critique:

> Leaving the responsibility of deciding on what is true effectively makes Facebook a gatekeeper that does just that—dictate their truth. (Kollegah, personal communication, April 07, 2017)

This statement emphasizes that shifting editorial capabilities to social network operators, both self-regulatory and regulatory, endows these actors with substantial responsibilities whose effects extend beyond the digital sphere. While platforms have rolled out a number of countermeasures in the wake of the #techlash movement, and testimonies by leading tech companies in front of congress, no specific measures for the German sphere were rolled out that were not directly promoted by the Network Enforcement Act.

CIVIL SOCIETY GROUPS AND INSULAR ACTIVISM

The aftermath of the 2016 US presidential campaign resulted in rising civic engagement in relation to misinformation and more policing of right-wing content, and advertising companies have emerged as media watchdogs in Germany. Gerald Hensel from the renowned advertising agency Scholz & Friends called for an advertising boycott of right-wing media. The campaign quickly became highly controversial as it was accused of serving as an instrument of censorship reminiscent of the Nazi boycotts of Jewish businesses (Hanfeld, 2016). Similarly, YouTube found itself at the center of an international advertising boycott against right-wing and extremist content. While the boycott found little public support in Germany, large German brands like Audi and Volkswagen participated (Rentz 2017). Nonprofit watchdog organizations like Mimikama, *correctiv*, and media organizations like the ARD have initiated fact-checking services and have launched fact databases (Bouhs, 2017). Schmalbart, a participatory online initiative that seeks to act as a counterbalance to misinformation and extremist content online, has launched more than 20 civic society projects (Rauschenberger, 2017). The Facebook group #ichbinhier (I am here) has made it its mission to counter hate speech and misinformation with objective, user-generated comments on the platform. Founded in December 2017, the group had <37,000 members at the time of writing (May 2018). While the list of civil society countermeasures in Germany is long and their scope ambitious, they stem from vocal but insular cases and hardly constitute a comprehensive movement.

Conclusion

Brexit and the 2016 US presidential election have spurred a cautious vigilance in relation to the manipulation of opinion in the digital sphere in Germany. Computational propaganda has become a controversially debated issue on the public agenda, with much media and political attention dedicated to its causes, agents, and countermeasures. The debate on computational propaganda itself has become a highly politicized proxy war in response to public concerns. Despite the ongoing debate and political efforts to regulate online manipulation of opinion, there is limited empirical evidence that computational propaganda is a serious problem in Germany. The research conducted concludes that the activity of highly automated bot accounts during the period of study was marginal. While junk news content accounted for some substantial traffic on Twitter, constituting roughly 20 percent of all political news and information on that platform, Germany lies far behind the United States with 50 percent of all traffic, and is on par with the United Kingdom.

Germany has emerged as a cautionary authority on concerns over computational propaganda. While direct threats from computational propaganda have yet to manifest, Germany is an outspoken advocate for preventative and precautionary countermeasures. Regulators and social networks have undertaken vigorous action to counter the causes and effects of computational propaganda. Yet, many of those measures lack legitimacy and suitable enforcement. In addition, experts fear that the approaches implemented or proposed are disproportionate, resulting in chilling effects on freedom of expression and the openness and freedom of the Internet.

Note

1. On methods see Neudert 2017: Fake News, Real Incentives Post-fact content in the transforming digital media system in Germany, unpublished.

References

Alejandro, J. (2014). Journalism in the Age of Social Media. Reuters Institute for the Study of Journalism. March 14, 2014. http://reutersinstitute.politics.ox.ac.uk/publication/journalism-age-social-media.

Allfacebook. (2018). Nutzerzahlen: Facebook, Instagram, Messenger und WhatsApp, Highlights, Umsätze, uvm. (Stand April 2018). allfacebook.de. April 26, 2018. https://allfacebook.de/toll/state-of-facebook.

Amann, M., Knaup, H., Müller, A.-K.,Marcel Rosenbach, M., & Wiedmann-Schmidt, W. (2016). Netzpolitik: Digitale Dreckschleudern. *Der Spiegel*, October 22, 2016. http://www.spiegel. de/spiegel/print/d-147472051.html.

Anderson, M., & Caumont, A. (2014). How Social Media Is Reshaping News. *Pew Research Center* (blog). September 24, 2014. http://www.pewresearch.org/fact-tank/2014/09/24/how-social-media-is-reshaping-news/.

BDZV. (2017). Zeitungswebsites. BDZV. 2017. http://www.bdzv.de/maerkte-und-daten/ digitales/zeitungswebsites/.

Beckedahl, M. (2017). Breites Bündnis Stellt Sich Mit Deklaration Für Die Meinungsfreiheit Gegen Hate-Speech-Gesetz. *Netzpolitik.Org* (blog). April 11, 2017. https://netzpolitik.org/ 2017/breites-buendnis-stellt-sich-mit-deklaration-fuer-die-meinungsfreiheit-gegen-hate-speech-gesetz/.

Bender, J., & Oppong. C. (2017). Digitaler Wahlkampf: Frauke Petry Und Die Bots. *FAZ.NET*. February 7, 2017. http://www.faz.net/aktuell/politik/digitaler-wahlkampf-frauke-petry-und-die-bots-14863763.html.

Beuth, P. (2016). Schluss Mit Fakebook Mark Zuckerberg Will Nun Doch Verstärkt Gegen Falschmeldungen in Seinem Sozialen Netzwerk Vorgehen. Der Facebook-CEO Stellt Mehrere Maßnahmen in Aussicht. *Die Zeit*, November 19, 2016, sec. Digital. http://www. zeit.de/digital/internet/2016-11/facebook-zuckerberg-massnahmen-gegen-fake-news.

Beuth, P. (2017). Heiko Maas: Auf Hass Gezielt, Die Meinungsfreiheit Getroffen. *Die Zeit*, March 16, 2017, sec. Digital. http://www.zeit.de/digital/internet/2017-03/ heiko-maas-gesetzentwurf-soziale-netzwerke-hass-falschnachrichten.

Boczkowski, P. J., & Mitchelstein, E. (2012). How Users Take Advantage of Different Forms of Interactivity on Online News Sites: Clicking, E-Mailing, and Commenting. *Human Communication Research*, 38(1), 1–22. https://doi.org/10.1111/j.1468-2958.2011.01418.x.

Bouhs, D. (2017). "Fake News"-Checker in Deutschland. Retrieved from https://www.ndr. de/fernsehen/sendungen/zapp/medienpolitik/Fake-News-Checker-in-Deutschland-,faktencheck146.html

bpb. (2011a). Geschichte der Kriegspropaganda | bpb. http://www.bpb.de/gesellschaft/medien-und-sport/krieg-in-den-medien/130707/geschichte-der-kriegspropaganda?p=all.

bpb, Bundeszentrale für politische. (2011b). Blick Über Die Mauer: Medien in Der DDR | Bpb. http://www.bpb.de/izpb/7560/blick-ueber-die-mauer-medien-in-der-ddr.

Braun, S. (2017). Netzpolitischer Wochenrückblick KW 4: Und Täglich Grüßt Der Social Bot. *Netzpolitik.Org* (blog). January 29, 2017. https://netzpolitik.org/2017/netzpolitischer-wochenrueckblick-kw-4-und-taeglich-gruesst-der-social-bot/.

Brien, J. (2016). Bundestagswahlkampf 2017: Angela Merkel nimmt Fake-News, Bots und Trolle ins Visier. *t3n News*. https://t3n.de/news/merkel-fake-news-bots-trolle-769925/.

Bright, J. (2016). "The Social News Gap: How News Reading and News Sharing Diverge." *Journal of Communication* 66 (3): 343–365. https://doi.org/10.1111/jcom.12232.

Bundeswahlleiter. (2017). Bundestagswahl 2017: Vorläufiges Ergebnis—Der Bundeswahlleiter. https://www.bundeswahlleiter.de/info/presse/mitteilungen/bundestagswahl-2017/32_ 17_vorlaeufiges_ergebnis.html.

Chandler, A. (2015). The "Worst" German Word of the Year. *The Atlantic*, January 14, 2015. https://www.theatlantic.com/international/archive/2015/01/the-worst-german-word-of-the-year/384493/.

Decker, F., & Lewandowsky, M. (2017). Rechtspopulismus: Erscheinungsformen, Ursachen Und Gegenstrategien | Bpb. http://www.bpb.de/politik/extremismus/rechtspopulismus/ 240089/rechtspopulismus-erscheinungsformen-ursachen-und-gegenstrategien.

Dexter, L. A. (2006). *Elite and Specialized Interviewing*. Colchester, UK: ECPR Press.

Die Zeit. (2016). Soziale Medien: Twitter nennt erstmals Nutzerzahlen für Deutschland. *Die Zeit*, March 21, 2016, sec. Digital. https://www.zeit.de/digital/2016-03/ soziale-medien-twitter-nutzerzahlen-deutschland.

Domainko, A. (2016). Wie computergesteuerte Propaganda Meinungen manipuliert. *sueddeutsche.de*, July 5, 2016, sec. digital. http://www.sueddeutsche.de/digital/internet-und-meinungen-der-bot-der-mich-liebte-1.3064164.

Eddy, M. (2017). How a Refugee's Selfie With Merkel Led to a Facebook Lawsuit. *The New York Times*, February 6, 2017. https://www.nytimes.com/2017/02/06/business/syria-refugee-anas-modamani-germany-facebook.html.

Gathmann, F., &Wittrock, P. (2016). Angebliche Russische Propaganda-Aktionen: Lügen, Gerüchte, Vorwürfe. *Der Spiegel*. http://www.spiegel.de/politik/deutschland/angebliche-russische-propaganda-aktionen-viele-vorwuerfe-wenig-fakten-a-1125494.html.

Gensing, P. (2017). Wahlkampf auf Facebook: "PARTEI" kapert 31 AfD-Gruppen. *tagesschau.de*. http://faktenfinder.tagesschau.de/inland/die-partei-afd-facebook-101.html.

Göttsche, K. (2017). Social Bots: Grüne Fordern Kennzeichnungspflicht. *Computerbild.De.* http://www.computerbild.de/artikel/cb-News-Internet-Social-Bots-Kennzeichnungspflicht-die-Gruenen-17209425.html.

Gries, D. G., & Rainer (Herausgeber). (1996). *Propaganda in Deutschland, Zur Geschichte der politischen Massenbeeinflussung im 20. Jahrhundert.* Darmstadt: Wissenschaftliche Buchgesellschaft Verlag,

Guilbeault, D., & Gorwa, R. (2017). Tinder Nightmares: The Promise and Peril of Political Bots. *WIRED UK*. http://www.wired.co.uk/article/tinder-political-bots-jeremy-corbyn-labour.

Hallin, D. C., & Mancini, P. (2004). *Comparing Media Systems: Three Models of Media and Politics.* Cambridge: Cambridge University Press. https://books.google.de/books?hl=de&lr=&id=PTRIBAAAQBAJ&oi=fnd&pg=PR8&dq=hallin+mancini&ots=3Y5MMgqKlV&sig=Yvn3EeyRT4wtLyQDCQpvbT5Cf5o.

Hammerstein, K. von, Höfner, R., & Rosenbach, M. (2017). March of the Trolls: Right-Wing Activists Take Aim at German Election. *Spiegel Online*, September 13, 2017, sec. International. http://www.spiegel.de/international/germany/trolls-in-germany-right-wing-extremists-stir-internet-hate-a-1166778.html.

Hanfeld, M. (2016). Boykottaufruf gegen "Rechts": Wirb nicht bei den Schmuddelkindern. *Frankfurter Allgemeine Zeitung*, December 15, 2016. http://www.faz.net/aktuell/feuilleton/debatten/scholz-friends-ruft-zum-werbeboykott-gegen-rechts-auf-14576102.html.

Hausding, G. (2017). Deutscher Bundestag—Kampf Gegen Fake News Und Social Bots. *Deutscher Bundestag*. https://www.bundestag.de/presse/hib/2017_01/-/490608.

Hegelich, S. (2016). Social Bots: Invasion Der Meinungsrobotor. http://www.kas.de/wf/de/33.46486/.

Hegelich, S., & Janetzko, D. (2016). Are Social Bots on Twitter Political Actors? Empirical Evidence from a Ukrainian Social Botnet. In *Tenth International AAAI Conference on Web and Social Media*. http://www.aaai.org/ocs/index.php/ICWSM/ICWSM16/paper/view/13015.

Hill, J. (2016). Cologne Attacks Put Spotlight on Germany's N African Migrants. *BBC News*, January 13, 2016, sec. Europe. http://www.bbc.com/news/world-europe-35298224.

Höig, S., & Hasenbrink, U. (2016). *Reuters Institute Digital News Survey 2016—Ergebnisse Für Deutschland.* Hamburg: Hans-Bredow-Verlag.

Horn, V. D. (2017). Facebook Markiert Fake News Jetzt Auch in Deutschland. *Tagesschau.De*. https://www.tagesschau.de/inland/facebook-fakenews-105.html.

Howard, P., & Kollanyi, B. (2016). Bots, #StrongerIn, and #Brexit: Computational Propaganda during the UK–EU Referendum. *ArXiv:1606.06356 [Physics]*, June. http://arxiv.org/abs/1606.06356.

Howard, P., & Woolley, S. (2016). Political Communication, Computational Propaganda, and Autonomous Agents. *International Journal of Communication*.

Howard, P., Woolley, S., & Kollanyi, B. (2016). Bots and Automation over Twitter during the Third U.S. Presidential Debate. *Political Bots* (blog). October 31, 2016. http://politicalbots.org/?p=769.

Howard, P., Bolsover, G., Kollanyi, B., Bradshaw, S., & Neudert, L.-M. (2017a). Junk News and Bots during the U.S. Election: What Were Michigan Voters Sharing Over Twitter? Data Memo 2017.1. Oxford, UK: Project on Computational Propaganda. http://comprop.oii. ox.ac.uk/2017/03/26/junk-news-and-bots-during-the-u-s-election-what-were-michigan-voters-sharing-over-twitter/.

Howard, P., Bolsover, G., Kollanyi, B., Bradshaw, S., & Neudert, L.-M. (2017b). Junk News and Bots during the U.S. Election: What Were Michigan Voters Sharing Over Twitter? Oxford, UK: Project on Computational Propaganda. http://comprop.oii.ox.ac.uk/2017/03/26/junk-news-and-bots-during-the-u-s-election-what-were-michigan-voters-sharing-over-twitter/.

Jagers, J., & Walgrave, S. (2007). Populism as Political Communication Style: An Empirical Study of Political Parties' Discourse in Belgium. *European Journal of Political Research, 46* (3), 319–345.

Jessen, J. (2017). Populismus: Der Hass Auf Die Da Oben. *Die Zeit*, March 5, 2017, sec. Kultur. http://www.zeit.de/2017/08/populismus-eliten-hass-spd-cdu-afd-kritik.

Karnitschnig, M. (2016). Cologne Puts Germany's 'Lying Press' on Defensive. *POLITICO*. January 20, 2016. http://www.politico.eu/article/cologne-puts-germany-lying-media-press-on-defensive-migration-refugees-attacks-sex-assault-nye/.

Kinkartz, S., Werkhäuser, N., & Hille, P. 2018. Martin Schulz: von 100 Prozent auf Null | DW | 09.02.2018. *DW.COM*. http://www.dw.com/de/martin-schulz-von-100-prozent-auf-null/a-42488754.

Klöckner, M.(n. d.) Die Große Meinungsvielfalt in Der Deutschen Presse Ist Geschichte. *Heise Online*. https://www.heise.de/tp/features/Die-grosse-Meinungsvielfalt-in-der-deutschen-Presse-ist-Geschichte-3373110.html.

Kohrs, C. (2017). Russische Propaganda Für Deutsche Zuschauer. *CORRECTIV*. January 4, 2017. https://correctiv.org/recherchen/neue-rechte/artikel/2017/01/04/medien-RT-RTdeutsch-russia-today/.

Kolb, M. (2017). AfD ist stärkste Partei in Sachsen—mit hauchdünnem Vorsprung. *sueddeutsche. de*, September 25, 2017, sec. politik. http://www.sueddeutsche.de/politik/bundestagswahl-afd-ist-staerkste-partei-in-sachsen-mit-hauchduennem-vorsprung-1.3681578.

Kurz, C. (2017). Diskussion Im Bundestag Über Fake News, Fake-Accounts Oder Social Bots. *Netzpolitik.Org* (blog). January 25, 2017. https://netzpolitik.org/2017/jetzt-diskussion-im-bundestag-ueber-fake-news-fake-accounts-oder-social-bots/.

Littig, B. (2008). Interviews with the Elite and with Experts. Are There Any Differences? *Forum Qualitative Sozialforschung / Forum: Qualitative Social Research, 9* (3). https://doi.org/10.17169/fqs-9.3.1000.

Mair, M. (2016). Propaganda-Roboter Als Wahlkampfhelfer: Social Bots in Der Politik. *Tagesschau.De*. https://www.tagesschau.de/multimedia/politikimradio/audio-35929.html.

Mascolo, G. (2017). Geheimdienste: Keine 'Smoking Gun' Aus Russland. *Tagesschau.De*. https://www.tagesschau.de/inland/deutsche-geheimdienste-russland-101.html.

McGuinness, D. (2016). Russia Steps into Berlin 'Rape' Storm Claiming German Cover-Up. *BBC News*, January 27, 2016, sec. Inside Europe Blog. http://www.bbc.com/news/blogs-eu-35413134.

Neuberger, C., Langenkohl, S., & Nuernbergk, C. (2014). *Social Media Und Journalismus*. Landesanstalt für Medien Nordrhein-Westfalen.

Neuberger, C., Langenohl, S., & Nuernbergk. C. (2014). *Social Media Und Journalismus*. Nordrhein-Westfalen: Landesanst. für Medien Nordrhein-Westfalen (LfM). http://www.lfm-nrw.de/fileadmin/lfm-nrw/Publikationen-Download/Social-Media-und-Journalismus-LfM-Doku-Bd-50-web.pdf.

Neudert, L,-M. (2017). Computational Propaganda in Germany: A Cautionary Tale. Oxford, UK: Project on Computational Propaganda. comprop.oii.ox.ac.uk.

Neudert, L-M., Howard, P., & Kollanyi, B. (2017). Junk News and Bots during the German Federal Presidency Election: What Were German Voters Sharing Over Twitter? Oxford, UK: Project on Computational Propaganda. comprop.oii.ox.ac.uk.

Nicola, S. (2016). Web Trolls Are Bombarding Angela Merkel With Abuse After Berlin Attack. *Bloomberg.Com*, December 22, 2016. https://www.bloomberg.com/politics/articles/2016-12-22/merkel-feels-hillary-s-pain-as-web-trolls-bombard-her-with-abuse.

Noworth, M. (2016). Ulrich Wickert: "Medien Haben Ein Falsches Verständnis von Toleranz." http://www.wiwo.de/politik/deutschland/ulrich-wickert-medien-haben-ein-falsches-verstaendnis-von-toleranz/12890660.html.

Qtiesh, A. (2011). Spam Bots Flooding Twitter to Drown Info About #Syria Protests [Updated]. *Global Voices Advocacy* (blog). April 18, 2011. https://advox.globalvoices.org/2011/04/18/spam-bots-flooding-twitter-to-drown-info-about-syria-protests/.

Rauschenberger. (2017). Wir gegen sie. *sueddeutsche.de*, January 16, 2017, sec. medien. http://www.sueddeutsche.de/medien/online-medien-wir-gegen-sie-1.3334911.

Reinemann, C., & Fawzi, N. (2016). Eine Vergebliche Suche Nach Der Lügenpresse. http://www.tagesspiegel.de/politik/analyse-von-langzeitdaten-eine-vergebliche-suche-nach-der-luegenpresse/12870672.html.

Rentz, I. (2017). Umfeldsicherheit Bei Youtube: OWM Unterstreicht Forderung Nach Mehr Brand Safety. *HORIZONT*. http://www.horizont.net/marketing/nachrichten/Youtube-OWM-unterstreicht-Forderungen-nach-mehr-Brand-Safety-156869.

Reuter, M. (2017). Hausfriedensbruch 4.0: Zutritt Für Fake News Und Bots Strengstens Verboten. *Netzpolitik.Org* (blog). January 17, 2017. https://netzpolitik.org/2017/hausfriedensbruch-4-0-zutritt-fuer-fake-news-und-bots-strengstens-verboten/.

Rosenbach, M., & Traufetter, G. (2017). Forderung Zu Meinungsrobotern: Betreiben von Social Bots Soll Unter Strafe Stehen. *Spiegel Online*, January 21, 2017, sec. Netzwelt. http://www.spiegel.de/netzwelt/netzpolitik/social-bots-laender-wollen-gegen-meinungsroboter-im-internet-vorgehen-a-1130937.html.

Rosenberg, Y. (2013). 62 Percent of All Web Traffic Comes from Bots. *The Week*. December 16, 2013. http://theweek.com/articles/454320/62-percent-all-web-traffic-comes-from-bots.

Saldana, J. (2012). *The Coding Manual for Qualitative Researchers*. 2nd edition. Los Angeles: Sage Publications.

Samuel, A. (2015). How Bots Took Over Twitter. *Harvard Business Review.* June 19, 2015. https://hbr.org/2015/06/how-bots-took-over-twitter.

Schöhauer. (2017). Kartenlegen Mit Kriminellen Ausländern. *Übermedien* (blog). January 16, 2017. http://uebermedien.de/11488/kartenlegen-mit-kriminellen-auslaendern/.

Schulte, B. R. (2016). Hasskommentare Gegen Flüchtlinge: Das Problem Der Social Bots. Audio. February 5, 2016. http://www.br.de/radio/b5-aktuell/sendungen/medienmagazin/fluechtlinge-social-bots-102.html.

Schweiger, W. (2017). *Der (Des)Informierte Bürger Im Netz—Wie Soziale Medien Die Meinungsbildung Verändern*. http://www.springer.com/de/book/9783658160579.

Silverman, C. (2015). Lies, Damn Lies, and Viral Content. How News Websites Spread (and Debunk) Online Rumors, Unverified Claims, and Misinformation. *Tow Center for Digital Journalism*.

Silverman, C., & Nardelli, A. (2017). Hyperpartisan Sites and Facebook Pages Are Publishing False Stories and Conspiracy Theories About Angela Merkel. *BuzzFeed*. https://www.buzzfeed.com/albertonardelli/hyperpartisan-sites-and-facebook-pages-are-publishing-false.

Smale, A., & Erlanger, S. (2016). As Obama Exits World Stage, Angela Merkel May Be the Liberal West's Last Defender. *The New York Times*, November 12, 2016. https://www.nytimes.com/2016/11/13/world/europe/germany-merkel-trump-election.html.

Stern, J. (2017). AfD Verzichtet Auf Meinungsroboter—Oder Nicht? Tagesschau.De. April 29, 2017. http://www.tagesschau.de/multimedia/video/video-283363~player.html.

Strathmann, M. (2018). Gegen den Hass im Netz | bpb. https://www.bpb.de/dialog/netzdebatte/264098/gegen-den-hass-im-netz.

Tretbar, C., Salmen, I., Schlegel, M., Portmann, K., & Schulz, J. 2018. Nach 171 Tagen hat Deutschland eine Bundesregierung. *Der Tagesspiegel Online*, March 14, 2018. https://www.tagesspiegel.de/politik/wahl-der-bundeskanzlerin-nach-171-tagen-hat-deutschland-eine-bundesregierung/21068952.html.

University of Würzburg, ed. (2017). *Tenor Medienvertrauen.* http://www.wiwi.uni-wuerzburg.de/lehrstuhl/professur_fuer_wirtschaftsjournalismus/medienvertrauen/.

Woolley, S C., & Howard, P. N. (2016). Automation, Algorithms, and Politics| Political Communication, Computational Propaganda, and Autonomous Agents—Introduction. *International Journal of Communication, 10,* 9.

World Economic Forum. (2014). 10. The Rapid Spread of Misinformation Online. *Outlook on the Global Agenda 2014* (blog). http://wef.ch/GJAfq6.

8

United States

Manufacturing Consensus Online

SAMUEL C. WOOLLEY AND DOUGLAS GUILBEAULT

Introduction

Political campaigns, candidates, and supporters have made use of bots in attempts to manipulate public opinion in the United States for almost a decade. The role of bots during the 2016 election, as tools for spreading disinformation, attacking users, and amplifying perspectives, has been much discussed in recent news media. This chapter seeks to build an understanding of the role of bots during this pivotal event. It focuses on bots as a tool for the proliferation of computational propaganda, best defined as the assemblage of social media platforms, autonomous agents, and big data tasked with the manipulation of public opinion.

This chapter seeks to fill crucial gaps in our understanding of how political bots, and computational propaganda in general, are shaping the political landscape in the United States, with global consequences. It reviews the history of bot interference in US politics, and focuses on the use of bots to influence the recent 2016 US election. The chapter is divided into two parts. The first part reports the results of nine months of ethnographic fieldwork on the campaign trail, including interviews with bot makers, digital campaign strategists, security consultants, campaign staff, and party officials. This on-the-ground investigation revealed that campaigners, citizens, and government representatives tell surprisingly inconsistent stories about the use of bots and their capacity to influence political processes. The second part provides a quantitative response to the question of whether bots were able to influence the flow of political information over Twitter during the election. Drawing on a dataset of over 17 million tweets, we show how bots were able to reach central positions of measurable influence within retweet networks during the US election. In the final section, we discuss the combined implications of our investigations, with particular concern for the policy implications surrounding the rising culture of computational propaganda in the United States and abroad.

When the political problem of bots is articulated effectively, concrete analyses can be undertaken to enrich qualitative reports about how bots shape the landscape of power and propaganda. In this chapter, we frame the problem of bot influence as a problem of how they influenced the informational dynamics of political discussion over Twitter. The mixed-methods approach we use provides a unique perspective on the role of bots in US politics. Ethnographic investigations expose the extent to which bots are nested within a complex system of political institutions and actors, with competing interests and conflicting stories. One of the most important observations to draw from this analysis is that, behind the scenes, bots have become an acceptable tool of campaigners and are a prime example of the new augmented age of computational propaganda. On the other hand, bots hold the promise of democratizing propaganda by taking it out of the hands of the elites and allowing citizens to spread their messages and boost their own voices via the megaphone effect. So far, however, bots have primarily been used to spread extremists' views in uncritical allegiance to dominant candidates, raising vital concerns about the use of bots to achieve what we call "manufactured consensus"—or the use of bots in creating the illusion of popularity for a candidate who might otherwise be on the political fringes.

While digital strategists and other technically savvy supporters have revealed that they use social media bots in attempts to change people's perspectives, they often did not know whether or not they actually drove people to consume information differently. The network analysis in this chapter reveals that bots did indeed have an effect over the flow of information among human users. The aim of the network analysis was to observe whether bots infiltrated the core of the discussion network over Twitter and thus the upper echelons of influence. The finding was yes—bots did infiltrate the upper cores of influence, and were thus in a position to significantly influence digital communications during the 2016 US election.

An Ethnographic Investigation of Bots and Campaigns in 2016

Halfway through nine months of fieldwork on the 2016 US presidential campaign trail, a light-bulb moment occurred. Cassidy, a digital strategist who did contract work for the Trump campaign, used the language of communication scholars to explain the unlikely political ascendance of Donald Trump. He brought up agenda setting, a theory which suggests that the more often something comes up in the media, the more likely the public is to consider it important (McCombs, Shaw, & Weaver, 1997). Agenda setting is generally about power, specifically the power of the media to define the significance of information.

Cassidy said that the Trump campaign turned the concept on its head. He said, "Trump's goal from the beginning of his candidacy has been to set the agenda of the media. His strategy is to keep things moving so fast, to talk so loudly— literally and metaphorically—that the media, and the people, can't keep up" (Cassidy, personal communication, November 2016). Cassidy made it clear that Trump's campaign wanted to create scenarios wherein the media couldn't resist covering him. Cassidy said that this was a conscious strategy. Trump inverted, or perhaps twisted, the typical structure of agenda setting. Cassidy argued that the candidate's fast-paced rhetoric and willingness to speak "off the cuff" gave an impression of authenticity that demanded attention. By defying expectations for what a presidential candidate should say and do, and doing so constantly, he set the media's agenda which in turn set the public's. As a report from the Harvard Shorenstein Center on Media, Politics, and Public Policy put it:

> Overall, Trump received 15 percent more coverage than [Clinton] did. Trump also had more opportunities to define Clinton than she had to define him. When a candidate was seen in the news talking about Clinton, the voice was typically Trump's and not hers. Yet when the talk was about Trump, he was again more likely to be the voice behind the message. "Lock her up" and "make America great again" were heard more often in the news than "he's unqualified" and "stronger together." (Patterson, 2016)

According to Cassidy and other digital strategists, candidates and campaigns are tirelessly working to stay up to date on a variety of evolving digital campaigning tools. Strategists associated with both the Republican and the Democratic campaigns said that interactive advertisements, live-streamed video, memes, and personalized messaging all played a role in the spread of partisan content during the 2016 election. According to the campaign officials, consultants and party employees have the tacit goal of using these tools to affect voter turnout. However, informants said that these tools were also used to achieve other, less conventional, goals: to sow confusion, to give a false impression of online support, to attack and defame the opposition, and to spread illegitimate news reports.

One tool has risen to prominence among those used to achieve these latter aims, that is, to spread propaganda online. That tool is the political bot. Previous research shows that political candidates and campaigns in the United States and abroad have made use of these automated software devices in attempts to manipulate public opinion on social media (Ratkiewicz et al., 2011; Woolley, 2016). The 2016 US election, however, was a watershed moment for the use of political bots and computational propaganda. Research from several sources suggests that political bot usage was at an all-time high during key moments of this particular election (Bessi & Ferrara, 2016; Howard et al., 2016; Ferrara et al., 2016).

CAMPAIGN FIELDWORK

The goal of this qualitative work is to study the ways in which political parties and their campaigns used digital media, bots, and automation during the 2016 US presidential election. This was achieved using a combination of field research methods. Observation, interview, participation, and process tracing were used from the beginning of February 2016, ending in the weeks after the election that November—a total of approximately ten months of material used to build understandings of the campaigns and their digital maneuvers. Time in the field was motivated by a desire to create a diagnostic, humanized view of the way in which people affiliated with the parties made use of bots.

This project aims to build a comprehensive understanding of digital campaign methods for communicating information. Particular interest is given to communication methods that make use of computational tools (automation, algorithmic design) and that attempt, often subtly, to manipulate public opinion. These efforts are part of spreading computational propaganda. Tools for dissemination and obfuscation, such as political bots, are of central interest to this research. But so are the strategies that these tools helped realize: the spread of false news reports, "shitposts" (highly negative memes), and attacks on journalists.

In order to understand where these tactics and tools originated, time was spent in several states during the primaries, and also at campaign gatherings, at digital strategy workshops, and at party nominees' home turf events in New York City. This allowed us to gain a sense of the culture of the campaigns through what Clifford Geertz (1973) called "deep hanging out." Participant observation formed a portion of this work. It began with spending time meeting people, volunteering, and learning about the structure of the campaign apparatus. This helped to gain access beyond the hordes of volunteers and to get in touch with those in the know about digital strategy who had the ability to make assertions about party and campaign strategy.

One part of this process involved volunteering and interacting with the campaigns: using applications like MiniVan to canvas for Bernie, knocking on doors in NYC's Chinatown and the Bowery, making calls and sending texts in Detroit for Clinton, and even hanging out with campaign folks at the preemptive

Michigan primary "victory" party that turned out to be a shocking precursor for the later electoral loss in that state. It meant corresponding with people working for the Trump campaign, going to their campaign headquarters—and being turned away—twice, and talking to crowds of red-cap-wearing supporters at various rallies. During the New York Republican primary, this also included attending a very sparse meet-up at a Chelsea tech store organized by a relatively unknown digital firm working for Ted Cruz. The company's chief data scientist and director of sales outlined, in deep detail, the firm's work in "behavioral analytics." The firm would turn up later in the campaign, and in many sensational media stories, when it began deploying its alleged "psychographic" digital tactics for the Trump campaign—known by the now familiar name Cambridge Analytica.

Other ways of staying up to date involved signing up for every mailer from the campaigns, following the candidates on social media, and religiously scouring digital messages and metadata. This led to familiarity with the regular re-tweeters and likers—especially those that showed signs of automation. Here, data gathering consisted of taking screen shots of public content and writing descriptive memos about what they showed. These, and other field notes, were stored using Zotero and organized with Microsoft Excel. It is worth noting that political bots are often short-lived. They either fulfill their task and are then taken down by their deployers to avoid a trail, or they are deleted by social media platforms because they violate terms of service when they show signs of spamming or of being used to harass other users. Several snapshots of these bots are included here to demonstrate particular tactics and types, but also to preserve now nonexistent automated accounts.

Important campaign events and important moments that could not be attended were followed online. News reports, community documents, and archived social media material were used to build further understandings of such events. All media reports on bots and US politics were captured using Zotero. Reflective accounts, through one-on-one interview, were gathered from experts who had been in attendance or who had worked with or for the campaigns. Contradictions in stories about how events played out, or about how automation or other social media tools were used, regularly occurred. This was a highly contested, and strategically ruthless, campaign. Parties and campaigns, and even factions who worked within them, disagreed about how things happened—and about what truth looked like. Cross-referencing and online research allowed for clarity when discrepancies in accounts arose. When possible, these contradictions are preserved rather than simplified, demonstrating the wide range of perspectives about the truth—especially as it relates to the use of bots in politics.

AGENDA SETTING AND THE CAMPAIGN

In writing their theory of agenda setting, McCombs and Shaw (1972) wrote specifically about the media's ability to guide voters through the information provided during the 1968 presidential campaign. The prescient and popular line from Cohen succinctly explains the role of the media in prioritizing information: the press "may not be successful much of the time in telling people what to think, but it is stunningly successful in telling its readers what to think about" (Cohen, 1963). McCombs and Shaw argue that during a heavily contested election, like the ones in 1968 and 2016, the power of the press to shape public attention is significant. They write that "the data suggest a very strong relationship between the emphasis placed on different campaign issues by the media (reflecting to a considerable degree the emphasis by candidates) and the judgment of voters as to the salience and importance of various campaign topics" (p. 181).

The question that arises is: who decides what the media reports on? The traditional answer from the discipline of communication is gatekeepers, editors, editorial boards, and the like. But during an election like the one in 2016, where the traditional campaign playbook is thrown out by one candidate, thus causing that candidate to draw extraordinary attention, that candidate gains a notable amount of power in driving media coverage.

Traditional media's willingness to cover Trump for free and to put him at the center of the presidential conversation was one part of his success. Another major portion, however, can be attributed to the way in which he and his supporters used social media. Twitter proved a crucial tool for Trump, a soapbox that bypassed gatekeepers and allowed him to circulate content regardless of form. This content was then legitimized by constant coverage by major TV news channels, national radio programs, and a new media tool—hordes of political bots, that is, automated social media accounts built to look like real users and used to artificially boost content.

Armies of bots allowed campaigns, candidates, and supporters to achieve two key things during the 2016 election: (1) to manufacture consensus and (2) to democratize online propaganda. Social media bots manufacture consensus by artificially amplifying traffic around a political candidate or issue. Armies of bots built to follow, retweet, or like a candidate's content make that candidate seem more legitimate, and more widely supported, than they actually are. This theoretically has the effect of galvanizing political support where this might not previously have happened. To put it simply: the illusion of online support for a candidate can spur *actual* support through a bandwagon effect. Trump put Twitter center stage in this election, and voters paid attention. As the *New York Times* put it, "For election day influence, Twitter ruled social media" (Isaac & Ember, 2016).

Political bots also made it possible for average citizens, people well outside of Washington or the professional campaign apparatuses, to amplify their own viewpoints online. The reach and sheer numerical strength of Twitterbots allowed anyone with some coding knowledge, or connections to groups using automation software, to create their own propaganda network. The question of whether campaigns themselves used political bots to spread "fake news" was, and continues to be, a smoking-gun issue in US politics. However, the democratization of online propaganda is also an especially salient issue. While government departments, academics, and journalists continue to search for evidence that campaigns used these means to manipulate public opinion, they tend to ignore the fact that anyone can launch a bot or spread fake news online. It was these citizen-built bots that probably accounted for the largest spread of propaganda, false information, and political attacks during the 2016 election.

According to many of the people interviewed for this chapter, including political bot makers and campaign personnel, the goals of bot-driven tactics are manifold: to create a bandwagon effect, to build fake social media trends by automatically spreading hashtags, and even to suppress the opinions of the opposition. Bots allow for the democratization of digital propaganda because they make it possible for one person or group to massively enhance their presence online. Open APIs, and laissez-faire approaches to automation on sites such as Twitter, allow regular people to deploy their opinions *en masse*. As one bot builder stated: if one person operating one profile can automate their profile to tweet every minute, just think what one person running one thousand automated profiles can do.

THE MEDIA AND THE CAMPAIGN

In order to understand the success of the Trump campaign's media strategy, it is useful to look to the early days of the campaign. In January 2016, Trump began gaining traction as a viable Republican candidate for the presidency. In an opinion article for the *New York Times* written that same month, Peter Wehner, a senior fellow at the conservative Ethics and Public Policy Center and employee of three Republican presidents, said he would never vote for Trump. He summed up the fears of the growing "Never Trump" movement taking hold within the Republican Party when he said that "no major presidential candidate has ever been quite as disdainful of knowledge, as indifferent to facts, as untroubled by his own benightedness" (Wehner, 2016).

Informants, including people who had done digital work for Republican presidential and senatorial candidates, saw Trump as a "loose cannon" willing to say and do anything. They echoed Wehner's concerns about his lack of military or government experience. So did key members of the Republican establishment.

Mitt Romney, the 2012 Republican presidential candidate, gave a speech in which he said: "Dishonesty is Donald Trump's hallmark . . . He's not of the temperament of the kind of stable, thoughtful, person we need as a leader. His imagination must not be married to real power" (Associated Press, 2016). Romney and his compatriots argued that it was only a matter of time before Trump did something so off-color that he would be drummed out of the race, but nothing seemed to be able to touch him. Media storms about Trump mimicking a disabled *New York Times* reporter, impugning Senator John McCain's war record, and harassing women did not stick. Any one of these stories might have undone another candidate. Suddenly, however, Trump would say or do something else and a misstep would be forgotten in the next day's media cycle.

Then, of course, Trump won the presidency.

Experts from every quarter have since weighed in on what caused the Trump win. Communication scholars have suggested it has to do with the fact that, despite his disregard for traditional advertising and what his supporters have derisively deemed "the mainstream media," he received far more media attention than any other candidate. According to MediaQuant, a firm that tracks media coverage of candidates, Trump received nearly five billion dollars' worth of free media attention compared to Clinton's three million (Harris, 2016). Scholars have also noted that the Trump campaign was innovative in its use of social media (Albright, 2016a; Beckett, 2016). An article in *Wired* magazine went as far as to say that sites like Facebook and Twitter won Trump the presidency (Lapowsky, 2016). The same article noted that "social media was Trump's primary communication channel." In a conversation with CBS's *60 Minutes* (2016), Trump himself said that Twitter and Facebook were key to his victory.

The numbers from the Wesleyan Media Project's (Franklin Fowler et al., 2017) report on campaign spending suggest that, as with the polls, the metrics by which advertising agencies seek insight into political wins proved to be misleading when it came to an actual outcome. Television advertising seemed to have very little bearing on success: Clinton spent $258 million to Trump's $100 million. On local cable, Trump had less than a one percent market share. Clinton even dominated digital ads (desktop, display, pre-roll) and had a 73 percent share of nationally focused digital ads, with Trump at only 27 percent.

Social media's affordances for democratizing communication and organization have long been discussed by scholars concerned with politics and the media (Benkler, 2006; Howard & Hussain, 2013; Owen, 2015). More recently, there has been a normalizing pattern on sites like Facebook and Twitter. That is, political elites have figured out how to harness social media to exert power and control (Karpf, 2012). Donald Trump used one digital tool in particular to circumvent the need for traditional political advertising. That tool was Twitter.

As one informant, a conservative social media expert named Clint, put it: "Trump used Twitter as a megaphone, as a tool to get his campaign message heard above all others" (Clint, personal communication, April 2016). However, suggesting that the Trump campaign's success in harnessing social media, an emergent version of political normalization, or the elite use of technology to manipulate public online won him the presidency is off the mark. In fact, a somewhat oppositional phenomenon, the democratization of propaganda, was also key to his success. Together, the campaign's creative use of social media and supporters' use of large-scale social automation allowed the agenda of the media to be set in favor of Trump.

THE MEGAPHONE EFFECT

Discussions about the Trump campaign's attempts to speak over all other news—what Clint called "megaphoning"—became a clear theme in interviews. For instance, another research informant, Al, echoed Clint's claims of this amplified communication tactic. Al was and is a high-ranking member of the Republican Party apparatus. Al explained that the campaigns he had worked on treated "digital" (online marketing) like the "Wild West." He said, "Anything goes as long as your candidate is getting the most attention."

Generally speaking, social media bots play a fairly heavy-handed role in amplifying political messages. The idea behind political botnets is one of numbers: if one account makes a splash with a message, then 1,000 bot-driven accounts make a flood. Armies of bots pretending to be human, what some call "sock-puppet accounts," computationally and automatically extend the ability of the deploying party to spread messages on sites like Twitter. Political botnets, large networked collections of bots, are no exception. During the 2016 election, numerous occurrences of bots were catalogued as being used to drive up traffic around a particular event or idea.

For instance, at the height of Pizzagate, the conspiracy that linked the Clinton campaign to an alleged human trafficking and child abuse ring, automated shell accounts rampantly spread memes putting Clinton campaign Chair John Podesta and the candidate herself at the center of the fabricated controversy. A disproportionate number of the accounts generating traffic on Pizzagate appeared to originate in Cyprus, the Czech Republic, and Vietnam (Albright, 2016b). According to the *Washington Post*, "[A]s the bots joined ordinary Twitter users in pushing out Pizzagate-related rumors, the notion spread like wildfire" (Fisher et al., 2017). Pro-Clinton bots also spread attacks on Donald Trump, though they were about a fifth as active as the pro-Trump bots during key election events (Howard et al., 2016).

One example of bots amplifying political messages during the campaign stands out. In April 2016, conservative political strategist Patrick Ruffini, webmaster of the 2004 Bush/Cheney campaign and former eCampaign Director of the RNC, sent out a series of tweets suggesting that bots were being used to attack Ted Cruz. The *Daily Caller* and the *National Review* quickly picked up the story, both suggesting that the bots were potentially part of a broader network of "fake" Trump Twitter traffic. Ruffini made a spreadsheet of nearly 500 allegedly automated accounts, many of which were deleted or became inactive just after he publicly shared the list. Most of the accounts in the document had no followers, copied one another's messages, and sent out advertisements alongside political content. Ruffini found that they were also being used to support the Trump campaign. The strategist noted that the bots sent out 400,000 messages about Trump, and nearly 2 million tweets in total, over the course of a month. The same accounts retweeted Dan Scavino, Trump's social media director, nearly 15,000 times.

Ruffini's main issue with the accounts was that they were urging those who had received Ted Cruz campaign robocalls to report him to the Federal Communications Commission for violating political media regulations. In a twist of irony, a group of automated Twitter accounts were being deployed to mobilize voters against automated campaign phone calls. The novel tactic of using bots to make assertions about campaign law had not been seen in two previous years of research about political bot use in other countries. Also interesting was the fact that this was a group of pro-Trump Republican bots being used to attack Ted Cruz, another Republican. In an interview with *Politico*, Ruffini said, "A lot of these unsavory tactics that you would see in international elections are being imported to the US." He also noted that "there is very clearly now a very conscious strategy to try to delegitimize opposition to Trump" (Schreckinger, 2016).

Ruffini's allegations, and his efforts to catalogue information about the accounts in question, provided a reason for further examination of party-focused or candidate-focused bots. There is evidence that US political actors have previously used bots in attempts to manipulate public opinion (Ratkiewicz et al., 2011; Metaxas & Mustafaraj, 2012). During the 2012 election cycle, Mitt Romney's campaign was accused of buying thousands of followers on Twitter in a bid to seem more popular (Coldewey, 2012). In 2010, researchers discovered a botnet purpose built to attack Martha Coakley, the former Massachusetts attorney general, by alleging she was anti-Catholic (Mustafaraj & Metaxas, 2010). At the time, Coakley was in a tight race with Scott Brown in the special election to fill Ted Kennedy's senate seat. Brown eventually won the race. In these cases, bots were used to support US political candidates, and even to attack the opposition. Was this a common campaign tactic, however?

The same week that the anti-Cruz botnet was launched, contact was made with a well-placed member of the Republican Party. The informant, Jane, had worked on several high profile political campaigns and was, at the time, employed by the Republican National Committee. When asked if she had seen campaigns use social media bots before, she answered bluntly, "Yes, absolutely. It's a common tactic, in both presidential campaigns and lower down the ladder" (Jane, personal communication, May 2016). She was, however, skeptical that using bots to boost candidates was actually effective. In fact, Jane said that doing so was, in her opinion, a waste of money and more a distraction than a benefit. She said, "[L]ikes and retweets don't equal votes." That said, she claimed that in her experience digital teams treated online strategy in a fairly ad hoc way. "We will throw anything against the wall and see what sticks," Jane said. "Bots are one tactic among many, and they aren't illegal."

There are two clear take-away points from the interview with Jane. The first is that, despite her own ambivalence about the efficacy of political bots, she openly admitted that bots were regularly used in campaigns at all levels of governance. Second, she was emphatic that digital campaign teams, again at all levels, commonly made use of a variety of tactics and treated the online space as a frontier for testing new marketing methods. This picture, one of experimentation and spontaneity, stands in stark contrast to the one painted later in the campaign by groups like Cambridge Analytica. Jane was not alone in this assessment; several other informants who worked in digital campaign contracting echoed her skepticism. Some went further, saying that claims of psychographic or psychometric targeting were largely exaggerated and that it was clear campaign messages and boots on the ground that led to votes, not fancy computational tactics.

However, it is a straw-man argument to denounce the political influence of digital tactics simply because a direct line cannot be drawn between social media activity and votes. First of all, some researchers have indeed made an effort to draw this line, and the results are increasingly exposing the influence of social media, and bots in particular (Bessi & Ferrara, 2016; Howard et al., 2016). Social media and automated agents of propaganda are part of much broader sociopolitical systems. These systems contain a vast diversity of actors, interests, techniques, and mechanisms of power. A more suitable question regarding the importance of bots is, do they have the capacity to influence the flow of political information over social media? The answer is important because this type of influence can make downstream contributions to a slew of political behaviors, including voting. Framed with this in mind, bots are a growing threat to American democracy, especially given that more than 60 percent of Americans now rely on social media for their political discussion (Gottfried & Shearer, 2016). If it can be shown that bots influence political discussion online, it becomes tenuous to view social media websites as neutral public spheres for the democratic market-place of ideas.

Modeling the influence of bots on real political processes has been a challenge. There have been efforts to use experimental methods to show how bots can influence Twitter discourse. For example, Messias et al. (2013) show that designing Twitterbots on the basis of simple feedback principles can enable them to reach positions of measurable influence. However, Messias et al. (2013) base their measures of influence on ready-made software packages such as Klout and Twitalyzer, which do not publicly reveal their methods for calculating influence. Mønsted et al. (2017) further demonstrate that networks of Twitterbots can be used to seed the spread of norms and misinformation, which spread in a complex, contagious fashion. Such methods establish the potential for bots to influence political discussion online. To understand how bots influenced specific political events of interest—in this case, the recent 2016 US election—it is important to focus analyses on data from this time period.

In order to study bots in actual Twitter networks, there have been efforts to automate bot detection. Some detection software can classify bots that deviate strongly from normal users in terms of click rate, message frequency, and time of operation (Ratkiewicz et al., 2011). Other software systems use network structure to detect bots. The Truthy team combined these detection methods into a machine-learning ensemble they recently made accessible as a public API (Davis et al., 2016). Using this classifier, Bessi and Ferrara (2016) found that almost one-fifth of Twitter discussion during the election was likely to come from bots. While these studies use network structures to distinguish between human and bot accounts, they have yet to undertake detailed analysis of the network influence that bots achieve within specific political events of interest, such as the recent US election.

Using the public API designed by Truthy, the second part of this chapter provides a transparent network analysis of the role of Twitterbots during the 2016 US election. As such, the goal is to provide a clear answer to the question of whether bots were capable of influencing the political discussion during the US election. The answer, as our results reveal, is yes.

A Network Analysis of Twitterbots During the 2016 Election

The data consists of approximately 4 million unique tweets, collected from November 1 to November 11, 2016. The election was on November 8, 2016. The data was collected using the Twitter streaming API, which provides access

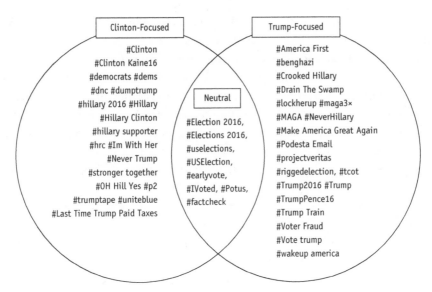

Figure 8.1 Political Valence of Hashtags Source: Authors' construction.

to one percent of the Twittersphere, tailored to the hashtags used to collect the data. In this way, the specific tweets collected using these hashtags are randomly filtered through the API. Hashtags were selected to provide a balance of Trump-related and Clinton-related data and to facilitate comparisons. Figure 8.1 is a display of the hashtags used during data collection. Hashtags highlighted on the left represent those associated with Clinton; those on the right are associated with Trump; and black hashtags are neutral.

BOT OR NOT?

The analysis procedure described in this chapter relies on three steps. First, we collected data from the Twitter streaming and rest API. Then, to classify bots, we ran this data through the BotOrNot API, which is a machine-learning ensemble for classifying bots that the Truthy team designed (Davis et al., 2016). Once our sample was classified, we constructed networks of retweeting among users to assess whether bots achieved influence over the flow of information during the 2016 US election. Each of these steps is discussed in detail below.

CLASSIFYING USERS

For our analysis, we extracted 1,991,748 unique retweets among 775,871 unique users, where we classified both the source and target of each retweet for whether they were likely to be a bot. We classified bots using the following three steps. First, we collected data from the Twitter streaming API. Then, to classify accounts as human or bot, we ran the profile data and 200 most recent tweets associated with each account through the BotOrNot API. The BotOrNot algorithm is the state-of-the-art in bot classification, as demonstrated by its recent adoption of large-scale analyses of Twitter focusing on the spread of false news (Vosoughi, Roy, & Aral, 2018). The BotOrNot system uses Twitter's rest API to obtain each account's recent history, including recent tweets from that account as well as mentions of that screen name. BotOrNot then processes the bot-likelihood score using the classification algorithm described below (see Davis et al., 2016).

BotOrNot recruits more than 1,000 statistical features using available metadata and information extracted from the social interactions and linguistic content. It groups its classification features into six main classes: features that concern user data, network structure, friend-based measures, temporal dynamics, and linguistic content. BotOrNot's classifier uses Random Forest, an ensemble supervised learning method that optimizes for feature selection by aggregating information across randomly generated classification trees. The features described above are used to train seven different classifiers: one for each subclass of features and one for the overall score. When the ensemble was originally tested, it performed with over 80 percent accuracy based on hand-coded and verified training data on both bot and human accounts (Davis et al., 2016). The BotOrNot ensemble scores accounts on a scale from 0 to 1, where scores closer to 1 indicate that an account is closer to being a bot.

A limitation in all methods of automated bot detection is that without back-end information owned and undisclosed by Twitter, it is impossible to have "ground truth" that a given account is a bot or a human (Guilbeault, 2016; Gorwa & Guilbeault, 2018). For this reason, the application of the BotOrNot algorithm to new data is best understood as detecting accounts that show strong signs of automated activity, rather than accounts that are bona fide bots. This can be viewed as its own strength, given that political actors often avoid bot detection by having humans intermittently operate their bot accounts so as to exhibit normal user behavior. Furthermore, automated bot detection using the rest API can only classify users whose accounts still exist. Bots are most affected by this, because bot accounts are more likely to be removed or deleted after the sampling period. A large number of participants also block their accounts from the rest API, further restricting analysis. The BotOrNot ensemble often categorizes organizational accounts, like @BarackObama, as bot accounts—and not always incorrectly, as these accounts regularly use software to automate responses. Lastly, the BotOrNot classifier was trained on mostly English-language tweets, so it is best suited to detecting bots that tweet in English. Since our data consists solely of English tweets, this bias was not an issue for this study. Due to these limitations, we supplemented BotOrNot's output by manually verifying that a random selection of accounts ranked as bots showed hallmark signs of automated activity.

After classifying all the accounts in our sample, we applied three metrics to measure the influence of automated accounts in retweet networks of human users. All retweet networks in this study were built by extracting the largest connected component, which refers to the largest continuous web of connections among users where every user has at least one connection. The networks used in our k-core decomposition were undirected and symmetric, which means that ties reflected the number of times that users mutually retweeted each other. The networks used to score between centrality and degree centrality were directed and thus asymmetric, where our measures accounted for differences between the number of users retweeting a given account and the number of users that given account retweeted. These directed networks allowed us to measure centrality in terms of positions in the network that mediated the flow of retweeted information between other users.

A BRIEF PRIMER ON NETWORK ANALYSIS

A network consists of a set of nodes (otherwise called vertices) and connections (otherwise called edges). The nodes and connections are defined with respect to the kind of network being built. In this chapter, we model the retweet network between users, where users represent the nodes and connections represent retweeting. Networks can be either directed or undirected. In the case of retweet networks, directed networks draw an edge between two users (nodes)—A and B—if A retweets B. In this chapter, undirected networks draw a connection between users if they have both retweeted each other. For a visualization, see Figure 8.2.

Network analysis consists of mathematical and statistical tools for examining the geometry and dynamics of connections within a network. One key measure concerns the degree of a node, which refers to the number of connections possessed by that node. For directed networks, it is possible to examine indegree (number of incoming connections) and outdegree (number of outgoing connections) separately. In the case of retweeting, indegree captures the number of people who retweeted a given user, and outdegree captures the number of people whom a given user retweeted. Network analysis also supplies methods for analyzing network influence, where influential nodes are more important for connecting others and controlling the flow of information. We deploy two methods for characterizing bot influence: k-core decomposition and

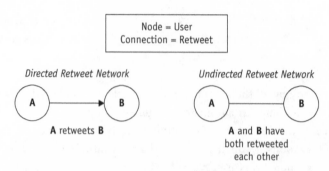

Figure 8.2 Building Blocks of Retweet Networks. Source: Authors' construction.

betweenness centrality. As is standard in network analysis, all retweet networks in this chapter are built by extracting the largest connected component, which refers to the largest continuous web of connections among users where every user has at least one connection in the network. Many of the measures we deploy require the object of analysis to be a single connected component.

K-CORE DECOMPOSITION

To determine how deeply the automated accounts penetrated networks of human users, we used a method in network analysis called k-core decomposition. K-core decomposition breaks a network down into separate layers where each layer (also known as a shell) consists of nodes that have the same number of connections or higher (see Figure 8.3). Figure 8.3 illustrates how each level of analysis proceeds. At the base of the decomposition procedure lie the most peripheral nodes. At the highest shells, we uncover nodes that are most central with respect to the number of connections they wield.

The output of k-core decomposition depends on the density and the degree distribution of networks, where degree refers to the number of connections each node has. The relative size of the core and periphery, and the communication dynamics that are created between the two, are critical for understanding political influence. The upper cores of a network integrate and disseminate the most information. It has been shown that the core of political networks online is capable of triggering cascades of recruitment during protests, where a cascade refers to a chain of users who cause their neighbors to not only join a protest but also to proselytize with them (González-Bailón et al., 2011). In other words, users in the upper core are in a position to serve as opinion leaders of political movements, where they can initiate bandwagon dynamics of public support around their political agenda. We aim to observe whether bots infiltrated the

(a)   (b)

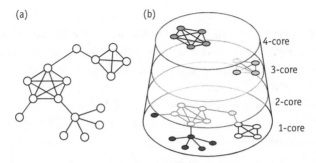

Figure 8.3 Graphic Illustration of K-Core Decomposition. Source: Barberá et al. (2015).
Note: This schematic represents k-core decomposition for a random network with 16 nodes and 24 edges.

upper cores of the network, with the ability to reach many people and thereby achieve politically significant influence.

BETWEENNESS CENTRALITY

Betweenness centrality represents the extent to which nodes "stand between" each other in a network, as gatekeepers of information (Freeman, 1979; Newman, 2010). A node has high betweenness centrality if it is necessary for linking many other nodes. As such, betweenness centrality is a robust measure of influence in a network, because nodes with high betweenness centrality have more control over the flow of information between other nodes. In terms of graph theory, betweenness centrality is based on measures of shortest paths, where a path refers to the number of people a message must travel through to get from person A to person B. For every pair of nodes in a single connected component, there exists at least one shortest path between nodes. The betweenness centrality for each node is the number of these shortest paths that pass through the node. See Newman (2010) for mathematical descriptions of this measure.

Using BotOrNot, we were able to classify a sample of 775,871 unique users. Three percent (N=23,276) of the accounts were detected as having been removed since the time of the retweets were produced. Two percent (N=15,517) of the accounts were listed as private, thus preventing access to their user content for classification. The remaining 95 percent of the accounts were able to be classified. Of this sample of classified users, 11 percent (N=77,330) of the accounts were identified as showing signs of automation by BotOrNot on the basis of its minimal criteria, where an account is 50 percent likely to be a bot. Using this threshold has been shown to reach the 80th percentile in terms of classification accuracy (Davis et al., 2016). However, given the size of our sample and the possibility of false positives, we decided to consider an account as likely to be a bot if its BotOrNot score was at least 70 percent or higher. With this more stringent criteria, three percent (N=25,169) of the accounts were flagged as bots.

To measure whether bots reached positions of structural influence, we undertook k-core decomposition analysis of the largest connected component of retweets within our network. We built an undirected network, where a link was formed between user A and user B if they had retweeted one other. The largest connected component contained 303,009 users and 1,966,158 retweet relationships. Within this largest connected component, we identified 8,127 potential bots. Because bots are often designed to retweet each other, their indegree and outdegree can be inflated when measuring degree centrality. For this reason, to gain a measure of whether bots entered the core of retweet networks among people, we removed all retweet relationships between bots from the largest connected component when examining the k-core distribution. The resulting network contained 302,815 unique accounts and 1,954,799 unique accounts, where 7,598 accounts were classified as potential bots. As Figure 8.4 displays, our k-core decomposition analysis reveals that bots are distributed throughout both the periphery and the core of the largest connected component. Over three-quarters of the bots in our sample were nested in layers with a degree of at least 10, and 13 percent of bots penetrated the upper ten shells of influence. These results indicate that bots infiltrated the core discussion network of our sample.

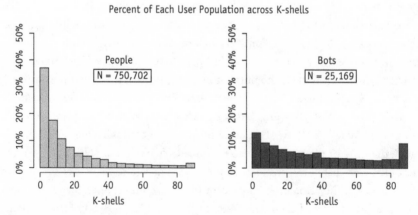

Figure 8.4 K-Core Distribution for Human and Bot Users. Source: Authors' construction. Note: This figure shows what percentage of the overall population for each type of user is located within a given k-shell. For example, here we see that, of the 34,922 humans, 50 percent (17,461) of them fell within the first k-shell (this does not mean that the first k-shell included 50 percent humans). This approach allows us to compare how the populations of humans and bots were distributed across the shells.

Next, we examined which bots achieved positions of high centrality within the retweet network, as evidence of their capacity to control the flow of information during the election. We focus our analysis on a directed model of the largest connected component in the retweet network. The directed network allows us to measure whether bots played a role in mediating the flow of information between users, where bots with high betweenness centrality are those that were potentially necessary for exposing users to tweets within the retweet network. By transforming betweenness centrality measures into z-scores, which indicate the number of standard deviations a score is from the mean, we find that 204 bots have a betweenness centrality score that is above the average score of all users, including humans. Figure 8.5 shows the top 20 potential bots with the highest betweenness centrality scores, as revealed by the first column indicating z-scores for betweenness centrality. We also found that 487 bots were above average in terms of their indegree (the number of users retweeting them) and 800 bots were above average in terms of their outdegree (the number of users they were retweeting). Bots thus reached positions of centrality because they were retweeting others and being retweeted. This raised the question of whether bots and humans were retweeting bots.

Next, we examined which bots achieved positions of high betweenness centrality within the largest connected retweet network. We focus our analysis on a directed model of the largest connected component in the retweet network, where retweets between bots are included in the model to allow for a full picture of the diffusion network. The directed network allows us to measure whether bots played a role in mediating the flow of information between users, where bots with high centrality were potentially necessary for exposing users to tweets within the retweet network. By transforming betweenness centrality measures into z-scores, we find that 213 bots reached a betweenness centrality score that is above the average score of all users, including people. Figure 8.5 displays the top 20 potential bots with the highest betweenness centrality scores, as revealed by the first column indicating z-scores for betweenness centrality. As expected, 39 percent of bots had higher than average outdegree (the number of users they were retweeting); we also found that seven percent of bots had higher than average indegree (the number of users retweeting them). Figure 8.6 displays the top 20 potential bots with the highest total degree (including both indegree and outdegree), as revealed by the first column indicating z-scores for betweenness centrality. Bots thus reached positions of centrality because they were retweeting others and being retweeted. This raised the question of whether both bots and humans were retweeting bots.

Next, we constructed a version of the retweeting network that only included connections where a human retweeted a bot. The result was a directed retweet network, where a connection represented a human retweeting a bot. Overall, this

Accounts Showing Signs of Automation with the Top 20 Betweenness Centrality (in z-scores)

User	Betweenness Centrality	In-degree	Out-degree
098James	73.0	16.8	15.5
DeplorableBride	32.3	13.9	6.3
Miami4Trump	29.9	66.2	4.0
RedNationRising	23.1	28.8	0.3
AMTrump4PRES	22.0	18.6	1.5
FreedomChild3	20.0	7.2	5.8
UnPoliticalPrty	19.5	8.1	4.4
GaetaSusan	15.7	4.4	42
winegir173	12.6	6.9	4.9
MynerStuff	11.8	5.6	4.9
ResistTyranny	10.7	14.4	1.2
RNRFlorida	10.3	1.8	1.5
NgullenR	9.8	0.3	0.3
THETXEMBASSY	9.5	4.0	0.5
EverySavage	8.9	0.6	0.1
FredZeppelin12	8.3	16.1	1.0
Indian4Trump	8.3	0.2	5.1
Dbargen	7.8	13.6	0.5
Masg66	6.8	0.0	4.9
LEFTH00K	6.0	0.6	8.1

Figure 8.5 Accounts suspected of automation with the top betweenness centrality scores. Source: Authors' calculations based on a Twitter sample of selected political hashtags collected between November 1–11, 2016. Note: This table represents the authors' calculations of the z-scores for each measure, where z-scores refer to the number of standard deviations a given user is from the mean measure for a given distribution. Negative values are standard deviations below the average, and positive values are above the average. These results were processed after thresholding out all bots that had not been retweeted more than twice. This facilitated clearer visualization, and it did not alter the accounts which appeared in the top 20 list here.

Username	In.degree	Out.degree	Total.degree	Total.Deg.Z	Btwn.Cent.Z	# times Retweeted
JohnKStahlUSA	1862	0	1862	22.18	−0.03	11207
magnifier661	1484	90	1574	18.73	78.53	6425
LeahR77	874	53	927	11	37.09	3364
Darren32895836	753	10	763	9.04	3.59	3370
healthandcents	609	20	629	7.44	6.72	2905
MAGA3X	590	9	599	7.08	7.07	3602
latinaafortrump	368	5	373	4.38	7.16	1362
USAforTrump2016	340	0	340	3.98	−0.03	1843
MightyBusterBro	301	0	301	3.52	−0.03	1599
greeneyes0084	271	16	287	3.35	9.51	1118
amrightnow	270	0	270	3.15	−0.03	1752
debsellsslc	228	14	242	2.81	9.52	1039
HalleyBorderCol	225	11	236	2.74	3.37	938
Dbargen	220	9	229	2.66	2.65	1126
HillaryforOH	209	4	213	2.47	0.25	1146
Don_Vito_08	191	18	209	2.42	13.53	902
jpm05880	202	0	202	2.33	−0.03	810
Thomas1774Paine	188	1	189	2.18	−0.02	809
HeHasntTweeted2	183	0	183	2.11	−0.03	992
true_pundit	143	2	145	1.65	-0.02	967

Figure 8.6 Accounts Suspected of Automation with the Top Scores for Total Degree.
Source: Authors' calculations based on a Twitter sample of selected political hashtags collected between November 1–11, 2016. Note: This table represents the authors' calculations of the z-scores for each measure, where z-scores refer to the number of standard deviations a given user is from the mean measure for a given distribution. Negative values are standard deviations below the average, and positive values are above the average. These results were processed after thresholding out all bots that had not been retweeted more than twice. This facilitated clearer visualization, and it did not alter the accounts which appeared in the top 20 list here.

network consisted of 81,935 people and 1,572 bots, indicating that over 10 percent of people in the network retweeted bots. Bots were retweeted an average of seven times and by approximately 2.3 people on average. As Figure 8.6 displays, we discovered 483 bots that were retweeted by humans more than 10 times. These same bots were retweeted 562 times on average, with retweet connections to an average of 378 people. Of particular note, as Figure 8.6 indicates, a number of the most retweeted bots were explicitly partisan in their handle, including @MAGA3X and @USAforTrump2016. Similarly, one of the suspected bots that people retweeted the most, @amrightnow, has been explicitly identified as a pro-Trump bot.

To model whether humans retweeted bots, we constructed a version of the retweeting network that only included connections where a human user retweeted a bot. The result was a directed retweet network, where a connection represented a human retweeting a bot. Overall, this network consisted of 15,904 humans and 695 bots. The average number of times that a given person retweeted a bot was five times. The average indegree of bots in this network was two, meaning that bots were retweeted by approximately two people on average. When examining only the bots who were retweeted by humans more than once, we discovered 122 bots (see Figure 8.7). These bots were retweeted 63 times on average, with connections to 40 different humans on average. These results confirm that bots won a significant amount of attention and interaction from human users. As Figure 8.7 shows, four out of the five most retweeted bots were explicitly pro-Trump in their Twitter handle: @TeamTrump, @Miami4Trump, @Bikers4Trump, and @RedNationRising.

THE RISE OF BOTS: IMPLICATIONS FOR POLITICS, POLICY, AND METHOD

The results of our quantitative analysis confirm that bots reached positions of measurable influence during the 2016 US election. Our k-core decomposition reveals that bots occupied both the periphery and the core of political discussion over Twitter. As members of the core, bots are in a position where they are capable of diffusing information that sets the agenda over Twitter (González-Bailón et al., 2011). Betweenness centrality measures indicate that bots also reached positions where they were able to control the flow of information between users. We then showed how bots were, in fact, retweeted by humans, adding further evidence to the finding that bots influenced meaningful political discussion over Twitter. Lastly, we provide preliminary evidence that bots were more actively involved in influencing the uptake of Trump-related hashtags than Clinton-related hashtags, with the potential to augment the megaphone effect, discussed earlier. Altogether, these results deepen our qualitative perspective on the political power bots can enact during major political processes of global significance. It is the task of future studies to explore in greater depth the downstream consequences of bot influence over social media on actual on-the-ground political behavior.

Most concerning is the fact that companies and campaigners continue to conveniently undersell the effects of bots. The quantitative analysis presented in this chapter aims to partially settle the question of bot influence so that we can begin to address the realities of bot manipulation more directly. Bots infiltrated the core

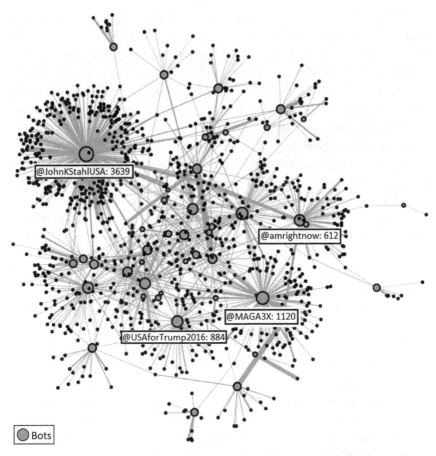

@JohnKStahlUSA: 3639

@amrightnow: 612

@MAGA3X: 1120

@USAforTrump2016: 884

Bots

Figure 8.7 Directed Retweet Network of People Retweeting Bots (with Threshold).
Source: Author's calculations based on a Twitter sample of selected political hashtags collected
between November 1–11, 2016. Note: In this figure, the bots are green and the humans are black.
A connection is drawn only if the human retweeted that bot. The bots with the highest number of
humans retweeting them are labelled, with the number of connections beside their name. *To facilitate a
clearer visualization, we removed all bots that were not retweeted at least seven times.* This is why thousands
of connections are not displayed for the bots with the highest indegree. *The weight of the connection
reflects the number of times a human user retweeted that bot.* The size of each node also reflects the
magnitude of the total degree for that bot. *Four of the bot hubs are labeled, and their overall indegree is
stated next to their handle. These bot hubs were selected from the list of the top 15 bots with the highest degree
centrality. See Figure 8.6 for a full list of these bots.*

of the political discussion over Twitter, where they were capable of disseminating
propaganda at mass scale. Bots also reached positions of high betweenness centrality, where they played a powerful role in determining the flow of information
among users. Several independent analyses show that bots supported Trump

much more than Clinton, enabling him to more effectively set the agenda. Our qualitative report provides strong reasons to believe that Twitter was critical for Trump's success. Taken all together, our mixed-methods approach points to the possibility that bots were a key player in allowing social media activity to influence the election in Trump's favor. Our qualitative analysis situates these results in their broader political context, where it is unknown exactly who is responsible for bot manipulation—Russian hackers, rogue campaigners, everyday citizens, or some complex conspiracy among these potential actors.

Despite growing evidence concerning bot manipulation, the Federal Election Commission in the United States showed no signs of recognizing that bots existed during the election. There needs to be, as a minimum, a conversation about developing policy regulations for bots, especially since a major reason why bots are able to thrive is because of laissez-faire API access to websites like Twitter. One of the efforts toward bot policy in the United States prior to the election is the US Anti-Bot Code of Conduct (ABCC), in relation to which a large number of representatives from major ISPs, and a noticeably smaller number of representatives from the US government, gathered to discuss concerns regarding bots of all kinds (Anti-Bot Code of Conduct, 2013).

However, the definition of bots in the ABCC is vague, including both compromised computers via viruses and possible social media interference. Nevertheless, the report exposes one of the possible reasons why we have not seen greater action taken toward bots on behalf of companies: it puts their bottom line at risk. Several company representatives fear that notifying users of bot threats will deter people from using their services, given the growing ubiquity of bot threats and the nuisance such alerts would cause. The conclusion of the report is that, for the time being, bot attacks should be viewed as the responsibility of the individual user. The problem is, much research shows that people are inherently and incurably poor at detecting bots online (Edwards et al., 2014; Guilbeault, 2016). Most curious of all is the ABCC's claim that one of the leading obstacles to bot policy is the fact that, in their words, "[Y]ou can't manage what you can't measure." We hope that the empirical evidence in this chapter—provided through both qualitative and quantitative investigation—can help to raise awareness and support the expanding body of evidence needed to begin managing political bots and the rising culture of computational propaganda.

Motivated in part by the research of Oxford's Computational Propaganda Project, recent legislation has been proposed to require social media companies to disclose and potentially remove accounts that may be bots. Please see the Bot Disclosure and Accountability Act, S.3127 – 115th Congress (2017–2018). This is a crucial development, and we hope that the findings of this research can help to further support effective policy interventions into bots and computational propaganda at large.

References

Albright, J. (2016a, November 11). What's Missing from the Trump Election Equation? Let's Start with Military-Grade PsyOps. Retrieved from https://medium.com/@d1gi/whats-missing-from-the-trump-election-equation-let-s-start-with-military-grade-psyops-fa22090c8c17.

Albright, J. (2016b, November 27). #Election2016 #FakeNews Compilation. Retrieved from https://medium.com/@d1gi/election2016-fakenews-compilation-455870d04bb#.hnmvtp7k3.

Anti-Bot Code of Conduct (2013). Retrieved July 5, 2017 from https://transition.fcc.gov/bureaus/.../CSRIC_III_WG7_Report_March_ percent202013.pdf

Associated Press. (2016, March 3). Transcript of Mitt Romney's Speech on Donald Trump. *The New York Times*. Retrieved from https://www.nytimes.com/2016/03/04/us/politics/mitt-romney-speech.html.

Beckett, C. (2016). What Does the Trump Triumph Mean for Journalism, Politics and Social Media? Retrieved from blogs.lse.ac.uk/polis/.

Benkler, Y. (2006). *The Wealth of Networks: How Social Production Transforms Markets and Freedom*. New Haven, CT: Yale University Press.

Bessi, A., & Ferrara, E. (2016). Social Bots Distort the 2016 U.S. Presidential Election Online Discussion. *First Monday*, 21(11). https://doi.org/10.5210/fm.v21i11.7090.

CBS 60 Minutes. (2016, November 12). Trump Says His Social Media Power Key to Victory. Retrieved from http://www.cbsnews.com/news/president-elect-trump-says-social-media-played-a-key-role-in-his-victory/.

Cohen, B. (1963). *Press and Foreign Policy*. Princeton, NJ: Princeton University Press.

Coldewey, D. (2012). Romney Twitter Account Gets Upsurge in Fake Followers, but from Where. *NBC News*. Retrieved from http://www.nbcnews.com/technology/technolog/romney-twitter-account-gets-upsurge-fake-followers-where-928605

Davis, C., Varol, E., Ferrara, E., Flammini, A., & Menczer, F. (2016). BotOrNot: A System to Evaluate Social Bots. In *Proceedings of the 25th International Conference Companion on World Wide Web* (pp. 273–274). New York, NY: Association for Computing Machinery (International World Wide Web Conferences Steering Committee). doi:10.1145/2872518.2889302.

Edwards, C., Edwards, A., Spence, P., & Ashleigh, K. (2014). Is that a Bot Running the Social Media Feed? Testing the Differences in Perceptions of Communication Quality for a Human Agent and a Bot Agent on Twitter. *Computers in Human Behavior*, 33(2014), 372–376. doi:10.1016/j.chb.2013.08.013.

Ferrara, E., Varol, O., Davis, C., Menczer, F., & Flammini, A. (2016). The Rise of Social Bots. *Communications ACM*, 59(7), 96–104. https://doi.org/10.1145/2818717

Fisher, M., Woodrow Cox, J., & Hermann, P. (2017, December 6). Pizzagate: From Rumor, to Hashtag, to Gunfire in D.C. Retrieved from https://www.washingtonpost.com/local/pizzagate-from-rumor-to-hashtag-to-gunfire-in-dc/2016/12/06/4c7def50-bbd4-11e6-94ac-3d324840106c_story.html.

Franklin Fowler, E., Ridout, T. N., & Franz, M. M. (2017). Political Advertising in 2016: The Presidential Election as Outlier? *The Forum*, 14(4), 445–469. https://doi.org/10.1515/for-2016-0040.

Freeman, Linton C. (1979). Centrality in Social Networks: Conceptual Clarification. *Social Networks*, 2(3), 215–239.

Geertz, C. (1973). *The Interpretation of Cultures: Selected Essays*. Basic Books.

González-Bailón, S., Borge-Holthoefer, J., Rivero, A., & Moreno, Y. (2011). The Dynamics of Protest Recruitment through an Online Network. *Scientific Reports, 1*(197). https://www.nature.com/articles/srep00197.

Gorwa, R., and Guilbeault, D. (2018, In Press) Unpacking the Social Media Bot: A Typology to Guide Research and Policy. *Policy and Internet.* https://arxiv.org/abs/1801.06863.

Gottfried, J., & Shearer, E. (2016). *News Use Across Social Medial Platforms 2016.* Pew Research Center.

Guilbeault, D. (2016). Growing Bot Security: An Ecological View of Bot Agency. *The International Journal of Communication, 10,* 5003–5021. http://ijoc.org/index.php/ijoc/article/view/6135.

Harris, M. (2016, November 14). A Media Post-Mortem on the 2016 Presidential Election. Retrieved from http://www.mediaquant.net/2016/11/a-media-post-mortem-on-the-2016-presidential-election/.

Howard, P. N., & Hussain, M. M. (2013). *Democracy's Fourth Wave?: Digital Media and the Arab Spring.* Oxford University Press. Retrieved from http://books.google.com/books?hl=en&lr=&id=ayHOyrmmT8kC&oi=fnd&pg=PP2&dq=howard+digital+activism+2013&ots=mJDwHv1nfa&sig=jvnGD3UO3Bg1GuzR2wayT4WD8pI.

Howard, P. N., Kollanyi, B., & Woolley, S. C. (2016). Bots and Automation Over Twitter during the US Election. Computational Propaganda Project: Working Paper Series.

Isaac, M., & Ember, S. (2016, November 8). For Election Day Influence, Twitter Ruled Social Media. *The New York Times.* Retrieved from https://www.nytimes.com/2016/11/09/technology/for-election-day-chatter-twitter-ruled-social-media.html.

Karpf, D. (2012). *The MoveOn effect: The Unexpected Transformation of American Political Advocacy.* Oxford University Press. Retrieved from http://books.google.com/books?hl=en&lr=&id=YReQ5quOFvUC&oi=fnd&pg=PP2&dq=The+moveon+effect&ots=GK-Vxi9cUm&sig=YfKIp3HYzKlIorhd4MjeEMjKbNU.

Lapowsky, I. (2016, November 15). This Is How Facebook Actually Won Trump the Presidency. *Wired Magazine.* Retrieved from https://www.wired.com/2016/11/facebook-won-trump-election-not-just-fake-news/.

McCombs, M. E., & Shaw, D. L. (1972). The Agenda Setting Function of Mass Media. *Public Opinion Quarterly, 36*(2), 176–187. https://doi.org/10.1086/267990.

McCombs, M. E., Shaw, D. L., & Weaver, D. H. (1997). *Communication and Democracy: Exploring the Intellectual Frontiers in Agenda-Setting Theory.* London, UK: Psychology Press.

Messias, J., Schmidt, L., Oliveira, R., & Benevenuto, F. (2013). You Followed my Bot! Transforming Robots into Influential Users on Twitter. *First Monday, 18*(7). Retrieved from http://firstmonday.org/ojs/index.php/fm/article/view/4217/3700#p4.

Metaxas, P. T., & Mustafaraj, E. (2012). Social Media and the Elections. *Science, 338*(6106), 472–473.

Mønsted, B., Sapieżyński, P., Ferrara, E., & Lehmann, S. (2017). Evidence of Complex Contagion of Information in Social Media: An Experiment Using Twitter Bots. *arXiv.* Retrieved from https://arxiv.org/abs/1703.06027

Mustafaraj, E., & Metaxas, P. T. (2010). From Obscurity to Prominence in Minutes: Political Speech and Real-time Search. Presented at the WebSci10. Retrieved from http://repository.wellesley.edu/computersciencefaculty/9/.

Newman, M. J. (2010). *Networks: An Introduction.* Oxford: Oxford University Press.

Owen, T. (2015). *Disruptive Power: The Crisis of the State in the Digital Age.* Oxford: Oxford University Press.

Patterson, T. E. (2016). News Coverage of the 2016 Election: How the Press Failed Voters. Shorestein Center on Media, Politics, and Public Policy. Harvard University, Cambridge: MA.

Ratkiewicz, J., Conover, M., Meiss, M., Goncalves, B., Patil, S., Flammini, A., & Menczer, F. (2011). Truthy: Mapping the Spread of Astroturf in Microblog Streams. In *Proceedings of the 20th International Conference Companion on World Wide Web* (pp. 249–252). ACM. Retrieved from http://dl.acm.org/citation.cfm?id=1963301.

Schreckinger, B. (2016, September 30). Inside Trump's "Cyborg" Twitter Army. Retrieved from http://politi.co/2dyhCD0.

Vosoughi, S., Roy D., and Aral, S. (2018). The Spread of True and False News Online. *Science* 359(6380): 1146–1151.

Wehner, P. (2016, January 14). Why I Will Never Vote for Donald Trump. *The New York Times.* Retrieved from https://www.nytimes.com/2016/01/14/opinion/campaign-stops/why-i-will-never-vote-for-donald-trump.html.

Woolley, S. C. (2016). Automating Power: Social Bot Interference in Global Politics. *First Monday,* 21(4). Retrieved from http://firstmonday.org/ojs/index.php/fm/article/view/6161.

9

China

An Alternative Model of a Widespread Practice

GILLIAN BOLSOVER

Introduction

The year 2016 has come to be seen as a year of political turmoil, and the point when long-standing fears about the negative effects of social media use on democratic politics were finally realized. In a referendum widely seen as marred by false promises based on misleading information (Helm, 2016), growing nationalism that led to the murder of an MP (Cobain & Taylor, 2016), and the manipulation of online public opinion through the use of online algorithms (Howard & Kollanyi, 2016), the United Kingdom voted, narrowly, to leave the European Union. Polemical billionaire Donald Trump won the US presidency for the Republican Party, in an election in which automated accounts, particularly in pro-Trump hashtags, dominated discourse on Twitter (Howard & Woolley, 2016), and junk news was shared as frequently as news from professional news producers (Howard, Bolsover, Kollanyi, Bradshaw, & Neudert, 2017).

In the face of this apparent turn in politics, 2017 started with widespread discussion in the media and among politicians, academics, and online platforms about how to best control this eruption of manipulation of the political process using online tools. Prominent online platforms such as Facebook, Twitter, and Google have announced measures to tackle false information, automation, and online harassment (Solon & Wong, 2016); the UK government has announced an inquiry into fake news distributed on social media (UK Parliament, 2017); and the German government is pursuing a law that would make social media sites responsible for illegal content (Faiola & Kirchner, 2017).

These new directions in attempts to control online information represent a reversal in established approaches to the governance of online information that has been brewing for some time. For years, the dominant discourse in Western democracies was that the Internet should be allowed to be a place for free speech. The use of the Internet was seen as potentially leading to more diverse information, and online free speech was understood as creating a marketplace of ideas in which "correct" information would rise to the top, resulting in stronger citizen political participation and strengthened democracies (Bolsover, 2017).

After the movement toward social media, many began to be worried about echo chambers, in which individuals are only exposed to online information that matches their existing perspectives (Adamic & Glance, 2005) and filter bubbles, in which sites tailor the information users see based on aggregate data (Pariser, 2012). There were also concerns about how these social media sites might aid extremists (Klausen, 2015) and lead to a domination by existing elites and the commercialization of online content and experiences (Bolsover, 2017; Cammaerts, 2008). Against this backdrop of increasing worries about the failure of the Internet to live up to its democratic potential, and the possibility that it might even be undermining established political processes, the events of 2016 brought new urgency to these fears. They also revealed new and more insidious practices such as fake news, automation, and computational propaganda, and have led to strident calls for change.

While to many this discourse of the Internet as a place for free and diverse information has seemed to be the dominant perspective, for more than a decade there has been an alternative model of governance and control of online information that is growing ever stronger and more influential—China.

The Chinese Internet

As the world's most populous country, China overtook the United States in having the world's largest population of Internet users in 2009. The Chinese Internet population is growing rapidly, particularly in rural areas with the influx of Internet-enabled smartphones, but just over half of the Chinese population remains offline (CNNIC, 2015). The Chinese approach to the governance of the Internet, politics, and political information is almost the polar opposite of that in Western democracies.

The Chinese state maintains high levels of control over the Internet, and discourses about the use of technology for politics rest on ideas about ideological correctness and hierarchy, in contrast to Western ideas about freedom of speech and equality (Bolsover, 2017). This approach is underpinned by "the Great Firewall," the most sophisticated regime of Internet censorship and control in the world, and the blocking and replacement of popular foreign platforms by domestic alternatives. The level of national specificity of the Chinese Internet has led scholars to argue that the idea of "the Internet" is dead, to be replaced by a "splinternet" with different countries exercising different levels of control over their national populations (Morozov, 2009).

In China, social media companies are held responsible for monitoring the legality of the content posted on them. They employ a large number of censors and collect identity data on registered users in order to achieve these aims (Fu, Chan, & Chau, 2013; Zhu et al., 2013). Sensitive topics and attempts at online protest are heavily censored online (King, Pan, & Roberts, 2012; Zhu et al., 2013). The message that Internet users receive from both the state and online platforms, therefore, emphasizes that the Internet is not a place for free speech, but rather that users in their online actions need to be cognizant of the state-set ideological priorities of society and the effects of their online actions (Bolsover, 2017).

Under Xi Jinping, there have been ever-increasing crackdowns on online political speech. Soon after his ascension as leader of the Chinese Communist Party (CCP) in late 2012, a major campaign against online rumors and misinformation was launched with high-profile arrests and state visits to the growing number of online opinion leaders (Nip & Fu, 2016). This crackdown appears to have precipitated a movement away from the Twitter-like microblogging giant Sina Weibo, toward more private mediums such as the (Tencent-owned) messaging service WeChat (Moore, 2014). In December 2016, regulations, specifically targeting both Weibo and WeChat, were announced that banned the distribution of user-generated audio or video content about current events (SARFT, 2016), media that had previously been important in challenging state dominance of information (Bolsover, 2013b).

This juxtaposition between "the Chinese Internet" and the emerging issues of computational propaganda, bots, algorithms and "fake news" in Western online spaces presents a key dilemma in understanding the current landscape of online political information and opinion manipulation. At its heart, the Internet is a global technology based on a global economy. Its hardware connects users across the world via wires and satellites. US-born Internet giants are familiar to most users, and even in China domestic alternatives mirror these US sites. Furthermore, this connectivity allows information and ideas to spread across national borders.

However, the Internet has also begun to seem nationally specific. For more than a decade China has been building an alternative Internet infrastructure that provides the online context in which more than 20 percent of the world's Internet users live, and is a model that has inspired other attempts at Internet control. However, much less is known about the state of the Internet in China than in Western democracies, and much of what is reported is myth. Now more than ever, with China growing in power on the international stage and Western democracies arguing about implementing strategies to control online information, it is important to understand how Chinese information control functions online and the way in which technology is used to influence and manipulate public opinion in and about China.

Established Wisdom on Public Opinion Manipulation on the Chinese Internet

Any attempt to understand the state of technology and politics in China must begin with the differences between approaches to politics, propaganda, media, and information control between China and the West. China has a distinctive political system, cultural heritage, and socioeconomic conditions. For thousands of years, China was governed by a dynastic system that was based on Confucian ideas of the ruler as the father of the people, with social relations centered on duty and filial piety. This cultural legacy has resulted in ideas of politics that focus on welfare rather than civil rights and that construct the state's duty as protecting the welfare and economic development of the people (Perry, 2008; Shue, 2004).

After a short-lived republican period in the early 1900s, China became a communist state under Mao Zedong. Following Mao's death in 1976, the country began a process of "opening up," under the leadership of Deng Xiaoping. These economic reforms have lifted more than 500 million people out of poverty and transformed China into one of the world's largest and fastest-growing economies in the space of a generation (World Bank, 2015). Despite these economic reforms, the Chinese state maintains high levels of control over information within the country and continues to follow a Marxist approach to the media, in which the truthfulness of the information is less important than the political effects of that information (Wilson, 1993; Xinhua, 2016).

Despite a commercialization of the media industry after 1994, professional news providers in China remain closely aligned with the party state and have to balance the needs of the Party with the need to make money (Winfield & Peng, 2005). Some have found that this leads to greater diversity of information within the country and encourages challenges to the status quo (Lu & Ma, 2015). In contrast, others argue that this solidifies the power of the Communist Party by making this information appear more unbiased, and by dividing the interests of the urban middle classes and rural poor based on a diet of consumer products and entertainment (Stockmann, 2012; Zhao, 2000). The situation in China with respect to propaganda and the manipulation of online public opinion is thus extremely complicated and opaque. Several myths persist about the control of online political information in China that have been refuted or challenged by recent research. The first myth is that all online criticism and political speech is censored.

Social media has proved a boon for the Communist Party in China, providing a great deal of information that is used to monitor public opinion, and allowing an efficient distribution mechanism for state entities (Song, 2015). The CCP has proved quite responsive to certain kinds of grievances aired on social media. For instance in 2007, the desperate parents of lost children suspected of being kidnapped posted an open letter online asking for "netizen" help in finding their children; the huge public response to this letter pressured the central government to take action, leading to police crackdowns on illegal brickmaking factories that freed thousands of young Chinese who had been forced into slavery by these business owners in collusion with local officials (Herold, 2008). Responding to criticism and evidence of wrongdoing online solidifies the control of the central government rather than undermining it, allowing the state to appear to be responding to citizens' problems and addressing minor grievances before they gain momentum.

A large number of Chinese Internet users' posts to social media are attempts to take action on small-scale political and social issues (Bolsover, 2017). However, these are restricted to relatively safe and sanctioned topics such as kidnapped children, rural poverty, local corruption, and animal cruelty. While political discussion and action related to popular nationalism, rights defense, corruption and power abuse, the environment, cultural contention, muckraking, and online charity are widely tolerated, content that challenges the state, such as human rights or illegal or unethical business practices that the state is unable to contain, is repressed (Yang, 2009). A study of social media found that criticism, even if it was vitriolic, of the state, its leaders, and its policies, was not more likely to be censored and that instead, the censorship regime was concerned with preventing collective action by deleting comments that spurred or reinforced offline mobilization (King et al., 2012).

It is not, however, the case that the state holds all the power in this process. The popularly held view among academics studying political speech on the Chinese Internet is that this technology has facilitated a negotiation between members of civil society and the state that results in a negotiation at the margins of permissible speech (Stern & Hassid, 2012; Yang, 2009). However, much of this research was conducted prior to the Xi premiership, which appears to have reduced the power of civil society that had hitherto been growing online (Bandurski, 2015; Moore, 2014).

A second myth about public opinion manipulation, which was recently challenged by an academic analysis of a leak of a local-level Internet propaganda department, is the idea of the "50-cent Party." For years, academics, journalists, and activists had written about the existence of this supposed army of individuals paid 50 cents per post to attack critics and support the state online. However, analyzing the content contained in this leak and using its contents to identify and contact other similar individuals, King, Pan, and Roberts (2016) found that rather than an army of users paid by the post, the "50-cent Party" seemed, in fact, to comprise government employees who posted pro-state content online as part of their regular jobs. Additionally, rather than attacking critical and anti-state content, it was found that these individuals engaged in a positive propaganda strategy that focused on distraction at times of potential unrest. However, unlike the cases of political opinion manipulation that are emerging on Twitter, the team concluded that despite looking extensively for evidence that these pro-state posts were created by automated means, evidence strongly indicated that each was written by a "specific, often identifiable, human being under direction from the government" (King et al., 2016, p. 11).

These are just two instances in which academic research has overturned or problematized established wisdom about how the Internet is used for the dissemination of propaganda and manipulation of public opinion in China. It is surprising that no academic research has found evidence of the use of robots and algorithms for computational propaganda in China, given the increasing instances of their use in Western countries and China's highly sophisticated regime of Internet control and propaganda. It is also the case that although some research has examined automated means for manipulating and controlling online public opinion in and about China, little of this research addresses this issue holistically or with an understanding of how propaganda is understood in Chinese theories and politics. This chapter attempts to address these questions by providing an overview of the current status of computational propaganda in China.

Key Concepts and Definitions

This chapter will address the following key questions:

1. Is computational propaganda being used in and about China?
2. Whose interests are furthered by this computational propaganda, and what is the effect of this computational propaganda on the landscape of online information in and about China?
3. How can the case of computational propaganda in China inform the current efforts of Western democracies to tackle fake news, online bots, and computational propaganda?

To answer these questions, I conducted an interview with a specialist in Chinese Internet censorship and an individual who had previously found evidence of Chinese computational propaganda on Twitter. I collected posts made on Twitter using one of 27 hashtags related to China and Chinese politics, in both English and Chinese, over a period of approximately seven weeks. This period included the Tomb-Sweeping Day Festival. I also collected comments left by Weibo users on posts made by one of 25 top media and state information providers on the platform over the Spring Festival period. I analyzed these data using both quantitative and qualitative methodologies to look for evidence of various forms of computational propaganda.

COMPUTATIONAL PROPAGANDA

The idea of propaganda has its roots in the Catholic Church in the 1600s, and refers to highly organized intellectual work that aims at "persuading large masses of people about the virtues (or vices) of some organization, cause, or person" (Jackall, 1995, p. 2). Propaganda works to influence the opinions and actions of individuals in society based on emotional appeals, rather than rationality (Institute for Propaganda Analysis, 1995).

Propaganda gained a negative connotation with its association with Nazi Germany; however, many scholars of propaganda see it as inevitable and neutral, rather than inherently negative (Lasswell, 1995). In China, propaganda is not generally seen as having the same negative connotations as it does in the West, but is rather viewed as an important tool of governance (Brady, 2009; Brady & Juntao, 2009).

The Internet has, however, changed how propaganda is used. Prior to the existence of the Internet, propaganda was a tool that was only really available to states and major political and commercial organizations. By lowering barriers to the publication of information, a much wider group of individuals and interest groups can now create and publish propaganda online. The Internet has also changed the distribution mechanism of propaganda. As both mass and individualized media, propaganda messages can rapidly gain a huge following online due to viral propagation. However, propaganda campaigns can now also be directed at specific individuals because of the targeting that the Internet and digital data makes possible, and which appears to increase the effectiveness of these propaganda messages.

This propaganda—designed and spread using new computer technologies—is "computational propaganda." Key tools of computational propaganda include robots, fake accounts, and "fake news." Robots are pieces of code designed to replicate human activity to promote a particular message or individual in online spaces, and fake accounts are manually administered social media accounts that are created and used for the purposes of manipulating online public opinion. "Fake news" is propaganda disguised as professional news. This misinformation is often distributed on social media. Evidence of the use of these tools to perpetuate computational propaganda has been found in relation to recent major political events in the United States and Europe (Howard et al., 2017; Howard & Kollanyi, 2016; Howard & Woolley, 2016).

Case 1: The Great Firewall and the Golden Shield

China is unique in the extent to which the state uses computational propaganda techniques to regulate the domestic Internet. "China operates the world's most sophisticated censorship apparatus," said Charlie Smith (a pseudonym), one of the two minds behind GreatFire.org, which has been monitoring Chinese Internet censorship and providing tools to circumvent these restrictions since 2011 (C. Smith, personal communication, 2017). "As a result, Chinese do not have free access to information and are often unaware of events taking place in their own country," he continued.

Smith breaks down the technologies of Internet censorship in China into two major programs: the Great Firewall, which blocks access to restricted foreign websites, and the Golden Shield Project, which regulates information on domestic sites. "Chinese companies who operate websites must self-censor and also monitor their websites for user-generated content that might not please the authorities," explains Smith. "When Chinese visit these websites and search for information, they will find sanitized information."

The technology of the Great Firewall works through IP blocking. If a user located in China tries to access a website that is restricted, they will often simply get a timed-out message; the website will never load. Smith thinks that as a result, Chinese individuals will not know that the site is being censored; they will just think that the foreign website is unstable, poorly coded, or simply slow to load because it is so far away, and as a result many people will eventually give up trying to visit foreign sites.

In early 2015, GreatFire also documented evidence of DNS poisoning being used as part of the Great Firewall. Instead of receiving a timed-out message, users attempting to access restricted sites would be redirected to a random IP address. A user trying to access GreatFire.org's site was redirected to a Korean government website, and a user trying to access Facebook tweeted that he was redirected to a German porn site (Percy, 2015). Smith thinks that the results of this DNS poisoning is similar to IP blocking: most users would not realize that the information they access is being censored, but simply think that this is a problem with the foreign site.

The Great Firewall is a very specific type of computational propaganda that is executed at the borders of China. Smith explained that it is not always easy to predict if or when a site will be blocked, but that one thing is certain—once a site is blocked it is almost never removed from the list. "Sometimes a site is blocked simply because it contains some information about a government official that that official wants blocked," Smith explained. "Perhaps the video featured a government official or the child of a government official. Or perhaps it was filmed in a government office. Perhaps the site was supposed to have been blocked long ago but just slipped through the cracks. The government does not have to justify the blocking of websites . . . and in many cases the Chinese are left simply wondering why?" This demonstrates that part of the effectiveness of the Chinese censorship system is its lack of transparency, and the uncertainty and instability that users experience over the continued functioning of the Internet within China and the information contained on it.

The domestic counterpart of the Great Firewall is the Golden Shield Project. Social media sites in China must actively monitor user-generated content to make sure that the information on these sites will not be deemed illegal or improper by the state. In particular, information related to political scandals, international events, and key political figures is often censored (Fu et al., 2013), as well as any attempt to organize offline protest or unite diverse grievances (King et al., 2012). Some of this censorship takes place automatically; for instance, certain sensitive keywords associated with the anniversary of the Tiananmen Square "incident" were reported as unable to be published on WeChat (Ng, 2015). Post-publication censorship by human censors is also used to control the content of information on social media (Zhu et al., 2013). The leaked 2012 memo Document Number Nine stipulates a target of five minutes for sensitive posts to be deleted by social media platforms (General Office of the Communist Party of China, 2012).

These automatic and manual censorship strategies work in tandem. When a newly sensitive topic emerges, Smith explained, a new automatic censorship filter will be created, which is followed by a period of manual adjustment to make sure that this filter censors out the necessary information and that not too much unnecessary information is censored along with the sensitive content. Smith believes that allowing this non-sensitive information to continue to be published is more important than most people think: "I don't think censorship is the most sinister part of this system," he said. "The most sinister part is that information still exists. When an individual searches for Xinjiang or Tibet and sees happy pictures of mountains and landscapes or holidaymakers eating local food, they don't think that there is censorship."

This demonstrates the complexity of the Chinese computational propaganda system. If content was simply blocked or deleted, users would soon realize that this content was missing and, perhaps, be more susceptible to influence by this kind of content if they did discover it.

This is part of a positive propaganda strategy that has been found to be used by the Chinese government domestically. Rather than attacking critics, the majority of the state's social media strategy seems to be posting positive information that fosters national pride and confidence in the achievements of the Chinese state. This positive propaganda strategy is particularly prominent during sensitive political events or national holidays, fostering distraction rather than engaged argument (King et al., 2016). This positive propaganda appears to be more important to the Chinese state's information strategy than the censorship of the Great Firewall or Golden Shield Project. The next case described in this chapter provides evidence that this positive propaganda strategy is also used internationally.

Case 2: Positive Propaganda on Twitter Aimed at Foreign Audiences
Angela Jenkins (a pseudonym) was working for the London-based organization Free Tibet in the summer of 2014, overseeing their online communications and social media campaigns. Jenkins had been working with Tibetan NGOs and the Tibetan community for some time and says she had "gotten quite used to seeing a lot of spam on Twitter that seemed to be intended to cover up any true stories about Tibet and any of the messages from the Tibetan exile community from the numerous Tibet NGOs" (A. Jenkins, personal communication, 2017). She had accepted this spam as part of the terrain but started to notice a different kind of computational propaganda strategy emerging online. "There didn't seem to be a lot we could do about it and it seemed very unsophisticated, just a lot of noise, really, designed to cloud out any genuine news," she said. "But then, there seemed to be a shift around 2014/2015 in general in the Tibetan movement. Instead of trying to engage in the Tibetans' arguments the Chinese government's strategy seemed to change."

This new strategy, Jenkins explained, focused on the distribution of positive propaganda, replacing the previous strategy of engaging with the arguments of the Tibetan community. As part of her job, Jenkins was seeing many positive news stories on Twitter, which she reported were all quite distorted. Then she noticed that many of the accounts that were sharing these news stories were "strange." They were all following each other but did not otherwise interact with each other; they were all sharing the same links from the same Tibetan information websites that painted a rosy picture of the situation in Tibet, and the profile photos of many of these accounts appeared to be fake (stock images, images taken from photographers' websites, celebrities, etc.).

Angela had found an organized group of about 100 fake accounts on Twitter that existed to retweet content that reflected the Chinese state's account of the situation in Tibet, sourced from Chinese websites and official state media. While it was not possible for the team to obtain evidence of who administered these fake accounts, Jenkins said the sophistication of the propaganda efforts led her to believe that they were Chinese state sponsored. Whether this is the case or not, their effect was the same. This spam dominated the information being shared on Twitter in Tibet and Tibet-related hashtags and, when searching for these hashtags, skewed the information that came up on the platform toward the perspectives of the Chinese state and away from the perspectives of the Tibetan exile community and those who work with them.

However, both Internet technology and Chinese politics move fast, and the use of fake and robot accounts on Twitter now appears much more sophisticated and widespread than the efforts that Jenkins found. The next section presents original research into computational propaganda on Twitter related to China.

Case 3: Anti-Chinese-State Bots on Twitter

Although Twitter is blocked in China, it is still used by some Chinese individuals, particularly as a subversive space for those who consciously want to engage in discussion about sensitive political issues (Sullivan, 2012). A random sample of 10,890 monthly active, non-private Twitter accounts found seven (0.15 percent) were used by individuals who were apparently located on the Chinese mainland (Bolsover, 2017). Twitter is also widely used in Hong Kong, with an estimated 24 percent of the population being active Twitter users (Statista, 2016), and was seen as an important place for political activism in Occupy Central and the subsequent Umbrella Movement that started in September 2014 (Lee, 2015; Lee & Chan, 2016).

In order to investigate the current state of computational propaganda on Twitter, we collected all the tweets posted to Twitter between February 21 and April 8, 2017, that used one of a set of hashtags associated with general Chinese social, political, and cultural topics. The hashtags were chosen based on a preliminary test that was designed to ascertain the most common hashtags used by Twitter users when posting about issues associated with Chinese politics. These hashtags for which data were collected can be divided into eight groups based on topic:

1. Commonly used locations in Chinese politics: #China, #Hongkong, #Beijing, #Shanghai, #Xinjiang, #Tibet, #Taiwan.
2. Commonly used locations in Chinese politics (in Mandarin): #中国, #香港, #北京, #上海, #新疆, #西藏.
3. Hashtags associated with Chinese culture and positive publicity: #ChinaCulture, #ChinaTravel, #panda.
4. Hashtags associated with areas of Chinese territorial disagreement: #SouthChinaSea, #Diaoyudao, #Senkaku.
5. Hashtags associated with Buddhism: #dalailama, #buddhism, #Kadampa.
6. Hashtags associated with Chinese premier Xi Jinping: #XiJinping, #习近平 and #XiVisit.

7. The hashtag #humanrights (in Mandarin): #人权.
8. The hashtag #AntiChina.

This dataset represents a snapshot of the information being shared in relation to China and Chinese politics over this six-week period. The final dataset contained 1,177,758 tweets from 254,132 unique accounts. Each of these users posted on average 4.6 tweets during the time period that contained one of the followed hashtags (an average of 0.1 posts per user per day.)

However, the information environment on Twitter in relation to China and Chinese politics is dominated by a small number of voices. More than half of the tweets that used one of these China-related hashtags were posted by users who posted 100 or more times during the data collection period, and 42 percent of posts were posted by users who posted more than 300 times during the data collection period.

Almost 30 percent of the tweets in the dataset came from one of the top 100 highest-posting users within these hashtags. Of these 100 users, 18 had been suspended (presumably by Twitter because of their high-posting and likely-automated nature). Each of the users that had not been suspended was an automated account. No pro-Chinese-state accounts were found within these top 100 posting users (Table 9.1); however, half of these users were automated accounts posting anti-Chinese-state content. Within these automated, anti-Chinese-state accounts there were two large bot groups: the 1989 group and the pan-Asia group.

THE 1989 BOT GROUP

Accounts in this group promote content about human rights in China, particularly related to keeping alive the memory of the 1989 student-led democracy movement that ended with the Tiananmen Square "incident" (see Figures 9.1–9.3). All of the posts of accounts in this group are in simplified Chinese, and information posted by these accounts dominates hashtags related to China and major Chinese cities in both English and simplified Mandarin (#China, #Hongkong, #Beijing, #Shanghai, #香港, #北京, #上).

Accounts in this group often use variations on the same profile name "民主, 人权" (democracy, human rights). These accounts also all use similar screen names (cnjs8, wib_dl, wib_s, cjss4, wib_z), similar profile pictures (often of generically attractive Asian women or photos with the words human rights or democracy), and similar or identical header pictures (images associated with human rights in China such as the famous "tank man" in Tiananmen Square). The 22 accounts that were among the top 100 posters in this dataset posted on average 118 tweets per day that used one of the hashtags monitored in this data

Table 9.1 **Top 100 Highest-Posting Accounts within China-Related Hashtags**

	Number of Accounts	Number of Posts	Proportion of Posts in Dataset (%)
Anti–Chinese State bots			
1989 group	22	117,578	10
Pan-Asia group	22	44,678	4
Independent anti–Chinese state bots	5	7,969	0.68
Both anti–Chinese state and commercial content	1	1,090	0.09
Other political bots			
Professional news bots	10	39,239	3
"Fake news" bots	4	10,213	0.87
Other non-political bots			
Commercial bots	8	34,860	3
Job bots	6	8,592	0.73
Other bots (non-political)	4	6,620	0.56
Account suspended			
Account suspended	18	64,170	5
TOTAL	100	335,009	28.44

collection. These accounts all utilized the Japanese-based service twitbot.net to post their content to Twitter.

Figure 9.1 shows the top four highest-posting accounts in this bot group within the analyzed hashtags across the data collection period, and shows how similar the

Figure 9.1 The Top Four Highest-Posting Accounts in the 1989 Bot Group.
Source: Author's screenshot June 16, 2017. Note: The 22 accounts in this group that were among the 100 highest-posting accounts in the dataset posted both original and retweeted content. All of the retweets of accounts in this group were originally posted by 吴仁华 (@wurenhua), a leader in the 1989 movement who fled to America following the protests and is now active in promoting democracy in China. Figure 9.2 shows two of these example posts. Both of the original posts by wurenhua have a picture from an important event from the 1989 pro-democracy movement. Accounts in this bot group retweet these messages, adding common hashtags such as #China, #Hongkong and #香港 (Hong Kong in simplified Mandarin) and #TFB, an abbreviation for "the follow back club," which indicates that if an account follows the user they will follow that user in return. This potentially might explain why all of the accounts in this group have a very similar number of friends and followers.

(a)

(b)

(c)

(d)

Figure 9.2 Examples of Forwarded Posts from the 1989 Bot Group. Source: Author's screen captures June 16, 2017. Note: While members of this group appear to retweet only posts from Wu Renhua, many of these bots also post frequent links to the Universal Declaration of Human Rights in Mandarin. All of these tweets are posted using the hashtags #China and #人权 (human rights in Mandarin); this means that, in particular, #人权 is dominated by this bot group. Eleven accounts in this bot group each posted more than 1,000 times using the hashtag 人权 during the data collection period.

accounts within this group appear. Three have almost identical screen names, two have identical profile pictures, and two have identical header images. The profile pictures and header images of all four accounts have a similar format. Three of the four accounts include a link to a blogspot.jp blog. While there is variation in the number of friends and followers between these accounts, each of these accounts has a very similar number of friends and followers, suggesting that they have gained followers through reciprocal following. Each of these accounts had posted at least twice in the previous 20 minutes and appeared to post frequently, having posted between 190,000 and 334,000 times since they were initially created.

THE PAN-ASIA GROUP

A second large bot group existed that aimed to disseminate information about the victims of the pan-Asian "Ponzi scheme." It has been reported that 220,000 people lost the money they had invested in the Kunming Pan Asia Nonferrous

Figure 9.3 Examples of Original Posts from the 1989 Bot Group. Source: Author's screenshots, June 16, 2017. Note: The existence of this coordinated bot group aimed at promoting human rights and democracy in China and keeping the aims of the 1989 protest movement alive is relatively surprising. Publishing in simplified Chinese, this group is presumably aimed at Chinese individuals, either those who jump the wall from the Chinese mainland to use Twitter or the Chinese diaspora (such as students studying abroad). As a result, information shared on Twitter with the hashtags commonly used by this bot group, such as #China and #人权 (human rights), appear to be dominated by this pro-democracy, anti–Chinese state information. Indeed, this is not the only anti-state group posting in simplified Mandarin on Twitter.

Metals Exchange when the exchange collapsed (China Economic Weekly, 2015; VOA Chinese, 2015). There have been many protests by those who lost money in the collapse and accusations that the local government was complicit in promoting the scheme and allowing it to continue.

This group appears to have a similar number of accounts (with both the 1989 group and the pan-Asia group having 22 accounts in the top 100 posting accounts in the dataset) but they post less frequently than the 1989 group. The 22 accounts in this group who were among the top 100 posters in the dataset post, on average, 43 times per day in one of the hashtags monitored in this data collection. This is lower than the cut-off point of 50 tweets per day used by some quantitative studies to identify likely bot activity. Additionally, accounts in this group do not appear to be using automation platforms or custom scripts to post to the platform, with the source of tweets for accounts in this group being either Twitter for Android or Twitter for iPhone.

Many of the accounts in this group utilize similar screen names that appear to be random strings of characters, such as GG8bjf0629Ehtvr, DkAvNtlRmLDHJYI, and 5KMGRvJX9mSYaoQ. However, other accounts in the group use more traditional names such as refugee_chinese, Sexymonkey793, and Devid98608606.

However, several of the accounts in this group present themselves as major Chinese news organizations in their profile name and display photos (using traditional Chinese characters) such as 雲南日報 (Yunan Daily News), 中國新聞 (China News), 中國·瑞麗 News (China Rili News), and CCTV or educational institutions such as 北京大学 (Peking University), 上海财经大学 (Shanghai University of Finance and Economics), or吉林大学 (Jilin University).

Figure 9.4 shows the top four highest-posting accounts in this group and demonstrates the similarity between accounts in this group. All four of these accounts have usernames composed of nonsensical strings of characters and numbers. However, three of the accounts have user names that suggest that they are media organizations. Despite publishing predominantly in simplified Chinese, each of these four accounts lists their location as being in the United States. Each of these accounts has approximately 1,000 friends and 300 followers and appears to post frequently, having posted between 14,000 and 37,000 tweets since their creation in either 2016 or 2017.

Figures 9.5 and 9.6 show examples of retweeted content from the pan-Asia group. These examples demonstrate the frequency of the activity of these accounts, the consistency of topic content, and the interrelations between these accounts, which appear predominantly to retweet content published by other accounts in the group.

OTHER ANTI-CHINESE STATE BOT ACTIVITY ON TWITTER

This analysis also found evidence of other independent anti-Chinese-state bots (such as pro-Uighur and pro-Hong Kong independence bots) on Twitter posting in simplified Chinese, Japanese, and English. One bot, which was perhaps associated with the 1989 group, posted quotes and links to the Universal Declaration of Human Rights in both simplified Chinese and Russian.

Restricting analysis to only the hashtags associated with Tibet and Buddhism (#dalailama, #buddhism, #Kadampa, and #Tibet) found no evidence of the pro-Chinese-state perspectives that were described in the previous section as having been prominent on Twitter in 2014/2015. Instead, within these Tibet- and Buddhism-related hashtags there was evidence of automation and groups

---

Figure 9.4 The Top Four Highest-Posting Accounts in the pan-Asia Group.
Source: Author's screenshots, June 16, 2017. Note: Several of these accounts used the same information in their profile descriptions, despite being created at different times. For instance, both China Ruili News, created in June 2016 with a stated location of California, US, and China Yunnan Mosuo (an ethnic minority) local conditions and customs. Devid, created in October 2016 with a stated location of New Jersey, US, had the same (nonsensical) profile description.

(a)

(b)

(c)

(d)

Figure 9.5 Example of Retweeted Content in the pan-Asia Group

working together to promote the messages of the Tibetan exile community and disseminating information about repression of ethnic Tibetans by China, predominantly in English.

Taken together, this analysis of computational propaganda in relation to Chinese political topics on Twitter seems to suggest that the Chinese state has given up the fight over discourse on Twitter, both in English and in Chinese. However, this content is aimed at a small number of Chinese users who have the technological means or desire to access Twitter. The next section examines evidence for the use of robots, fake accounts, and public opinion manipulation on China's version of Twitter: Weibo.

Case 4: Domestic Public Opinion Manipulation on Weibo

Although it is sometimes referred to as the Chinese Twitter, (Sina) Weibo, the largest microblogging platform in China, provides different affordances for

Figure 9.6 Example of Retweeted Content in the pan-Asia Group. Note: Accounts in this group tweeted with a wide variety of hashtags. This group showed up frequently in the dataset for their use of hashtags such as #北京 (Beijing) and #习近平 (Xi Jinping). However, as the screenshots above demonstrate, accounts in this group also post frequently in hashtags that were not monitored as part of this data collection.

political speech and public opinion manipulation than Twitter. It also has a very different user base, with high levels of penetration in urban and affluent areas of the Chinese mainland (Bolsover, 2017). Weibo has been seen as important in a variety of political events in China, such as the death of migrant Sun Zhigang in 2003 (which resulted in the abolition of the custody and repatriation system) and the release of blogger Guo Baofeng after a 2009 postcard-writing campaign (Yang & Calhoun, 2007; Zheng & Wu, 2005; Zhou, Chan, & Peng, 2008). Many commentators have pointed to the emergence of an online civil society on Weibo that encourages a renegotiation of acceptable political speech in China, with society constraining the state as much as the other way around (Yang, 2009, p. 45; Zheng, 2007).

Weibo is also more explicitly part of a strategy of political governance, with state mouthpieces encouraged to use the platform to promote their messages to citizens, and social media used to monitor public opinion. The state has also shown itself to be responsive to the political information posted online (Herold, 2008). Given its prominent place within Chinese politics and its supposed potential to challenge the existing balance of political power in Chinese society, it is unsurprising that there has been evidence of computational propaganda and public opinion manipulation on Weibo and other social media platforms in China. It has been estimated that individuals employed by the Chinese state post almost 500 million messages to social media every year as if they were the genuine opinions of ordinary people; 53 percent of these posts were on government-run websites and 47 percent on commercial websites (half of which were posted to Sina Weibo) (King et al., 2016).

Fake accounts also appear to be frequently employed to manipulate information on Weibo. In an analysis of networks of news dissemination from major information providers, evidence of retweeting from fake accounts was found in three of the 50 analyzed stories, and 30 percent of accounts that acted as opinion leaders for disseminating news information were fake (Bolsover, 2013a). The fake accounts identified in this research were highly clustered, with accounts within a particular group all following each other. Accounts within a group often used the same or similar profile pictures. These accounts had far below the average number of followers on the platform. Accounts within a particular group would "all post the same commentary on the same message, often posting 20 messages within several minutes . . . never posted original messages, only retweeted others' content, and they had no interaction with other users on their profiles" (Bolsover, 2013a). The activity of these fake accounts meant that some news stories appeared much more popular on the platform and may have been included in site trending topics, and thus seen and forwarded by many more individual Weibo users due to the influence of these fraudulent accounts.

These fraudulent accounts are recognized as a major problem on Weibo; however, it is hard to estimate the scale of the issue. The platform itself deletes known fraudulent accounts to prevent this activity (Yu, Asur, & Huberman, 2012), and the posts of some accounts that appear to have been marked by the platform as fraudulent are hidden from user timelines (Bolsover, 2017). It is estimated that close to or even more than five percent of accounts on Weibo may be fake (Bolsover, 2017).

These pieces of quantitative research provide an indication of the scale of public opinion manipulation that occurs on Weibo but cannot speak to the actual content and drive of the actions of these fraudulent accounts. They also cannot speak to a particularly important functionality of Weibo in relation to online political information—comments. A major difference between Twitter and Weibo that is particularly relevant to its political position in the country is that Weibo posts provide threaded inline commenting functions at the site of the original post. These comments can be sorted by most popular, verified users, or the logged in user's connections. While retweeting and participating in conversations via hashtags are seen as the most important affordances for political conversation on Twitter, comments are a particularly important part of political and social discourse on Weibo.

In order to investigate whether evidence of computational propaganda appears in Weibo comments, the posts of 25 major information providers—news organizations, government departments, and official mouthpieces—were collected over the Spring Festival period. Prior research has suggested that there are higher levels of state-led public opinion manipulation in China during official holidays (King et al., 2016). This dataset contained 6,145 posts from these major information providers between January 26 and February 7, 2017. Comment data for each of these posts was collected (at least two weeks after comments were originally posted to ensure that commenting had finished on these stories). This dataset contained 1,543,165 comments by 815,776 unique users. These users posted on average 1.89 comments across the collected news stories during the time period.

This dataset revealed little evidence of automation within the comments on these news stories. In all, 145 users posted 100 or more comments across all the examined news stories. These users did not appear to be using automated means to make these posts. However, the content of the posts of the highest-posting users indicates that there may be significant trolling within these comments. For instance, the majority of comments left by the highest-posting users in this dataset were generic attacks on other users, and were not all left on the same news story but spanned multiple news stories analyzed within the dataset. The majority of comments from the highest-posting user were attacks on the intelligence or honor of another named poster, such as "Reply @username: Everyone in your family has a hole in their brain, your father and mother's brain issues are especially serious, how can they have given birth so such a low quality person" or "Reply @username: I will kill your father, I can say that too."

Other comments by this user appeared to indicate strong nationalism and support for the state, such as "China is so great, during Spring Festival the whole world will be busy! Go China, China is mighty [emoji for heart] [emoji for heart]." Another post by the same user on a different news story held a similar sentiment: "China celebrates Spring Festival, the whole world will be more lively, China is great, go China!" While the majority of users who posted comments on these stories appear to be genuine individuals posting their opinions and thoughts, this evidence of high posting by some troll accounts would probably drive the conversation away from productive discussions about these political issues.

Conclusions

Computational propaganda is a growing phenomenon in Western politics. An increasing number of political campaigns and issue movements have been shown to employ fake accounts, robots, and propaganda to further their causes on social media and influence the political process. This chapter presents the first ever summary of computational propaganda in and about China.

The political potential of China's domestic Internet is highly controlled, using sophisticated censorship and filtering technologies, a complex legislative regime, and the personnel and cooperation of major domestic media companies. Fake accounts are common on China's microblogging giant Sina Weibo, and are active in disseminating certain information, both political and commercial. Chinese state employees also post large amounts of positive propaganda online to social media, state websites, and newspaper websites, particularly around sensitive times.

China, however, appears to have given up the computational propaganda fight on Twitter, in both English and Chinese. However, large and well-organized groups use computational propaganda on Twitter to promote information and perspectives that run counter to Chinese state messages—the 1989 democracy movement, Tibetan rights, and the victims of the pan-Asia scheme. Additionally, independent bots promote Uighur and Hong Kong independence. Much of this content is in simplified Chinese and presumably aimed at the Chinese diaspora as well as the population of mainland Chinese who "jump the wall" to use blocked foreign platforms.

The case of China presents several lessons for Western democracies looking to tackle "fake news," bots, and other hallmarks of computational propaganda. First, the Chinese state's active efforts to control online information are reminiscent of many of the strategies currently proposed to combat computational propaganda in the West. These strategies have been relatively successful in controlling the online information environment, but their employment would run counter to democratic principles. It may, however, be possible to learn from the technological, legislative, and practical successes of Chinese computational propaganda without tending toward authoritarianism.

Additionally, the contrasting cases of the pro-state Tibet spam accounts and anti-state human rights accounts show that Twitter is a battleground for public opinion and that political players apparently see a lot to gain in the use of these computational propaganda techniques to influence the online information environment, particularly in flooding discourse on Twitter with certain information about a particular issue. These computational propaganda techniques are rapidly becoming more widespread and more sophisticated, and greater attention needs to be turned to understanding the landscape of online opinion before these nascent online public spheres are entirely undermined by these largely automated propaganda efforts.

References

Adamic, L.A., & Glance, N. (2005). The Political Blogosphere and the 2004 US Election: Divided They Blog. In *Proceedings of the 3rd international Workshop on Link Discovery* (pp. 36–43). Retrieved from http://dl.acm.org/citation.cfm?id=1134277

Bandurski, D. (2015, December 9). How Xi Jinping Sees the Internet. China Media Project. Retrieved from http://cmp.hku.hk/2015/12/09/39451/.

Bolsover, G. (2013a). *News in China's New Information Environment: Dissemination Patterns, Opinion Leaders and News Commentary on Weibo* (SSRN Scholarly Paper No. ID 2257794). Rochester, NY: Social Science Research Network. Retrieved from http://papers.ssrn.com/abstract=2257794.

Bolsover, G. (7 June 2013b). Exposing Wrongdoing and Controlling Public Opinion Through Online Video in China. Retrieved from http://politicsinspires.org/china-exposing-wrongdoing-and-controlling-public-opinion-through-online-video/

Bolsover, G. (2017, January). *Technology and Political Speech: Commercialisation, Authoritarianism and the Supposed Death of the Internet's Democratic Potential.* Working Paper. University of Oxford, UK.

Brady, A.-M. (2009). *Marketing Dictatorship: Propaganda and Thought Work in Contemporary China.* Rowman & Littlefield Publishers. Retrieved from https://books.google.com/books?hl=es&lr=&id=v4jFCwAAQBAJ&oi=fnd&pg=PR5&dq=marketing+dictatorship&ots=Bn6if2fYb8&sig=_u7AuoncpkhHNaPlGSOO_xOefXk.

Brady, A.-M., & Juntao, W. (2009). China's Strengthened New Order and the Role of Propaganda. *Journal of Contemporary China, 18*(62), 767–788.

Cammaerts, B. (2008). Critiques on the Participatory Potentials of Web 2.0. *Communication, Culture & Critique, 1*(4), 358–377. https://doi.org/10.1111/j.1753-9137.2008.00028.x.

China Economic Weekly. (2015). The Pan Asia Crisis: A 40 Billion "Ponzi Scheme"? (泛亚危机：400亿的"庞氏骗局"？). September 21, 2015. *China Economic Weekly* (中国经济周刊). Retrieved from http://news.xinhuanet.com/finance/2015-09/21/c_128252059.htm.

CNNIC. (2015). 中国互联网络发展状况统计报告 (Statistical report on China's Internet development).

Cobain, I., & Taylor, M. (23 November 2016). Far-Right Terrorist Thomas Mair Jailed for Life for Jo Cox Murder. *The Guardian*. Retrieved from https://www.theguardian.com/uk-news/2016/nov/23/thomas-mair-found-guilty-of-jo-cox-murder.

Faiola, A., & Kirchner, S. (5 April 2017). How Do You Stop Fake News? In Germany, with a Law. *Washington Post*. Retrieved from https://www.washingtonpost.com/world/europe/how-do-you-stop-fake-news-in-germany-with-a-law/2017/04/05/e6834ad6-1a08-11e7-bcc2-7d1a0973e7b2_story.html.

Fu, K., Chan, C., & Chau, M. (2013). Assessing Censorship on Microblogs in China: Discriminatory Keyword Analysis and the Real-Name Registration Policy. *Internet Computing, IEEE*, 17(3), 42–50.

General Office of the Communist Party of China. (2012). *Communiqué on the Current State of the Ideological Sphere* (Document no. 9). Retrieved from https://chinacopyrightandmedia.wordpress.com/2013/04/22/communique-on-the-current-state-of-the-ideological-sphere-document-no-9/.

Helm, T. (2016, September 10). Brexit camp abandons £350m-a-week NHS funding pledge. *The Guardian*. Retrieved from https://www.theguardian.com/politics/2016/sep/10/brexit-camp-abandons-350-million-pound-nhs-pledge.

Herold, D. K. (2008). Development of a Civic Society Online?: Internet Vigilantism and State Control in Chinese Cyberspace. Retrieved from http://repository.lib.polyu.edu.hk/jspui/handle/10397/4434.

Howard, P.N., Bolsover, G., Kollanyi, B., Bradshaw, S., & Neudert, L.-M. (2017). Junk News and Bots during the US Election: What Were Michigan Voters Sharing over Twitter? *COMPROP Data Memo* 2017.1.

Howard, P.N., & Kollanyi, B. (2016). Bots, #StrongerIn, and #Brexit: Computational Propaganda during the UK–EU Referendum. *SSRN*. Retrieved from https://papers.ssrn.com/sol3/papers.cfm?abstract_id=2798311.

Howard, P.N., & Woolley, S.C. (2016). Bots and Automation over Twitter during the US Election. Retrieved from http://politicalbots.org/wp-content/uploads/2016/11/Data-Memo-US-Election.pdf.

Institute for Propaganda Analysis. (1995). How to Detect Propaganda. In R. Jackall (Ed.), *Propaganda* (pp. 217–224). Basingstoke and London: Macmillan.

Jackall, R. (1995). *Propaganda*. Basingstoke and London: Macmillan.

King, G., Pan, J., & Roberts, M. (2012). How Censorship in China Allows Government Criticism but Silences Collective Expression. In *APSA 2012* annual meeting paper. Retrieved from http://papers.ssrn.com/sol3/papers.cfm?abstract_id=2104894.

King, G., Pan, J., & Roberts, M. E. (2016). How the Chinese Government Fabricates Social Media Posts for Strategic Distraction, Not Engaged Argument. Retrieved from http://gking.harvard.edu/files/gking/files/50c.pdf?m=1464086643.

Klausen, J. (2015). Tweeting the Jihad: Social Media Networks of Western Foreign Fighters in Syria and Iraq. *Studies in Conflict & Terrorism*, 38(1), 1–22.

Lasswell, H. D. (1995). Propaganda. In R. Jackall (Ed.), *Propaganda* (pp. 13–25). Basingstoke and London: Macmillan.

Lee, F. L. (2015). Social Movement as civic Education: Communication Activities and Understanding of Civil Disobedience in the Umbrella Movement. *Chinese Journal of Communication*, 8(4), 393–411.

Lee, F. L., & Chan, J. M. (2016). Digital Media Activities and Mode of Participation in a Protest Campaign: A Study of the Umbrella Movement. *Information, Communication & Society*, 19(1), 4–22.

Lu, F., & Ma, X. (2015). Keep Silent and Make a Big Fortune: Partially Free Media and an Authoritarian Intra-Elite Election. Retrieved from http://xiao-ma.me/s/Author.pdf.

Moore, M. (2014, January 30). China Kills Off Discussion on Weibo after Internet Crackdown. Retrieved from http://www.telegraph.co.uk/news/worldnews/asia/china/10608245/China-kills-off-discussion-on-Weibo-after-internet-crackdown.html.

Morozov, E. (2009). Think Again: Twitter. August 7, 2009. *Foreign Policy*. Retrieved from http://foreignpolicy.com/2009/08/07/think-again-twitter/.

Nip, J. Y., & Fu, K. (2016). Challenging Official Propaganda? Public Opinion Leaders on Sina Weibo. *The China Quarterly, 225*, 122–144.

Ng, J. (2015). Tracking Censorship on WeChat's Public Accounts Platform. Retrieved from https://citizenlab.org/2015/07/tracking-censorship-on-wechat-public-accounts-platform/.

Pariser, E. (2012). *The Filter Bubble: What the Internet Is Hiding from You*. London: Penguin. Retrieved from http://www.amazon.co.uk/The-Filter-Bubble-Internet-Hiding/dp/0241954525.

Percy. (9 January 2015). GFW Upgrade Fail—Visitors to Blocked Sites Redirected to Porn. *GreatFire Analyzer*. Retrieved from https://en.greatfire.org/blog/2015/jan/gfw-upgrade-fail-visitors-blocked-sites-redirected-porn.

Perry, E. J. (2008). Chinese Conceptions of: From Mencius to Mao—and Now. *Perspectives on Politics, 6*(01), 37–50. https://doi.org/10.1017/S1537592708080055.

SARFT. (2016, December 16). 国家新闻出版广电总局发布微博、微信等网络社交平台传播视听节目的管理规定 (The National Press and Publication Administration of Radio, Film and Television issues management requirements for the dissemination of audio-visual programs on Weibo, Wexin and other social networking platforms). Retrieved from http://www.sarft.gov.cn/art/2016/12/16/art_113_32237.html.

Shue, V. (2004). Legitimacy Crisis in China? In S. Rosen & P.H. Gries (Eds.), *State and Society in 21st Century China* (pp. 24–49). London: Routledge.

Solon, O., & Wong, J. C. (2016). Facebook's Plan to Tackle Fake News Raises Questions over Limitations. December 16, 2016. *The Guardian*. Retrieved from https://www.theguardian.com/technology/2016/dec/16/facebook-fake-news-system-problems-fact-checking.

Song, F. (22 May 2015). State Governance in the Internet Era. *Red Flag Manuscripts*. (R. Creemers, Trans.) Retrieved from https://chinacopyrightandmedia.wordpress.com/2015/06/01/state-governance-in-the-internet-era/.

Statista. (2016). Penetration of Leading Social Networks in Hong Kong as of 4th Quarter 2016. Retrieved from https://www.statista.com/statistics/412500/hk-social-network-penetration/.

Stern, R. E., & Hassid, J. (2012). Amplifying Silence Uncertainty and Control Parables in Contemporary China. *Comparative Political Studies, 45*(10), 1230–1254.

Stockmann, D. (2012). *Media Commercialization and Authoritarian Rule in China*. New York: Cambridge University Press.

Sullivan, J. (2012). A Tale of Two Microblogs in China. *Media, Culture & Society, 34*(6), 773–783.

UK Parliament. (30 January 2017). "Fake news" Inquiry Launched. Retrieved from https://www.parliament.uk/business/committees/committees-a-z/commons-select/culture-media-and-sport-committee/news-parliament-2015/fake-news-launch-16-17/.

VOA Chinese. (2015, September 22). The Pan-Asia Ponzi Scheme (泛亚"庞氏骗局"：22万投资人的家当有望讨回吗？). *VOA Chinese* (美国之音). Retrieved from http://www.voachinese.com/a/fanya-metal-exchange-20150921/2973451.html.

Wilson, G. (1993). The Mass Media in China: An Evolution that Failed. *Journal of Northwest Communication Association, 1993*, 21–33.

Winfield, B. H., & Peng, Z. (2005). Market or Party Controls? Chinese Media in Transition. *Gazette, 67*(3), 255–270.

World Bank. (25 March 2015). *China Overview*. Retrieved from http://www.worldbank.org/en/country/china/overview.

Xinhua. (2016, February 19). At the Party's news and public opinion work conference, Xi Jinping stresses persisting in the correct orientation, innovating methods and means, and raising the dissemination strength and guidance strength of news and public opinion (习近平:坚持正确方向创新方法手段　提高新闻舆论传播力引导力). *People's*

Daily (人民日报). Retrieved from http://politics.people.com.cn/n1/2016/0219/c1024-28136159.html.

Yang, G. (2009). *The Power of the Internet in China: Citizen Activism Online*. New York: Columbia University Press.

Yang, G., & Calhoun, C. (2007). Media, Civil Society, and the Rise of a Green Public Sphere in China. *China Information, 21*(2), 211–236. https://doi.org/10.1177/0920203X07079644.

Yu, L.L., Asur, S., & Huberman, B.A. (2012). Artificial Inflation: The Real Story of Trends and Trend-Setters in Sina Weibo. In 2012 International Conference on Privacy, Security, Risk and Trust (PASSAT) and 2012 International Conference on Social Computing (SocialCom) (pp. 514–519). *IEEE*. Retrieved from http://ieeexplore.ieee.org/xpls/abs_all.jsp?arnumber=6406395.

Zhao, Y. (2000). From Commercialization to Conglomeration: The Transformation of the Chinese Press within the Orbit of the Party State. *Journal of Communication, 50*(2), 3–26.

Zheng, Y. (2007). Technological empowerment: The Internet, state, and society in China. Stanford University Press. Retrieved from http://dl.acm.org/citation.cfm?id=1564953.

Zheng, Y., & Wu, G. (2005). Information technology, public space, and collective action in China. Comparative Political Studies, 38(5), 507–536. https://doi.org/10.1177/0010414004273505.

Zhou, X., Chan, Y.-Y., & Peng, Z.-M. (2008). Deliberativeness of online political discussion. Journalism Studies, 9(5), 759–770. https://doi.org/10.1080/14616700802207771.

Zhu, T., Phipps, D., Pridgen, A., Crandall, J.R., & Wallach, D.S. (2013). The velocity of censorship: High-fidelity detection of microblog post deletions (arXiv e-print No. 1303.0597). Retrieved from http://arxiv.org/abs/1303.0597.

Part III

CONCLUSIONS

Conclusion

Political Parties, Politicians, and Computational Propaganda

SAMUEL C. WOOLLEY AND PHILIP N. HOWARD

Can Democracy Survive Computational Propaganda?

We find several distinct global trends in computational propaganda. While it is true that social media are significant platforms for political engagement, crucial channels for disseminating news content, and the primary media over which young people develop their political identities, they are also—and perhaps in part because of these affordances—vessels for control. In some countries this problem is exacerbated because companies such as Facebook have effectively become monopoly platforms for public life. In several democracies the majority of voters use social media to share political news and information, especially during elections (Bakshy, Messing, & Adamic, 2015). In countries where only small proportions of the public have regular access to social media, such platforms are still fundamental infrastructure for political conversation among the journalists, civil society leaders, and political elites (Farhi, 2009; Hermida, 2010). With this confluence of communication and sense making comes efforts to co-opt the flow of communication.

Social media are actively used as a tool for public opinion manipulation, though in diverse ways and on different topics. In authoritarian countries, social media platforms are a primary means of social control. This is especially true during political and security crises but is generally true in day to day life. In democracies, social media are actively used for computational propaganda either through broad efforts at opinion manipulation or targeted experiments on particular segments of the public. In every country we found civil society groups trying, but struggling, to protect themselves and respond to active misinformation campaigns.

We face new challenges in the investigation of automation and fake accounts on social media. Bots and sock-puppet accounts—fake accounts run by people—are key tools for spreading computational propaganda. Automation and anonymity allow for large scale amplification of some ideals or candidates for office alongside suppression of others. We have found that political actors are adapting their automation in response to our research. This suggests that the campaigners behind fake accounts and the people doing their "patriotic programming" are aware of the negative coverage that this gets in the news media.

We have also found several kinds of bot networks that are quite active but that fall below our formal threshold of what counts as a bot—or highly automated. For countries where Twitter is not a particularly important social media platform, it seems that bots are prevalent but not performing as efficiently as bot networks in countries with lots of Twitter users. Bots do not necessarily need to message at high rates in order to adversely affect public opinion or trending algorithms. Large numbers of automated accounts can be run by one person, converge on a topic or hashtag, and through this affect the flow of political communication.

Increasingly, bots supported via close attention from human operators—cyborg accounts—are being used to circumvent algorithms set to detect automation. Headless browsing bots get around these mechanisms by logging on to social media sites rather than via the application programming interface (API). Coordinated human-run accounts have also been successful in political hashtag bombing and trend manipulation (Musgrave, 2017). In many countries there are large numbers of "sleeper bots" (Woolley & Howard, 2016; Bradshaw & Howard, 2017). These are accounts that have only tweeted a few times, usually in scattered ways, and have other account features that suggest automation.

It is difficult to put research findings into service for public policy recommendations in consistent ways across countries, because the legal questions about computational propaganda vary greatly from country to country. During the 2015 election in Canada, comedienne Sarah Silverman encouraged Canadians to vote for the National Democratic Party over Twitter (Itzkoff, 2018). Is she a foreigner influencing voters in contravention of the Canada Elections Act? If bots propagate her message after campaigning is supposed to stop, are platforms or bot writers interfering with the election? When political bots are built and launched using crowd-sourced or open-source code, who is responsible for their actions? Also, how can we preserve democratically beneficial bots? It has been argued that bots can act as social scaffolding for journalists and democratic activists (Hwang & Woolley, 2016; S. Woolley et al.,

2016)? However, positive uses are threatened by attempts to prevent malicious uses of social automation.

The advantage of cross-national comparisons is in yielding evidence about which policy responses can work well. In Taiwan the government has responded with an aggressive media literacy campaign, and bots that will check facts for the public. In Ukraine the government response has been minimal, but there are a growing number of private firms trying to make a business of fact checking and protecting social media users—Youscan.io, ContextMedia, Noksfishes, SemanticForce, and InfoStream. In the United States, platforms like BotoMeter, NewsbotAI, and botcheck.me are becoming industry standards for detecting nefarious bots as well as disinformation. However, it is important to note, whether solutions are short term or long term, that global society needs fixes that are social as well as technological—the Taiwanese case being a good example of this two-pronged approach. Moreover, our research shows this is not simply an issue that can be solved by giving users access to more or better information. Companies and governments have a crucial role in combating computational propaganda through new policies and interventions.

Automated political communication involves the creation, transmission, and controlled mutation of significant political symbols over expansive social networks. Indeed, the impact of digital information infrastructure on how political culture is produced is at least as interesting, though under-studied, as the impact of infrastructure on how political culture is consumed. While we can theorize about the ways in which computational propaganda may violate political values or the social contract writ large, it is difficult to quantify these effects. But the case studies in this collection of working papers demonstrate the origins and very concrete consequences of computational propaganda.

It is time for social media firms to design for democracy. For democracies, there will always be big elections ahead. Let's assume that authoritarian governments will continue to use social media as a tool for political control. But for democracies, we should assume that encouraging people to vote is a good thing. Promoting political news and information from reputable outlets is crucial. Ultimately, designing for democracy, in systematic ways, will help restore trust in social media systems.

Computational propaganda is now one of the most powerful tools against democracy. Social media firms may not be creating this nasty content, but they are the platform for it. The Facebook Newsfeed, and Trending features on sites like Twitter and YouTube, produce curated content (Gillespie, 2010). This means that these features prioritize, or control, the information that people see. Because social media companies have made decisions to control what information or news people see, these entities have responsibility for making sure this information is not harmful, harassing, or false. This is especially true during pivotal political events like elections, but also true in general.

Platforms need to significantly redesign themselves if democracy is going to survive social media. Moreover, they cannot rely upon tired defenses about being technology not media companies. Trending features, algorithmic curation, and personalized news feeds mean that companies do, to use their language, arbitrate truth. Because they control information flow, they are media companies. To solve these problems, social media companies must confront their role as media platform. They must design for democracy.

Remaining Questions

Cross-country comparison is a powerful way of understanding real trends and lived political experience. Yet all of the case studies here have conclusions that beg more questions, some theoretical and others practical. How should democracies advance security while protecting privacy? When should reasonable forms of surveillance be implemented, and under what circumstances? What technological design principles might provide both collective and personal security? How can we make algorithmic decision-making transparent, fair, and accountable? How can we create regulations to keep pace with innovation to safeguard our rights to be treated fairly by algorithmic decision-making systems?

Research Challenges Ahead

While the researchers in this collection have demonstrated the global spread of political propaganda that takes advantage of the affordances of social media algorithms, there are several important political communication research questions that need answering. We know very little about the actual influence of highly automated accounts on individual political attitudes, aspirations, and behaviors. In short, it is hard to demonstrate that any particular tweet, Facebook post, or other social media message has a direct effect on a voter. Notably, this test is one that many political communication researchers dismiss as misinformed when it comes to print, radio, or television, but it has reappeared as an expectation of social media research. But more broadly, making a causal claim from social media use to citizen engagement, trust in institutions, or voter sophistication is proving difficult to do even in countries for which there are significant amounts of data. In democracies across the global south, understanding these dynamics are an important research challenge.

Cross-Case Comparison

Table C.1 summarizes the various national contexts we have investigated, and the consequences of having important political actors in each country develop and apply algorithms and automation in public discourse. The precise applications also vary—from referenda and elections to policy debates and national security crises. There are also some disturbing similarities between the contexts and consequences among countries we would normally distinguish as being democracies or authoritarian regimes.

Indeed, we have argued elsewhere that technology use and policy has become the most important defining feature of regime type, since technology use and policy has become the best, most consistent evidence on how a governance system prioritizes human rights, media freedoms, election interference, and the myriad other features we use to determine regime type.

Conclusion

Democracy itself is under assault from foreign governments and internal threats, such that democratic institutions may not flourish unless social data science puts our existing knowledge and theories about politics, public opinion, and political communication to work. These threats are current and urgent, and, if not understood and addressed in an agile manner, will further undermine European democracies. Given current trends, it is likely that some political actors will begin using machine learning applications to produce political content during elections, or fully fake videos that are indistinguishable from real news, to undermine the public confidence in shared information and reasoned debate. Most democratic governments are preparing their legal and regulatory responses. Yet, unintended consequences from over-regulation may be as damaging to democratic systems as the threats themselves.

Technology innovation often provides new opportunities to dream of possible political futures. It invariably inspires new research questions in those of us who study public life, especially when new information technologies appear to exacerbate social inequalities and cause social problems rather than mitigate or solve them. The causes and consequences of computational propaganda certainly vary from country to country, and we are eager to develop a large research community that is normatively committed to redress social inequalities, solve public problems, and strengthen democratic institutions.

Table C.1 **Country Specific Breakdowns of Computational Propaganda**

Country	Domestic Political Actors Involved	Foreign Political Actors Involved	Prominence of Computational Propaganda in Political Communication	Observations
China	State	N/A	Low	Much more human-driven propaganda campaigns on behalf of the party than those facilitated by bots.
Brazil	Parties, Firms, Lobbyists	N/A	High	Active use of automation, trolls, on social media since 2014, implicated in several presidential elections, impeachment process, and 2016 mayoral race in Rio.
Canada	Parties, Firms, Civil Society groups	N/A	Low	Though political bots are not as active in Canada as in some cases, they still retain influence. Several types of distinct political bots exist and are outlined.
Germany	Parties	N/A	Moderate	Computational propaganda played less of a role than expected during the 2017 German election— potentially because of public awareness, a robust public media, and other factors.
Poland	Parties, Firms	Russian	Moderate	Like Ukraine, Poland is near enough to Russia to experience propaganda from the Kremlin. Internal Polish parties and firms make and deploy computational propaganda.
Taiwan	Parties	Chinese	High	Taiwan experiences propaganda over social media from the Chinese mainland, and likely the Chinese state. It is mostly human driven.

Table C.1 **Continued**

Country	Domestic Political Actors Involved	Foreign Political Actors Involved	Prominence of Computational Propaganda in Political Communication	Observations
United States	Parties, Firms, Lobbyists, Civil Society Groups	Russian	Moderate	Computational propaganda played a significant role in the 2016 US presidential election, with numerous political actor types deploying and using bots in attempting to manipulate public opinion.
Ukraine	Parties, State, Firms, Civil Society Groups	Russian	High	Ukraine is on the frontline of computational propaganda, and myriad offline problems, from Russia. It is perhaps the most advanced, and worrisome, case of computational propaganda explored here.
Russia	Parties, State	N/A	High	The Russian government, and entities including the Internet Research Agency, have developed new strategies for computational propaganda and honed kompromat strategies from the Cold War in attempts to influence both domestic and foreign political events over social media.

References

Bakshy, E., Messing, S., & Adamic, L. (2015). Exposure to Ideologically Diverse News and Opinion on Facebook. *Science*, aaa1160. https://doi.org/10.1126/science.aaa1160.

Bennett, W. L., & Segerberg, A. (2013). *The Logic of Connective Action: Digital Media and the Personalization of Contentious Politics.* Cambridge University Press. Retrieved from http://books.google.co.uk/books?hl=en&lr=lang_en&id=nZFtAAAAQBAJ&oi=fnd&pg=PR8&dq=the+logic+of+connective+action&ots=RpxfX64PVh&sig=0sme_CHVXxqs4hhrlFhJAiBovTE.

Bradshaw, S., & Howard, P. (2017). *Troops, Trolls and Troublemakers: A Global Inventory of Organized Social Media Manipulation* (Computational Propaganda Project Working Paper Series No. 2017.12) (p. 37). Oxford: University of Oxford. Retrieved from http://comprop.oii.ox.ac.uk/2017/07/17/troops-trolls-and-trouble-makers-a-global-inventory-of-organized-social-media-manipulation/.

Farhi, P. (2009). The Twitter Explosion: Whether they are reporting about it, finding sources on it or urging viewers, listeners and readers to follow them on it, journalists just can't seem to get enough of the social networking service. Just how effective is it as a journalism tool? *American Journalism Review, 31*(3), 26–32.

Gillespie, T. (2010). The Politics of "Platforms." *New Media & Society, 12*(3), 347–364. https://doi.org/10.1177/1461444809342738.

Hermida, A. (2010). Twittering the News. *Journalism Practice, 4*(3), 297–308. https://doi.org/10.1080/17512781003640703.

Howard, P. N. (2010). *The Digital Origins of Dictatorship and Democracy: Information Technology and Political Islam.* New York: Oxford University Press. Retrieved from http://books.google.com/books?hl=en&lr=&id=T6xoAgAAQBAJ&oi=fnd&pg=PR9&dq=Philip+N.+Howard&ots=_fUmO-NrDz&sig=0RaOk-uotRBxQN6eqDPTkJiTJbs.

Hwang, T., Woolley, S., & Borel, B. (2016, March 8). How Politicians Should and Shouldn't Use Twitter Bots. *Slate.* Retrieved from http://www.slate.com/articles/technology/future_tense/2016/03/how_politicians_should_use_twitter_bots.html.

Itzkoff, D. (2018, January 20). Sarah Silverman on Bernie or Bust, and the Joke She Didn't Tell. *The New York Times.* Retrieved from https://www.nytimes.com/2016/07/27/arts/television/sarah-silverman-bernie-or-bust-democratic-national-convention-hillary-clinton.html.

Musgrave, S. (2017, August 9). "I Get Called a Russian Bot 50 Times a Day." *POLITICO Magazine.* Retrieved from http://politi.co/2viAxZA.

Woolley, S. C. (2016). Automating Power: Social Bot Interference in Global Politics. *First Monday, 21*(4). Retrieved from http://firstmonday.org/ojs/index.php/fm/article/view/6161.

Woolley, S. C., & Howard, P. N. (2016). Automation, Algorithms, and Politics| Political Communication, Computational Propaganda, and Autonomous Agents—Introduction. *International Journal of Communication, 10*(0), 9.

Woolley, S. C., boyd, danah, Broussard, M., Elish, M., Fader, L., Hwang, T., . . . Shorey, S. (2016, February 23). How to Think About Bots. Retrieved from http://motherboard.vice.com/read/how-to-think-about-bots.

Author Bios

Dan Arnaudo is a senior program manager at the National Democratic Institute. He is a research fellow at the University of Washington's Center for Global Studies and the Igrapé Institute of Rio de Janeiro. His research focuses on Internet governance, cybersecurity, and information and communication technologies for development (ICT4D). He earned master's degrees in information management and international studies at University of Washington by completing a thesis on Brazil and its Bill of Rights for the Internet, the Marco Civil. In the past, he has worked for the Arms Control Association, the Carnegie Endowment for International Peace, and the Carter Center.

Gillian Bolsover is a former researcher on the computational propaganda project at the Oxford Internet Institute (OII), University of Oxford. She holds a DPhil from OII and a master's degree in media and communications from the London School of Economics. Her current work investigates the use of bots, algorithms, and other forms of automated online political opinion manipulation, with a particular focus on China.

Elizabeth Dubois is an assistant professor at the University of Ottawa. Her work examines digital media, influence, and political engagement. She is a graduate of the Oxford Internet Institute at the University of Oxford where she completed a DPhil (PhD) in information, communication, and the social sciences as well as an MSc in the social sciences of the Internet (distinction). She has a BA Hons. specialization in communication (summa cum laude) from the University of Ottawa. Elizabeth was a SSHRC doctoral fellow, Clarendon fellow, and Killam fellow (Fulbright Canada).

Robert Gorwa is a DPhil student in the department of politics and international relations at the University of Oxford. His doctoral work looks at the effects of technology on various international relations phenomena, with a focus on the Internet and its implications for international security, diplomacy, and conflict. He is particularly interested in the way that governments and other actors use social media to exert international influence. He holds a BA in international relations from the University of British Columbia and an MSc from the Oxford Internet Institute, where he focused on the politics, policy, and political economy of social bots.

Douglas Guilbeault is a PhD researcher at the Annenberg School for Communication at the University of Pennsylvania and a research associate at the Digital Intelligence Lab at the Institute for the Future. He studies social bots in the Network Dynamics Group at Penn. He holds an MA in cognitive linguistics from the University of British Columbia and a BA in philosophy, rhetoric, and cognitive science from the University of Waterloo. Doug's research is funded through a Joseph-Armand Bombardier, PhD Scholarship from the Social Sciences and Humanities Research Council of Canada.

Philip N. Howard is director and statutory professor of Internet studies at the Oxford Internet Institute and a senior fellow at Balliol College at the University of Oxford. He has published eight books and over 120 academic articles and public essays on information technology, international affairs, and public life. Howard's books include *The Managed Citizen* (Cambridge, 2006), the *Digital Origins of Dictatorship and Democracy* (Oxford, 2010), and most recently, *Pax Technica: How the Internet of Things May Set Us Free or Lock Us Up* (Yale, 2015).

Fenwick McKelvey is an assistant professor in information and communication technology policy in the department of communication at Concordia University. Investigating the machines, bots, artificial intelligence, algorithms, and daemons that make up the Internet's infrastructure, his research takes him from debates at the Canadian Radio and Television Commission to data centers and from Gilles Deleuze to John Dewey. His recent and ongoing studies have focused on the daemons that manage Internet flows and their role in network neutrality debates, the new software and social media platforms that mediate political engagement, and the algorithms and AIs that govern the discoverability of online content.

Nicholas J. Monaco is a research associate at Graphika and at the Digital Intelligence Lab at the Institute for the Future where he studies automation, disinformation, and online political communication. He received his master of science in computational linguistics from the University of Washington and his BA in linguistics from the University of Wisconsin at Madison. Previously, he worked for Pacific Social Architecting Corporation on research around the political use of social bots. His research interests include Chinese, French and German linguistics, political bots, automation/AI, computational propaganda, and foreign affairs. He had written about these topics for commentary venues such as *Fortune* and *TechCrunch*.

Lisa-Maria N. Neudert is a researcher on the computational propaganda project at the Oxford Internet Institute (OII), University of Oxford and a DPhil student at OII. Selected as a Fulbright Scholar, Lisa-Maria studied communication technologies & diplomacy at the Georgetown University, Washington DC, and holds a BA in communication science from the Ludwig-Maxmilians-University, Munich. She has worked in various fields in the (digital) communications sector including radio & broadcast news journalism (ARD), communication consulting (Allianz Singapore), and marketing (Coca-Cola, BBDO). She has conducted research at SDA Bocconi, Milan, the National University of Singapore and Ludwig-Maximilians-University, Munich.

Dariya Orlova is a senior lecturer and media researcher at the Mohyla School of Journalism at the National University of Kyiv and a former visiting professor at the Center for Russia, East European, and Eurasian Studies at Stanford University. She received her PhD in mass communication in 2013 from the Autonomous University of Barcelona and National University of Kyiv-Mohyla Academy with a thesis on "Representation of 'Europe' in the Mediatized Discourse of Ukrainian Political Elites." Her research interests include political communication, media transformations in post-Soviet countries, journalism culture, media and national identity.

Sergey Sanovich is a PhD student in the Wilf family department of politics at New York University. He studies institutions and policies that enable authoritarian regimes to stay in power. Specifically, he is interested in how governments manage potential threats from organized opposition through election fraud as well as formal electoral rules manipulation. At New York University, he conducts research for the Social Media and Political Participation (SMaPP) Lab. At SMaPP he studies tools employed to counter opposition activity in social media. Sergey holds a bachelor in economics and master's in public policy from Higher School of Economics (Moscow) and master's in social sciences from the University of Chicago.

Samuel C. Woolley is the director of the Digital Intelligence Lab at the Institute for the Future, a research associate at the Oxford Internet Institute, University of Oxford and a visiting scholar at University of California, Berkeley's Center for Information Technology Research in the Interest of Society (CITRIS). In the fall of 2019 he will join the Journalism School at the Moody College of Communication at the University of Texas as an Assistant Professor. He is the co-founder and the former director of research of the computational propaganda project at the Oxford Internet Institute, University of Oxford. He is a Belfer fellow at the Anti-Defamation League's Center for Technology and Society Research, a research fellow at the TechPolicy Lab at the University of Washington. He is a former fellow at Google Jigsaw, the Institute for the Future, and the Center for Media, Data and Society at Central European University. He researches automation and political communication and has published widely on the subject of computational propaganda. He holds a PhD from the University of Washington.

Mariia Zhdanova is a researcher for StopFake.org, a Ukrainian fact checking site that looks at how propaganda influences Ukraine and other countries worldwide. She is the head of digital at Vogue Ukraine. She has an interest in the verification of information, the raising of media literacy in Ukraine, and the establishment of a clear red line between journalism and propaganda. Previously, Mariia worked as a communications manager at the British Council and a digital project manager for a Ukrainian television channel. She holds a master's degree in sociology from the University of Glasgow.

Index

ABCC. *See* Anti-Bot Code of Conduct
ABIN. *See* Brazilian Intelligence Agency
advertising
    amplifier bots and, 76
    elections and, 76–77
    interactive, 187
    networks for, mapping of, 12
    in US presidential election (2016), 102
AfD. *See* Alternative für Deutschland party
agenda setting, theory of, 187
Akamai Technologies, 110
Akhmetov, Rinat, 49
Akin, David, 67, 72
Alexander, L., 54
algorithmic distribution, 14
algorithms, 6–7
    online experience governed by, 92–93
    political role of, 9
    public service uses of, 14
    See also bots
Alternative für Deutschland party, 155, 156, 157,
    165, 166
alt-right media (US), 89
amplifier bots, 53, 54, 59, 70–72, 74, 76–78, 80,
    97, 190, 193
analysis bots, 74
anonymity, 7
Anonymous, 69, 71, 76
Anonymous Asia, 110
Anti-Bot Code of Conduct (US), 208
Antifa, 91
application programming interfaces (APIs), 8,
    88, 160, 191, 196–97, 208, 242
ARD (Germany), 178
astroturfing, 4, 10, 99, 100, 109
Atlantic Council, 23
Audi, 178

authoritarian governments, computational
    propaganda and, 14
automated social actors, 4

/b/, 88
Baidu Tieba (China), 25, 119
Barlow, John Perry, 130
Batkivshchyna Party (Ukraine), 46
behavioral analytics, 189
Berkman Center for Internet & Society (Harvard
    University), 25
Bernier, Maxime, 68
Bērziņš, J., 42
Bessi, A., 196
betweenness centrality, 199–206
Bitcoin ransomware attacks, 110
Bitkom (Germany), 177
Black Lives Matter, 69
Boczkowski, P. J., 160
Bolsa Familia (Brazil), 131
Bot Disclosure and Accountability Act
    (US), 208–9
botnets, 69, 71–72, 75, 76, 128–29, 135–38, 139,
    142, 163
    political, 196
    sleeping, 167
bot networks, 130, 166, 167, 242
Bot or Not (University of Indiana), 144, 145,
    146, 197, 198–99, 201–2
bots, 4, 218–19, 242
    acceptability of, 186
    adaptability of, 167
    in Brazil, 130, 133–47
    builders of, 10
    in Canada, 64–65, 68–79
    candidate-focused, 194–95 (*see also* Trump,
        Donald: social media and)

bots (*cont.*)
  in China, 223–30
  combating fake news with, 113–14
  commercial tasks of, 162–63
  complaints and, 53
  content of, 140
  criminalization of, 176
  deployment of, strategy for, 32
  detection of, 22, 53, 167, 196–99, 243
  effectiveness of, in affecting opinion, 10, 186,
    195–96, 207–8
  Facebook and, 48, 53–54, 56, 111–12
  free speech and, 76
  fully automated, 31
  functions of, 6, 88
  in Germany, 162–68
  goals of, 191
  human retweeting of, 203–7
  humanlike behavior of, 8, 9
  identification of, 31–32, 48
  influence of, 52, 186, 199
  influencing political discussion,
    195–96, 207–8
  labeling obligation for, 176
  law and, 74–79, 194
  legitimate uses for, 162
  life span of, 189
  manufacturing consensus, 190
  and MH17 crash, 55–56
  multiplier figures and, 166–68
  operation of, 143
  party-focused, 194
  in Poland, 97
  programming of, 6
  in public discourse, 74
  public awareness of, 81
  in Russia, 28–32
  self-promotion and, 50
  selling of, 10 (*see also* fake accounts)
  in Taiwan, 105, 111–12
  as threat to American democracy, 195–96
  traffic generated by, 7–80
  on Twitter, 7, 48, 53, 88
  types of, 43, 53
  in Ukraine, 48, 49, 51, 52–53, 59, 163
  understanding of, 101
  in the US, 185–208
  user responsibility for, 208
  See also political bots
boyd, danah, 112
Brasil Liker, 137
Brazil, 13
  bots in, 130, 133–47
  cybercrime in, 135
  Cyber Defense Center, 134–35
  dictatorial legacy of, 134
  digital bill of rights in, 130

  economics of, 129, 131, 132
  Facebook in, 130, 133, 134, 136, 137,
    139, 141–42
  fake news in, 130, 141
  hashtags in, 140–41, 143–46
  impeachment in, 129–32, 137–41, 147
  international press in, 133
  Internet influence of, 129
  Internet participation in, 130, 134
  local elections in (2016), 131, 141–42
  media environment in, 130
  media market in, 132–33
  polarization in, 140
  political reform in, 136, 142–43, 148
  politics in, 129–48
  presidential election in (2014), 131, 135–38
  presidential election in (2016), 131
  protests in, 134, 135, 138–40, 144
  ruling party opposition in, 138–39
  social media in, 130
  social networks in, 133, 134
  Twitter in, 136, 143–47
  WhatsApp in, 134, 136, 138, 142
  YouTube in, 133, 134
Brazilian Intelligence Agency, 134
Brazilian Socialist Party, 132
Brexit, 112, 128, 129, 155, 163, 212
Bright, J., 160
Brown, Scott, 194
Bund Deutscher Zeitungsverleger, 171
Bündnis 90 / Die Grünen (Germany), 156, 157,
  165, 176
butlers. *See* servant bots

Cambridge Analytica, 112, 129, 189, 195
Canada
  algorithms and public service in, 14
  bot law in, 74–79
  bots in, 64–65, 68–79
  data sharing in, 79
  digital news in, 65
  Facebook in, 66, 67, 68
  governmental use of social media in, 67–68
  Instagram in, 67
  Internet use in, 67
  journalism in, 65, 72
  LinkedIn in, 67
  media ownership in, 65–66
  news sources in, 65–66
  political and economic context of, 65–66
  political discourse in, 67, 81
  social media use in, 67, 68
  as target for foreign influence, 77
  Twitter in, 66, 67–68
  YouTube in, 66
Canadian Anti-Spam Law, 76
Canadian Centre for Child Protection, 73–74

Canadian Charter of Rights and Freedoms, 79
Canadian Radio-television and
    Telecommunications Commission, 77
Car Wash scandal (Brazil), 129
CASL. *See* Canadian Anti-Spam Law
Castells, Manuel, 159
CBC/Radio-Canada, 65
CCP. *See* Chinese Communist Party
CDCiber. *See* Cyber Defense Center
CDU/CSU. *See* Christlich Demokratische Union
    / Christlich-Soziale Union
Center for Strategic and International Studies, 22
Centre for International Relations (*Centrum
    Stosunków Międzynarodowych*; Poland), 94
CERT. *See* Computer Emergency
    Response Team
Channel One (Russia), 42
chat bots, 6, 48, 64, 72, 81
Chaturvedi, Swati, 116
Chen, Adrian, 89
Chen, H.-H., 105, 109
Chiang Kai-Shek, 106
child exploitation, online, 73–74
China (People's Republic of China [PRC]), 106
    anti-state content in, 223–31
    bots in, 223–30
    censorship in, 216, 219–21
    computational propaganda used by, 14,
        219–30, 234–35
    cross-Strait propaganda from, 114–24
    culture of, 215
    economy of, 215
    Facebook in, 119
    fake accounts in, 221–30, 232–34
    fake news in, 232
    freedom ranking of, 106
    Great Firewall in, 22, 219–21
    human rights in, 223
    Internet control in, 11, 22, 219–21
    Internet use in, 213–17
    manual propaganda in, 115
    media control in, 24, 215–16
    online content, responsibility for, 214, 219–21
    online harassment from, 115–16
    opinion manipulation in, 215–16
    political information in, 215–16
    political speech in, renegotiation of, 232
    politics in, 215, 216, 222–27, 230–35
    propaganda in, 107, 114–15, 218, 220–22
    public opinion manipulation in, 233
    sending computational propaganda to
        Taiwan, 114–24
    social media in, 115, 214, 216, 220
    social media propaganda in, 115
    Taiwan and, 107, 116
    trolls in, 34n10
    Twitter and, 119, 218, 221–30, 235

China Military, 116
Chinese Communist Party, 124, 214, 215–16
Chinese Nationalist Party (KMT), 106, 107
Christlich Demokratische Union / Christlich-
    Soziale Union (Germany), 156, 157,
    165, 176
Christmas market attack (Germany, 2016),
    166, 167
Chu, Z., 8
Church of Scientology, 69
Civic Platform party (*Platforma Obywatelska*
    [PO]; Poland), 91, 93
Clark, Christy, 71
Clarke, Amanda, 65
Clement, Tony, 67–68
clickbait, 89
Clinton, Hillary, 7, 187
Clinton campaign (2016), 188–89, 192, 193, 197
Coakley, Martha, 194
Coalition Avenir Québec party (Canada), 71
Coderre, Denis, 71
Cohen, B., 190
Collor de Mello, Fernando, 139
comments
    paid, 49–51
    spam and, 92
commercial messages, 76
Communist Youth Party (China), 114
complainers, 53, 59
computational propaganda, 4–5
    algorithmic distribution of, 14
    automation and, 7
    components of, 5
    control of, 175–78, 234–35
    cyborg theory of, 123
    definitions of, 4–7, 43, 87, 105, 153–54, 185
    effect of, on democracy, 243–44
    global trends in, 241
    hallmarks of, 5–6
    history of, 7
    human curation of, 14
    legal questions and, 242–43
    by nonpolitical nonactors, effectiveness of, 56
    study of, 11–12
    tools of, 218–19 (*see also* bots; fake accounts;
        fake news; propaganda)
    understanding, 52, 89
    uses of, 7, 14, 219–30, 234–35
    worldwide, 7
Computational Propaganda Project (University
    of Oxford), 107, 159, 208
computational social science, 12
Computer Emergency Response Team
    (Brazil), 135
Computer Emergency Response Team
    (Poland), 95
ComScore, 133

consensus
    astroturfing and, 10
    impression of, 4, 6, 9
    manufacturing of, 190 (*see also* manufactured
        consensus)
Conservative Party (Canada), 65, 71
content
    algorithms attached to, 92–93
    automation of, 5, 31
    promotion of, 53, 54 (*see also* multiplier
        figures, bots and)
ContextMedia, 49
copyright laws, 78
correctiv (Germany), 177, 178
crawler bots, 74, 111. *See also* general bots
Crimea, Russian annexation of, 41, 45
Crivella, Marcelo, 142
Cruz, Ted, 189, 194
curation, human, 14
cyber armies, 108–9, 123
cyberattacks, 74
cyberbullying, 69
cybercrime, 135
cyber defense, 33
Cyber Defense Center (Brazil), 134
cybersecurity, attribution and, 77
cyborg accounts, 8, 123, 134, 141–42, 242

Dai, Leon, 115–16
dampener bots, 68–70, 74, 75–76, 80
Danwei, 116
DARPA. *See* Defense Advanced Research
    Projects Agency
data
    analysis of, critical stance toward, 5
    protection of, 13
data mischief, 75
Dcard (Taiwan), 108
DDoS. *See* distributed denial of service attacks
Defense Advanced Research Projects Agency
    (US), 22
Deloire, Christophe, 104
democracy
    assault on, 245
    computational propaganda's effect on, 243
    digital technologies and, 3
    social media designing for, 243–44
    social media undermining, 3
democratic governments, computational propa-
    ganda and, 14
Democratic National Committee (US), 21, 28
Democratic Progressive Party (Taiwan), 106, 107
Deng Xioaping, 215
Diba (China), Facebook expedition of,
    116, 119–24
Die Linke (Germany), 156, 165
Die Partei (Germany), 166

DiffEngine bots, 72
digital campaigning, tools of, 187. *See also* bots
digital divides, 10
Digital Forensic Research Lab (Atlantic
    Council), 23
digital literacy, 168. *See also* media literacy
digital propaganda gap, 22
digital technologies, democracy and, 3
Dilma. *See* Rousseff, Dilma
disinformation, 4, 6, 87, 93–94
    attribution of, 95–96
    in Ukraine, 41–42, 45, 57
    undermining opposition through, 7
    See also fake news; junk news
distributed denial of service (DDoS) attacks, 69,
    75–76, 110
DNS poisoning, 219
Document Number Nine (China), 220
Donetsk People's Republic, 45
Dp.ru, 42
DPP. *See* Democratic Progressive Party
D64 (Germany), 177
Dubois, D., 65
Durov, Pavel, 30
Dvorkovich, Arkady, 27

echo chambers, 3, 4, 12, 213
Echo of Moscow, 26
8chan, 7
Eight Honors and Eight Shames, 121, 123
Elections Act (Canada), 76–77
Elections Canada, 77–78, 81
emails, hacking of, 21, 27–28
Endireita Brasil (Righting Brazil), 139
EuroMaidan revolution, 41, 44–45, 47, 53, 95
Europe, political fringe in, 153
European Parliament, 22
Eurozone, 155

Facebook, 25, 128, 163
    acknowledging false amplifiers on, 99–100
    amplifier bots on, 54
    artificial identities on, 87
    automation and, 8
    ban requests with, 53
    bots and, 53–54, 56, 72, 111–12, 176
    in Brazil, 130, 133, 134, 136, 137, 139,
        141, 141–42
    buying likes on, 71
    in Canada, 66, 67, 68
    chat bots on, 72
    in China, 119
    criminalizing bots on, 176
    curated content on, 243–44
    fake accounts and, 8, 96
    fake news detection tools on, 177
    in Germany, 166, 168, 173–74

impact bots on, 54
internal report of, 99–100
in Poland, 87, 90, 91–92
political advertising on, 80
in Russia, 30–31
self-regulation of, 212
in Taiwan, 107, 111–12, 116, 119–24
Trump victory and, 192
in Ukraine, 47, 48
in the US, 67, 192
user information gathered from, 111–12
fact-checking services, 55, 177, 178
Factum Group Ukraine, 47
fake accounts, 8, 87, 89, 96, 218, 221–30,
    232–34, 242
creation of, 97–99
flagging of, 100
sale of, 167
in Ukraine, 43, 44, 51, 52
Fakebook, 174
fake news, 14, 87, 89, 93–94, 112–14, 130, 141,
    168–69, 218, 219, 232
bots for combating, 113–14
campaigns' spread of, 191
countering, 112–13, 161, 177
evaluation of, 162
in Germany, 168, 169–75
methodological assessment of, 169–73
in the US, 188
See also junk news; misinformation
Falun Gong, 116
Fawzi, N., 156
FDP (Germany), 157, 165
Fedchenko, Yevhen, 56
Federal Election Commission (US), 208
federal government, 65
Federal Republic of Germany (West
    Germany), 158
Federal University of Espírito Santo (Brazil),
    135, 139, 142
Federal University of Minas Gerais (Brazil), 143
Fedor, J., 28
Ferrara, E., 196
50-cent-ers, 27
50-cent Party (China), 114–15, 119, 216–17
filter bubbles, 213
Firtash, Dmytro, 46
Fiverr, 10
flagging wars, 91–92
Folha de São Paulo (Brazil), 135–36
Ford, H., 65
4Chan, 88
France
cyber defense in, 22
misinformation in, 173
Fredheim, R., 28
Freedom House, 25, 106, 107

Freedom of the Press ranking (Freedom World),
    25, 107
freedom of speech, 75–76, 92
Freedom in the World (Freedom House), 106
Free Tibet (London), 221
Freixo, Marcelo, 142

Gauthier, Ursula, 116
gay marriage, digital politics and, 107
Gazeta Wyborcza, 92
@gccaedits bot, 64–65, 72, 78
GDR. *See* German Democratic Republic
Geertz, Clifford, 188
general bots, 43
Gerasimov, Valery, 22
German Democratic Republic (East
    Germany), 158
Germany
addressing misinformation, 156
bots in, 162–68
commercial market in, for bots, 167
computational propaganda in, 154, 156
control in, of online propaganda, 175–76
cyber defense in, 22
Facebook in, 166, 168, 173–74
fake (junk) news in, 168, 169–75
journalists in, media literacy of, 167, 168
media climate in, 157–58
media regulation in, 169–70, 176–78
misinformation in, 168, 169–75
political bots in, 156
political culture of, 154–55, 157, 174
propaganda and, 158
Russia's digital influence in, 172–75
social (political) bots in, 163–68
social media regulation in, 212
social networking regulation in, 176–78
Twitter in, 159–60, 163–66, 168–73
Globe and Mail, 72
Globo Network (Brazil), 132–33, 134
Golden Shield Project (China), 219, 220
#GoodRiddanceHarper, 69
Google, 25, 212
Gorchinskaya, Katya, 57–58
Gorwa, R., 88
g0v.tw, 113–14
GreatFire.org, 219
Great Firewall of China, 116, 121,
    213–14, 219–21
Green Party (Germany). *See* Bündnis 90 /
    Die Grünen
Guilbeault, D., 88
Guo Baofeng, 232

hackers, 7, 69, 161
Harper, Stephen, 69, 70
hate campaigns, 6, 75

headless browsing bots, 242
Hegelich, Simon, 43, 163
Hensel, Gerald, 178
hoaxes, 93
Hong Kong, Twitter in, 222
Hoskins, A., 42
Ho Wan-see, 121
Howard, Philip N., 10, 43, 119, 159
Hromadske TV (Ukraine), 47, 57–58
Huang Kuo-chang, 107
Hu Jintao, 121
Hung Hsiu-chu, 120

I Am a Troll (Chaturvedi), 116
#ichbinhier, 178
ICQ, in Ukraine, 48
#IdleNoMore movement, 69
If That Then This, 146
Ignacio de Silva, Lula. *See* Lula
impact bots, 53, 54, 59
Incapsula, 7
"Information Operations and Facebook"
    (Facebook), 99–100
InfoOps, 4–5
InfoStream, 49
Instagram, 67, 163
Inter Media group (Ukraine), 46
Internet
    free speech and, 213, 214
    as global technology, 134, 214
    propaganda and, 218 (*see also* propaganda)
    social control via, 10–11
    undermining political processes, 213
IP blocking, 219–20
Iran, Internet control in, 11
IRC channels, 79

Janetszko, D., 43
Jansen, Sandra, 68
Jobs, Steve, 26
journalists, attacks on, 188
J-Source (Canada), 72
Junge Freiheit, 173
junk news, 5, 9–10, 13. *See also* fake news;
    misinformation

Kalsnes, Bente, 68
k-core decomposition analysis, 199–202
Kelly, J., 42
Khan, Aamir, 116
King, Gary, 105, 115, 119, 123, 217
Klimenko, German, 34n11
Klout, 196
KMT (Kuomintang), 105. *See also* Chinese
    Nationalist Party
Ko, M.-C., 105, 109
Kolomoysky, Ihor, 46

Ko Wen-je, 105, 107, 109–12, 124
Kunming Pan Asia Nonferrous Metals
    Exchange, 226–31
Kuomintang (Taiwan), 105. *See also* Chinese
    Nationalist Party

Larsson, Anders Olof, 68
Lasswell, H. D., 11
Latin America, Internet in, 129
Lava Jato scandal (Brazil), 129, 131, 132, 145–48
Law and Justice party (*Prawo i Sprawiedliwość*
    [PiS]; Poland), 91, 93, 97
Lawrow, Sergey, 175
Lazarsfeld, P., 11
least effort, principle of, 121
Legatum Institute (UK), 22
Le Pen, Marine, 155
Lewis, R., 88
Liang, Johnson, 113
libel, 75
Liberal Party (Canada), 65, 71
Lien, Sean, 109–12
LINE, 107–8, 112, 113–14, 116, 123
LinkedIn, in Canada, 67
LiveJournal, 25, 26, 28, 30, 50
Low Orbital Ion Cannon, 69
Lucas, E., 42
Lügenpresse (lying press), 155–56
Luhansk People's Republic, 45
Lula (Ignacio de Silva), 129, 131, 132
lying press, 155–56
Lyovochkin, Serhiy, 46

Maas, Heiko, 176
Macron, Emmanuel, 153
Maksimov, Sergei, 27–28
manufactured consensus, 186
Mao Zedong, 106, 121, 215
Marco Civil da Internet (Internet Bill of Rights;
    Brazil), 130, 147
Martinsen, Joel, 116
Marwick, A., 88
mass public participation online, 76
May, Theresa, 153
McCain, John, 192
McCombs, M. E., 190
media
    shaping public attention, 190
    Trump setting agenda for, 187, 192,
        193, 207–8
media ecosystems, network perspective on, 159
media literacy, 81, 113, 177–78, 243
MediaMiser, 73
Medvedev, Dmitry, 26–29, 34n12
megaphone effect, 186, 193, 206
Meister, S., 42
memes, as campaign tools, 187, 188

MentionMapp, 71–72
Merkel, Angela, 155–56, 157, 165, 166, 167, 173–74, 175
message bombs, 9
messengers, 48
Messias, J., 196
MH17, crash of, 53, 55–56, 59
microtargeting, 112
Midia Ninja (Brazil), 134
Mimikama, 178
misinformation, 89
  in Germany, 168, 169–75
  as social concern, 9, 13, 168
  solutions to, 112–13
  travel of, 12
  See also fake news; junk news
Mitchelstein, E., 160
Modamani, Anas, 173–74
Modi, Narendra, 116
Monaco, N., 119
Mønsted, B., 196
Moro, Sergio, 141
Mourinho, Robert, 133
Movimento Brasil Livre (Free Brazil Movement), 139
Muda Mais, 135–36
multiplier figures, bots and, 166–68

Nagy, P., 75, 79
Nardelli, A., 173
Narodny Front party (Ukraine), 45–46
NaszaKlasa ("Our Class"; Poland), 90
National Council for TV and Radio Broadcasting (Ukraine), 47
nationalism, 68, 96, 155, 216, 233–34
National Research Council (Canada), 73
NATO, 94
Navalny, Alexey, 30, 35n14
NDP. *See* New Democratic Party
Neff, G., 75, 79
Nelson, E., 28
Net DG. *See* Network Enforcement Act (Germany)
network analysis, 199–206
network automation, 10
Network Enforcement Act (Germany), 154, 156, 176–77, 178
Neuberger, C., 159
Never Trump movement, 191
Neves, Aécio, 132, 135–36, 137
New Democratic Party (Canada), 65, 68–69, 71, 77
Newman, M. J., 201
New Power Party (Taiwan), 106, 107
news portals, online, 92
Nexalogy, 71
Nicola, S., 167

Nimmo, B., 42
NoksFishes, 49
No Other Love (dir. Zhao), 115–16
Novodvorski, Alex, 57
NPD (Germany), 165
NPP. *See* New Power Party

Obama, Barack, 133
Occupy Central, 222
Odnoklassniki, 25, 47
Olgino trolls, 42–43, 54
O'Loughlin, B., 42
online content
  class-based gap and, 10
  control of, 213
online support, illusion of, 190
OpAnonDown, 69
Operation Serenade of Love (Brazil), 147–48
opinion leaders, targeting of, 98–99
Opposition Bloc (Ukraine), 46
Orkut, 130

Pan, Jennifer, 105, 115, 217
Parkhomenko, Sergey, 56
Parsons, Rehtaeh, 69
Partido Movimento Democratico Brasileiro (PMDB [Brazilian Democratic Movement Party]), 129
Party of Regions (Ukraine), 46
Party of the Republic (Brazil), 131–32
Patten, Steve, 68
People's Daily (China), 114, 116
People's Liberation Army (China), 116
Perrin, Benjamin, 69
personal information, 78–79. *See also* privacy
Personal Information Protection and Electronic Documents Act (Canada), 78–79
Petrobras (Brazil), 132
Petro Poroshenko Bloc (Ukraine), 45–46
Philosphia Perennis, 173
Pinchuk, Viktor, 46
PIPEDA. *See* Personal Information Protection and Electronic Documents Act
PiS. *See* Law and Justice party
PIT (Taiwan), 123
Pizzagate, 193
"PL Espião" (the Big Spy Bill; Brazil), 147
Plurk (Taiwan), 108
PMDB (Brazil), 131
Podesta, John, 28, 193
Poland
  bots in, 97
  Facebook in, 87, 90, 91–92
  fake accounts in, 97–100
  "fake news" in, 93–94
  hate speech in, 92
  Internet and politics in, 87

Poland (*cont.*)
  Internet use in, 90
  media climate in, 93–94
  nationalist groups in, organizing online, 92
  online harassment in, 95
  online-only news portals in, 92
  paid posters in, 97
  politics in, 13, 87, 90–92
  Russia's cyber involvement in, 94–97
  Twitter in, 90, 97
  Ukraine and, 94
Polish Ministry of Education, 93
political botnets, 193. *See also* botnets
political bots, 3, 6, 43, 64–65, 74, 88, 114,
    117, 163
  effectiveness of, 99
  goal of, 193
  hate campaigns and, 6
  issues involving, 74–75
  sleeping networks of, 167
political environment, upheavals in, 4
Pomerantsev, P., 42
Popova, Tetyana, 58
populism, 155
Poroshenko, Petro, 43, 45–46, 58
post-truth, 41
privacy, protection of, 13, 78–79, 130
Privacy Act (Canada), 78
Progressive Party (Brazil), 132
Project Arachnid (Canada), 73–74
Project on Computational Propaganda, 162, 163
propaganda, 5, 218
  classification of, 96
  democratization of, 186, 190–93, 218
  Internet's changing of, 218
  positive, 221–22
  study of, 11
provincial government, 65
PSDB. *See* Social Democracy Party of Brazil
psychographic targeting, 195
psychometric targeting, 195
PsyOps, 4–5
PT. *See* Workers' Party
PTT (Taiwan), 108, 109, 116
public opinion, manipulation of, 9, 49, 86, 169,
    241–42. *See also* bots; computational prop-
    aganda; fake news
Public Policy Forum, 65
Puschmann, C., 65
Putin, Vladimir, 24, 26, 29, 43

Radical Party (Ukraine), 46
Radio Liberty, 31
Random Forest, 198
Ratkiewicz, J., 10
RBC, 43
Reconquista Germanica, 155

Reddit, 79
regulation, consequences of, 3–4
Reinemann, C., 156
Reporters Without Borders, 104
retweets, network analysis of, 199–203
Revoltados ONLINE (Revolted Online; Brazil),
    137, 139
Roberts, Margaret E., 105, 115
Roberts, N., 217
robocalling, bots and, 77–78
Robocalling Scandal, 77, 80
robot etiquette, 79
Romney, Mitt, 192
Romney campaign (2012), 194
Rosie (Brazil), 147–48
Roskomnadzor (Russia), 30, 43
Rousseff, Dilma, 13, 129, 131, 132, 135–37,
    139–40, 145
RT, 21, 23–24, 28, 31, 42
Ruest, Nick, 72
Ruffini, Patrick, 194
Russia
  annexing Crimea, 41, 45
  and attack on MH17, 55–56, 59
  blogosphere in, 25–26, 27, 33
  bots in, 28–32
  computational propaganda campaigns by,
      14, 57–58
  conducting disinformation campaign against
      US, 153
  cyber operations of, 21–22, 94–97, 153
  disinformation from, 7, 42, 87
  economic competition in, 33
  edge of, in digital propaganda, 22–23
  email hacking and, 27–28
  Facebook in, 30–31
  foreign online services and, 25–26
  foreign responses to, 22
  Freedom House ranking of, 25
  and German media, 158
  influence of, in German elections, 172–75
  information wars and, 14
  Internet use in, 24–25
  market competition in, 23
  media control in, 23–25, 29–31, 42
  motivation of, in cyber activities, 96
  nationalism in, 29
  online information flow in, 22, 24–25
  opposition suppression in, 29–31
  political competition in, 23
  pro-government bots and trolls
      deployed in, 27
  propaganda abilities of, 23–24
  protests in, 29, 30
  search engine optimization industry in, 27, 28
  spam industry in, 27
  state-run propaganda machine of, 21–22

tech sector in, 24–25, 33
trolls in, 27, 34n10, 42–43, 89
Twitter in, 13, 24, 30–32
youth movements in, recruited as trolls, 27
Russian Internet Research Agency, 42–43
Russian media factory, 43
Russia Today, 175

Sadovy, Andriy, 46
Samopomich party (Ukraine), 46
Sberbank, 30
scalper bots, 79
Scavino, Dan, 194
Schmalbart, 178
Schradie, J., 10
Schulz, Martin, 157, 165
SemanticForce, 49
servant bots, 73–74, 78–79, 80
service bots, 53–54, 59
Shattered Mirror, The (Public Policy Forum), 65
Shaw, D. L., 190
shitposts, 188
Shorenstein Center on Media, Politics, and
     Public Policy (Harvard University), 187
Sia, S., 119
Silva, Marina, 132
Silverman, C., 173
Silverman, Sarah, 77, 242
Sina Weibo, 214. *See also* Weibo
Singapore, Internet control in, 11
Skype, in Ukraine, 48
sleeper bots, 242
Smith, Nicola, 113
Snapdeal, 116
social bots, 6, 8, 43, 88, 97
   astroturfing and, 10
   communication and, 9
   countering, 161
   public service and, 14
   See also social media bots
social control, 10–11
social data science, 5
Social Democracy Party of Brazil, 131, 132
Socialist Conception of Honors and Shames, 121
social media
   bots' presence on, 7–8 (*see also* bots)
   Chinese Communist Party and, 215–16
   concerns about, 212–13
   designing for democracy, 243–44
   disinformation and, 4
   fake accounts and, 5, 8 (*see also* fake accounts)
   information campaigns on, success of, 23
   junk news and, 9–10
   as media business, 244
   political normalization of, 10–11, 192–93
   political use of, 3
   public opinion manipulation and, 241–42

role of, improving, 5
sensationalistic content and, 9, 168
Trump campaign and, 192–97, 207–8
undermining democracy, 3
social media analytics, journalism's use of, 80
social media bots, 13, 88, 193. *See also* social bots
social media monitoring, in Ukraine, 48–49
Social Media and Political Participation Lab
     (NYU), 31
social network analysis, 12
social networking, content on, responsibility
     for, 177–78
social news gap, 160
sock puppets, 10, 89, 193, 242
Sonnad, Nikhail, 119
Sozialdemokratische Partei Deutschlands,
     156, 157
Spamhaus Project, 135
SPD. *See* Sozialdemokratische Partei
     Deutschlands
splinternet, 214
Sputnik News Agency, 21, 22, 23, 42, 175
Sputnik.pl, 95
Steinmeier, Frank-Walter, 175
StopFake.org, 57
StratCom, 47
streaming API, 160
Stukal, Denis, 31
Sunflower Movement (Taiwan), 107, 116
Sun Zhigang, 231
surveys, 12–13
Symantec, 135
symbiotic agency, 75
Syria, social bots in, 163
Szefernaker, Paweł, 97
Szefernaker's Eggs (Poland), 97

Tagesschau, the (Germany, 163
Taipei, mayoral race in (2014), 109–12, 124
Taiwan (Republic of China), 106
   bots in, 105, 111–12
   China's interest in, 107
   cross-Strait propaganda campaigns in, 105–6,
      107, 114–24
   cyber armies in, 105, 108–9, 123
   DDoS attacks in, 110
   democratic society in, 104
   digital media and politics in, 105
   Facebook in, 107, 111–12, 116, 119–24
   fake news in, 112–14
   freedom ranking of, 106
   freedom of speech in, 113
   future of, 104
   gay marriage in, messaging campaign on,
      106, 107
   internal campaigns in. of computational
      propaganda, 105–14

Taiwan (Republic of China) (*cont.*)
LINE in, 116
manual propaganda in, 108–9, 123
media in, 106–7
media literacy campaign in, 243
online harassment in, from China, 115–16
political bots in, 117
politics in, 106–7
press freedom in, 107
propaganda accounts in, 117–20, 123–24
PTT in, 116
social media landscape in, 107–8
Twitter in, 107, 116–20, 123–24
Tang, Audrey, 113
technology, as target of criminal activity, 75
Telegram, in Ukraine, 48
Temer, Michel, 129, 131, 132, 141, 148
Texty.org.ua, 57
Thales Group, 73
Thieltges, Andree, 163
Timakova, Natalya, 27
Tinder, 8
"Torquemada Hell" (Sergei Maksimov), 27–28
trackers, 53, 59
transparency bots, 64, 72, 74, 78, 80
trolling, 4, 27, 31, 34n10, 42–43, 49, 88–89, 91–92, 97, 116
Trudeau, Justin, 69
Trump, Donald J., 7, 14, 43, 89, 155, 212
concern about, 191–92
free media attention for, 192
media coverage of, 190
setting media's agenda, 187, 193, 207–8
social media and, 190
Twitter and, 190
Trump campaign, 129, 186–87, 189, 191–93, 207–8
Truthy, 196, 197
Tsai Ing-wen, 107, 117–20
Tsvetkova, M., 88
Tucker, Joshua, 31
Turing Test, 9
TVP (Poland), 93–94, 95
Twitalyzer, 196
Twitter
APIs and, 8, 88, 117, 160, 196–98
automation and, 8
bots on, 7, 31, 53, 88
bots' influence over, 186
in Brazil, 136, 143–47
in Canada, 66, 67–68
in China, 119, 218, 221–30, 235
curated content on, 243–44
fake accounts on, 221–30
in Germany, 159–60, 163–66, 168–73
in Hong Kong, 222
in Poland, 90, 97

rest API, 197, 198
retweeting rate on, for Russian bot accounts, 54
in Russia, 30–32
self-regulation of, 212
streaming API, 160, 196–97, 198
in Taiwan, 107, 116–20, 123–24
trending topics section, 54
Trump and, 190, 192–97, 207–8
in Ukraine, 47, 48, 53
in the US, 173, 185–86, 192–208
Tymoshenko, Yuliya, 46

Ukraine
affecting Polish–Russian relations, 94
banning Russian Web services and social media, 58
bots in, 49, 51, 52–53, 59, 163
brainwashing in, 22
computational propaganda in, 13–14, 42–49, 52
conflict of, with Russia, 42, 44–45, 47
digital agencies in, 50–52
disinformation in, 41–42, 45, 57
fake accounts in, 44, 49–52
Internet Army project, 56
Internet use in, 42, 47
media market in, 46–47
messengers in, 48
oligarchs in, 46–47
online political communication in, 45, 50
paid commenters in, 49–51, 57
pluralism by default in, 46
political parties in, and social media, 51
politicians in, Facebook presence of, 54
post-truth conditions in, 41
public manipulation in, industry for, 50–51
public relations consultants in, 54–55
recent history in, 41–42, 44–46
response of, to computational propaganda, 56–58
social media in, 47–50, 243
trolls in, 49
Twitter in, 53
Ukraine–European Union Association Agreement, 94
Ukrayinska Pravda (Ukraine), 47, 50
Umbrella Movement, 222
United Kingdom
Brexit vote in, 128 (*see also* Brexit)
fake news in, 212
misinformation in, 173
social media as news source in, 158
United States
bot detection in, 243
bots in, 185–208
cyber defense in, 22

democracy in, bots as threat to, 195–96
elections in, presidential (2016), 128
Facebook in, 67, 192
fake news in, 188
freedom ranking of, 106
propaganda democratized in, 191–93
Russian involvement in elections of, 128
social media as news source in, 158
Twitter in, 173, 185–86, 192–208
See also US elections
UOL network (Brazil), 133
US elections
1968 presidential, 190
2010 congressional, 10
2010 Senate, 194
2012 presidential, 194
2016 presidential election, 7, 14, 112, 153, 163, 173, 185–208
Usenet, 88

VCR. *See* Voter Contact Registry
Vem Pra Rua (Go to the Street; Brazil), 137, 139
Viber, in Ukraine, 48
virality, 28
Vkontakte (VK), 14, 25, 30, 47, 48
Volkswagen, 178
Volozh, Arkady, 34n13
Voter Contact Registry (Canada), 77–78, 79
voters, manipulation of, 10

WannaCry ransomware attacks, 110
WeChat (China), 214, 220
Wehner, Peter, 191
Weibo (Sina Weibo; China), 25, 115–16, 218, 230–34
Wesleyan Media Project, 192
WhatsApp, 48, 134, 136, 138, 142
Wikipedia, edits to, bots tracking, 6, 53, 65
Woolley, Samuel, 43, 119
Workers' Party (*Partido dos Trabaladores* [PT]; Brazil), 129, 131, 132, 137
World Economic Forum, 168
Wynne, Kathleen, 73

Xi Jinping, 214

Yandex, 25, 28, 30, 34n12
Yandex.Blogs, 26
Yanukovych, Viktor, 44–45, 46, 94
YouScan.io, 49
YouTube
in Brazil, 133, 134
in Canada, 66
curated content on, 243–44
extremist content on, boycott of, 178
in Russia, 28

Zhanggong Propaganda Office, 119
Zhao Wei, 115–16